THE MACARTHUR NEW TESTAMENT COMMENTARY

ROMANS 9-16

John MacArthur

MOODY PUBLISHERS/CHICAGO

All Scripture quotations, unless otherwise indicated, are taken from the *New American Standard Bible®*, Copyright © The Lockman Foundation 1960, 1962, 1963, 1968, 1971, 1972, 1973, 1975, 1977. Used by permission. (www.Lockman.org)

Scripture quotations marked NIV are taken from the *Holy Bible, New International Version®*. NIV®. Copyright © 1973, 1978, 1984 by International Bible Society. Used by permission of Zondervan. All rights reserved.

Scripture quotations marked KJV are taken from the King James Version.

ISBN: 978-0-8024-0768-9

We hope you enjoy this book from Moody Publishers. Our goal is to provide high-quality, thought-provoking books and products that connect truth to your real needs and challenges. For more information on other books and products written and produced from a biblical perspective, go to www.moodypublishers.com or write to:

Moody Publishers
820 N. LaSalle Boulevard
Chicago, IL 60610

Printed in the United States of America

Contents

Preface

It continues to be a rewarding divine communion for me to preach expositionally through the New Testament. My goal is always to have deep fellowship with the Lord in the understanding of His Word, and out of that experience to explain to His people what a passage means. In the words of Nehemiah 8:8, I strive "to give the sense" of it so they may truly hear God speak and, in so doing, may respond to Him.

Obviously, God's people need to understand Him, which demands knowing His Word of truth (2 Tim. 2:15) and allowing that Word to dwell in us richly (Col. 3:16). The dominant thrust of my ministry, therefore, is to help make God's living Word alive to His people. It is a refreshing adventure.

This New Testament commentary series reflects this objective of explaining and applying Scripture. Some commentaries are primarily linguistic, others are mostly theological, and some are mainly homiletical. This one is basically explanatory, or expository. It is not linguistically technical, but deals with linguistics when this seems helpful to proper interpretation. It is not theologically expansive, but focuses on the major doctrines in each text and on how they relate to the whole of Scripture. It is not primarily homiletical, though each unit of thought is generally treated as one chapter, with a clear outline and logical flow of thought. Most truths are illustrated and applied with other Scripture. After establishing the context of a passage, I have tried to follow closely the writer's development and reasoning.

My prayer is that each reader will fully understand what the Holy Spirit is saying through this part of His Word, so that His revelation may lodge in the minds of believers and bring greater obedience and faithfulness—to the glory of our great God.

The Tragic Unbelief of Israel (Romans 9:1-5)

1

I am telling the truth in Christ, I am not lying, my conscience bearing me witness in the Holy Spirit, that I have great sorrow and unceasing grief in my heart. For I could wish that I myself were accursed, separated from Christ for the sake of my brethren, my kinsmen according to the flesh, who are Israelites, to whom belongs the adoption as sons and the glory and the covenants and the giving of the Law and the temple service and the promises, whose are the fathers, and from whom is the Christ according to the flesh, who is over all, God blessed forever. Amen. (9:1-5)

Romans 9-11 is one of the most fascinating passages in the New Testament, filled with essential and very practical doctrine and focused on Israel, God's chosen people.

Throughout church history, however, this passage has often been greatly misunderstood. Some commentators and expositors all but ignore it. Others treat it as a parenthesis that has little, if any, connection to the rest of the letter. They take it as an aside in which Paul expresses personal concerns and insights about his fellow Jews. According to those interpreters, the central message of justification by faith is interrupted at the beginning of chapter 9 and resumes at the beginning of chapter 12. They argue that Paul's beautiful and climactic paean of praise, hope, and assurance in 8:38-39 flows naturally into 12:1.

It is true that if Paul had left out chapters 9-11, the argument and the flow of the letter would still seem unbroken. But, as we will see, it is also true that these three chapters are integrally related to the rest of the letter. Paul did not want to continue his teaching on justification by faith until he clarified some related truths regarding Israel and Israelites. As part of that clarification, the apostle needed to contradict some prevailing falsehoods over which many Christians, especially those who were Jewish, were stumbling.

Paul no doubt had taught the basic truths of Romans 9-11 many times, and, although he had yet to visit Rome in person (1:13), numerous believers there had known Paul personally and had heard those truths spoken from his own lips. It is possible that some of his letters to other churches had been read by Christians in Rome. And because Paul had received previous opposition to these truths, he anticipated the questions and arguments that some of the Roman church members were sure to raise and answers them in the inspired words of these chapters. An initial look at these questions and a brief suggestion of their answers may provide a helpful start to this section.

First, he anticipated the argument that, if the gospel of Jesus Christ offered salvation to all Gentiles, then God must have forsaken His ancient people Israel. Jews who heard the gospel concluded that the doctrine of justification by faith was a new idea that was valid only for Gentiles and that Christians believed the ceremonies and works righteousness of Judaism had no merit before God. They were sure the gospel implied that Jews no longer had a unique place or purpose in God's plan of redemption.

These Jews were quite right, of course, that the gospel discounts Jewish ritual and works righteousness as a means of salvation. But ritualism and legalism, even the keeping of God's divinely-revealed law, had *never* been a means of salvation, only a means of expressing or symbolizing obedience to God. As Paul makes clear earlier in this letter (see especially chaps. 3-5), God has never justified any person, Jew or Gentile—not even Abraham—on any other basis than His grace made effective by personal faith. It was also true that the New Covenant in the blood of Christ had replaced the Old Covenant and that God was calling out a new people for His name from among all nations and peoples.

In his introduction to this letter, Paul states unambiguously that Christ had given him a unique apostleship to the Gentiles (1:1-5; cf. Gal. 1:16). But the book of Acts clearly indicates that he also was called to bring the gospel to "the sons of Israel" (9:15). It is therefore not strange that, whenever possible, this apostle to the Gentiles began a new ministry by first preaching the gospel to Jews, in a synagogue or other meeting place (see, e.g., Acts 9:20; 13:5, 14; 14:1; 16:13; 17:1-2; 19:8). He was genuinely, passionately concerned for Israel's spiritual condition and so was eager to answer the questions he knew they were asking.

Near the end of Romans 11 Paul asserts with divine authority that the Savior of the world came from Zion (that is, was a Jew) and that ultimately "all Israel will be saved," just as the prophet Isaiah had declared (Rom. 11:26; cf. Isa. 59:20-21; 27:9). Early in His earthly ministry, Jesus told the Samaritan woman that "salvation is from the Jews" and that He was the promised Jewish Messiah who would offer salvation not only to Jews but to all mankind (John 4:22-26). Paul was doubtless familiar with that declaration by his Lord, and he assures the Romans that it is inconceivable that God could reject and forget His people Israel. True Christianity and anti-Semitism are therefore contradictory terms in the most absolute sense.

Paul anticipated and answered a second question he knew would arise in the minds of many of his readers, namely, "If salvation is *from* the Jews and is first of all *to* the Jews, why did Israel, including her highest religious leaders, reject Jesus as their Messiah, Savior, and King?" If, as Paul said, "the gospel... is the power of God for salvation to everyone who believes, to the Jew first and also to the Greek" (Rom. 1:16), and if God grants "glory and honor and peace to every man who does good, to the Jew first and also to the Greek" (2:10), why are most Jews still in unbelief? Why is the uniquely chosen and blessed nation of Israel, who knows the law and the prophets so well, not only rejecting the gospel of Jesus Christ but zealously persecuting fellow Jews who believe it?

As we will study in detail in a later chapter, Paul's response to such thinking was: "What shall we say then? That Gentiles, who did not pursue righteousness, attained righteousness, even the righteousness which is by faith; but Israel, pursuing a law of righteousness, did not arrive at that law. Why? Because they did not pursue it by faith, but as though it were by works. They stumbled over the stumbling stone" of salvation by faith (9:30-32). Continuing his explanation, the apostle says, "Brethren, my heart's desire and my prayer to God for them [fellow Jews] is for their salvation. For I bear them witness that they have a zeal for God, but not in accordance with knowledge. For not knowing about God's righteousness, and seeking to establish their own, they did not subject themselves to the righteousness of God. For Christ is the end of the law for righteousness to everyone who believes" (10:1-4).

Because Paul well understood that most of his fellow Jews trusted in their descent from Abraham and in their good works, he asserts in unmistakable terms that "he is not a Jew who is one outwardly; neither is circumcision that which is outward in the flesh. But he is a Jew who is one inwardly; and circumcision is that which is of the heart, by the Spirit, not by the letter; and his praise is not from men, but from God" (Rom. 2:28-29). In other words, the true Jew is a spiritual Jew, a Jew whose heart and mind have been cleansed and purified ("circumcised") by the Spirit and who therefore belongs to God by faith. Neither physical circumcision nor physical lineage from Abraham can save a person. They can, in fact, easily become barriers to salvation by giving a false sense of spiritual security. Trusting in such human things kept Jews from receiving Jesus Christ.

Because the gospel is clear that both Jews and Gentiles are saved by faith, the Jews must turn from their trust in their own religious achievement, humbling themselves, rejecting the intimidating pressure of the tradition they lived by. They rejected that gospel and thus rejected their Messiah.

This salvation was not new. "Apart from the Law the righteousness of God has been manifested," Paul says, "being witnessed by the Law and the Prophets, even the righteousness of God through faith in Jesus Christ for all those who believe; for there is no distinction" (Rom. 3:21-22). The individual Jew has never been saved on any other basis than personal faith in God, no matter how pure and well documented his physical descent from Abraham. "We maintain that a man is justified by faith apart from works of the Law. Or is God the God of Jews only? Is He not the God of Gentiles also? Yes, of Gentiles also, since indeed God who will justify the circumcised by faith and the uncircumcised through faith is one" (3:28-30). God creates Jews and Gentiles alike, and He saves them alike, in faith, apart from works and rituals. The Jews were not saved because the barriers of ceremonies, traditions, and legalism in general blocked their way.

The apostle later asks rhetorically, "I say then, they [Israel] did not stumble so as to fall, did they? May it never be! But by their transgression salvation has come to the Gentiles, to make them jealous" (11:11). In other words, Israel's failure to come to Jesus Christ in faith, tragic as it has been, is not permanent or irreversible. In fact, because Israel's failure opened the door of the gospel to the Gentiles, jealousy of the Gentiles eventually will have a part in leading Israel to turn to the Savior God through faith in Christ, to receive at last the Messiah they rejected at His first coming.

Not only that, the apostle says, but, "if their transgression be riches for the world and their failure be riches for the Gentiles, how much more will their fulfillment be!" (v. 12). If Israel's unbelief brought so many Gentiles to the Lord, how many more will be brought to Him when Israel finally believes. John reveals that the number will be incalculable. "After these things I looked, and behold, a great multitude, which no one could count, from every nation and all tribes and peoples and tongues, standing before the throne and before the Lamb, clothed in white robes, and palm branches were in their hands" (Rev. 7:9).

This question could be stated another way: "If Abraham is the father of those who are truly saved by faith, how can his descendants largely reject God's way of salvation as set forth in the gospel of Jesus Christ?" The apostle had answered that question in chapter 4, saying,

> What then shall we say that Abraham, our forefather according to the flesh, has found? For if Abraham was justified by works, he has something to boast about; but not before God. For what does the Scripture say? "And Abraham believed God, and it was reckoned to him as righteousness." Now to the one who works, his wage is not reckoned as a favor, but as what is due. But to the one who does not work, but believes in Him who justifies the ungodly, his faith is reckoned as righteousness. . . . And he [Abraham] received the sign of circumcision, a seal of the righteousness of the faith which he had while uncircumcised, that he might be the father of all who believe without being circumcised, that righteousness might be reckoned to them. (Rom. 4:1-5, 11)

In other words, large numbers of Jews reject the gospel of Christ because they trust in the outward rite of circumcision and, as already mentioned, in their physical descent from Abraham, rather than in the unqualified faith in God that brought salvation to Abraham and made him "the father of *all* who believe without being circumcised," Gentile as well as Jew (v. 11, emphasis added).

Paul knew that a third and closely related question would also arise in the minds of Jews: "Granted that individual Jews must be saved by personal faith, what about the *nation* of Israel? Has God discarded His ancient chosen nation?" Paul's response to that question is given in chapter 9. It is the "Israelites," he explains, "to whom belongs the adoption as sons and the glory and the covenants and the giving of the Law and the temple service and the promises, whose are the fathers, and from whom is the Christ according to the flesh, who is over all, God blessed forever. Amen" (9:4-5). It has always been a unique blessing and privilege to be a Jew, and the nation of Israel has always held "favored status" before God among the nations of the world.

But that favored position has not prevented God from disciplining that nation or from temporarily putting it aside "until the fullness of the Gentiles has come in" (Rom. 11:25). Once that has occurred, the Lord "will pour out on the house of David and on the inhabitants of Jerusalem, the Spirit of grace and of supplication, so that they will look on

Me whom they have pierced; and they will mourn for Him, as one mourns for an only son, and they will weep bitterly over Him, like the bitter weeping over a first-born" (Zech. 12:10). Then "the sovereignty, the dominion, and the greatness of all the kingdoms under the whole heaven will be given to the people of the saints of the Highest One; His kingdom will be an everlasting kingdom, and all the dominions will serve and obey Him" (Dan. 7:27).

In this section Paul shows that the nation of Israel was temporarily set aside by God because of her continued impenitence and unbelief, most especially for her rejection of the Messiah. In His gracious sovereignty, however, and with divine certainty, God will preserve for Himself a remnant of Israel. That nation, in the form of an ordained remnant of its people, will be brought by faith not only into the purified and restored kingdom of "David's greater Son" but into the eternal kingdom of God.

Paul also reminds his readers that, just as Isaiah prophesied, "Though the number of the sons of Israel be as the sand of the sea, it is the remnant that will be saved" (Rom. 9:27; Isa. 10:22). Through His prophets God had made clear that only a remnant of the nation would ultimately come to Him in genuine faith. Through Isaiah He had promised that "in the last days, then it will happen on that day that the Lord will again recover the second time with His hand the remnant of His people, who will remain, from Assyria, Egypt, Pathros, Cush, Elam, Shinar, Hamath, and from the islands of the sea. And He will lift up a standard for the nations, and will assemble the banished ones of Israel, and will gather the dispersed of Judah from the four corners of the earth" (Isa. 11:11-12; cf. v. 16). Through Jeremiah He promised: "Then I Myself shall gather the remnant of My flock out of all the countries where I have driven them and shall bring them back to their pasture; and they will be fruitful and multiply" (Jer. 23:3; cf. Mic. 2:12; Zech. 8:11-12). And because "the gifts and the calling of God are irrevocable" (Rom. 11:29), Israel has the divine guarantee that this remnant, representing the nation, *will* be saved. God's plan from eternity past has always been that Israel's rejection of Him would be both partial and temporary.

In those answers to fellow Jews, Paul also answered a question he knew would arise in the minds of many Gentile believers. "If God did not keep His promises to His chosen people Israel," they would wonder, "how can we expect Him to keep His promises to us as Gentile believers?" The problem, of course, is in the question. God *did not fail* in His promises to Israel or to individual Jews. His promises were given to *faithful* Israel and to *faithful,* believing Jews, to those who were spiritual, not simply physical, descendants of Abraham. Because he was such a model of faithfulness, Abraham not only was the father of the faithful who lived after him but, in a prevenient sense, the father even of the faithful who lived before him. Abraham's faith reached forward, as the Lord Jesus Christ Himself tells us that, "Abraham rejoiced to see My day, and he saw it and was glad" (John 8:56).

As we shall learn, these questions and many more are answered with profound wisdom and holy reason.

So overwhelmed is he with what the Lord has given him to write, Paul ends this three-chapter section on Israel (Rom. 9-11) with a majestic, triumphant doxology of praise and thanksgiving to God: "Oh, the depth of the riches both of the wisdom and knowledge of God! How unsearchable are His judgments and unfathomable His ways! For who has known the mind of the Lord, or who became His counselor? Or who has first given to Him that it might be paid back to him again? For from Him and through Him and to Him are all things. To Him be the glory forever. Amen" (Rom. 11:33-36).

In the first of these three chapters, Paul focuses first on the tragedy of Israel's unbelief (Rom. 9:1-5). He then declares that this unbelief is part of God's eternal plan of redemption (vv. 6-13) and demonstrates that this divine plan for Israel's unbelief is not capricious or unfair but is perfectly just (vv. 14-29).

In expressing his deep sorrow over Israel's spiritual condition, the apostle first declares his love for her people as fellow Jews.

PAUL'S PERSONAL CONNECTION WITH UNBELIEVING ISRAEL

I am telling the truth in Christ, I am not lying, my conscience bearing me witness in the Holy Spirit, that I have great sorrow and unceasing grief in my heart. For I could wish that I myself were accursed, separated from Christ for the sake of my brethren, my kinsmen according to the flesh, (9:1-3)

As just noted, Paul begins this section on Israel by declaring his personal grief over the unbelief of his beloved kinsmen. He has just presented eight chapters of divine truths that are thrilling to those who believe but devastating to all unbelievers, particularly so to unbelieving Jews, who felt totally secure in their racial heritage from Abraham, in their legalistic performance of ceremony, and in their adherence to rabbinical traditions. An unbelieving Jew who took seriously Paul's words in chapters 1-8 would likely feel that the gospel rendered him an utter outcast, written off by God.

Paul had once been the most zealous persecutor of Jews who named the name of Christ, relentlessly "breathing threats and murder against the disciples of the Lord" (Acts 9:1). Now he had been completely transformed, gladly counting himself among the disciples of Christ and strongly condemning the legalism and false security of traditional Judaism. To unbelieving religious Jews, Christianity would be viewed as an anti-Jewish conspiracy. In their eyes, Paul utterly contradicted the teaching of Moses, preaching such things as, "Let it be known to you, brethren, that through Him [Christ] forgiveness of sins is proclaimed to you, and through Him everyone who believes is freed from all things, from which you could not be freed through the Law of Moses" (Acts 13:38-39). Paul, a former Pharisee (Acts 23:6; Phil. 3:5) and zealous defender of traditional Judaism (Acts 8:1, 3; 9:1-2), was now considered the traitor of traitors to his people, more despised than a pagan Gentile. He was the great betrayer, the Judas of Judaism and the archenemy of Israel (see, e.g., Acts 9:23; 13:50; 20:3; 2 Cor. 11:24).

Still today, Jews look upon Christianity as inherently anti-Semitic. When they hear Jesus proclaimed as their long-awaited Messiah, the great Savior and Deliverer of Israel, they become highly incensed. Instead of seeing the gospel as the perfect fulfillment and completion of Judaism, they see it as a destructive threat. Unfortunately, their many persecutions throughout history at the hands of professed Christians exacerbates that resentment.

Paul had great concern not just for Israel as a nation but an incredibly profound love for Israelites as individuals. And he knew that before unbelieving Jews would listen to anything else he had to say, they first would have to be convinced that he truly cared for them and was far from leading an anti-Jewish conspiracy. In his preaching and writing the apostle irrefutably undermined the two basic pillars of popular Judaism, physical descent from Abraham and works righteousness under the law. Like Jesus during His earthly ministry, Paul stripped bare the hypocritical and legalistic sham of rabbinical Judaism. Also like Jesus, he knew he had to assure unbelieving Jews of his genuine love for them. He had to convince them that he proclaimed the gospel as a friend who wanted to protect and rescue them, not as an enemy who sought to condemn and destroy them. He had to show them his heart before he could give them his theology.

He begins by assuring them of his personal honesty and integrity, saying, **I am telling the truth in Christ, I am not lying.** Paul certified his genuineness by declaring that this **truth** was told **in Christ.** He called his Lord and Savior, Jesus Christ, as an indisputable witness. He was saying that everything he thought or did or felt was done for and through his Lord. Paul's union with Christ was the orbit within which his emotions moved and the fountain from which they flowed. In other words, Christ, who was the apostle's very life and breath, would attest to the truth of what he was about to teach. His omniscient, righteous, sovereign, and gracious Lord, who perfectly knew Paul's heart and motives, would affirm the truthfulness of the apostle's limitless love for his fellow

Jews. In the words of the nineteenth-century Swiss commentator and theologian Frederic Godet, "In the eyes of Paul there is something so holy in Christ, that in the pure and luminous atmosphere of His felt presence no lie, and not even any exaggeration, is possible" (*Commentary on St. Paul's Epistle to the Romans* [New York: Funk & Wagnalls, 1883], 338).

Paul frequently called God as his witness. In the opening of this letter he assured the Roman church that "God, whom I serve in my spirit in the preaching of the gospel of His Son, is my witness as to how unceasingly I make mention of you, always in my prayers" (1:9-10). For Paul, a promise made was a promise kept. In his second letter to Corinth, he wrote, "I call God as witness to my soul, that to spare you I came no more to Corinth" (2 Cor. 1:23). Later in that same letter he again assured his readers of his truthfulness by declaring, "The God and Father of the Lord Jesus, He who is blessed forever, knows that I am not lying" (11:31).

Giving the same assurance in 9:1, Paul insisted **I am not lying.** The apostle would not say or do anything simply for the sake of expediency or to make a favorable impression. He was not trying to entice his Jewish readers to accept what he said by flattering them or by making insincere and exaggerated claims for himself. He would not say anything that was untruthful or hypocritical in order to gain their attention or their agreement. His words exactly expressed his mind and heart.

Next he calls his own **conscience** as a **witness.** While defending himself before the Sanhedrin in Jerusalem, "Paul, looking intently at the Council, said, 'Brethren, I have lived my life with a perfectly good conscience before God up to this day'" (Acts 23:1). It was not Paul's conscience in itself that was reliable. His conscience was consistently clear and uncondemning because he lived in consistent obedience to the Lord. "For our proud confidence is this," he said, "the testimony of our conscience, that in holiness and godly sincerity, not in fleshly wisdom but in the grace of God, we have conducted ourselves in the world, and especially toward you" (2 Cor. 1:12).

Contrary to the common advice, "Let your conscience be your guide," the natural human conscience is far from being a reliable guide. It can be "seared" (1 Tim. 4:2), covered with insensitive scar tissue. Like every other aspect of man's fallen nature, it is tainted and corrupted by sin. "To the pure, all things are pure," Paul explained to Titus; "but to those who are defiled and unbelieving, nothing is pure, but both their mind and their conscience are defiled" (Titus 1:15). Through neglect of fellowship with God and disobedience to His Word, even a believer's conscience can become insensitive and unreliable. That is why Paul does not allow for believers to violate conscience, even in regard to nonmoral things. To do so is to train yourself to reject conscience (cf.

Rom. 14:20-23). All believers should be able to say with Martin Luther, "My conscience is captive to the Word of God."

A conscience surrendered to God's Word is a conscience that is subject to **the Holy Spirit,** whom Paul next invokes as a witness to his truthfulness and to the reliability of his conscience.

The human conscience by itself is neutral. It is activated by and according to the nature of the person to whom it belongs. The conscience of an evil, unregenerate man is no guard against sinful thoughts and actions. The conscience of a faithful believer, on the other hand, is reliable, because it is activated by the truths and standards of God's Word and is energized by the power of God's indwelling **Holy Spirit.** When we live in the Spirit, walk in the Spirit, and obey the Spirit, we can trust our conscience because it is under divine control. The Spirit's perfect prompting will either commend or condemn what we are doing or are planning to do.

Because what he is about to say seems so unbelievable—at best, highly exaggerated—Paul has an important reason for summoning such an array of witnesses.

His introductory statement is believable enough. Few Christians who knew Paul would doubt that he had **great sorrow and unceasing grief** in his **heart** for his unbelieving fellow Jews. As noted above, although he was a specially appointed apostle to the Gentiles, he also was commissioned to proclaim the gospel to "the sons of Israel" (Acts 9:15). As he makes clear in this present passage, it would have torn his heart out were he not to have opportunity to proclaim the way of salvation to his fellow sons and daughters of Israel. Even *with* the opportunity for witness, he could not assuage the **great sorrow and unceasing grief** he felt for those Jews who refused to believe.

It was that same kind of grief that the prophet Samuel had for Saul. We read that "Samuel did not see Saul again until the day of his death; for Samuel grieved over Saul. And the Lord regretted that He had made Saul king over Israel" (1 Sam. 15:35). By his own arrogance and disobedience, Saul had made himself an outcast before God and his people. But out of deep love for the Lord's anointed, Samuel never stopped grieving on the king's behalf. In the massive psalm that so highly exalts God's Word, the writer confesses: "My eyes shed streams of water, because they [Israel] do not keep Thy law" (Ps. 119:136).

Jeremiah is called the weeping prophet because of his deep grief over the unbelief and wickedness of his people. "Oh, that my head were waters," he mourned, "and my eyes a fountain of tears, that I might weep day and night for the slain of the daughter of my people!" (Jer. 9:1). Later he implores: "Listen and give heed, do not be haughty, for the Lord has spoken. Give glory to the Lord your God, before He brings darkness and before your feet stumble on the dusky mountains, and while you are hoping for light He makes it into deep darkness, and turns it into gloom. But if you will not listen to it, my soul will sob in secret for such pride; and my eyes will bitterly weep and flow down with tears, because the flock of the Lord has been taken captive" (Jer. 13:15-17).

Israel's rejection of her Messiah weighed so heavily on Paul's heart that he called on two members of the Trinity to attest to his unrelenting anguish. And he knew that, but for God's gracious intervention on the Damascus road, he not only would still be among those unbelieving Jews but would still be leading them in persecuting those who had acknowledged their Messiah.

The full depth and genuineness of Paul's grief is expressed in his almost unbelievable declaration that **I could wish that I myself were accursed, separated from Christ for the sake of my brethren, my kinsmen according to the flesh.** As indicated by his opening qualifier, **I could wish,** Paul knew he could not reject his salvation and again become **accursed** (devoted to destruction in eternal hell) and thus forever **separated from Christ.**

It was for the salvation of his fellow Jews that Paul expresses himself in hyperbole, saying he was willing even to forfeit his salvation, if, somehow, that could save them from God's condemnation. No one, of course, knew better than Paul that salvation is a believer's most precious treasure and that only Christ's sacrificial death has the power to save. But here he was speaking emotionally, not theologically, and there is no reason to doubt that his awesome statement of self-sacrifice was the expression of a completely honest heart. Paul felt such love that he was willing to relinquish his own salvation and spend eternity in hell if somehow that could bring his fellow Jews to faith in Christ! He knew, of course, that, even if such a thing were possible, his being separated from Christ would have no power in itself to bring a single person to Christ. The apostle also knew that the obvious impossibility and worthlessness of such a sacrifice would cause some of his critics to accuse him of safely offering to sacrifice that which he knew was impossible to lose. It was doubtless to counter such accusations that he had called Christ and the Holy Spirit to witness his sincerity.

Paul's passion to offer such an ultimate sacrifice reflected the gracious heart of God, who so loved the unloving and evil world that He sent His only begotten Son to provide for its redemption (John 3:16). It also reflected the equally gracious heart of the Son, who, in obedience to the Father, gave His life that others might live. Paul had just finished rejoicing in the believer's absolute security in Christ, from which "neither death, nor life, nor angels, nor principalities, nor things present, nor things to come, nor powers, nor height, nor depth, nor any other created thing" can "separate us from the love of God, which is in Christ Jesus our Lord" (Rom. 8:38-39). Yet his love for the lost in Israel gave him the willingness to surrender those intimate, inestimable, and eternal blessings, if doing so would bring his Jewish brethren to Christ.

It was exactly Paul's great love for the lost that made him such a powerful instrument in the hands of God. Evangelism has little effect if the evangelist has little love for the lost. John Knox reflected Paul's great love when he prayed, "Give me Scotland or I die," Henry Martyn when he said, "O that I were a flame of fire in the hand of God," and David Brainerd, who prayed that he might burn out for God, which he did before he was thirty years old.

Moses loved the fickle, ungrateful, and disobedient Israelites in much the same way that Paul loved them centuries later. Interceding for them after they built and worshiped the golden calf during the very time he was on Mount Sinai receiving the tablets of the law from God, Moses pleaded with the Lord on their behalf, "Now, if Thou wilt, forgive their sin—and if not, please blot me out from Thy book which Thou hast written!" (Ex. 32:32).

Some years ago, a young woman in our area was stabbed and killed while jogging near her apartment. Both the woman and her husband were Christians, but the woman's parents were not, and she had a great burden for their salvation. Shortly before she was killed she had confided to her husband that she would be willing to die if her death could be used by God to win her parents to Himself. After the memorial service, in which the gospel was proclaimed, her mother did indeed receive Christ as Lord and Savior.

Only Christ's own gracious love in the hearts of those who belong to Him can produce such self-sacrificing devotion. The more we obey His Word and surrender to His will, the more we will love as He loves.

GOD'S PERSONAL CONNECTION WITH UNBELIEVING ISRAEL

who are Israelites, to whom belongs the adoption as sons and the glory and the covenants and the giving of the Law and the temple service and the promises, whose are the fathers, and from whom is the Christ according to the flesh, who is over all, God blessed forever. Amen. (9:4-5)

Paul next expresses his deep sorrow over Israel's unbelief because of their personal connection with God. He not only loved Jews because they were his physical kinsmen but even more because they are God's chosen people. He loved whomever God loves, and because God loves Israel uniquely, Paul loved Israel uniquely.

In these two verses the apostle sets forth nine marvelous privileges that belong to Israel, graciously bestowed on them by a loving God.

First, they are privileged simply to be **Israelites,** descendants of Abraham through Isaac and then through Jacob, whose name was changed to Israel (Gen. 32:28).

Throughout history, Israelites (or Jews, as they came to be called after the Exile in Babylon) have distinguished themselves in virtually every field of human endeavor—in science, the arts, music, business, education, political leadership, and countless other areas. They have always been a noble people and have produced a disproportionate share of the world's geniuses. When God prepared His special earthly vineyard, "He planted it with the choicest vine," namely, Israel (Isa. 5:2).

Second, it is Israelites **to whom belongs the adoption as sons.** Beyond their patriarchal ancestry, Jews are privileged to have **adoption as** God's **sons.** God commanded Moses to "say to Pharaoh, 'Thus says the Lord, "Israel is My son, My first-born" ' " (Ex. 4:22). Through Hosea, the Lord declared that "when Israel was a youth I loved him, and out of Egypt I called My son" (Hos. 11:1). At the covenant at Sinai, when the law was given through Moses, God declared to Israel, "You shall be to Me a kingdom of priests and a holy nation" (Ex. 19:6). Israel was separated out to be His unique and righteous witness to the rest of the world.

It is clear from the context of those verses, as well as from countless other parts of Scripture, that the *nation* of Israel was, in some respect, God's child. Salvation has always been on an individual basis. One person cannot be saved by another's faith. As Paul makes clear a few verses later, "They are not all Israel who are descended from Israel" (Rom. 9:6). Yet, while not in the sense of salvation, it was as a nation that God sovereignly bestowed on Israel His special calling, covenant, blessing, and protection.

The Old Testament does not refer to God as the Father of individual Jews—in the way the New Testament does of God as Father of individual Christians—but as the Father of Israel. It was for that reason, among others, that the Jewish leaders were so incensed when Jesus referred to God in a personal relationship as His Father.

But Israel poorly fulfilled that calling, wasting its privilege. Through Isaiah the Lord lamented, "Listen to Me, O house of Jacob, and all the remnant of the house of Israel, you who have been borne by Me from birth, and have been carried from the womb; even to your old age, I shall be the same, and even to your graying years I shall bear you! I have done it, and I shall carry you; and I shall bear you, and I shall deliver you" (Isa. 46:3-4).

Third, God blessed Israel by revealing to her His own presence in the Shekinah glory. In that unique and inexplicable way, God dwelt in the midst of His people. In the wilderness, "the glory of the Lord appeared [to Israel] in the cloud" (Ex. 16:10). It was in His glory that He appeared to Israel at Sinai (Ex. 24:16-17), and His glory was present in the tent of meeting, where He spoke "with the sons of Israel" (Ex. 29:42-43; Lev. 9:23). His glory was supremely present in the Holy of Holies in the Tabernacle and then the Temple, manifested in light between the wings of the cherubim on the ark of the covenant (see Ex. 25:22; 40:34; 1 Kings 8:11).

Fourth, Israel was privileged to have been given **the covenants.** The first covenant was with Abraham, the physical father of all Jews (Gen. 12:15-17) and the spiritual father of all who believe (Rom. 4:11). Through Moses, Israel was given the covenant of law at Mount Sinai (Ex. 19-31; cf. Deut. 29-30). Through David Israel was given the covenant of an eternal kingdom (2 Sam. 7:8-16). It would even be through Israel that God's supreme covenant of redemption through His Son would come (Jer. 31:31-34; Ezek. 37:26). No other nation has or ever will be blessed with such covenants. As one commentator has observed, no aspect of Israel's history pointed out their uniqueness as the recipients of redemptive revelation more than these covenants.

Fifth, Israel was privileged by **the giving of the Law** of God to them through Moses. In that **Law** Israel not only was taught the Ten Commandments but countless other principles and standards, the obeying of which would honor God and bring blessing on the people. They were shown the way of blessing and prosperity, not only morally and spiritually but also materially. To disobey was to be cursed (cf. Deut. 27-28).

As Israel was encamped on the plains of Moab, shortly before entering the Promised Land, Moses reminded the people:

> See, I have taught you statutes and judgments just as the Lord my God commanded me, that you should do thus in the land where you are entering to possess it. So keep and do them, for that is your wisdom and your understanding in the sight of the peoples who will hear all these statutes and say, "Surely this great nation is a wise and understanding people." For what great nation is there that has a god so near to it as is the Lord our God whenever we call on Him? Or what great nation is there that has statutes and judgments as righteous as this whole law which I am setting before you today? (Deut. 4:5-8)

As Paul had already told his readers, Israel had the incomparable privilege of being custodian of the "oracles of God" (Rom. 3:2), which not only included the books of Moses but all of what we now call the Old Testament.

Sixth, Israel was uniquely blessed by being entrusted with **the temple service,** through which she worshiped and dealt with sin before the Lord. **The temple service** refers to the entire ceremonial system that God revealed through Moses—the sacrifices, offerings, cleansings, and other means of worship and repentance administered by the priests and Levites. When Israel obediently and sincerely worshiped the Lord, He promised: "I will meet there [at the tent of meeting] with the sons of Israel, and it shall be consecrated by My glory. And I will consecrate the tent of meeting and the altar; I will also consecrate Aaron and his sons to minister as priests to Me. And I will dwell among the sons of Israel and will be their God. And they shall know that I am the Lord their God who brought them out of the land of Egypt, that I might dwell among them; I am the Lord their God" (Ex. 29:43-46).

Seventh, Israel was given **the promises** of God in a distinct and unique way. Although Paul does not explain the nature of **the promises,** it seems likely that he was referring to the promised Messiah, who would come out of Israel, and to His promised kingdom, as well as to eternal life. That is the promise of which Peter reminded his audience in Jerusalem at Pentecost, saying, "For the promise is for you and your children, and for all who are far off, as many as the Lord our God shall call to Himself" (Acts 2:39). Later in the book of Acts, Luke reports Paul's message to Jews in Galatia: "We preach to you the good news of the promise made to the fathers, that God has fulfilled this promise to our children in that He raised up Jesus, as it is also written in the second Psalm, 'Thou art My Son; today I have begotten Thee.' And as for the fact that He raised Him up from the dead, no more to return to decay, He has spoken in this way: 'I will give you the holy and sure blessings of David'" (Acts 13:32-34; cf. 2 Sam. 7:8-17).

Eighth, Paul reminds his readers that it was from Israel that God raised up **the fathers,** beginning with the first great patriarchs, Abraham, Isaac, and Jacob/Israel. It was through those men that the foundations of all the blessings were laid.

Ninth, and finally, Israel was privileged to provide the lineage of **Christ according to the flesh.** Christ was not incidentally born a Jew but was preordained to be a human descendant of Abraham and of David. It is for that reason that Matthew gives the genealogy of Jesus' adoptive father, Joseph (1:1-17) and that Luke gives the genealogy of His natural mother, Mary (Luke 3:23-38). As noted above, Jesus Himself told the Samaritan woman that "salvation is from the Jews" and that He was the promised Jewish Messiah who would offer salvation to all mankind (John 4:22-26).

In closing this abbreviated but comprehensive account of Israel's special blessings, Paul declares that Jesus Christ—by far their greatest blessing, the blessing in whom all the others find their full meaning—**is over all, God blessed forever. Amen.**

Those words are not so much a benediction as an affirmation of Christ's divine majesty and lordship. Without exception in Scripture, both in the Hebrew Old Testament and the Greek New Testament, a doxology always places the word "blessed" *before* the name of God. Here, Paul uses the reverse form, **God blessed,** indicating beyond doubt that the apostle intentionally equates **Christ** with **God.** The antecedent of **God** is **who,** and the antecedent of **who** is **Christ.**

He was the supreme blessing, yet they rejected Him! Tragic unbelief that grieved the heart of Paul and grieves the heart of God Himself.

Israel's Unbelief Is Consistent with God's Plan—part 1 It Is Consistent with His Promises (Romans 9:6-13)

2

But it is not as though the word of God has failed. For they are not all Israel who are descended from Israel; neither are they all children because they are Abraham's descendants, but: "through Isaac your descendants will be named." That is, it is not the children of the flesh who are children of God, but the children of the promise are regarded as descendants. For this is a word of promise: "At this time I will come, and Sarah shall have a son." And not only this, but there was Rebekah also, when she had conceived twins by one man, our father Isaac; for though the twins were not yet born, and had not done anything good or bad, in order that God's purpose according to His choice might stand, not because of works, but because of Him who calls, it was said to her, "The older will serve the younger." Just as it is written, "Jacob I loved, but Esau I hated." (9:6-13)

While the major theme of chapters 9-11 is God's dealing with His elect nation, the underlying theme, especially of chapter 9, is God's sovereignty in doing so. It demands more than a superficial understanding. And yet, when the deepest meaning and implications of this passage are carefully considered, especially its unambiguous declaration of God's absolute and unrestricted sovereign power, even the most devoted believer is left with some profound mysteries.

In 1948, Jews reestablished the nation of Israel in part of the ancient land that God had promised them through Abraham. In the Six-Day War of 1967, they acquired more of that land, including full control over their holy city of Jerusalem.

But the modern state of Israel is not a theocracy, with God as its sovereign Lord, or even a nation ruled by God-serving leaders. Although it contains large and influential religious groups, it is, like most nations of today, a secular state.

Some Israelis are openly atheistic. Others cherish their religious, biblical heritage and see it as the key to justify their right to the land. Some even believe the state of Israel itself is the Messiah spoken of figuratively in the Old Testament, the promised deliverer who would regain Jewish rights and influence in a world where the nation has so long been persecuted and suppressed.

One such group even draws parallels between that national view and the claims of Christians that the historical person Jesus Christ is the Messiah. It is claimed, for instance, that, like Jesus Christ, the nation of Israel was sovereignly called, or destined, into existence as its own messiah. That nation faced destruction by famine and was protected in Egypt, just as the infant Jesus faced destruction by Herod and was taken by Joseph and Mary to Egypt for protection. That nation/messiah became despised and hated by the world and was crucified, as it were, by the Romans in A.D. 70, just as Jesus had been crucified by the Romans some forty years earlier. Finally, just as Jesus was resurrected to life on the third day, the nation/messiah of Israel was raised up to national life in the third millennium (the general timing of 1948-76).

On the other hand, many religious Jews in Israel are still awaiting the first coming of their promised king, the messiah. Yet they look forward to a man who will come as their deliverer from human oppression, not from sin. They believe he will someday triumphantly enter the eastern gate of Jerusalem and that he will establish his throne in that city, setting in place their nation's supremacy from which he will rule the world.

In the land of God's own promise to them, few Jews acknowledge their true Messiah. They live where the prophets lived and walk where Jesus walked, but they do not truly believe the prophets (honoring only their memories) and, far worse, they reject the truth of the sacrifice of Messiah's own life made for sin.

Many Israelis pragmatically appreciate evangelical Christians who strongly support the state of Israel. But Jewish gratitude for such Christian patronage is based largely on its power to help them achieve their own economic and political ends.

Questions that Jews everywhere might express to Christians could be phrased something like these:"If, as you say, God sent His Son to earth as the promised King and Savior to redeem Israel and the world to Himself, how could His ancient chosen people possibly have not recognized and accepted Him? How could Jews—which Christians themselves acknowledge to be God's uniquely elect race—conceivably have rejected their promised and long-awaited Hope and even put Him to death? If the Jewish leaders of Jesus' time, as well as the vast majority of other Jews of that day and of every age since, have not recognized Him as their own Messiah, then it is utterly irrational to believe that Jesus of Nazareth was, much less still is, who Christians claim Him to be."

Because they assume that those very dilemmas themselves disprove that Jesus could have been the Messiah, Jews conclude that Christianity is nothing more than a perversion of the true, God-given religion of Judaism.

Two further reasons that Jews do not accept Christianity are that it supersedes the Old Covenant of Moses and that it opens the door for Gentiles to come directly to God on the same terms as Jews and thereby become full and unqualified members of the family of God without passing through the vestibule of Judaism. To accept the New Covenant in Jesus Christ was to recognize that it fulfilled and replaced the Old Covenant, that it completely nullified the ceremonies and all the manmade rabbinical traditions, and that it set aside Israel as God's uniquely chosen nation in order to call out a new people from the Gentiles, who were thus offered equal access to God's grace and favor.

In the minds of most Jews of Jesus' and Paul's day, Christianity, as it soon came to be called (see Acts 11:26), was nothing less than a heretical movement that attempted to abrogate God's ancient covenant and promises given through Abraham and reiterated to the other patriarchs as well as the covenant and law that He gave through Moses and to David. Most Jews, therefore, considered Christianity to be the total denigration of God's integrity and faithfulness.

Because the Judaism of his day was so deeply steeped in the legalistic works righteousness of rabbinical traditions, and because God's plan to offer salvation on equal terms to Gentiles was a mystery not fully revealed in the Old Testament, Paul devotes chapters 9-11 of Romans to clarifying the place of Israel in the present church age.

As the apostle explained to the church at Ephesus,

> By revelation there was made known to me the mystery, as I wrote before in brief. And by referring to this, when you read you can understand my insight into the mystery of Christ, which in other generations was not made known to the sons of men, as it has now been revealed

to His holy apostles and prophets in the Spirit; to be specific, that
the Gentiles are fellow heirs and fellow members of the body, and
fellow partakers of the promise in Christ Jesus through the gospel.
(Eph. 3:4-6)

In Romans 9:6-33 Paul gives four basic reasons why the gospel of
Jesus Christ is not blasphemous heresy and in particular why its rejection by most individual Jews and by Israel as a nation does not impugn
God's righteous and just character, does not vitiate His revelation given
in the Jewish Scriptures (the Old Testament), does not alter the means
of salvation, and does not relinquish the place of Israel in His ultimate
plan of redemption.

First, Paul declares that the unbelief of Israel is consistent with
God's promises (9:6-13); second, that it is consistent with His Person
(vv. 14-24); third, that it is consistent with God's prophetic revelation
(vv. 25-29); and fourth, that it is consistent with God's prerequisite of
salvation by faith (vv. 30-33).

**But it is not as though the word of God has failed. For
they are not all Israel who are descended from Israel; neither
are they all children because they are Abraham's descendants,
but: "through Isaac your descendants will be named." That is, it
is not the children of the flesh who are children of God, but the
children of the promise are regarded as descendants. For this is
a word of promise: "At this time I will come, and Sarah shall have
a son." And not only this, but there was Rebekah also, when she
had conceived twins by one man, our father Isaac; for though
the twins were not yet born, and had not done anything good or
bad, in order that God's purpose according to His choice might
stand, not because of works, but because of Him who calls, it
was said to her, "The older will serve the younger." Just as it is
written, "Jacob I loved, but Esau I hated."** (9:6-13)

As discussed in the previous chapter, Paul began his correction
of Jewish false belief about the gospel of Jesus Christ by declaring his
own unequivocal love for unbelieving Israel (Rom. 9:1-5). Almost incon-
ceivably, calling the Holy Spirit as witness, he declared that, because of
his "unceasing grief" over their eternal alienation from God, he would
gladly sacrifice his own salvation, if doing so could redeem his fellow
Jews, his "brethren, [his] kinsmen according to the flesh" (vv. 1-3). Apart
from Jesus' own statements during His incarnation, no greater human
testimony of compassion and willing sacrifice for the sake of others is
recorded in all of Scripture.

The apostle could not, of course, accomplish such a thing, but
he was compelled to assure unbelieving Jews of his great love for them

and his desire for their salvation before he declared to them the more than unwelcome news that all of their gracious and unique God-given advantages and blessings were of no avail before Him if they rejected His own Son as Savior and Lord (vv. 4-5). By implication he was saying that, in rejecting Jesus Christ, Israel rejected God and lost her status as God's favored, divinely blessed nation. She would no longer be the apple of God's eye, no longer be the people upon whom God would pour out His great blessings of care and protection. The question is, "Doesn't this rejection by God constitute a violation of His promises and thereby sacrifice His integrity?" It was on the basis of such reasoning that Jews rejected Jesus as their Messiah and felt justified in that rejection because they concluded it was based on sound defense of the character of God. And, they reasoned, such almost unanimous rejection had to prove Jesus was not the Messiah.

The first of the reasons mentioned above that Paul gives for contradicting the prevalent Jewish idea that Israel's rejection of Jesus proved He could not have been the true Messiah is that Israel's unbelief as a nation was perfectly consistent with God's ancient promises.

He begins by declaring, **It is not as though the word of God has failed** (or, more literally, "has fallen"). Paul was referring to Israel's "adoption as sons and the glory and the covenants and the giving of the Law and the temple service and the promises" (v. 4). The Lord had not abrogated or in any way invalidated the ultimate fulfillment of His unconditional promises to the Jews. Through Jeremiah, He had long ago assured His people that, "just as I brought all this great disaster on this people, so I am going to bring on them all the good that I am promising them" (Jer. 32:42). Through Isaiah He said, "My word ... which goes forth from My mouth ... shall not return to Me empty, without accomplishing what I desire, and without succeeding in the matter for which I sent it" (Isa. 55:11). Even God's cutting off unbelieving Israel was perfectly consistent with His covenant promises to them. Chastening and punishment are elements of His divine faithfulness, integrity, and love and are not to be questioned.

Our own day has witnessed irrefutable proof that, although God has punished the nation for its unbelief, He has not allowed the many trials and dispersions of His people—the deportation of Jews from Israel, first by Assyria in 722 B.C. and by Babylon in 586, and subsequently by Rome, partially in A.D. 70 and all but entirely in 132—to obliterate Israel as a distinct people. After nearly two thousand years (by 1948), the Lord reestablished her in her own land and she was recognized by the world community as an independent and sovereign state.

God's bringing Israel back into her own land, however, does not prove that, as a nation, she is once again pleasing in His eyes. And, as already mentioned, mere physical descent from Abraham has *never* made an individual Jew a member of God's holy family. But as we will see, her salvation *will* come, along with the kingdom that God promised.

As Paul continues to explain how Jewish unbelief does not discredit God's Word, he writes: **They are not all Israel who are descended from Israel; neither are they all children because they are Abraham's descendants, but: "Through Isaac your descendants will be named." That is, it is not the children of the flesh who are children of God, but the children of the promise are regarded as descendants.**

But even being in the line of Isaac through Jacob, who became Israel, did not make a person a true child of the promise. **They are not all Israel who are descended from Israel.** Not all physical Israelites are true heirs of the promise (see the discussion of Romans 2:28-29 in the previous commentary volume).

Because Jews were so familiar with them, Paul chooses familiar Old Testament texts to support his point. The first male descendant of Abraham was Ishmael, whom he had by Hagar, the Egyptian maid of his wife Sarah. Disbelieving God's promise that Abraham would have an heir through her, the barren Sarah gave Hagar to Abraham as another wife and insisted that her husband would father a male heir through her (Gen. 16:1-3). As soon as Hagar became pregnant, however, Sarah became resentful and jealous. In due time Ishmael was born, and, had he been Abraham's only son, would have become the only heir. Sarah soon demanded that Hagar and her newly-weaned son be driven out of the household (vv. 4-6).

Although Ishmael was a son of Abraham, and although Sarah was past the age of normal child-bearing, it was through her, Abraham's true wife, that God gave assurance that the true son of His promise would be born: "Sarah your wife shall bear you a son, and you shall call his name Isaac; and I will establish My covenant with him for an everlasting covenant for his descendants after him....My covenant I will establish with Isaac, whom Sarah will bear to you at this season next year" (17:19, 21; cf. 18:10-14).

It was to that specific passage that Paul referred when he reminded his readers of God's declaration to Abraham that **through Isaac your descendants will be named.** As Abraham's son, Ishmael would receive his own special blessings from God (Gen. 17:18), but he was not and never could have been the heir of God's promise. After Sarah died, Abraham had six other sons by a new wife, Keturah (25:1-2); but, like Ishmael, none of those could have been the heir of promise.

Not only could the descendants of those sons not be the children of God's promise, but even the privileged descendants of Sarah through Isaac could not become full heirs of the promise merely by their physical lineage.

God has always known that Jews would be spiritually dead and cut off from the promise and from salvation. **Neither are they all children because they are Abraham's descendants** states the same truth. Because some Jews reject Jesus does not prove He is not Messiah, nor does it denigrate the integrity of God. He knew there would be unbelieving Jews throughout all Israel's history.

To illustrate that reality, Paul turns back to Isaac. Because Isaac was Abraham's only child of the divine **promise** of Genesis 17:19-21, Paul here refers to Isaac's children as **Abraham's descendants** (the Jews) and therefore the only true **children of God** in a racial sense. The entire *nation* of Israel was elected and brought into *divine privilege.*

It was not **the children of the flesh,** Abraham's other children by Hagar and Keturah, but the children of Isaac, the child of promise, who were **the descendants** of the promise. The point is that, just as not all of Abraham's physical children are to inherit the promise of belonging to the people of God physically, only those of Isaac, so neither do all of Abraham's children through Isaac belong to the people of God spiritually. The unbelief, sin, rejection, and hostility of Israel toward Christ is not proof He is not Messiah. To the contrary, they fit perfectly with God's promise, which anticipated that not all Jews would believe in Jesus and be saved.

That truth was remarkably illustrated during the time of Elijah. Because of the continual threats against his life, not only by the priests of Baal but also by King Ahab and Queen Jezebel of Israel, Elijah became convinced that all Israel had become apostate. Later in the book of Romans, Paul reminds his readers of the prophet's fearful complaint and of God's assuring reply: "'Lord, they have killed Thy prophets, they have torn down Thine altars, and I alone am left, and they are seeking my life.' But what is the divine response to him? 'I have kept for Myself seven thousand men who have not bowed the knee to Baal'" (Rom. 11:3-4; cf. 1 Kings 19:10, 18). In other words, even during the ministry of that great miracle-working prophet, the vast majority of Israel was thoroughly and openly pagan.

From the very time of the Fall, long before God's covenant with Abraham, God established that the only way a person can become righteous before Him is by faith. The writer of Hebrews explains that, in regard to Adam's own sons, the sacrifice of Abel was accepted by God because it was offered in faith and that the sacrifice of Cain was rejected because it was not offered in faith: "By faith Abel offered to God a better sacrifice than Cain, through which he obtained the testimony that he was righteous, God testifying about his gifts, and through faith, though he is dead, he still speaks" (Heb. 11:4).

Isaac also is an excellent illustration of the true child of God because, long before he was even conceived, he was divinely chosen among the descendants of Abraham to be the heir of promise. His becoming the spiritual child of God was just as sovereignly and supernaturally preordained as his becoming the physical child of Abraham. That sovereign election, made effective through faith, is true of every person who has been saved, both before and after Isaac.

Even before Jesus met Nathanael, He said of him, "Behold, an Israelite indeed, in whom is no guile!" (John 1:47). "Indeed" translates *alēthōs,* which means genuine. In other words, of the multiplied thousands of Jews in Israel at that time, Jesus identified Nathanael as a true, genuine Israelite—declaring by implication that most other Jews were not, no matter how impeccable their genealogy from Abraham. Nathanael was spiritually without "guile," without deceit or pretense, a spiritual descendant of Abraham who trusted in God rather than in his human lineage or works.

In stark contrast to Nathanael, the religious leaders who confronted Jesus while He was teaching in the Temple treasury (John 8:20) were incensed by His declaration that they needed to receive His truth in order to be free. "We are Abraham's offspring," they replied, "and have never yet been enslaved to anyone; how is it that You say, 'You shall become free?'" When Jesus explained that He was speaking of freedom from sin, from which only He, God's Son, could deliver them, they indignantly appealed to presumed righteousness based on their physical descent from Abraham. But Jesus said to them, "If you are Abraham's children, do the deeds of Abraham. But as it is, you are seeking to kill Me, a man who has told you the truth, which I heard from God; this Abraham did not do" (see vv. 8:32-40). A few moments later, He called those unbelieving Jewish leaders sons of their "father the devil" and charged that, by their rejection of Him and His gospel, that they were "not of God" (see vv. 43-47).

Paul's assertion in Romans 9 echoes what Jesus said to those unbelieving Jews in the Temple and what he himself had emphasized some years earlier in his letter to the Galatian churches: "Even so Abraham believed God, and it was reckoned to him as righteousness. Therefore, be sure that it is those who are of faith who are sons of Abraham" (Gal. 3:6-7).

Paul's point in Romans 9:6-33 is that Israel's rejection of Jesus as the Messiah did not prove Jesus was not of God but, to the contrary, that unbelieving Israel and Israelites were not of God. Their rejection did not abrogate God's promise but simply gave further evidence that His promise had always been to those who believed as Abraham believed, not to those who were merely his physical progeny. At the end of the chapter in Galatians cited above, Paul reiterates that "if you belong to

Christ, then you are Abraham's offspring, heirs according to promise" (Gal. 3:29).

God's just and righteous character does not allow the possibility of His failing in any of His promises. In addition to the primary problems of love of sin and lack of faith, the great obstacle for the Jews of Paul's day, as with the great majority of Jews today, was failure to understand the true meaning of God's promises.

The prophets repeatedly made clear that, just as only Isaac, the elect son of Abraham, would be the physical heir of promise, so only a divinely elected remnant would qualify as the recipients of God's promise to Abraham. Near the end of Romans 9, Paul wrote that "just as Isaiah foretold, 'Except the Lord of Sabaoth had left to us a posterity [a remnant], we would have become as Sodom, and would have resembled Gomorrah'" (Rom. 9:29).

As noted above, Paul's reference to God's **word of promise** was His declaration to Abraham that **at this time I will come, and Sarah shall have a son** (see Gen. 18:10, 14). As seen earlier, in His previous statement of that promise, the Lord even told Abraham that the son's name would be Isaac (17:19, 21).

God always raises up, at the right time and place, those whom He chooses to use in His divine plan. The Lord led Ruth to return to Judah with Naomi, her mother-in-law, in order that she might become an ancestor of King David. Mordecai sensed that truth when he told his niece, Esther, "Who knows whether you have not attained royalty for such a time as this?" (Esther 4:14).

God's supreme raising up of the right person at the right time was the sending of His own Son to bring salvation to Israel and the world: "When the fulness of the time came," Paul reminded the Galatians, "God sent forth His Son, born of a woman, born under the Law, in order that He might redeem those who were under the Law, that we might receive the adoption as sons" (Gal. 4:4-5).

And not only this, Paul continues with a second illustration of this truth, **but there was Rebekah also, when she had conceived twins by one man, our father Isaac.** Although she lived in the land of Padan-Aram, God specifically chose Rebekah not only to become Isaac's wife but to bear him twin sons. Yet, instead of allowing those twins to be equal heirs of Isaac, the Lord sovereignly chose Jacob above Esau—even when **the twins were not yet born, and had not done anything good or bad, in order that God's purpose according to His choice might stand, not because of works, but because of Him who calls, it was said to her, "The older will serve the younger."**

God did not choose both sons to continue the physical line of promise but sovereignly elected Jacob and passed over Esau before they were even born. And just as He chose them without any regard for what they would do in their lives, but purely **that God's purpose . . . might stand** with no regard for any human work, so God has chosen some Jews, not all, for salvation.

Unconditionally, and completely apart from any consideration of human merit, God elects those who will become His heirs of promise. Jacob and Esau not only had the same father and mother but were born at the same time. Technically, Esau was born slightly ahead of Jacob, but God purposely disregarded that fact, telling their mother that, contrary to the custom of those days, **the older will serve the younger** (cf. Gen. 25:23).

Esau's own life and the lives of his descendants give clear evidence that they rejected God. And God's statement that Esau would serve his younger brother extended to their progeny as well. There is no biblical record of Esau's being personally subservient to Jacob, but much evidence that the nation of Edom, which descended from Esau, was often in direct or indirect subservience to and in conflict with the nation Israel, which derived from Jacob, whose name was later changed to Israel.

The Edomites soon became idolatrous, and centuries later the prophet Amos declared to them:"Thus says the Lord,'For three transgressions of Edom and for four I will not revoke its punishment, because he pursued his brother with the sword, while he stifled his compassion; his anger also tore continually, and he maintained his fury forever. So I will send fire upon Teman, and it will consume the citadels of Bozrah [the ancient capital of Edom]'" (Amos 1:11-12). Obadiah warned them that, "because of violence to your brother Jacob, you will be covered with shame, and you will be cut off forever" (Obad. 10).

Because He is a God of truth and justice, the Lord did not condone Jacob's and his mother's later deceit of his blind father in order to receive the blessing of the first-born. Yet, as He often does, God used Jacob's deception to fulfill His own divine purposes—which He would have accomplished perfectly in any case, without sinful human intervention.

Jacob's sin did not abrogate God's promise in the least degree, but it brought many painful and unnecessary problems to Jacob himself and to many others. Unlike his twin brother, Jacob sought God and had a heart for God, but he suffered because of his lack of trust in God to accomplish His own purposes in His own holy way and in His own divine time.

Paul's next statement, summarizing what he has just written, is quoted from Malachi 1:2-3 and seems shocking and completely contrary to most people's view of God's impartiality: **Just as it is written, "Jacob I loved, but Esau I hated."** But just as God's prediction that the elder Esau would serve the younger Jacob did not directly apply to those two individuals but rather to their descendants, so the Lord's declaration here seems to apply in the same way. The book of Genesis mentions no divine hatred of Esau himself. Obadiah's declaration that God hated Esau was written over a thousand years after Esau lived, and the most reasonable interpretation of the prophet's statement would seem to indicate that the Lord's hatred is against Esau's idolatrous descendants. In the same way, the Lord's love of Jacob would refer to Jacob's descendants, who, although often rebellious and sometimes idolatrous, were His sovereignly elected people through whom the world's Redeemer would come.

In an analogous way, through the illustrations of Isaac and Jacob, Paul shows that out of the loins of Abraham, Isaac, and Jacob would come an elect remnant of redeemed Jews and that others would remain in unbelief and thereby forfeit the spiritual promises of God.

But Paul has already declared unambiguously that God's justification for choosing Jacob over Esau was not based on their personal characteristics or works but solely on the basis of His divine and infallible prerogative (v. 13)—a mystery that our finite human minds cannot fathom. Out of their loins came two nations, one of whom God chose for divine blessing and protection and the other whom He chose for divine judgment.

Paul has already established the absolute necessity for human faith in salvation, Abraham being the spiritual father of all those who trust in God (Rom. 4:11). But the power of salvation is entirely from God's grace, and the primary purpose of salvation is to give Him glory.

Self-centered man rebels at such a notion, and even many Christians vainly try to explain away the clear truth that God is God and that, by definition, whatever He does can be nothing but just and righteousness. He needs no justification for anything He does—including calling some men to salvation and not calling others. He has always acted thus.

We can only acknowledge with Paul, with full belief but with far from full understanding, that "God is faithful, through whom [we] were called into fellowship with His Son, Jesus Christ our Lord" (1 Cor. 1:9).

Israel's Unbelief Is Consistent with God's Plan—part 2 It Is Consistent with His Person (Romans 9:14-24)

3

What shall we say then? There is no injustice with God, is there? May it never be! For He says to Moses, "I will have mercy on whom I have mercy, and I will have compassion on whom I have compassion." So then it does not depend on the man who wills or the man who runs, but on God who has mercy. For the Scripture says to Pharaoh, "For this very purpose I raised you up, to demonstrate My power in you, and that My name might be proclaimed throughout the whole earth." So then He has mercy on whom He desires, and He hardens whom He desires. You will say to me then, "Why does He still find fault? For who resists His will?" On the contrary, who are you, O man, who answers back to God? The thing molded will not say to the molder, "Why did you make me like this," will it? Or does not the potter have a right over the clay, to make from the same lump one vessel for honorable use, and another for common use? What if God, although willing to demonstrate His wrath and to make His power known, endured with much patience vessels of wrath prepared for destruction? And He did so in order that He might make known the riches of His glory upon vessels of mercy, which He prepared beforehand for glory, even us, whom He also called, not from among Jews only, but also from among Gentiles. (9:14-24)

Paul's second point in explaining that Israel's unbelief is not inconsistent with God's revealed plan is that her unbelief in no way reflects against or demeans God's person, in particular His sovereign power and justice. In this passage the apostle answers two anticipated questions that are often raised about God's electing some people for salvation while others are left to damnation.

THE FIRST ANTICIPATED QUESTION ANSWERED

What shall we say then? There is no injustice with God, is there? May it never be! For He says to Moses, "I will have mercy on whom I have mercy, and I will have compassion on whom I have compassion." So then it does not depend on the man who wills or the man who runs, but on God who has mercy. For the Scripture says to Pharaoh, "For this very purpose I raised you up, to demonstrate My power in you, and that My name might be proclaimed throughout the whole earth." So then He has mercy on whom He desires, and He hardens whom He desires. (9:14-18)

The question behind this paragraph is a question of God's fairness. If He only chose some to be the heirs of promise, and not others, people will say He is unfair. Paul had just reminded his Jewish readers that God sovereignly chose Isaac above Ishmael and Jacob above his twin brother Esau before they were born (Rom. 9:13-16). They were not chosen or rejected because of who they were or would be or because of what they had done or would do, "but because of Him who calls" (v. 11), that is, wholly on the basis of God's sovereign will. Isaac and Jacob were "the children of the promise" (v. 8); Ishmael and Esau were not. So, in the sense of spiritual salvation, God has chosen some to believe.

The natural human response is to assert that God was unjustly arbitrary in choosing one over the other long before they would have opportunity to trust or reject Him or to be obedient or disobedient. That natural response, however, is tantamount to saying that there is **injustice with God.** So Paul asks rhetorically if we have a right to accuse God of being unjust.

That accusation has been raised throughout the history of the church and is still heard today when God's election and predestination are proclaimed. How can God elect one person and reject another before they are even born? In light of human wisdom and standards, especially in democratic societies, where all people are considered equal before the law, the ideas of election and predestination are repulsive and unacceptable. Those doctrines, it is claimed, could not possibly characterize a God who is truly just and righteous. To the saved but ignorant or immature mind, God simply could not do such a thing, and to the unsaved mind, a god like that would not be worthy of recognition, much less worship.

Soon after his great afflictions began, Job's wife advised him to "Curse God and die!" (Job 2:9), implying that God was grossly unfair and did not deserve the worship of a faithful man who was allowed to be so tormented.

In light of such human objections and conjectures, Paul proceeds to defend God's person. **May it never be!** he declares, using the strongest Greek negative *(mē genoito),* which he employs some ten times in this epistle. The phrase sometimes is translated idiomatically (as in the KJV) as "God forbid!" The idea is that of "No, no, a thousand times no!" The very idea that God could be unjust or unrighteous to the slightest degree is blasphemy. Even with his limited understanding of God, long before any of His revealed Word was recorded, Abraham affirmed rhetorically, "Shall not the Judge of all the earth deal justly?" (Gen. 18:25).

Because God Himself is the measure of righteousness and justice, He has no capacity for unrighteousness or injustice. It is His very character to be gracious, compassionate, merciful, and loving. The psalmists repeatedly declared that cardinal truth. David asserted that "the righteous God tries the hearts and minds" (Ps. 7:9) and "The Lord is gracious and merciful; slow to anger and great in lovingkindness" (145:8). Other psalmists proclaimed: "Thy right hand is full of righteousness" (48:10); "Thy righteousness, O God, reaches to the heavens" (71:19); "Gracious is the Lord, and righteous" (116:5); "Righteous art Thou, O Lord, and upright are Thy judgments" (119:137); and "Thy righteousness is an everlasting righteousness" (119:142).

With equal certainty Jeremiah testified, "Thus says the Lord, 'Let not a wise man boast of his wisdom, and let not the mighty man boast of his might, let not a rich man boast of his riches; but let him who boasts boast of this, that he understands and knows Me, that I am the Lord who exercises lovingkindness, justice, and righteousness on earth'" (Jer. 9:23-24). By His very nature, God always has been and always will be righteous and just. As He reveals through Malachi, "I, the Lord, do not change" (Mal. 3:6).

As he did with the previous point, in response to the accusation that God's sovereign election is unfair, Paul cites two texts from the Old Testament Scriptures that clearly illustrate otherwise. He does not resort to rational argument or to philosophical apologetics but bases his assertion directly on God's own Word.

First, he cites Exodus 33:19, declaring, **For He [God] says to Moses, "I will have mercy on whom I have mercy, and I will have compassion on whom I have compassion."**

Moses had just come through a very trying experience. While he had been on Mount Sinai receiving the two tablets of the testimony from God, his brother Aaron, the high priest, led the impatient people of Israel to melt down their gold jewelry to make a calf to worship as if it represented the true God (Ex. 32:2-6). In response to that great apostasy, God commanded that "about three thousand men" be put to death (v. 28). He would have been perfectly justified in killing all the Israelites who had participated in the idolatry, but He sovereignly chose to execute only those three thousand as a warning to the others and to preserve His witness nation.

Horrified by that "great sin," Moses made intercession for his people, praying, "Now, if Thou wilt, forgive their sin—and if not, please blot me out from Thy book which Thou hast written!" (vv. 30-31). The Lord replied, "Whoever has sinned against Me, I will blot him out of My book. But go now, lead the people where I told you. Behold, My angel shall go before you; nevertheless in the day when I punish, I will punish them for their sin" (vv. 33-34).

Despite God's assurance that He would lead and protect His people as they entered and conquered the Promised Land (33:1-3), and despite Moses' own nearness to the Lord, who spoke to him "just as a man speaks to his friend" (v. 11), this loyal man of God deeply sensed his own inadequacy for such a formidable task and his own and his people's need for the Lord's continual presence, guidance, and power (vv. 12-13). In reply to that additional entreaty, God gave assurance, tempered by the declaration of His divine prerogative: "I Myself will make all My goodness pass before you, and will proclaim the name of the Lord before you; and I will be gracious to whom I will be gracious, and will show compassion on whom I will show compassion" (v. 19). In other words, His sparing the people and continuing to guide and protect them was purely reflective of His mercy and grace. He had the absolute right to condemn or to save as He divinely saw fit. God's sovereignty and His grace not only are compatible but are inseparable.

Because all men are sinful and deserve God's condemnation, no person is wronged or treated unjustly if God chooses to condemn him. That is justice. His mercy toward any person is purely by His grace.

Mercy and **compassion** are essentially synonymous, but **mercy** refers primarily to action, whereas **compassion** refers more to the feeling or disposition behind that action.

Continuing simply to declare God's truth, rather than fruitlessly trying to explain the logic of what is beyond human comprehension, Paul goes on to say, **So then it does not depend on the man who wills or the man who runs, but on God who has mercy.** It is not man's choice or pursuit but God who initiates mercy for the sinner. Salvation is never initiated by human choice or merited by zealous human effort. It always begins in God's sovereign, gracious, and eternal will. Those who receive God's **mercy** receive it solely by His grace. Ishmael desired the blessing but failed to receive it. Esau ran for the blessing, as it were, but also failed to receive it (see Gen. 27).

As the writer of Hebrews explains, "By faith Abraham, when he was tested, offered up Isaac; and he who had received the promises was offering up his only begotten son; it was he to whom it was said, 'In Isaac your descendants shall be called'" (Heb. 11:17-18).

The same writer also makes clear, however, that God's choosing must be confirmed by man's faith. "By *faith* Isaac blessed Jacob and Esau, even regarding things to come. By *faith* Jacob, as he was dying, blessed each of the sons of Joseph" (Heb. 11:20-21, emphasis added). Esau received *a* blessing from his father but not *the* blessing he sought with tears, because he was ungodly and sought the blessing without repentance or faith (12:16-17).

Next, Paul cites another supporting passage from Exodus, this time from chapter 9, verse 16: **For the Scripture says to Pharaoh, "For this very purpose I raised you up, to demonstrate My power in you, and that My name might be proclaimed throughout the whole earth."** Being an absolute monarch, Pharaoh assumed that, certainly within his own realm, everything he said and did was by his own free choice to serve his own human purposes. But the Lord made clear through Moses that Pharaoh was divinely raised up to serve a divine purpose, a purpose of which the king was not even aware.

Exegeirō **(raised . . . up)** carries the idea of bringing forward or lifting up and was used of the rise of historical figures to positions of prominence. The word is used several times in the Septuagint. Speaking of the Messiah, Balaam declared to Balak, the king of Moab, "One from Jacob *shall have dominion*, and shall destroy the remnant from the city" (Num. 24:19). Through the prophet Nathan, the Lord told David that, because of his murder of Uriah and taking his wife, Bathsheba, for himself, "I will *raise up* evil against you from your own household" (2 Sam. 12:11). One of Job's "comforters" rightly said of God that "He *sets on high* those who are lowly, and those who mourn are lifted to safety" (Job 5:11). In much the same way that He raised up Pharaoh, the Lord also *raised up* "the Chaldeans" to do His will (Hab. 1:6) and one day will "*raise up* a shepherd [Antichrist] in the land who will not care for the perishing, seek the scattered, heal the broken, or sustain the one standing, but will devour the flesh of the fat sheep and tear off their hoofs" (Zech. 11:16).

The **Pharaoh** of whom Moses and Paul were speaking was probably Amenhotep II, whom the Lord sovereignly raised to prominence and power. **For this very purpose,** God declared, **I raised you up, to demonstrate My power in you, and that My name might be**

proclaimed throughout the whole earth." The Lord of all history put that king into a position of great authority in order to **demonstrate** His far greater divine power and authority that would bring glory to His **name . . . throughout the whole earth.**

It is that very divine redemptive power that Jews have celebrated for millennia in Passover, remembering the Lord's gracious delivering power, as shown by His saving them from the oppressive hand of Pharaoh. That feast is the Old Testament benchmark of redemption—the physical deliverance of Israel from human bondage, and it foreshadowed Christ's infinitely greater spiritual deliverance of men from sin's spiritual bondage.

Using Pharaoh's proud arrogance, the Lord demonstrated that His miraculous power was far greater than the Satan-empowered miracles of Pharaoh's magicians. He made a path through the Red Sea to deliver His people and then brought back that same sea to rush over and drown Pharaoh's entire army. Celebrating that gracious deliverance,

> Moses and the sons of Israel sang this song to the Lord, and said, "I will sing to the Lord, for He is highly exalted; the horse and its rider He has hurled into the sea. The Lord is my strength and song, and He has become my salvation; this is my God, and I will praise Him; my father's God, and I will extol Him. The Lord is a warrior; the Lord is His name. Pharaoh's chariots and his army He has cast into the sea; and the choicest of his officers are drowned in the Red Sea. The deeps cover them; they went down into the depths like a stone. Thy right hand, O Lord, is majestic in power, Thy right hand, O Lord, shatters the enemy." (Ex. 15:1-6)

The song continues through verse 18, declaring God's sovereign mercy in behalf of His people and His divine wrath against their enemies. Israel sang, "The peoples have heard, they tremble; anguish has gripped the inhabitants of Philistia. Then the chiefs of Edom were dismayed; the leaders of Moab, trembling grips them; all the inhabitants of Canaan have melted away" (Ex. 15:14-15). Just as the Lord had predicted, that great deliverance caused **His name [to] be proclaimed throughout the whole earth.** He became known even by the pagans as the awesome and fearful God who delivered Israel from Egypt (cf. Josh. 9:9).

Even earlier in Israel's history, as the conquest of Canaan began, the Gentile prostitute Rahab verified that the Lord's intention was being fulfilled, telling the Israelite spies in Jericho,

I know that the Lord has given you the land, and that the terror of you has fallen on us, and that all the inhabitants of the land have melted away before you. For we have heard how the Lord dried up the water of the Red Sea before you when you came out of Egypt, and what you did to the two kings of the Amorites who were beyond the Jordan, to Sihon and Og, whom you utterly destroyed. And when we heard it, our hearts melted and no courage remained in any man any longer because of you; for the Lord your God, He is God in heaven above and on earth beneath. (Josh. 2:9-11)

Psalms 105, 106, and 136 all celebrate God's sovereign demonstration of His power and glory by delivering His people from Egypt. As one commentator has observed, Pharaoh was the open adversary of God, an avowed enemy following his own designs; yet a divine purpose was being fulfilled in his life. Only that purpose, and nothing else, can explain Pharaoh's very being.

That mighty act of God demonstrated two great truths. He delivered Israel to exhibit His sovereign **mercy on [those] whom He desires,** and He raised up and destroyed Pharaoh to exhibit the corollary truth that **He hardens** those **whom He desires.** Only His divine desire determines which it will be.

Moses was a Jew, whereas Pharaoh was a Gentile; but both of them were sinners. Both were murderers, and both witnessed God's miracles. Yet Moses was redeemed and Pharaoh was not. God raised up Pharaoh in order to reveal His own glory and power, and God had mercy on Moses in order to use him to deliver His people Israel. Pharaoh was a ruler, whereas Moses' people were slaves under Pharaoh. But Moses received God's mercy and compassion, because that was God's will. The Lord's work is sovereign, and He acts entirely according to His own will to accomplish His own purposes. The issue was not the presumed rights of either men but rather the sovereign will of God.

Hardens translates *sklērunō,* which literally means to make hard and metaphorically means to render stubborn and obstinate. The Exodus account of Moses' confrontation with Pharaoh speaks ten times of God's hardening that ruler's heart (see, e.g., 4:21; 7:3,13). That same passage also informs us that Pharaoh hardened his own heart (see, e.g., 8:32; 9:34), confirming God's act by his own. Such passages point up the humanly unreconcilable tension between God's sovereignty and man's will. Esau was rejected before he was born, and, also before he was born, Judas was appointed to betray Christ (see Acts 1:16; John 6:70-71). Yet both men themselves chose to follow sin and unbelief.

During His incarnation, Jesus clearly revealed that God's choosing of men always precedes their choosing Him. He told a group of unbelieving Jews, "No one can come to Me, unless the Father who sent Me draws him; and I will raise him up on the last day" (John 6:44). On a later occasion, He explained to His disciples, "You did not choose Me, but I chose you, and appointed you" (John 15:16). But He also said to unbelieving Jews, "You shall die in your sins; for unless you believe that I am He, you shall die in your sins" (John 8:24). In the familiar words of John 3:18, Jesus said that "he who does not believe has been judged already, because he has not believed in the name of the only begotten Son of God." Because of men's natural and willing unbelief, God is just in condemning those who already deserve it.

The Second Anticipated Question Answered

So then He has mercy on whom He desires, and He hardens whom He desires. You will say to me then, "Why does He still find fault? For who resists His will?" On the contrary, who are you, O man, who answers back to God? The thing molded will not say to the molder, "Why did you make me like this," will it? Or does not the potter have a right over the clay, to make from the same lump one vessel for honorable use, and another for common use? What if God, although willing to demonstrate His wrath and to make His power known, endured with much patience vessels of wrath prepared for destruction? And He did so in order that He might make known the riches of His glory upon vessels of mercy, which He prepared beforehand for glory, even us, whom He also called, not from among Jews only, but also from among Gentiles. (9:18-24)

The second question, or objection, that Paul anticipates and responds to is: **Why does God then still find fault? For who resists His will?** In other words, if God sovereignly **has mercy on whom He desires and hardens whom He desires,** how can human beings be held responsible? How can they be blamed for their unbelief and sin, when their destiny has already been divinely determined? Again, such reasoning challenges God's justice and righteousness.

As Israel was conquering Canaan, "Joshua waged war a long time with all these [Canaanite] kings. There was not a city which made peace with the sons of Israel except the Hivites living in Gibeon; they took them all in battle. For it was of the Lord to harden their hearts, to meet Israel in battle in order that he might utterly destroy them, that they might receive no mercy, but that he might destroy them, just as the Lord had commanded Moses" (Josh. 11:18-20).

Such commands of God, with which the Old Testament abounds, seem totally capricious and cruel to worldly, carnal minds, which accept only what fits their preconceived ideas of right and wrong, justice and injustice. Consequently, they judge even God by their own finite, biased, and sin-tainted standards.

God's utterly sovereign will is just as clearly taught in the New Testament. Later in this letter to Rome, Paul tells his readers: "That which Israel is seeking for, it has not obtained, but those who were chosen obtained it, and the rest were hardened" (Rom. 11:7). In his first letter to Thessalonica, he declares that "God has not destined us [believers] for wrath, but for obtaining salvation through our Lord Jesus Christ" (1 Thess. 5:9).

In His perfect wisdom, and in perfect righteousness and justice, God has destined some people for salvation by His grace and, because of their sin and unbelief, has left others to damnation by His wrath. Speaking of unrepentant unbelievers, Peter writes, "These, like unreasoning animals, born as creatures of instinct to be captured and killed, reviling where they have no knowledge, will in the destruction of those creatures also be destroyed" (2 Pet. 2:12).

Many critics of such doctrine, supposedly coming to the defense of God's justice, fail to acknowledge that every human being since the Fall has deserved nothing but God's just condemnation to an eternity in hell. If God were to exercise *only His justice,* no person would ever be saved. It is therefore hardly unjust if, according to His sovereign grace, He chooses to elect some sinners for salvation.

It is not, of course, that we can fully understand what God reveals about His sovereign election and predestination. It can only be accepted by faith, acknowledging its truth simply because God has revealed it to be true. As believers, we know that, in ourselves, we deserve only God's rejection and condemnation. But we also know that, for His own sovereign reasons, God has elected us to be His children and, in His own time and way, brought us to saving faith in Jesus Christ. On the other hand, we also know that our human will had a part in our salvation. Jesus said, "All that the Father gives Me shall come to Me." That is the choice of God's will. But Jesus immediately went on to say that "the one who comes to Me I will certainly not cast out" (John 6:37). That is the choice of man's will, which God graciously accedes to for all who believe in His Son.

Continuing simply to proclaim God's sovereign righteousness and justice rather than trying to explain it, Paul turns a question back on those who would question the Lord. **On the contrary,** he says, **who are you, O man, who answers back to God?** In other words, it is blasphemous even to question, not to mention deny, God's right to hold men accountable when they are captives of His sovereign will.

It is obvious from Paul's wording that the ones who might be asking such questions would not be seeking God's truth but rather self-

justification. Attempting to excuse their own unbelief, sinfulness, ignorance, and spiritual rebellion, they would be apt to accuse God of injustice.

But because human understanding is so limited, even sincere
questions about God's sovereign election and predestination ultimately must go unanswered. As already noted, it is one of the many
truths about God that we must accept by faith, simply because He has
revealed it in His Word.

Again taking support from the Old Testament, Paul continues his
rebuke of presumptuous unbelievers by showing the absurdity of anyone's questioning God's rights. **The thing molded will not say to the
molder, "Why did you make me like this," will it? Or does not the
potter have a right over the clay, to make from the same lump one
vessel for honorable use, and another for common use?**
Many centuries earlier, the prophet Isaiah had used that analogy:

> For all of us have become like one who is unclean, and all our righ-
> teous deeds are like a filthy garment; and all of us wither like a leaf,
> and our iniquities, like the wind, take us away. And there is no one
> who calls on Thy name, who arouses himself to take hold of Thee;
> for Thou hast hidden Thy face from us, and hast delivered us into the
> power of our iniquities. But now, O Lord, Thou art our Father, we are
> the clay, and Thou our potter; and all of us are the work of Thy hand.
> (Isa. 64:6-8)

Also using that figure, Jeremiah wrote,

> Then I went down to the potter's house, and there he was, making
> something on the wheel. But the vessel that he was making of clay was
> spoiled in the hand of the potter; so he remade it into another vessel,
> as it pleased the potter to make. Then the word of the Lord came to
> me saying, "Can I not, O house of Israel, deal with you as this potter
> does?" declares the Lord. "Behold, like the clay in the potter's hand, so
> are you in My hand, O house of Israel." (Jer. 18:3-6)

Although it is to an infinitely greater degree, God is the creator of
men much as a potter is the creator of his clay vessels. And it is no more
rational, and far more arrogant and foolish, for men to question the
justice and wisdom of God than, if such were possible, for a clay bowl
to question the motives and purposes of the craftsman who made it.

To his humanist friend Erasmus, Martin Luther said,

Mere human reason can never comprehend how God is good and merciful; and therefore you make to yourself a god of your own fancy, who hardens nobody, condemns nobody, pities everybody. You cannot comprehend how a just God can condemn those who are born in sin, and cannot help themselves, but must, by a necessity of their natural constitution, continue in sin, and remain children of wrath. The answer is, God is incomprehensible throughout, and therefore His justice, as well as His other attributes, must be incomprehensible. It is on this very ground that St. Paul exclaims, "O the depth of the riches of the knowledge of God! How unsearchable are His judgments, and His ways past finding out!" Now, His judgments would not be past finding out, if we could always perceive them to be just. (See *Martin Luther on the Bondage of the Will,* trans. J. I. Packer and O. R. Johnston [Westwood, N.J.: Revell, 1957], 314-15.)

To fully understand God, we would have to be equal to the God who made us—a notion even more absurd than a clay pot's being equal to the potter who molded it.

Whatever God's sovereignty may mean in its fullness, it does not mean and cannot mean that He chose for men to become sinful. The perfectly holy and righteous God is not responsible in the slightest way for the sinfulness of His creatures. Making that truth plain, James declares, "Let no one say when he is tempted, 'I am being tempted by God'; for God cannot be tempted by evil, and He Himself does not tempt anyone" (James 1:13). "Thine eyes are too pure to approve evil," Habakkuk said of the Lord, "and Thou canst not look on wickedness with favor" (Hab. 1:13).

As in the rest of Romans 9—indeed, as in the rest of Scripture—the closing three verses of this passage do not attempt to show the source or origin of evil or try to explain the humanly-inexplicable consistency of God's justice with His righteousness. The apostle simply makes a declaration in the form of a rhetorical question: **What if God, although willing to demonstrate His wrath and to make His power known, endured with much patience vessels of wrath prepared for destruction?**

Paul then gives two reasons for, although not a complete explanation of, God's allowing sin to enter and contaminate His universe. The Greek term behind **willing** is much stronger than this English word connotes. The Greek word carries the idea of determined intent, not indifferent or helpless acquiescence.

First, Paul says, God determined to allow sin in His creation because it gave Him the opportunity **to demonstrate His wrath.** God is glorified in displaying **His wrath,** just as surely as in displaying His grace, because both of those attributes, along with all the others, comprise His divine nature and character, which are perfectly and permanently self-consistent and are worthy of adoration and worship. Even God's anger, vengeance, and retribution poured out on sinners are glorious, because they display His majestic holiness.

Second, God allowed sin to enter the world in order **to make His power known.** His **power** is manifested in His judgment and punishment of sin. The vivid and sobering events found in the closing chapters of Revelation depict God's ultimate judgmental wrath. The plagues, the fiery judgment, and all the other curses of the apocalypse leave no doubt that the Lord will judge and remove all sin and sinners from the earth before He establishes His millennial kingdom. When Christ comes from heaven in His bloodstained garments, riding a white horse and carrying a sword, He will defeat Antichrist and all his ungodly followers. God's **power,** originally displayed in creation, will be equally glorious in destruction. It will be awesomely manifested in His vengeful, but wholly righteous and justified, conquest of all enemies who would attempt to conquer Him.

God has every right to act gloriously in such judgment, but He has, by His mercy, **endured with much patience** a world of sinners. He has **endured** their unbelief, rejection, hatred, blasphemy, and iniquity, while patiently allowing time for repentance (cf. Ps. 103:8; 2 Pet. 3:9).

Vessels of wrath prepared for destruction is surely one of the most tragic identifications of unbelievers in all of Scripture. Paul, of course, is speaking of ungodly and unrepentant *human* **vessels,** all of whom will feel the ultimate **wrath** of God, for which they have been **prepared for destruction** by their own rejection of Him. As already noted, it is not that God *makes men sinful* but that He leaves them *in their sin* unless they repent of it and turn to His Son for deliverance.

The Greek verb rendered **prepared** is passive. God is not the subject doing the preparing. There is the very clear sense in this use of the passive voice to relieve God of the responsibility and to put it fully on the shoulders of those who refuse to heed His Word and believe in His Son. They are **prepared** *by their own rejection* for a place (hell) prepared by God, not originally for them but "for the devil and his angels" (Matt. 25:41).

The corollary of that sobering truth regarding unbelievers is the comforting truth regarding believers: **And He did so in order that He might make known the riches of His glory upon vessels of mercy, which He prepared beforehand for glory, even us, whom He also called, not from among Jews only, but also from among Gentiles.**

God allowed sin to enter the world not only to demonstrate His wrath and to make His power known but also to demonstrate **the riches of His glory** by bestowing His grace **upon vessels of mercy** (cf.

Eph. 2:6-7). These are people **which He prepared beforehand for glory.** In this instance, the Greek verb rendered **prepared** is in the active voice, and the subject doing the action is specifically God **(He).** The great work God did in saving the elect puts His glory on display before all angels and all men (cf. Rev. 5:9-14). He has the absolute right to reveal and demonstrate His character in any way He chooses, whether by His just condemnation of unbelievers or by His gracious redemption of believers.

Scripture makes clear that no person is saved apart from faith in Christ, because God sovereignly requires that human response to His grace. But the primary purpose of salvation is not the benefit it brings to those who are saved but rather the honor it brings to the God who saves them, by making **known the riches of His glory upon vessels of mercy.** Believers are saved without any merit or work of their own, in order that God may have a means of displaying **His glory,** which is seen in the grace, the mercy, the compassion, and the forgiveness that He alone grants to those who come to Christ.

Paul closes this passage by identifying **us**—that is, himself and all other believers—as God's preordained **vessels of mercy.** Every believer is among those **whom He also called, not from among Jews only, but also from among Gentiles.** That is the glorious truth of the universal offer of God's grace.

The unfathomable truth that God chooses some men for salvation and others for destruction is not revealed to confuse us or upset us, and certainly not to tempt us to question the character of God's person. That truth is given to demonstrate God's glory and sovereignty to all men. It is also given to make believers thankful that He has chosen us, who, in ourselves, were not and are not more worthy of salvation than those who remain lost.

In showing mercy and in judging sin, God makes no distinctions based on race, ethnic background, nationality, intelligence, or even moral or religious merit. He distinguishes only between those whom He has chosen and those whom He has not. That is a hard truth to accept, because it runs directly counter to man's natural inclinations and standards. To the natural man it seems grossly unfair, and even the best-taught and most faithful believer cannot fully explain it. But the truth is fully biblical and is among the truths taught by Paul that Peter says are "hard to understand, which the untaught and unstable distort, as they do also the rest of the Scriptures, to their own destruction" (2 Pet. 3:16).

For those who receive God's Word as inerrant, there will always be a tension between fully acknowledging God's sovereign will and fully acknowledging His requirement of human faith. We can only believe what Scripture teaches, accepting in our hearts what we cannot explain with our minds.

And although Scripture makes clear that God elects and rejects solely on the basis of His divine sovereignty, it makes equally clear that God has no pleasure in the death of the wicked (Ezek. 18:32) and has no desire that even one person should perish (2 Pet. 3:9). Without compromising either His holiness or His justice, Jesus assures us that "the one who comes to Me I will certainly not cast out" (John 6:37).

> And they sang the song of Moses the bond-servant of God and the song of the Lamb, saying, "Great and marvelous are Thy works, O Lord God, the Almighty; righteous and true are Thy ways, Thou King of the nations. Who will not fear, O Lord, and glorify Thy name? For Thou alone art holy; for all the nations will come and worship before Thee, for Thy righteous acts have been revealed." (Rev. 15:3-4)

Israel's Unbelief Is Consistent with God's Plan—parts 3-4 It Is Consistent with His Prophetic Revelation and His Prerequisite of Faith
(Romans 9:25-33)

4

As He says also in Hosea, "I will call those who were not My people, 'My people,' and her who was not beloved, 'beloved.'" "And it shall be that in the place where it was said to them, 'You are not My people,' there they shall be called sons of the living God." And Isaiah cries out concerning Israel, "Though the number of the sons of Israel be as the sand of the sea, it is the remnant that will be saved; for the Lord will execute His word upon the earth, thoroughly and quickly." And just as Isaiah foretold, "Except the Lord of Sabaoth had left to us a posterity, we would have become as Sodom, and would have resembled Gomorrah."

What shall we say then? That Gentiles, who did not pursue righteousness, attained righteousness, even the righteousness which is by faith; but Israel, pursuing a law of righteousness, did not arrive at that law. Why? Because they did not pursue it by faith, but as though it were by works. They stumbled over the stumbling stone, just as it is written, "Behold, I lay in Zion a stone of stumbling and a rock of offense, and he who believes in Him will not be disappointed." (9:25-33)

Continuing his argument that Israel's unbelief is not inconsistent with God's promised covenant of redemption, Paul proceeds to give two more features from the Old Testament that support divine integrity. He confirms the truth that Israel's unbelief is perfectly consistent with God's revelation through the Old Testament prophets. He then confirms that Israel's unbelief is consistent with God's eternal prerequisite of faith on the part of those He saves.

Israel's Unbelief Is Consistent with God's Prophetic Revelation

As He says also in Hosea, "I will call those who were not My people, 'My people,' and her who was not beloved, 'beloved.'" "And it shall be that in the place where it was said to them, 'You are not My people,' there they shall be called sons of the living God." And Isaiah cries out concerning Israel, "Though the number of the sons of Israel be as the sand of the sea, it is the remnant that will be saved; for the Lord will execute His word upon the earth, thoroughly and quickly." And just as Isaiah foretold, "Except the Lord of Sabaoth had left to us a posterity, we would have become as Sodom, and would have resembled Gomorrah." (9:25-29)

Paul uses two quotations from Hosea and two from Isaiah to show that Israel's unbelief and rejection of the Messiah and His gospel fit what the prophets had predicted.

Paraphrasing the prophet, Paul declares that **He,** that is, God, **says also in Hosea, "I will call those who were not My people, 'My people,' and her who was not beloved, 'beloved'"** (see Hos. 2:23).

To understand the full meaning of that truth it is necessary to look at the first chapter of Hosea, where we read, "The Lord said to Hosea, 'Go, take to yourself a wife of harlotry, and have children of harlotry; for the land commits flagrant harlotry, forsaking the Lord'" (Hos. 1:2). It is not clear from the text whether Gomer, Hosea's wife, was a harlot before she married him or became one after the marriage. In either case, the Lord commanded the prophet to keep her as his wife, despite her adultery—or more correctly, because of it.

> So [Hosea] went and took Gomer the daughter of Diblaim, and she conceived and bore him a son. And the Lord said to him, "Name him Jezreel; for yet a little while, and I will punish the house of Jehu for the bloodshed of Jezreel, and I will put an end to the kingdom of the house of Israel."...Then she [Gomer] conceived again and gave birth to a daughter. And the Lord said to him, "Name her Lo-ruhamah, for I will

no longer have compassion on the house of Israel, that I should ever forgive them." ... When she had weaned Lo-ruhamah, she conceived and gave birth to a son. And the Lord said, "Name him Lo-ammi, for you are not My people and I am not your God." (Hos. 1:3-4, 6, 8-9)

Gomer's moral unfaithfulness to Hosea provided a vivid analogy to Israel's spiritual unfaithfulness to God. By His sovereign design and provision, she would bear Hosea a son whose name means "God sows" (referring to the scattering of seeds, as well as to the place where Jehu murdered Ahab's sons). Hosea then had a daughter whose name means "not pitied" or "not having obtained compassion," and another son whose name means "not My people." Those three names represented God's attitude toward Israel, His chosen but disobedient people. For a divinely determined period of time, they would be scattered like sown seeds, unpitied by the world, and forsaken by God.

The Lord goes on to promise, however, that His people will not be permanently forsaken. Applying the analogy to unfaithful and spiritually adulterous Israel God says, "I will allure her, bring her into the wilderness, and speak kindly to her," and speaking to Israel, He adds, "And I will betroth you to Me forever; Yes, I will betroth you to Me in righteousness and in justice, in lovingkindness and in compassion" (Hos. 2:14, 19). Just as Hosea protected and supported Gomer, even during her harlotries, and one day bought her as a slave on the block in the open market, naked and full of shame, so God someday will redeem Israel.

Until that time, God not only will treat Israel as not being His children but will treat Gentiles, who were not His people, *as* His people. It is that converse truth, found in Hosea 2:23, that Paul paraphrases: **"I will call those who were not My people, 'My people,' and her who was not beloved, 'beloved.' And it shall be that in the place where it was said to them, 'You are not My people,' there they shall be called sons of the living God."**

Hosea already had witnessed the Assyrian conquest and devastation of the northern kingdom of Israel, which occurred in 722 B.C., some twelve years before the prophet wrote his book. That pagan nation became the rod of God's anger (see Isa. 10:5), which He used to chastise His rebellious people. When God removed His protective hand, Israel became subject to the military expansionism of Assyria and thereby became, for a while, not God's people. Israel was scattered, unpitied, and forsaken by God, just as He had declared. In 586 B.C. the southern kingdom of Judah would meet a similar fate at the hands of the Babylonians. Only after many years of exile in foreign lands would God bring His chosen people back to their promised land. Even today, He has not yet redeemed them from the slave market of sin.

It is important to understand that Paul is here speaking about Israel as a nation and that they will be the focus of his message through the end of chapter 11. Paul's purpose is to show that Israel's unbelief was no surprise to God and was in no way inconsistent with His divine plan for His chosen people or for the world.

Paul was also referring to Israel's rejection of the Messiah, Jesus Christ, at His first coming. Rejecting God's own Son was Israel's supreme unfaithfulness to God, her consummate act of spiritual adultery, in which she still lived when Paul wrote his letter to Rome and still lives today. Like her rejection of God in the time of Hosea, Israel's rejection of Christ in the time of Paul was perfectly consistent with God's divine plan. Israel responded to Christ exactly as the prophets had predicted hundreds of years earlier.

Paul says, in effect, "We are not surprised when we see Jewish unbelief and we see them denying the gospel. We are not surprised when they enter into unbelief and sever themselves from God." Through the prophet Hosea, the Lord revealed what kind of people they would be. The prophet saw and understood Israel's unfaithfulness and God's scattering and rejection of her during that ancient time, and through Paul, the Holy Spirit applies to New Testament times what Hosea both envisioned and witnessed in regard to the Israel of his day. In A.D. 70, about ten years after Paul wrote to the Romans, the city of Jerusalem, including its magnificent temple, was totally destroyed by the Roman general Titus, under direct orders from the emperor. At that time a large percentage of the surviving Jews fled Israel, and in 132 the remainder of them were forcefully expelled by Rome. They remained a scattered people until 1948, when the modern state of Israel was formed and became recognized as such by most of the world.

Yet the great majority of Jews do not now live in Israel but are still scattered throughout the world. And that nation still rejects her Messiah and is not yet again the people of God. But, as Paul explains later in this epistle, God has not permanently rejected His people. One day, when "the fulness of the Gentiles has come in, ... all Israel will be saved" (Rom. 11:25-26). God promises through Hosea and through Paul that those who had become, for a long time, **not My people** would, by His gracious plan, someday become again **My people.**

Drawing from the same passage in Hosea and referring to that same divine graciousness, the Lord says through Peter, "For you once were not a people, but now you are the people of God; you had not received mercy, but now you have received mercy" (1 Pet. 2:10). Here the words refer to the church, God's chosen **people** of this present age.

Paul's focus, however, is Israel. When the Jews rejected God and became scattered, unpitied, and **not My people,** they became just like the Gentiles as far as their relation to God was concerned, scattered and unsaved.

Paul continues to explain that **it shall be that in the place where it was said to them, "you are not My people," there they shall be called sons of the living God.** Paul again quotes from Hosea, but this time does not paraphrase, using the prophet's own words almost verbatim (see Hos. 1:10). **The place** of which Hosea spoke was every place to which the Jews had been scattered. In those places they have been called **not My people,** but one day they will in those same places **be called sons of the living God.**

As Hosea did with his wife, after the scattering of God's people in Hosea's day, God eventually brought them back. And after their present scattering, He will again bring them back, not only to their own land but to their true Lord, as **sons of the living God.** The redemption of Israel will come.

But Paul's emphasis in this passage is not Israel's ultimate restoration to God but her present alienation from God. As already noted, the apostle's primary point is that the unbelief of Israel that caused her alienation and scattering was not inconsistent with God's sovereign plan for His people. On the contrary, historically and in regard to the time of Messiah, God foresaw and predicted Jewish rejection and its consequences long before it occurred.

Paul next cites another prophet, a contemporary of Hosea, saying, **Isaiah cries out concerning Israel, "Though the number of the sons of Israel be as the sand of the sea, it is the remnant that will be saved"** (see Isa. 10:22). The Greek term *krazō* **(cries out)** behind Paul's quotation of Isaiah carries the sense of crying out with great emotion, as from fear or pain, and was often used of a scream of despair and agony. The truth he was divinely called to proclaim tore at the prophet's heart. When he uttered that sorrowful truth, he doubtless wept for his brethren. Of the vast number of the human descendants of Abraham through Isaac—a **number** as great **as the sand on the sea**—only **the remnant,** a very small remnant at that, **will be saved.**

Beginning about 760 B.C., Isaiah prophesied to the southern kingdom of Judah for some forty-eight years. Like Hosea, he was given the divine revelation that God's people in Judah, just as those in Israel, would be conquered, scattered, and temporarily forsaken by God because of their unbelief. It is likely that Isaiah, as Hosea, personally understood that truth as relating to a judgment that would come in his own age, when Judah's rejection of God would lead to her conquest and exile by Nebuchadnezzar, king of Babylon.

Paul is saying that as important and tragic as those two scatterings were, they were only previews of Israel's immeasurably greater and more tragic rejection of the Messiah, and the subsequent conquest, slaughter, and scattering of Jews that has followed.

Quoting from the following verse in Isaiah 10, Paul declares, **For the Lord will execute His word upon the earth, thoroughly and quickly** (see Isa. 10:23). When God used the Babylonians to judge Israel for her unbelief and unfaithfulness, His justice was thorough and fast, and only a few, the remnant of true believers, escaped. So also was it in the destruction of Jerusalem and devastation of Palestine in A.D. 70.

The prophet Amos, who prophesied in Judah shortly before Isaiah, declared, "Thus says the Lord God, 'An enemy, even one surrounding the land, will pull down your strength from you and your citadels will be looted.' Thus says the Lord, 'Just as the shepherd snatches from the lion's mouth a couple of legs or a piece of an ear, so will the sons of Israel dwelling in Samaria be snatched away—with the corner of a bed and the cover of a couch!'" (Amos 3:11-12).

If a shepherd could not rescue a sheep from a predator, he would make every effort to snatch at least part of the carcass to take back to the owner as proof that the sheep was indeed attacked and devoured by a wild animal, rather than stolen or sold by the shepherd.

Just as a shepherd snatches a small part of a sheep from a lion's mouth, God will snatch for Himself, as it were, only a small part of Israel from unbelief and condemnation.

To further press home the truth he is declaring, Paul quotes again from **Isaiah,** who **foretold, "Except the Lord of Sabaoth had left to us a posterity, we would have become as Sodom, and would have resembled Gomorrah"** (see Isa. 1:9).

Lord of Sabaoth is often translated "Lord of hosts" and refers to God's all-encompassing lordship of the universe, of everything He has created. **Posterity** translates *sperma,* which literally means "seed" but, by extension, can also refer to the descendants of the seed or sperm. The Jews of Isaiah's day and, even more so the Jews of Christ's day, faced terrible judgment for their unbelief. They not only killed many of God's ancient prophets but even killed God's very Son, their Messiah and Savior. And since that day, all Jews who reject Christ continue to face the same terrible judgment.

But the **Lord of Sabaoth** graciously **left to us a posterity,** a remnant, apart from which no one would be saved but every human being, Jew and Gentile alike, **would have become as Sodom, and would have resembled Gomorrah**—divinely judged and destroyed. The Lord's destruction of those two morally perverted cities became a byword for total annihilation without a trace remaining. Only God's grace has prevented such ultimate and total destruction of the entire world.

The swift and sudden destruction of Sodom and Gomorrah in Abraham's time, and of Israel and Judah in A.D. 70, illustrate how **the Lord will execute His word** of judgment **upon the earth, thoroughly and quickly,** when the time has come. Only God's sovereign mercy spares the remnant.

Israel's unbelief, therefore, is not inconsistent with God's revelation through His prophets. They predicted it, stretching all the way from their own day to the day of Messiah.

ISRAEL'S UNBELIEF IS CONSISTENT WITH GOD'S PREREQUISITE OF FAITH

What shall we say then? That Gentiles, who did not pursue righteousness, attained righteousness, even the righteousness which is by faith; but Israel, pursuing a law of righteousness, did not arrive at that law. Why? Because they did not pursue it by faith, but as though it were by works. They stumbled over the stumbling stone, just as it is written, "Behold, I lay in Zion a stone of stumbling and a rock of offense, and he who believes in Him will not be disappointed." (9:30-33)

Paul's fourth and final point in this section is that God's prerequisite of faith for salvation does not conflict with or violate His divine plan of redemption but has always been an inseparable requirement of that plan.

God's demand for faith on the part of men is in no way inconsistent with His sovereignty. By His own sovereign decree, His gracious offer of salvation becomes effective only when it is willingly received by faith. In regard to salvation, the other side of divine sovereignty is human responsibility. From the human standpoint there is a tension, even a seeming contradiction, between those two realities. By human reasoning, they seem mutually exclusive. But both of them are clearly taught in God's Word, and when one is emphasized to the exclusion of the other, the gospel is invariably perverted. By His own determination, God *cannot save* a person who does not believe in His Son, and a person *cannot save* himself simply by the act of his own will, no matter how sincere and heartfelt. In God's sovereign order, both His gracious provision and the exercise of man's will are required for salvation. Like many other revelations in Scripture, those two truths cannot be fully harmonized by reason, only accepted by faith.

Paul therefore declares, **What shall we say then? That Gentiles, who did not pursue righteousness, attained righteousness, even the righteousness which is by faith.**

Paul is not implying that Gentiles are saved on a different basis than Jews. He is simply stating the human requirement for salvation that has always been the only means of attaining the **righteousness** that is necessary for salvation—**the righteousness which is by faith.**

Pursue is from *diōkō*, which means to run swiftly after something, and was therefore frequently used of hunting. It was also used metaphorically of earnestly seeking a desired goal or objective.

The implication for Jews was that they did not **pursue . . . the righteousness which is by faith,** but instead relied on their birthright as Jews or on their supposed good works in obedience to God's law. But no person has ever been saved, at any time, under any dispensation or covenant, on any other basis than **faith** exercised in response to God's gracious call. It is that truth that the writer of Hebrews makes so clear. From Abel through the prophets, men "gained [God's] approval through their faith" (Heb. 11:4-39). As Paul explicitly establishes earlier in this letter, Abraham, "the father of all who believe," was saved by his faith, which God "reckoned as righteousness"—before He required the rite of circumcision and long before He gave His law through Moses (Rom. 4:1-11).

Paul is not saying, of course, that the pagan Gentiles naturally sought God's righteousness through faith. Whether Jew or Gentile, the natural man *never* seeks God by his own independent choice. "The mind set on the flesh is hostile toward God; for it does not subject itself to the law of God, for it is not even able to do so; and those who are in the flesh cannot please God" (Rom. 8:7-8; cf. 5:10). Despite their being called as God's chosen people and their having received His divine revelation through Moses, the psalmists, the prophets, and other inspired men of God, the Jews were no more naturally inclined to seek or to obey God than was the most pagan Gentile.

In fact, when the gospel came through Christ, far more Gentiles than Jews believed. The greatest obstacle to salvation is self-righteousness. The person who thinks he is already righteous and pleases God will see no need for salvation. As noted above, because most Jews thought they had satisfied God by their Jewishness or their works righteousness, they felt no need for the gospel of grace through faith.

Consequently, **Israel, pursuing a law of righteousness, did not arrive at that law.** What a tragic commentary on a wasted effort. God's righteousness cannot be achieved by man's works, because they are always sin-tainted and fall short of God's perfect and holy standard. By his own effort, *no* person can **arrive at that law.**

Why did self-righteous Jews fail? **Because they did not pursue it by faith, but as though it were by works. They stumbled over the stumbling stone.** The only thing that any person, Jew or Gentile, can do to be saved is to believe that he can do nothing to merit salvation and to cast himself at God's feet for His mercy for the sake of Christ. Jews were incensed at the gospel of grace made effective by **faith** because it nullified all the good **works** by which they thought they could please God. Several years before he wrote the epistle to Rome, Paul had reminded the church at Corinth that "For indeed Jews ask for signs, and Greeks search for wisdom; but we preach Christ crucified, to Jews a stumbling block, and to Gentiles foolishness" (1 Cor. 1:22-23).

Again quoting from Isaiah, Paul explains that, **Just as it is written, "Behold, I lay in Zion a stone of stumbling and a rock of offense, and he who believes in Him will not be disappointed"** (see Isa. 28:16; cf. 8:14; 1 Pet. 2:8). Long before their Messiah came, the Lord had predicted in many ways and through many prophets that Israel would reject Him. Far from being inconsistent with God's Word, Israel's unbelief verified that Word. Just as Isaiah declared, she tripped over the **stone of stumbling,** refusing to receive her Savior and Lord, because He did not fit their understanding of the Messiah and because, **as a rock of offense,** He declared their works to be worthless. Daniel completes the picture by adding that the One who was the stone over which the Jews stumbled and the rock that offended them will, in the future, be the Stone that will break in pieces all the kingdoms of the world (Dan. 2:45).

But the good news of the gospel is that, unlike those who reject Him, **he who believes in Him**—the one who has faith in the Lord Jesus Christ, the divine stumbling stone and rock of offense—**will not be disappointed.**

The issue on the human side is faith, which alone can bring the salvation that God's grace provides. Man is justified by grace through faith. But Israel's unbelief, her lack of faith, did not surprise the Lord or nullify His plan. God's prerequisite of faith has always been the same, and His choosing a remnant in Israel for salvation was in perfect harmony with His omniscient awareness that only a few would believe in His Son and be saved. That is the way God knew it would be and planned it to be, and that, of course, is the way it turned out to be.

Israel's Failure—part 1 Ignorance of the Person of God: His Righteousness (Romans 10:1-3)

5

Brethren, my heart's desire and my prayer to God for them is for their salvation. For I bear them witness that they have a zeal for God, but not in accordance with knowledge. For not knowing about God's righteousness, and seeking to establish their own, they did not subject themselves to the righteousness of God. (10:1-3)

As he continues his theme explaining the place of Israel in God's plan, Paul now focuses on what might be called Israel's failure, or ignorance.

It will be helpful to begin by looking at a crucial issue in Scripture, namely, the matter of truth. In the introduction to his gospel, John pronounced that Jesus was "full of grace and truth" (John 1:14). While teaching in the treasury of the temple, "Jesus therefore was saying to those Jews who had believed Him, 'If you abide in My word, then you are truly disciples of Mine; and you shall know the truth, and the truth shall make you free'" (John 8:31-32). In other words, Jesus declared Himself to be the source and the measure of truth, and that "everyone who is of the truth hears My voice" (John 18:37). "I am the way, and the truth, and the life," He said on another occasion, and "no one comes to the Father, but through Me" (John 14:6).

Jesus promised His disciples that "when He, the Spirit of truth, comes, He will guide you into all the truth; for He will not speak on His own initiative, but whatever He hears, He will speak; and He will disclose to you what is to come" (John 16:13). In their behalf He prayed to His heavenly Father, "Sanctify them in the truth; Thy word is truth" (John 17:17). In many other instances, Jesus emphasized the truthfulness of His teaching, introducing His instruction with such words as, "Because I speak the truth, you do not believe Me" (John 8:45) and "I tell you the truth" (John 16:7).

Paul declared that "those who perish," do so "because they did not receive the love of the truth so as to be saved" (2 Thess. 2:10) and that those who are saved are sanctified "by the Spirit and faith in the truth" (2:13). No matter how erudite, religious, and sincere they may be, those who rely on their own knowledge and understanding are destined to be "always learning and never able to come to the knowledge of the truth" (2 Tim. 3:7).

The gospel puts a high premium on God's truth. The gospel is the life-changing, sin-cleansing, salvation-giving, soul-transforming, heaven-opening truth that comes only through trust in Jesus Christ as Savior and Lord.

No group of people in history has been more concerned about religious truth than the Jews (see Rom. 2:17-20). From ancient times, centuries before the time of Christ, Jewish children, especially boys, were meticulously instructed in the Old Testament. But they were also carefully instructed in Jewish tradition, which often wrongly interpreted and even contradicted the Old Testament. Those traditions taught by the rabbis, along with their commentaries on Scripture, were considered by most Jews to be essential for comprehending God's truth.

Leading rabbis, who often were scribes, were thought to be the possessors and the purveyors of religious truth, and consequently they had great power and influence over the Jewish people. Paul relates that he had studied at the feet of the famed rabbi Gamaliel (Acts 22:3). Young boys who aspired to be teachers themselves would travel great distances to study under noted rabbis, the most renowned of which were usually found in Jerusalem. That holy city of the Jews had become a citadel of learning, and its rabbis and scribes were honored and venerated. Those teachers were held in such esteem that their interpretations of Scripture and their religious instructions were seldom questioned, regardless of how much their ideas may have contradicted the clear message of God's own Word. Because those teachers were thought to have esoteric powers of spiritual discernment that most Jews did not possess, their word became virtual law.

A simple story in the Talmud illustrates the extreme admiration most Jews had for the scribes. The Day of Atonement was the most sacred day of the Jewish year, when the high priest went alone into the Holy of Holies and sprinkled blood on the mercy seat as atonement for his own sins and those of all the people. It is told that, on the eve of one Day of Atonement, the high priest was going to his home, followed by a large and admiring crowd. But when two beloved scribes passed by, the crowd left the high priest and followed the scribes.

The scribes were given the prestigious titles of *rabbi,* which means teacher, and even of *master* and *father* (cf. Matt. 23:1-12). So great was their influence that some historians believe that it was a group of zealous scribes that incited the Jewish riots against Rome in A.D. 66, a rebellion that led to the destruction of Jerusalem and its temple four years later.

The scribes always sat in the places of highest honor at banquets and religious feasts. In the synagogue they would sit with their backs to the cupboards that contained the scrolls of the Torah, the sacred law of Moses, indicating their unique position as its sole interpreters. Even the tombs of famous rabbis were venerated with a superstitious awe, and their memories were embellished with fictitious legends about their wisdom and works.

Because the Old Testament was written in Hebrew whereas most Jews of New Testament times spoke only Aramaic, the scribes had an additional advantage in their interpretation of Scripture. Part of their responsibility was translating the Scriptures into Aramaic, making the people almost completely reliant on those leaders for any knowledge of God's Word.

As will be studied later in this chapter in more detail, Paul speaks of Israel, typified by such scribes and their followers, as having "a zeal for God, but not in accordance with knowledge" (10:2). Of another group of Jewish religious leaders, the Sadducees, Jesus said, "You are mistaken, not understanding the Scriptures, or the power of God" (Matt. 22:29). In other words, with all their effort and presumed intense study of the Scriptures, they were ignorant of their true meaning. They could not truly know God's Word, because they did not know God Himself. "You know neither Me, nor My Father," Jesus said to their faces; "if you knew Me, you would know My Father also" (John 8:19). A short while later the Lord answered their charge of blasphemy by declaring, "If I glorify Myself, My glory is nothing; it is My Father who glorifies Me, of whom you say, He is our God'; and you have not come to know Him, but I know Him; and if I say that I do not know Him, I shall be a liar like you, but I do know Him, and keep His word" (John 8:54-55; see also 9:39-41).

After healing the cripple at the gate of the Temple, Peter explained to the wondering Jews who gathered around, "The God of Abraham, Isaac, and Jacob, the God of our fathers, has glorified His servant

Jesus, the one whom you delivered up, and disowned in the presence of Pilate, when he had decided to release Him. But you disowned the Holy and Righteous One, and asked for a murderer to be granted to you. ...Now, brethren, I know that you acted in ignorance, just as your rulers did also" (Acts 3:13-14,17).

Countless other passages in both testaments speak of Israel's spiritual ignorance and its terrible consequences. Through Isaiah the Lord declared, "Therefore My people go into exile for their lack of knowledge; and their honorable men are famished, and their multitude is parched with thirst" (Isa. 5:13), and through Hosea, "My people are destroyed for lack of knowledge. Because you have rejected knowledge, I also will reject you from being My priest. Since you have forgotten the law of your God, I also will forget your children" (Hos. 4:6).

Throughout their history, the Jews thought they knew God's truth. But Isaiah declared to his people, "Listen, O heavens, and hear, O earth; for the Lord speaks, 'Sons I have reared and brought up, but they have revolted against Me. An ox knows its owner, and a donkey its master's manger, but Israel does not know, My people do not understand.' Alas, sinful nation, people weighed down with iniquity, offspring of evildoers, sons who act corruptly! They have abandoned the Lord, they have despised the Holy One of Israel, they have turned away from Him" (Isa. 1:2-4). And through the psalmist He declared, "For forty years I loathed that generation, and said they are a people who err in their heart, and they do not know My ways" (Ps. 95:10).

Centuries later, Jesus said to unbelieving descendants of those Jews, "[You invalidate] the word of God by your tradition which you have handed down; and you do many things such as that" (Mark 7:13). On another occasion, He said, "These people honor me with their lips, but their hearts are far from me. They worship me in vain; their teachings are but rules taught by men" (Matt. 15:8-9 NIV). Their leaders had so modified and explained away God's revelation that the resulting religious traditions frequently nullified His truth. Consequently, Israel has walked a path of pain and turmoil, sorrow, and suffering—dispossessed, hated, and maligned. Because they believe they already know God and are favored by Him, such suffering and persecution have always been hard for Jews to understand.

Sanford C. Mills, himself a Hebrew Christian, has commented, "Israel wants to be the captain of her own soul, the master of her own ship. But Israel lost both her rudder and her compass, and now, with her vessel of state careening about in a maelstrom of sin, what is to save her from being drawn into the vortex of hell? Yet this is the condition of Israel today, even as it was in Paul's day" (*A Hebrew Christian Looks at Romans* [Grand Rapids: Dunham, 1968], 333).

Paul confessed to Timothy his own rejection and spiritual igno-rance before coming to salvation: "I thank Christ Jesus our Lord, who has strengthened me, because He considered me faithful, putting me into service; even though I was formerly a blasphemer and a perse-cutor and a violent aggressor. And yet I was shown mercy, because I acted ignorantly in unbelief" (1 Tim. 1:12-13). Paul makes clear that his own spiritual ignorance, like that of all other Jews, was due to unbelief. In other words, ignorance of God does not bring rejection of Him, but rather rejection of God brings spiritual ignorance of Him.

In Romans 9, Paul focuses on God's sovereign election and on the elect's response of faith in Him. The corollary is that because God has not elected all Jews, all Jews have not had saving faith. As we have seen earlier, because Paul knew how offensive that truth would be to most Jews, he began that chapter of Romans with great compassion and sorrow, testifying that he would gladly sacrifice his own salvation if doing so would bring salvation to his unbelieving kinsmen according the flesh (9:1-3).

Romans 10 is equally offensive to Jews, because the apostle here focuses on Israel's willing unbelief and the spiritual ignorance and divine condemnation that this unbelief brings.

PAUL'S PRAYER FOR ISRAEL

Brethren, my heart's desire and my prayer to God for them is for their salvation. (10:1)

Again (see 9:1-3) Paul begins by declaring his great love for fel-low Jews, saying, **Brethren, my heart's desire and my prayer to God for them is for their salvation.** The antecedent of **them** is Israel (see 9:31), God's chosen nation through Abraham.

Paul did not have a cold and indifferent acquiescence to God's sovereign election. He had a compelling, heartfelt longing to bring his physical kinsmen to Christ. His deepest **heart's desire** was that every Jew be saved, and his earnest **prayer to God** on their behalf was **for their salvation.** *Deēsis* **(prayer)** conveys the idea of pleading and entreaty, of persistent petition to God. Paul was not making a hopeless plea that he did not expect God to answer. He prayed because he fully believed God could save all Israel, that, no matter how seemingly un-likely, the people of Israel *could be saved* if they would place their trust in their Messiah and Savior.

Although Paul's foremost calling was to be the apostle to the Gentiles (Rom. 11:13; cf. Acts 9:15), that did not lessen at all his unbounded love for the salvation of his fellow Jews. He was doubtless well aware of Jesus' last earthly commission to the other apostles just before He ascended into heaven: "You shall be My witnesses both in Jerusalem, and in all Judea and Samaria, and even to the remotest part of the earth" (Acts 1:8). He also knew that Jesus had declared that "salvation is from the Jews" (John 4:22). Paul had already proclaimed that "the gospel ... is the power of God for salvation to everyone who believes, to the Jew first and also to the Greek" (Rom. 1:16). In his earlier ministry, Paul always preached the gospel first in a synagogue or other place of Jewish worship if he could find one (see, e.g., Acts 9:20; 13:14; 14:1; 16:13).

As He was dying on the cross, Jesus prayed for those who placed Him there, saying, "Father, forgive them; for they do not know what they are doing" (Luke 23:34). That was a prayer for the salvation of His murderers! Following his Lord's example, Stephen prayed with his dying breath, "Lord, do not hold this sin against them!" (Acts 7:60). That, too, was a prayer for his killers' salvation. With that same forgiving compassion, Paul held no grudge against fellow Jews who maligned and persecuted his Lord or himself, but rather prayed for their salvation.

No apostle better understood or more fully declared God's sovereignty than did Paul. Yet he knew with certainty that, perfectly consistent with God's sovereign power and grace, Israel's salvation was not impossible. The apostle did not try to reconcile rationally the seeming incongruity between God's sovereign election and man's willing faith.

The elective decree of God is absolute and certain, but it is a secret choice that He alone knows. It is not our responsibility to try to determine whom God has chosen but to proclaim the saving gospel to every person who will hear it, praying with Paul's earnestness that they will all receive Christ and be saved. Our responsibility is to diligently preach, teach, testify, and intercede, fully believing with Paul that "God our Savior. ... desires all men to be saved" (1 Tim. 2:3-4) and with Peter that "the Lord is not slow about His promise, as some count slowness, but is patient toward you, not wishing for any to perish but for all to come to repentance" (2 Pet. 3:9). We should be able to say with Paul, "I endure all things for the sake of those who are chosen, that they also may obtain the salvation which is in Christ Jesus and with it eternal glory" (2 Tim. 2:10).

Believers are to pray for and witness to all unbelievers, knowing that God will faithfully save those who believe in His Son. God's redemptive program is not one-dimensional. To isolate God's sovereign choice from the believer's personal faith is to foolishly and presumptuously separate what God has inextricably united. A theology that does not reflect genuine, heartfelt compassion for the lost and a deep desire for their salvation is a theology that is unbiblical.

THE IGNORANT ZEAL OF ISRAEL

For I bear them witness that they have a zeal for God, but not in accordance with knowledge. (10:2)

Paul earnestly desired and prayed for Israel's salvation because he bore **them witness that they** [had] **a zeal for God, but not in accordance with knowledge.** The apostle knew from his own experience as a radically zealous Pharisee that most Jews of that day were very religious but yet far from God. He testified to the Galatians: "For you have heard of my former manner of life in Judaism, how I used to persecute the church of God beyond measure, and tried to destroy it; and I was advancing in Judaism beyond many of my contemporaries among my countrymen, being more extremely zealous for my ancestral traditions" (Gal. 1:13-14). He gave a similar testimony to the Philippians: "[I was] circumcised the eighth day, of the nation of Israel, of the tribe of Benjamin, a Hebrew of Hebrews; as to the Law, a Pharisee; as to zeal, a persecutor of the church; as to the righteousness which is in the Law, found blameless" (Phil. 3:5-6). As far as legalistically fulfilling the outward demands of the law, Paul was blameless. Yet with the other Jews of his day, he had no understanding of spiritual truth and genuine godliness. He not only did not know and follow God's way but vehemently opposed it, persecuting the church of God.

Before the angry crowd of Jews in Jerusalem, Paul declared, "I am a Jew, born in Tarsus of Cilicia, but brought up in this city, educated under Gamaliel, strictly according to the law of our fathers, being zealous for God, just as you all are today" (Acts 22:3). Some years later, before the Roman commander Festus, King Herod Agrippa, and his wife Bernice in Caesarea, the apostle gave similar testimony: "All Jews know my manner of life from my youth up, which from the beginning was spent among my own nation and at Jerusalem; since they have known about me for a long time previously, if they are willing to testify, that I lived as a Pharisee according to the strictest sect of our religion" (Acts 26:4-5).

By his own words, Paul had been a zealous member of the most zealous Jewish sect. No one understood better than he what it was to **have a zeal for God, but not in accordance with knowledge.** The Jews had a certain degree or kind of knowledge (*gnōsis*), an intellectual awareness of the outward demands of God's law. But they did not have the discerning spiritual **knowledge** (*epignōsis*) that comes only from a saving relationship to God. They had the kind of superficial religious knowledge that causes pride and arrogance (1 Cor. 8:1), but not the godly **knowledge** that both comes from and produces humility and holiness.

In behalf of the Ephesian church, Paul prayed "that the God of our Lord Jesus Christ, the Father of glory, may give to you a spirit of wisdom and of revelation in the knowledge [*epignōsis*] of Him. I pray that the eyes of your heart may be enlightened, so that you may know [another term is used here for mature, full knowledge] what is the hope of His calling, what are the riches of the glory of His inheritance in the saints" (Eph. 1:17-18). True salvation brings with it a true "knowledge of Him" that opens the door to spiritual wisdom and enlightenment.

THE IGNORANT UNRIGHTEOUSNESS OF ISRAEL

For not knowing about God's righteousness, and seeking to establish their own, they did not subject themselves to the righteousness of God. (10:3)

Lack of knowledge is tied to lack of faith. Paul has already made clear that Israel's failure in righteousness was due to failure in faith. "Israel, pursuing a law of righteousness," he had said earlier, "did not arrive at that law. Why? Because they did not pursue it by faith, but as though it were by works. They stumbled over the stumbling stone" (Rom. 9:31-32).

Israel's rejection by God was not due to arbitrary divine election, as though He had withheld His grace from His chosen people. The entire Jewish Scriptures are a testimony to God's calling Israel to Himself. He called her over and over again—through the law, the prophets, and the other sacred writings. Of all people on earth, Israel was entrusted with the very oracles of God (Rom. 3:2). She was therefore uniquely responsible for her rejection by God, who made every effort to bring her to Himself.

As with the rest of the world (cf. Rom. 1:18-21), Israel rejected God before God rejected Israel. The tragedy in the history of Israel was squandering the immeasurable privilege of having *directly received the very Word of God*—first His written Word in the Scriptures, and even more tragically the living Word, God's only Son, Jesus Christ.

Israel was willingly and inexcusably ignorant of **God's righteousness** because she sought **to establish** her **own** righteousness and refused to **subject** herself **to the righteousness of God.** Such a charge was a terrible blow to a people who prided themselves in knowing the truth about God and in being His chosen ones.

Paul makes clear that Israel's most serious ignorance was about **God's righteousness,** the central nature of His personhood. In light of having received the full revelation of the Old Testament, it is shocking to think that the Jews would underestimate God's holiness and righteous perfection. But they had brought God's holiness and purity down to their own sinful level, and their basic spiritual and moral flaw was in thinking that God was less holy and more tolerant of sin than He had clearly revealed Himself to be.

Through Jeremiah, the Lord warned His people, "'Let not a wise man boast of his wisdom, and let not the mighty man boast of his might, let not a rich man boast of his riches; let him who boasts boast of this, *that he understands and knows Me,* that I am the Lord who exercises lovingkindness, justice, and righteousness on earth; for I delight in these things,' declares the Lord" (Jer. 9:23-24, emphasis added). Man's only cause for boasting is in **God's righteousness,** never his own.

But most Jews of that day *did* boast in their own righteousness and considered themselves pleasing to God simply because they were His ancient chosen people. For that same reason they thought the many rabbinical traditions they had substituted for God's Word were perfectly acceptable to Him. Not only were they willingly ignorant of **God's righteousness,** but they also had no understanding of their own unrighteousness. They thought they were more holy and righteous than they were and therefore fully believed that any deficit in their own merit could be met by their own good works—measured by **their own** standard of righteousness.

Consequently, they felt no need for a Messiah to save them from sin but rather a Messiah to deliver them from their earthly oppressors, namely Rome. That heinous misjudgment and ignorance about God's righteousness and their own unrighteousness was the basis for their whole system of legalistic self-righteousness. Through their rabbinical traditions they had brought the infinitely holy standards of God, which no man can achieve by his own efforts, down to a man-made level which they could achieve without divine grace.

Despite the clear and unambiguous teaching of the Old Testament, Jews chose to **establish their own** standards of holiness and righteousness and thereby **did not submit themselves to the righteousness of God.** They knew that Moses declared, "Who is like Thee among the gods, O Lord? Who is like Thee, majestic in holiness, awesome in praises, working wonders?" (Ex. 15:11). But they chose instead to **submit themselves** to the much less demanding standards of their own traditions.

Jews knew of the earnest entreaty that the godly King Jehoshaphat made to his people: "Listen to me, O Judah and inhabitants of Jerusalem, put your trust in the Lord your God, and you will be established. Put your trust in His prophets and succeed.... Give thanks to the Lord, for His lovingkindness is everlasting" (2 Chron. 20:20-21). They probably often intoned, "Sing praise to the Lord, you His godly ones, and give thanks to His holy name" (Ps. 30:4), but in their hearts they praised themselves for their own presumed worthiness.

Righteousness and holiness are basically synonymous, but they can carry slightly different connotations. Someone has said that righteousness is "transitive, manifest holiness." In other words, holiness can be said to be the standard and righteousness its active fulfillment. Or it might be said that God's holiness is His complete separation from all that is evil and sinful, and that His righteousness is the manifestation of that holiness. He is "majestic in holiness, awesome in praises, working wonders" (Ex. 15:11).

It is not that any man can begin to fully understand God's holiness or His righteousness. Yet that very inability to comprehend God's perfection should be reason enough to fall down at His feet in awe and praise. Men *are able* at least to *acknowledge* that God's holiness and righteousness are absolutely perfect and flawless, because He has revealed that truth about Himself. As Paul declared earlier, "The wrath of God is revealed from heaven against all ungodliness and unrighteousness of men, who suppress the truth in unrighteousness, *because that which is known about God is evident within them; for God made it evident to them.* For since the creation of the world His invisible attributes, His eternal power and divine nature, have been clearly seen, being understood through what has been made, so that they are without excuse. For even though they knew God, they did not honor Him as God, or give thanks; but they became futile in their speculations, and their foolish heart was darkened" (Rom. 1:18-21, emphasis added).

God has also clearly revealed that His perfect holiness abhors all evil and that He therefore hates even the smallest manifestation of sin. That realization alone should drive a person to his knees in repentance, knowing that God's divine righteousness stands in judgment of his own sinfulness.

The Jews of Paul's day were not much different than most people of any day, including our own. Because men think God is less holy than He is and that they are more holy than they are, they believe they can achieve acceptance with Him. They measure both God and themselves by human standards of right and wrong and are deceived in both regards. The psalmist Asaph wrote of such self-deception:

> To the wicked God says, "What right have you to tell of My statutes, and to take My covenant in your mouth? For you hate discipline, and you cast My words behind you. When you see a thief, you are pleased with him, and you associate with adulterers. You let your mouth loose in evil, and your tongue frames deceit. You sit and speak against your brother; you slander your own mother's son. These things you have

done, and I kept silence; you thought that I was just like you; I will reprove you, and state the case in order before your eyes." (Ps. 50:16-21)

The true God is not like the gods that men invent to accommo-
date their sinfulness. The boastful self-righteous "shall not stand before
[God's] eyes; [who hates] all who do iniquity" (Ps. 5:5), because "God is
a righteous judge, and a God who has indignation every day" (Ps. 7:11).

The natural man abhors such a God, just as he abhors the idea
that he is inherently sinful and stands condemned under God's holy
wrath. He much prefers a lesser god of his own making that will tolerate
his moral and spiritual shortcomings.

Tragically, much Christian teaching and evangelism today proclaim God's love and mercy at the expense of His perfect holiness and
His righteous judgment. People do not like to hear that, in His perfect
righteousness, God condemns all unrepentant and unforgiven men to
eternity in hell.

Not surprisingly, a weakened understanding of God's righteousness brings a weakened view of His judgment. When we do not see God
as He really is, we cannot see man as he really is. When Isaiah came face-
to-face with the holy God, he cried, "Woe is me, for I am ruined! Because
I am a man of unclean lips, and I live among a people of unclean lips;
for my eyes have seen the King, the Lord of hosts" (Isa. 6:5). When Peter
witnessed Jesus' miraculous filling of their nets with fish, "he fell down at
Jesus' feet, saying, 'Depart from me, for I am a sinful man, O Lord!'" (Luke
5:8). When he saw Jesus' awesome deity manifested, Peter became ter-
rified of his own sinfulness. When a sinner comes into the presence of
a holy God, he becomes fearfully aware of his own unholiness. In fact,
man can never be aware of his own unholiness apart from an awareness
of God's perfect holiness.

All other attributes of God function in concert with His divine
perfection. He is love, and His love is perfect love. He is wise, and His
wisdom is perfect wisdom. He is all-powerful, and His power is perfect
power. He is omniscient, and His knowledge is perfect knowledge. He
is just, and His justice is perfect justice. He is gracious, and His grace is
perfect grace.

Not only is God Himself perfect, but He demands perfection of
all men. Jesus said, "Therefore you are to be perfect, as your heavenly
Father is perfect" (Matt. 5:48). Quoting from Leviticus, Peter wrote, "It is
written, 'You shall be holy, for I am holy'" (1 Pet. 1:16; cf. Lev. 11:44).

Only the most arrogant fool would claim to be perfectly holy. Yet
perfect holiness is the only standard acceptable to God. For that reason
it becomes obvious that, apart from God's graciously granting that holiness, no man can hope to achieve it.

Israel's Failure—part 2
Ignorance of the Provisions of Christ
Ignorance of the Place of Faith
(Romans 10:4-10)

6

For Christ is the end of the law for righteousness to everyone who believes. For Moses writes that the man who practices the righteousness which is based on law shall live by that righteousness. But the righteousness based on faith speaks thus, "Do not say in your heart, 'Who will ascend into heaven?' (that is, to bring Christ down), or 'Who will descend into the abyss?' (that is, to bring Christ up from the dead)." But what does it say? "The word is near you, in your mouth and in your heart"—that is, the word of faith which we are preaching, that if you confess with your mouth Jesus as Lord, and believe in your heart that God raised Him from the dead, you shall be saved; for with the heart man believes, resulting in righteousness, and with the mouth he confesses, resulting in salvation. (10:4-10)

As Paul stresses in the first three verses of chapter 10, the Jews of his day were ignorant of the person of God, in particular His perfect holiness and righteousness. Consequently, they also were ignorant of the divine standard of holiness that He demands of men. If anything, God's standard for Israel was higher than for Gentiles, because Israel had the great privilege and advantage of being "entrusted with the oracles of God" (Rom. 3:2) and because, under the Old Covenant, it was Israel "to whom belongs the adoption as sons and the glory and the covenants and the giving of the Law and the temple service and the promises" (9:4).

But proud arrogance led most Jews to disregard "God's righteousness" and seek to "establish their own" (10:3). As Paul had already declared, they sought "a law of righteousness, [but] did not arrive at that law. Why? Because they did not pursue it by faith, but as though it were by works" (9:31-32).

ISRAEL WAS IGNORANT OF THE PROVISION OF CHRIST

For Christ is the end of the law for righteousness (10:4a)

Because of that arrogant self-satisfaction and self-righteousness, Jews were blind to the marvelous truth of the New Covenant, that **Christ is the end of the law for righteousness.** "They stumbled over the stumbling stone, just as it is written, 'Behold, I lay in Zion a stone of stumbling and a rock of offense'" (Rom. 9:32-33; cf. Isa. 8:14-15; 28:16). Just as Jesus **Christ,** "the stumbling stone," had declared early in His earthly ministry, the man-made self-righteousness characterized by the scribes and Pharisees was repugnant to God and would qualify no one to "enter the kingdom of heaven" (Matt. 5:20). To the Pharisees who criticized Him for eating with "tax-gatherers and sinners," Jesus said sarcastically, "It is not those who are healthy who need a physician, but those who are sick" (Matt. 9:11-12). In other words, those who think they are already righteous and acceptable to God will be ignorant of God's true provision for righteousness.

Paul explained to the church at Philippi that before his conversion he was "a Hebrew of Hebrews; as to the Law, a Pharisee; . . . as to the righteousness which is in the Law, found blameless" (Phil. 3:5-6). But he went on to say that he now counted "all those things to be loss in view of the surpassing value of knowing Christ Jesus my Lord" and that he no longer relied on "a righteousness of [his] own derived from the Law, but that which is through faith in Christ, the righteousness which comes from God on the basis of faith" (vv. 8-9).

Until a person acknowledges his own unrighteousness in light of divine and perfect righteousness, he will see no need for a Savior to liberate him from sin and provide him with God's own righteousness. No preacher, teacher, or evangelist can faithfully or effectively present the gospel if he does not first convince his hearers of their damning unrighteousness apart from Christ.

Jews in New Testament times sought to fulfill **the law** by their own efforts and thereby attain a righteousness acceptable to God. But Paul declares that **Christ** is the only **end,** the only fulfillment, of perfect, divinely acceptable **righteousness.**

Some interpreters believe Paul is here referring to the fulfillment of the law of which Jesus spoke when He said, "Do not think that I came to abolish the Law or the Prophets; I did not come to abolish, but to fulfill. For truly I say to you, until heaven and earth pass away, not the smallest letter or stroke shall pass away from the Law, until all is accomplished" (Matt. 5:17-18). Others maintain that the apostle is speaking of Christ's fulfillment of the Old Covenant through the New Covenant of the gospel.

Paul cannot be speaking of Christ's historical fulfillment of the law, as important as that truth is. Christ did indeed historically fulfill **the law** and the entire Old Covenant by His perfect, sinless life—whether anyone believed in Him or not. But that accomplishment does not provide anyone else with saving righteousness. Rather, as indicated at the end of verse 4, Paul is saying that belief in Christ as Savior and Lord brings to an end the sinner's futile quest for **righteousness** through his own imperfect attempts to fulfill **the law.** When a sinner receives Christ, he also receives the gift of Christ's own **righteousness.**

Paul here uses the term **law** in its most general sense, as representing the totality of God's commands and requirements under the Old Covenant, including such things as observance of the temple sacrifices and the feasts.

Those who try to please God and thereby attain salvation through legalism or religious ritual—even behavior and forms commanded by Him—pursue an absolutely vain quest, because the best righteousness fallen man can hope to achieve on his own is worth no more than "a filthy garment" in God's eyes (Isa. 64:6). Anticipating the provision by Christ, Isaiah declared that "only in the Lord are righteousness and strength" (45:24). The glorious truth of the gospel is that God "made Him [Christ] who knew no sin to be sin on our behalf, that we might become the righteousness of God in Him" (2 Cor. 5:21).

"It was for freedom that Christ set us free," Paul reminded the Galatian believers; "therefore keep standing firm and do not be subject again to a yoke of slavery" (Gal. 5:1). In different words, he explained the same basic truth to the church at Colossae: "When you were dead in your transgressions and the uncircumcision of your flesh, [God] made you alive together with [Christ], having forgiven us all our transgressions, having canceled out the certificate of debt consisting of decrees against us and which was hostile to us; and He has taken it out of the way, having nailed it to the cross" (Col. 2:13-14). In his letter to Rome, Paul has already proclaimed that "by the works of the Law no flesh will be justified in His sight; for through the Law comes the knowledge of sin. But now apart from the Law the righteousness of God has been manifested, being witnessed by the Law and the Prophets, even the righteousness of God through faith in Jesus Christ for all those who believe" (Rom. 3:20-22).

Being willfully ignorant of Christ and His righteousness, the Jews cut themselves off from redemption.

ISRAEL WAS IGNORANT OF THE PLACE OF FAITH

to everyone who believes. For Moses writes that the man who practices the righteousness which is based on law shall live by that righteousness. But the righteousness based on faith speaks thus, "Do not say in your heart, 'Who will ascend into heaven?' (that is, to bring Christ down), or 'Who will descend into the abyss?' (that is, to bring Christ up from the dead)." But what does it say? "The word is near you, in your mouth and in your heart"—that is, the word of faith which we are preaching, that if you confess with your mouth Jesus as Lord, and believe in your heart that God raised Him from the dead, you shall be saved; for with the heart man believes, resulting in righteousness, and with the mouth he confesses, resulting in salvation. (10:4b-10)

Because Israel was ignorant of God's holiness and of His provision for salvation through His Son, Jesus Christ, she was also ignorant of the place of faith in God's plan of salvation. Because they relied on their own works-righteousness, Jews saw no need for faith. As Paul already had pointed out, "Israel, pursuing a law of righteousness, did not arrive at that law. Why? Because they did not pursue it by faith, but as though it were by works. They stumbled over the stumbling stone," Jesus Christ (Rom. 9:31-32). Consequently, they cut themselves off from Christ and thereby also cut themselves off from the righteousness that He imparts **to everyone who believes** in Him. To reject Christ is to forfeit the perfect righteousness that only He can provide.

Believers receive as a gracious gift from God what they never could have achieved by their own efforts. **Everyone who believes** in Him, signs, as it were, the new and eternal covenant that Christ sealed with His own blood (see Heb. 12:24; 13:20), thereby making His righteousness our own.

To verify the place of faith in God's eternal plan for man's redemption, Paul reminds his readers that **Moses writes that the man who practices the righteousness which is based on law shall live by that righteousness.** The Lord also declared through Moses: "You shall keep My statutes and My judgments, by which a man may live if he does them" (Lev. 18:5). In other words, whoever relies on his own obedience to the **law** is held accountable for everything that the **law** requires. Quoting again from Deuteronomy, Paul testifies that "as many as are of the works of the Law are under a curse; for it is written, 'Cursed is everyone who does not abide by all things written in the book of the law, to perform them'" (Gal. 3:10; cf. Deut. 27:26).

The righteousness which is based on law demands absolute perfection in every detail of the **law.** For that reason, James says, "Whoever keeps the whole law, and yet stumbles in one point, he has become guilty of all" (James 2:10). In other words, if such were possible, a person who failed in only one point of the law would remain just as lost as a person who failed in *every point* of the law.

Anyone who is not utterly self-deceived realizes the impossibility of never stumbling even in the smallest way. And the foolish person who does presumptuously rely on his own obedience to the **law** will attain only the imperfect and unacceptable **righteousness** that his imperfect obedience merits. In God's sight, such righteousness is wholly *unrighteous* and can never remove sin or earn divine favor. "That no one is justified by the Law before God is evident" (Gal. 3:11).

Because of the countless rabbinical traditions that had been developed over the previous several hundred years, the Jews of Paul's time had so lowered and replaced with tradition Goal's divine standard of righteousness that many Jews actually believed they lived in satisfactory obedience to the law. After Jesus cited several Old Testament commandments, the rich young ruler told Him with doubtless sincerity, "All these things I have kept" (Matt. 19:20).

The truths that Paul emphasizes here may be summarized as follows: First, the man who pursues salvation by trying to keep the law will be judged on the basis of that effort. Second, it is impossible to keep all the law. Third, the inevitable failure of works-righteousness results in eternal damnation.

The idea that even the most ardent Pharisee was unable to keep God's law and was therefore cursed was unthinkable to Jews. Many Jews believed they were acceptable to God *simply because they were Jews,* members of His chosen race through physical descent from Abraham. In their thinking, the most reprobate Jew was more pleasing to God than the most upright Gentile.

But as Paul makes clear earlier in this epistle, "The Law brings about wrath" (Rom. 4:15). The law both demonstrates and incites man's natural lawlessness and releases God's wrath against him. The law justifies no one, redeems no one, provides mercy for no one. By the law, man is left to his own resources, all of which are imperfect, sinful, and powerless to save, which necessitates salvation by faith.

Personifying **the righteousness based on faith,** Paul says that it **speaks thus, "Do not say in your heart, 'Who will ascend into heaven?' (that is, to bring Christ down), or 'Who will descend into the abyss?' (that is, to bring Christ up from the dead)"** (cf. Deut. 30:12-14).

Calling His people to faithful obedience, God said to Israel, "The Lord your God will prosper you abundantly ... if you obey the Lord your God to keep His commandments and His statutes which are written in this book of the law, *if you turn to the Lord your God with all your heart and soul"* (Deut. 30:9-10, emphasis added).

In His law, God set the standards for holy living and has always required heart obedience, so that the promises to Israel just mentioned were contingent on her faith, evidenced by seeking the Lord "with all [her] heart and soul." As Paul pointed out earlier, "Abraham believed God, and it was reckoned to him as righteousness" (Rom. 4:3; cf. Gen. 15:6). The physical father of Israel became the spiritual "father of all who believe without being circumcised, that righteousness might be reckoned to them" (Rom. 4:11), because "the promise to Abraham or to his descendants that he would be heir of the world was not through the Law, but through the righteousness of faith" (Rom. 4:13).

Even the commandments in the Old Testament books of the law (the Pentateuch) are not primarily a call to external obedience. They are, above all, a call to heartfelt, adoring faith in the God of mercy and lovingkindness, who desires obedience and who graciously forgives sin. External observance of the law without internal faith in the God who gave the law results in condemnation for sin without mercy, not salvation from it.

On the plains of Moab, Moses proclaimed: "Hear, O Israel! The Lord is our God, the Lord is one! And you shall love the Lord your God with all your heart and with all your soul and with all your might" (Deut. 6:4-5). A short while later he reminded the people:

> The Lord did not set His love on you nor choose you because you were more in number than any of the peoples, for you were the fewest of all peoples, but because the Lord loved you and kept the oath which He swore to your forefathers, the Lord brought you out by a mighty hand, and redeemed you from the house of slavery, from the hand of Pharaoh king of Egypt. Know therefore that the Lord your God, He is God, the faithful God, who keeps His covenant and His lovingkindness to a thousandth generation with those who love Him and keep His commandments. (7:7-9; see also 9:4-5; 10:15; 14:2; 15:15-16)

The framework of Deuteronomy—and of all the rest of Scripture—is God's sovereign grace. Salvation and divine blessing *always* begun with God's grace, which is made effective for the sinner when he comes to God in faith.

Paul's point in Romans 10:6-7 is that, even if such things were possible, men could not come to salvation by searching for **Christ in heaven, . . . to bring [Him] down,** or by descending **into the abyss,** the depths of the earth or of the oceans, to raise Him **up from the dead.** The righteousness of faith does not require some mystical, esoteric, and impossible journey through the universe to find Christ. No matter what form it takes, "righteousness which is based on law" (v. 5) denies Christ's incarnation and denies His resurrection. Consequently, works-righteousness is also a denial of the gracious salvation Christ has provided by His own blood. As Geoffrey Wilson observes, "The sheer perversity of unbelief is shown by the many who prefer to undertake an impossible odyssey rather than put their trust in an accessible Christ" *(Romans: A Digest of Reformed Comment* [London: Banner of Truth Trust, 1969], 177).

Continuing his personification of "the righteousness based on faith" (v. 6), Paul asks, **What does it say? "The word is near you, in your mouth and in your heart"—that is, the word of faith which we are preaching.** In other words, men do not have to ascend or descend to find it, because God's way of salvation had already been clearly and abundantly revealed. His chosen people had been engulfed in and surrounded by **the word of faith** that Paul was now **preaching.** Even under the Old Covenant men could claim God's grace simply by receiving it in **faith.**

Much of western society today is like the Israel of Paul's day. Although most unbelievers have a limited and often distorted concept of Christianity, they have a general idea of its claims and have access to Bibles, churches, and Christians—through which they could easily discover the gospel if they honestly desired to. Tragically, however, men still choose works-righteousness and "suppress the truth in unrighteousness, because that which is known about God is evident within them; for God made it evident to them. For since the creation of the world His invisible attributes, His eternal power and divine nature, have been clearly seen, being understood through what has been made, so that they are without excuse" (Rom. 1:18-20).

The way to be saved and to secure the righteousness God requires is the supreme essential. There is great confusion in much of the church today about God's way of salvation, but it is the same as it was when Paul wrote to Roman believers: **If you confess with your mouth Jesus as Lord, and believe in your heart that God raised Him from the dead, you shall be saved; for with the heart man be-**

lieves, resulting in righteousness, and with the mouth he confesses, resulting in salvation. Salvation and its attendant righteousness are appropriated by confession and by faith.

Following the order of verse 8, which quotes Deuteronomy 30:14, Paul speaks first of confession, which is **with the mouth,** and then of faith, which is in the **heart.** In verse 10, however, he mentions them in reverse order, which is the chronological order of redemption. First, **with the heart man believes** and is granted **righteousness;** second, **with the mouth he confesses** and is granted **salvation.**

Paul has been speaking about true and false righteousness. False righteousness is based on the law (Rom. 10:5), which is impossible for man to fulfill. True righteousness, on the other hand, is based on faith in Christ (vv. 6-8), who bestows His own perfect righteousness on those who believe in Him. It is therefore of great significance that in verse **10** Paul equates **righteousness** and **salvation.** Only the person who is righteous before God is truly saved.

Those two truths represent the positive and the negative sides of God's redemptive grace. The positive side reflects His own perfect **righteousness,** which He graciously imputes to and bestows on those who believe in His Son, Jesus Christ. The believer is simultaneously *declared* righteous (justified) and *made* righteous (regenerated). It is about that complete divine righteousness that Paul exults to the Philippians: "I count all things to be loss in view of the surpassing value of knowing Christ Jesus my Lord, for whom I have suffered the loss of all things, and count them but rubbish in order that I may gain Christ, and may be found in Him, not having a righteousness of my own derived from the Law, but that which is through faith in Christ, the righteousness which comes from God on the basis of faith" (Phil. 3:8-9).

The negative side of God's work in the believer is **salvation,** divine deliverance from the sin that separates fallen man from holy God.

Righteousness has to do with what we become, and **salvation** has to do with what we escape. The first has to do with the eternal life we receive but do not deserve, the second with the eternal punishment we deserve but do not receive. The first relates to entering into blessedness, the second relates to escaping cursedness.

Unfortunately, those two aspects are often out of balance in evangelism and personal witnessing. When deliverance from sin and hell is made paramount, God's gracious bestowal of His **righteousness** on believers is left in the shadows. Consequently, unbelievers who have been repeatedly asked by Christians, "Are you saved?" might well give an ear to the gospel if they were asked instead, "Have you been made holy in Christ?" On the other hand, when God's love and grace are presented to the virtual exclusion of the need for **salvation** from sin and its judgment, cheapening of the gospel is almost inevitable.

Another contrast between the two verses is that, whereas verse 9 is a personal invitation to **believe,** focusing on the individual **(you),** verse 10 presents gospel truth concerning **man** in general.

Scripture never approves, much less commends, contentless faith, a "faith in faith" as it is often described. Paul here specifies two truths that must be believed in order to be saved. The first is that **Jesus is Lord,** the second that **God raised Him from the dead.**

Many people acknowledge that Jesus is both the Son of God and Lord of the universe. But Paul is speaking of the deep, personal, abiding conviction that, without any reservation or qualification, will **confess . . . Jesus as Lord,** that is, will confess that **Jesus** is the believer's *own* sovereign, ruling **Lord,** in whom alone he trusts for salvation and to whom he submits.

James teaches that even demons acknowledge truth about God. In a purely factual sense, they are completely orthodox in their theology. "You believe that God is one," he writes. "You do well; the demons also believe, and shudder" (James 2:19). In other words, demons are monotheists. Satan and his fallen angels are also confirmed creationists, having watched God form the heavens and the earth simply by speaking them into existence. Demons have observed more of God's work and know more about His nature and power than all human beings combined, apart from the incarnate Christ. And, having originally dwelt there, they know exactly what heaven is like. They also know with great certainty that they are destined for judgment, and, knowing something of what judgment means, they "shudder."

James's point is that men can hold such demon belief, belief that is theologically correct but that does not include reception of Jesus as Lord. People may be well aware of their sin, be under deep conviction about it, and even have a great emotional sense of guilt from which they long to be delivered. But they do not repent and forsake the sin that causes the guilt, nor do they trust in the Savior who can forgive and remove the sin. Speaking about such people, the writer of Hebrews gives one of the most sobering warnings to be found in Scripture: "For in the case of those who have once been enlightened and have tasted of the heavenly gift and have been made partakers of the Holy Spirit, and have tasted the good word of God and the powers of the age to come, and then have fallen away, it is impossible to renew them again to repentance, since they again crucify to themselves the Son of God, and put Him to open shame" (Heb. 6:4-6).

In other words, a person can hold orthodox theology, lead a moral life, acknowledge his sin, desire eternal life, be scrupulously religious, and yet go to hell. Jesus encountered such superficial and spurious "believers" early in His ministry. "When He was in Jerusalem at the Passover, during the feast, many believed in His name, beholding His signs which He was doing. But Jesus, on His part, was not entrusting Himself to them, for He knew all men" (John 2:23-24). Those disciples apparently acknowledged that Jesus was the Messiah (believing "in His name"), and, unlike the Pharisees (see Matt. 12:24), they believed that His supernatural powers were from God. But they did not submit themselves to Him as their Lord and Savior.

That was also the response of the rich young ruler, who appeared willing to do what Jesus told him in order to inherit eternal life— except acknowledge his sin and repent, as well as relinquish the riches which were his first love and then serve Jesus as Lord (see Matt. 19:16-22). Similarly, three other men professed willingness to follow Jesus but put their own preferences above His authority, proving themselves to be false disciples (Luke 9:57-62).

The Father repeatedly declared publicly that He had committed authority, power, judgment, and lordship into the hands of His Son, Jesus Christ. At Jesus' baptism the Father announced from the heavens, "This is My beloved Son, in whom I am well-pleased" (Matt. 3:17). After Jesus manifested His glory at the transfiguration, the Father said to the awe-struck Peter, James, and John, "This is My beloved Son, with whom I am well-pleased; listen to Him!" (Matt. 17:5).

Submitting to Christ's lordship is such an integral part of salvation that Paul testified, "I make known to you, that no one speaking by the Spirit of God says, 'Jesus is accursed'; and no one can say, 'Jesus is Lord', except by the Holy Spirit" (1 Cor. 12:3). When the Holy Spirit brings faith and salvation to a heart, that heart proclaims the lordship of Christ. "For to this end Christ died and lived again," Paul says, "that He might be Lord both of the dead and of the living" (Rom. 14:9).

In Philippians, Paul teaches that God has bestowed on Jesus Christ "the name which is above every name," a name that requires bowing submission (2:9-11). Obviously, that name is "Lord." God gave Christ that name, and all men must acknowledge it and bow to it to be saved.

Contrary to much teaching today, Scripture never separates Christ's lordship from His saviorhood. **Lord** is from *kurios*, which signifies sovereign power and authority. In the book of Acts, Jesus is twice referred to as Savior but ninety-two times as Lord. In the entire New Testament, He is referred to some ten times as Savior and some seven hundred times as Lord. When the two titles are mentioned together, *Lord* always precedes *Savior*. And even if, as some erroneously contend, *Lord* were simply a synonym for *God*, the very term *God* by definition includes the idea of sovereign authority, that is, of lordship. (For a full treatment of this issue, see the author's book *The Gospel According to Jesus* [Grand Rapids: Zondervan, 1988].)

The second truth that must be believed in order to be saved is that **God raised Him [Jesus] from the dead.** There are many important truths about Jesus that Christians are to believe. The New Testament makes clear, for example, that Christ became incarnate, that He was conceived by the Holy Spirit to a mother who was a virgin, and that He experienced every kind of temptation while living a sinless life.

But the truth of Jesus' resurrection **from the dead** was the supreme validation of His ministry. At the beginning of this letter, Paul states that Jesus Christ "was declared the Son of God with power by the resurrection from the dead, according to the Spirit of holiness, Jesus Christ our Lord" (Rom. 1:4). When **God raised Him from the dead,** the Father was declaring again that the Savior was His beloved Son, with whom He is well pleased.

The resurrection of Christ also demonstrated that He was eternally victorious over sin, death, and Satan. It was "for our sake also, to whom it will be reckoned, as those who believe in Him who raised Jesus our Lord from the dead" (Rom. 4:24). Men must believe the resurrection of Christ because it proves that He accomplished their salvation on the cross. To believe that **God raised** Christ **from the dead** is to identify ourselves with the One who purchased our redemption on the cross and rose to share His eternal life with those for whom He is Lord and Savior. Had Jesus not been raised, sin and death would have been victorious over fallen mankind, who then would have had no hope of attaining the perfect righteousness that God requires.

In Antioch of Pisidia, Paul told the assembled Jews in the synagogue, "We preach to you the good news of the promise made to the fathers, that God has fulfilled this promise to our children in that He raised up Jesus, as it is also written in the second Psalm, 'Thou art My Son; today I have begotten Thee'" (Acts 13:32-33). Proclaiming the same foundational truth of the gospel, Peter said, "Blessed be the God and Father of our Lord Jesus Christ, who according to His great mercy has caused us to be born again to a living hope through the resurrection of Jesus Christ from the dead, to obtain an inheritance which is imperishable and undefiled and will not fade away, reserved in heaven for you" (1 Pet. 1:3-4).

Apart from Christ's resurrection, there could be no salvation. Paul warned the church at Corinth that "If Christ has not been raised, then our preaching is vain, your faith also is vain. Moreover we are even found to be false witnesses of God, because we witnessed against God that He raised Christ, whom He did not raise, if in fact the dead are not raised. For if the dead are not raised, not even Christ has been raised; and if Christ has not been raised, your faith is worthless; you are still in your sins" (1 Cor. 15:14-17).

The resurrection was the Father's final stamp of approval on His Son and the final feature in the provision of salvation for those who trust in Him. The resurrection divinely certifies that Jesus is the Messiah, the only Savior, the sovereign and sinless Lord, the sacrificial Lamb who paid the price for our redemption, the judge of all men, the conqueror of death, the coming King of kings.

Verses 9 and 10 both clearly state that *true belief* in Christ's lordship and in His resurrection comes from the **heart.** The Hebrews considered the heart to be the core of personhood and the residence of the soul, the deepest, innermost part of man—where thought, will, and motive are generated. That is why the ancient writer admonished his fellow Israelites, "Watch over your heart with all diligence, for from it flow the springs of life" (Prov. 4:23).

It is **with the heart** that **man believes,** and it is therefore with his heart that man determines his eternal destiny. Early in His ministry Jesus spoke the beautiful words, "God so loved the world, that He gave His only begotten Son, that whoever believes in Him should not perish, but have eternal life" (John 3:16). Later He declared, "I am the light of the world; he who follows [believes in] Me shall not walk in the darkness, but shall have the light of life" (John 8:12). In both instances the positive and the negative aspects of the gospel are again clearly seen. In 3:16, "eternal life" is the positive and "perish" is the negative. In 8:12, "the light of life" is the positive and walking "in the darkness" is the negative.

John's very purpose for writing the fourth gospel was that "you may believe that Jesus is the Christ, the Son of God; and that believing you may have life in His name" (John 20:31). Belief in Christ brings an entirely different kind and quality of life—a holy life, a righteous life, an eternal life.

It is **with the mouth** that man **confesses,** Paul says. *Homologeō* **(confess)** has the root meaning of speaking the same thing, of being in agreement and accord with someone. The person who confesses Jesus as Lord (v. 9) agrees with God the Father, and that confession mixed with genuine trust brings **salvation.**

Israel misunderstood the place of this saving faith. So do many people today.

Israel's Failure—part 3
The Parameters
of Salvation
The Predictions
of Scripture
(Romans 10:11-21)

7

For the Scripture says, "Whoever believes in Him will not be disappointed." For there is no distinction between Jew and Greek; for the same Lord is Lord of all, abounding in riches for all who call upon Him; for "Whoever will call upon the name of the Lord will be saved." How then shall they call upon Him in whom they have not believed? And how shall they believe in Him whom they have not heard? And how shall they hear without a preacher? And how shall they preach unless they are sent? Just as it is written, "How beautiful are the feet of those who bring glad tidings of good things!"

However, they did not all heed the glad tidings; for Isaiah says, "Lord, who has believed our report?" So faith comes from hearing, and hearing by the word of Christ. But I say, surely they have never heard, have they? Indeed they have; "Their voice has gone out into all the earth, and their words to the ends of the world." But I say, surely Israel did not know, did they? At the first Moses says, "I will make you jealous by that which is not a nation, by a nation without understanding will I anger you." And Isaiah is very bold and says, "I was found by those who sought Me not, I became manifest to those who did not ask for Me." But

as for Israel He says, "All the day long I have stretched out My hands to a disobedient and obstinate people." (10:11-21)

Continuing to discuss Israel's failure to believe the gospel, Paul digs deeper into the issue of salvation, showing its extent and pointing out that Israel's failure was not a surprise, but long beforehand was predicted in Scripture.

THE PARAMETERS OF SALVATION

For the Scripture says, "Whoever believes in Him will not be disappointed." For there is no distinction between Jew and Greek; for the same Lord is Lord of all, abounding in riches for all who call upon Him; for "Whoever will call upon the name of the Lord will be saved." How then shall they call upon Him in whom they have not believed? And how shall they believe in Him whom they have not heard? And how shall they hear without a preacher? And how shall they preach unless they are sent? Just as it is written, "How beautiful are the feet of those who bring glad tidings of good things!"
However, they did not all heed the glad tidings; for Isaiah says, "Lord, who has believed our report?" So faith comes from hearing, and hearing by the word of Christ. But I say, surely they have never heard, have they? Indeed they have; "Their voice has gone out into all the earth, and their words to the ends of the world." (10:11-18)

Paul next explains the parameters, the extent, of salvation.

Because most Jews strongly rejected the idea that God's grace extended to Gentiles, they were willingly ignorant of the full measure and extent of His provision for redemption. Because they were God's specially chosen people, they believed they were also His only saved people. They knew, of course, that Ruth, a Moabite, was the great-grandmother of David and therefore in the line of the Messiah. But they insisted that such Gentiles who converted to Judaism and were blessed by God were exceptions that proved the rule.

Consequently, just as they had rejected Jesus and His teaching, they also vehemently rejected the teaching of Paul, a former zealous Pharisee and persecutor of the church, who now not only claimed that Jesus was the Messiah, the Christ, but that Christ had appointed him to be "a chosen instrument ... to bear [His] name before the Gentiles" (Acts 9:15; cf. Gal. 1:16).

But Paul declares that God's extending His salvation to *all* Gentiles was nothing new. That gracious offer did not begin with the all-inclusive gospel of Jesus Christ, which Christians, most of whom were Jews, were then proclaiming to everyone who would hear. To the contrary, as Paul had already cited (9:33), **The Scripture says** through Isaiah, **"Whoever believes in Him will not be disappointed"** (cf. Isa. 28:16). God had always been calling to Gentiles **(whoever).** In fact, Israel was to have been His witness nation, "a kingdom of priests and a holy nation" (Ex. 19:6), to preach salvation in the true God to the rest of the world.

The Old Testament Scripture, as "witnessed by the Law and the Prophets," had long testified that "the righteousness of God through faith in Jesus Christ [is] *for all those who believe; for there is no distinction"* (Rom. 3:21-22, emphasis added). In other words, salvation through faith in Him *for anyone* **(whoever believes)** has always been God's plan. As Paul declared earlier, "I am not ashamed of the gospel, for it is the power of God for salvation to *everyone* who believes, to the Jew first *and also to the Greek"* (Rom. 1:16, emphasis added). And as he assured the believers at Corinth, many of whom were Gentiles, "If *any man* is in Christ, he is a new creature; the old things passed away; behold, new things have come" (2 Cor. 5:17, emphasis added). From eternity past, God's Word invariably has accomplished His divine goal, which has *always included* His loving and gracious desire that no human being would perish but that "all [would] come to repentance" (2 Pet. 3:9).

That wondrous truth is a balance to the great emphasis Paul has been placing on God's sovereignty (see, e.g., Rom. 9:6-26). Although the two truths seem mutually exclusive to our finite minds, God's sovereign choice of every person who is saved is, in His infinite mind, perfectly consistent with His promise that **whoever believes in Him will not be disappointed.** Both the Old and the New Testaments make clear that salvation is granted only to those who trust in God and that He offers His gracious redemption to all mankind, Jew and Gentile. No one who **believes in Him will** ever **be disappointed** by the salvation that He so graciously and universally offers.

The barrier to salvation, therefore, is not racial or cultural but personal rejection of the God who offers it. People perish because they refuse to "receive the love of the truth so as to be saved" (2 Thess. 2:10). Yet it was that very universal aspect of the gospel that many Jews resented. The classic biblical example of Jewish religious and racial pride and reluctance to reach Gentiles is found in the prophet Jonah when he responded to the Lord's call to preach to Nineveh.

Jonah lived in Israel during the reign of Jeroboam II, who ruled from 793 to 753 B.C. It was a prosperous time for the nation, which had expanded its boundaries northeastward to include Damascus. Because the Assyrians periodically made raids into Israel, Jews developed a special hatred for Nineveh, the capital of Assyria.

That immense city of perhaps 600,000 inhabitants is said to have taken three days to traverse on foot. Ninevites, like all other Assyrians, were noted for their immorality and idolatry, and Assyrian soldiers were infamous for their merciless brutality. Nahum spoke of Nineveh as "the bloody city, completely full of lies and pillage; her prey never departs" (Nah. 3:1).

Therefore, when the Lord called Jonah to preach to that wicked Gentile city, the prophet immediately took ship to travel in the opposite direction. Because of the hatred of Assyrians that he shared with his fellow Israelites, Jonah's concern was not that his preaching might fail but that it would surely succeed. It is not surprising, therefore, that the remarkable repentance of the Ninevites, from the king to the lowest servant, "greatly displeased Jonah, and he became angry. And he prayed to the Lord and said, 'Please Lord, was not this what I said while I was still in my own country? Therefore, in order to forestall this I fled to Tarshish, for I knew that Thou art a gracious and compassionate God, slow to anger and abundant in lovingkindness, and one who relents concerning calamity'" (Jonah 4:1-2). At the very time he was forced to testify to God's grace and compassion, he disdainfully refused to emulate those virtues himself.

God's miraculous work in the hearts of the Ninevites was an object lesson to Israel in several ways. First of all, it demonstrated that great power for salvation was in God and His proclaimed Word, not in the prophet who proclaimed that word. Second, it doubtless was also intended to shame Jonah and all other self-righteous, hard-hearted Israelites. One extremely reluctant prophet went one time to preach one message and God caused the entire city to repent!

By tragic contrast, despite all the blessings in being God's called people, with whom He made covenant and to whom He gave His law and sent His prophets, Israel repeatedly turned away from Him into idolatry and every other form of ungodliness. Yet Nineveh, which was thoroughly pagan and had no such advantages, in one day "believed in God; and they called a fast and put on sackcloth from the greatest to the least of them" (Jonah 3:5).

Some eight centuries later, Jews still held unabated disdain for Gentiles. When returning to Israel from another country, Jews would shake the dust from their robes and feet, lest they carry any defiled earth into their land. They would not enter a Gentile house, eat or drink from a Gentile vessel, or so much as touch a Gentile hand. Every morning many Jewish men would pray, "I thank God that I am not a woman, a slave, or a Gentile." Jews were reluctant to have any dealings with Gentiles, and were especially loath to share the redemptive truth of their God, lest, as Jonah feared, their "gracious and compassionate God, slow to anger and abundant in lovingkindness," would cause even pagans to repent and be saved.

Paul knew that it was the Lord's plan for the gospel to be preached first "in Jerusalem, and in all Judea and Samaria, and even to the remotest part of the earth" (Acts 1:8), making "disciples of all the nations" (Matt. 28:19). As already noted, Paul had testified at the beginning of Romans that "the gospel ... is the power of God for salvation to everyone who believes, to the Jew first *and also to the Greek*" (Rom. 1:16, emphasis added). But it was doubtless also for another reason that Paul always witnessed first in a synagogue or other place of Jewish worship. Had he preached first to Gentiles, Jewish indignation would have been so strong that they would never have listened to him.

As more and more Jews believed in Jesus and were saved, many more turned more fiercely against Him and His Jewish followers. Just as Jesus had warned, "They will make you outcasts from the synagogue, but an hour is coming for everyone who kills you to think that he is offering service to God" (John 16:1-2). When Paul took four Jewish men who were under a vow into the temple for ritual purification, "Jews from Asia, upon seeing him in the temple, began to stir up all the multitude and laid hands on him, crying out, 'Men of Israel, come to our aid! This is the man who preaches to all men everywhere against our people, and the Law, and this place; and besides he has even brought Greeks into the temple and has defiled this holy place.' For they had previously seen Trophimus the Ephesian in the city with him, and they supposed that Paul had brought him into the temple" (Acts 21:27-29).

In the modern state of Israel, most Jews, including many who are not religious, still strongly resent and oppose Christian missionary work in their country. Although Jews consider all other religions to be false, they are particularly fervent in their opposition to Christianity. Like the Jews in Jerusalem who decried Paul's visit to the temple, they view Christianity as a Gentile religion that is specifically "against [their] people, and the Law" (Acts 21:28). And they make little or no effort to convert Gentiles to Judaism.

Nothing could have been more devastating to Jews than to be reminded that God makes **no distinction between Jew and Greek; for the same Lord is Lord of all, abounding in riches for all who call upon Him.** Those whose greatest pride was in the belief that they were far superior to all other peoples could not tolerate that humbling truth.

Proclaiming the same message to the Galatian church, Paul wrote, "There is neither Jew nor Greek, there is neither slave nor free man, there is neither male nor female; for you are all one in Christ Jesus."

Not only that, but shockingly he went on to say that believing Gentiles, just as much as believing Jews,"are Abraham's offspring, heirs according to promise" (Gal. 3:28-29).

To Gentile believers in the church at Ephesus Paul declared, "Therefore remember, that formerly you, the Gentiles in the flesh, who are called 'Uncircumcision' by the so-called 'Circumcision,' which is performed in the flesh by human hands—remember that you were at that time separate from Christ, excluded from the commonwealth of Israel, and strangers to the covenants of promise, having no hope and without God in the world. But now in Christ Jesus you who formerly were far off have been brought near by the blood of Christ" (Eph. 2:11-13). Later in that letter he said,"I, Paul, [am] the prisoner of Christ Jesus for the sake of you Gentiles" (3:1). The great "mystery of Christ," which Jews so intensely hated, is that "Gentiles are fellow heirs and fellow members of the body, and fellow partakers of the promise in Christ Jesus through the gospel" (see vv. 4-6).

The same Lord who called out Abraham and his descendants to be His chosen people, is **Lord of all** who believe in Him. But because most Jews were looking for a national deliverer rather than a universal Savior, the gospel of Jesus Christ, which He extends to **all who call upon Him,** was unacceptable.

Not only is Christ the Savior and **Lord of all** who believe but He is also **abounding in riches for all who call upon Him.** Gentile believers have God's equal blessing as well as His equal salvation. And just as God sovereignly calls all believers to Himself, all must **call upon Him** in faith.

To further emphasize the universal outreach of the salvation message, Paul quotes another prophet, Joel, who centuries earlier had declared to Israel the extent of saving grace when he said that **whoever will call upon the name of the Lord will be saved** (see Joel 2:32).

In the Old Testament, the phrase **call upon the name of the Lord** was especially associated with right worship of the true God. It carried the connotations of worship, adoration, and praise and extolled God's majesty, power, and holiness. Emphasizing the negative side of that phrase, the imprecatory psalmist cried to God,"How long, O Lord? Wilt Thou be angry forever? Will Thy jealousy burn like fire? Pour out Thy wrath upon the nations which do not know Thee, and upon the kingdoms *which do not call upon Thy name*" (Ps. 79:5-6, emphasis added). Again the psalmist exulted,"Oh give thanks to the Lord, *call upon His name*; make known His deeds among the peoples" (105:1, emphasis added). Still another time in the Psalms we read that he *"called upon the name of the Lord,"* praying, "'O Lord, I beseech Thee, save my life!' Gracious is the Lord, and righteous; yes, our God is compassionate" (116:4-5, emphasis added).

In the four references just cited from Joel and the Psalms, the word *Lord* represents God's covenant name, Yahweh, or Jehovah—which is rendered in many translations in large and small capital letters *(Lord).* Therefore to **call upon the name of the Lord** was not a desperate cry to just any deity—whoever, whatever, and wherever he or she might be—but a cry to the one true God, the Creator-Lord of all men and all things. As Paul has just stated, it is by the confession of "Jesus as Lord" and belief in one's "heart that God raised Him from the dead" that any person "shall be saved" (Rom. 10:9). He is the one true **Lord** on whom faithful Jews had always called in penitence, adoration, and worship. To **call upon the name** of Jesus as Lord is to recognize and submit to His deity, His authority, His sovereignty, His power, His majesty, His Word, and His grace. Everyone, Jew or Gentile, who does so **will be saved.**

Forms of the Hebrew word *yasha,* most commonly translated **save**, is found some 160 times in the Old Testament, and forms of the corresponding Greek term *sōzō* **(saved)** are found well over a hundred times in the New Testament. Paul alone uses the term forty-five times.

To further explain the universal extent, or parameters, of God's saving grace, the apostle asks rhetorically, **How then shall they call upon Him in whom they have not believed? And how shall they believe in Him whom they have not heard? And how shall they hear without a preacher? And how shall they preach unless they are sent?**

With simple, progressive logic Paul establishes that only those who **call upon the name of the Lord** can **be saved,** only those who have **believed** in Him can call upon Him, only those who have **heard** of Him can **believe in Him,** only those who have **a preacher** can rightly **hear** of Him, and finally no preacher can **preach** the true gospel who has not been sent by God. Viewed from the other direction, Paul is saying that if God did not send preachers no one could hear, if no one could hear no one could believe, if no one could believe no one could call on the Lord, and if no one could call on Him no one could be saved.

The capstone of Paul's argument in this passage is that a clear message which gives understanding of the truth must precede saving faith. He reminds his Jewish readers that God called Abraham and his descendants in order that "the whole earth shall be blessed" (Gen. 12:3) and that He called those descendants (Israel) to be His witnesses before the whole earth, as "a kingdom of priests and a holy nation" (Ex. 19:5-6). Just as He did in the Old Testament, God still sends His preachers to witness to the farthest corners of the earth.

Again gathering Old Testament support, Paul quotes from Isaiah, **Just as it is written, "How beautiful are the feet of those who**

bring glad tidings of good things!" (see Isa. 52:7). It is not the physical **feet** of God's preachers that are **beautiful,** but the wondrous **glad tidings of good things** that those feet carry to the ends of the earth.

That verse from Isaiah was written in celebration of Israel's deliverance from years of captivity and bondage, first in Assyria and then in Babylon. But for Paul's purpose, an even greater fitness of that verse is seen in Isaiah's subsequent declaration of a future day when "The Lord has bared His holy arm in the sight of all the nations, that *the ends of the earth may see the salvation of our God*" (Isa. 52:10, emphasis added). In that day, we learn from John, "the four living creatures and the twenty-four elders [will fall] down before the Lamb, having each one a harp, and golden bowls full of incense, which are the prayers of the saints. And they [will sing] a new song, saying, 'Worthy art Thou to take the book, and to break its seals; for Thou wast slain, and didst purchase for God with Thy blood *men from every tribe and tongue and people and nation*'" (Rev. 5:8-9, emphasis added).

Changing from a note of great rejoicing to one of great sorrow, Paul reminds his Jewish readers that **They did not all heed the glad tidings; for Isaiah says, "Lord, who has believed our report?"** (see Isa. 53:1). **Heed** translates *hupakouō,* which has the basic meaning of listening attentively and the derived meaning of submission or obedience. Tragically, the offer of salvation that is proclaimed to all men is not heeded by all men.

As do many other passages of Scripture, this verse makes clear that, even in His omnipotent sovereignty, God chooses not to exercise absolute control over human affairs. Contrary to the idea of a divine determinism, such as that of ultra-Calvinism, God's **glad tidings** must be received in faith by those who hear it. Only lopsided and unbiblical theologies put everything on God's side or everything on man's side. In order to produce salvation, God's unmerited grace demands man's positive response. Inherent in God's eternal plan of salvation is man's obedient faith. In perhaps the most concise and beautiful statement of the gospel, Jesus said, "For God so loved the world, that He gave His only begotten Son, that *whoever believes in Him* should not perish, but have eternal life" (John 3:16, emphasis added).

Luke reports that in the very early church, "The word of God kept on spreading; and the number of the disciples continued to increase greatly in Jerusalem, and a great many of the priests were becoming obedient to the faith" (Acts 6:7). The phrase "obedient to the faith" is here a synonym for becoming saved. Near the opening to his letter to Rome, Paul declared that "through Jesus Christ our Lord . . . we have received grace and apostleship to bring about the obedience of faith among all the Gentiles, for His name's sake, among whom you also are the called of Jesus Christ" (Rom. 1:4-6). Here again we see both sides of salvation. Those who are "obedient to the faith" are believers who have been "called of Jesus Christ." Later in the letter, Paul declares the corollary truth: "To those who are selfishly ambitious and do not obey the truth, but obey unrighteousness, [God's] wrath and indignation" (2:8). Later still, the apostle says, "Do you not know that when you present yourselves to someone as slaves for obedience, you are slaves of the one whom you obey, either of sin resulting in death, or of obedience resulting in righteousness? Thanks be to God that though you were slaves of sin, you became obedient from the heart to that form of teaching to which you were committed" (6:16-17).

Paul assured the church at Thessalonica that, "when the Lord Jesus shall be revealed from heaven with His mighty angels in flaming fire, [He will deal] out retribution to those who do not know God and to those who do not obey the gospel of our Lord Jesus" (2 Thess. 1:7-8). Similarly, the writer of Hebrews speaks of Christ as having become "to all those who obey Him the source of eternal salvation" (Heb. 5:9). Scripture makes clear that saving faith is marked by submissive obedience to God's righteous truth, and that unbelief is marked by disobedience to that truth (cf. 2 Thess. 2:10-12).

John declares that "If we say that we have fellowship with Him and yet walk in the darkness, we lie and do not practice the truth; but if we walk in the light as He Himself is in the light, we have fellowship with one another, and the blood of Jesus His Son cleanses us from all sin" (1 John 1:6-7). As the apostle goes on to say, true salvation does not bring sinless perfection in this life. "If we say that we have no sin," he explains, "we are deceiving ourselves, and the truth is not in us. If we confess our sins, He is faithful and righteous to forgive us our sins and to cleanse us from all unrighteousness. If we say that we have not sinned, we make Him a liar, and His word is not in us" (1:8-10). When they fall into sin, genuine believers go to the Lord to seek and receive the forgiveness He continually offers to those who are His.

To be saved is to submit oneself to the lordship of Jesus Christ. Jesus will not and cannot be Savior of those who will not receive Him as Lord. "No one can serve two masters," Jesus attested; "for either he will hate the one and love the other, or he will hold to one and despise the other. You cannot serve God and mammon" (Matt. 6:24). On another occasion Jesus declared to a group of Jews who claimed to believe in Him: "If you abide in My word, then you are truly disciples of Mine; and you shall know the truth, and the truth shall make you free" (John 8:31-32). When they claimed to be free already, "Jesus answered them, 'Truly, truly, I say to you, everyone who commits sin is the slave of sin'" (v. 34). To their claim to be Abraham's offspring, He said, "I know that you are Abraham's offspring; yet you seek to kill Me, because My word has no place in you" (v. 37). To their claim that Abraham was their father,

He said,"If you are Abraham's children, do the deeds of Abraham. But as it is, you are seeking to kill Me, a man who has told you the truth, which I heard from God; this Abraham did not do" (vv. 39-40). And to their claim that God was their Father, He responded,"If God were your Father, you would love Me; for I proceeded forth and have come from God, for I have not even come on My own initiative, but He sent Me.... You are of your father the devil, and you want to do the desires of your father. He was a murderer from the beginning, and does not stand in the truth, because there is no truth in him" (8:41-42, 44).

To have one spiritual father is to have one spiritual lord. Those relationships are inseparable. There is no such thing as partial father-hood or partial lordship. In the same way, to have Christ as Savior is to have Him as Lord. Christ does not exist in parts and cannot be accepted in parts. Those to whom Christ is not *both* Savior and Lord, He is *neither* Savior nor Lord. Those who have not accepted Him as Lord have not accepted Him as Savior. Those who have not accepted the Son as Lord have no claim on the Father but are still slaves to sin and are still under the fatherhood and lordship of Satan.

When Isaiah wrote the words quoted by Paul in Romans 10:16, the prophet was speaking of the suffering, dying, substitutionary Savior, who "was pierced through for our transgressions, [and] was crushed for our iniquities; the chastening for our well-being fell upon Him, and by His scourging we are healed" (Isa. 53:5). The **report** of which Isaiah and Paul speak is **the glad tidings** of the gospel, the good news of Christ's dying that we might live, the glorious truth that "God so loved the world, that He gave His only begotten Son, that whoever believes in Him should not perish, but have eternal life. For God did not send the Son into the world to judge the world, but that the world should be saved through Him" (John 3:16-17). But because Jews as well as Gentiles **did not all heed the glad tidings,** Jesus went on to declare that "he who does not believe has been judged already, because he has not believed in the name of the only begotten Son of God" (John 3:18). Later in his gospel account John reported that Jesus "had performed so many signs before them, yet they were not believing in Him; that the word of Isaiah the prophet might be fulfilled, which he spoke,'Lord, who has believed our report? And to whom has the arm of the Lord been revealed?'" (12:37-38).

As Paul and Barnabas explained to unbelieving Jews in Antioch of Pisidia,"It was necessary that the word of God should be spoken to you first; [but] since you repudiate it," that is, reject **the glad tidings** "and judge yourselves unworthy of eternal life, behold, we are turning to the Gentiles" (Acts 13:46).

Summarizing what he had said in verses 1-16, Paul declared, **So faith comes from hearing, and hearing by the word of Christ.**

Salvation does not come by intuition, mystical experience, meditation, speculation, philosophizing, or consensus but by **hearing** and having **faith in the word of Christ.** To proclaim the saving **word of Christ** is therefore the central and essential purpose of evangelism to "go therefore and make disciples of all the nations, baptizing them in the name of the Father and the Son and the Holy Spirit, teaching them to observe all that I commanded you" (Matt. 28:19-20). Paul reminded the elders of the church at Ephesus that, in obedience to that commission, he solemnly testified "to both Jews and Greeks of repentance toward God and faith in our Lord Jesus Christ" (Acts 20:21).

The purpose of evangelism is not to use human persuasion and clever devices to manipulate confessions of faith in Christ but to faithfully proclaim the gospel of Christ, through which the Holy Spirit will bring conviction and salvation to those who hear and accept **the word of Christ.** It is tragic that many appeals to salvation are a call for trust in someone and something they know nothing about. Positive responses to such empty appeals amount to nothing more than faith in faith—a blind, unrepentant, unsubmissive trust in a contentless message that results in a false sense of spiritual security. Such false evangelism cruelly leads the unsaved to believe they are saved, and leaves them still in their sin, without a Savior and without salvation.

Paul next asks rhetorically, **But I say, surely they have never heard, have they?** and then answers by quoting from the Septuagint (Greek) version of Psalm 19:4, **Indeed they have; "Their voice has gone out into all the earth, and their words to the ends of the world."** In other words, even David understood the universal parameters of God's offer of salvation, which already **has gone out** (a past tense) **into all the earth.** David opens that psalm with the declaration that "The heavens are telling of the glory of God; and their expanse is declaring the work of His hands. Day to day pours forth speech, and night to night reveals knowledge. There is no speech, nor are there words; their voice is not heard" (vv. 1-3). **Their voice** and **their words** refer to God's revelation of Himself that **has gone out into all the earth** and has been proclaimed **to the ends of the world**—to all men and women who have ever or will ever live.

That is the same truth Paul emphasizes so strongly in the first chapter of Romans. For "those who suppress the truth in unrighteousness . . . that which is known about God is evident within them; for God made it evident to them. For since the creation of the world His invisible attributes, His eternal power and divine nature, have been clearly seen, being understood through what has been made, so that they [unbelievers] are without excuse" (1:18-20). All men have both internal and external evidence of God. Just as the heavenly bodies touch all the earth and extend to the ends of the world with God's natural revelation, so His gospel touches all the earth and extends to the ends of the world with His special revelation. God cannot be unfair or unjust. Those who refuse to trust in Him do so because they "suppress the truth in unrighteousness" (v. 18).

The way of salvation has always been offered to all men everywhere. As the Lord graciously promised through Jeremiah, "You will seek Me and find Me, when you search for Me with all your heart" (Jer. 29:13). God's absolute and universal assurance to all men is that no person who sincerely seeks for Him will fail to find Him. The incarnate Christ "was the true light which, coming into the world, enlightens *every man*" (John 1:9, emphasis added), and the incarnate Christ Himself declared that "this gospel of [His] kingdom shall be preached in the whole world for a witness to all the nations" (Matt. 24:14). Even in the first century Paul could therefore declare, "the word of truth, the gospel... has come to you, just as in all the world also it is constantly bearing fruit and increasing" (Col. 1:5-6). Although the apostle was probably speaking here only of the part of "the world" to which the full gospel had been proclaimed, the benefit of the gospel was available to **all the earth** and **the ends of the world.**

In Romans 10:11-18, Paul affirms that the gospel is not just one more local invention or one more pagan mystery religion but is the good news of salvation that God always has sought to be proclaimed to every nation and to every person, Jew and Gentile alike.

It is that universal extent of the gospel that caused many Jews to reject Jesus as their Messiah. The Pharisees reprimanded the officers who reported Jesus' authoritative teaching and work, arrogantly saying, "No one of the rulers or Pharisees has believed in Him, has he?" (John 7:48). In other words, an ordinary Jew was presumptuous to believe and trust in a Messiah who was not recognized by their religious leaders. Tragically, many Jews today reject Jesus as their Messiah for the same foolish reason.

When Galileo was summoned before the Roman Catholic inquisition for teaching that the earth revolved around the sun rather than the sun around the earth, he was charged with heresy. When he offered to demonstrate the truth of his findings by having them look through his telescope, they refused. Their minds were already made up, and they refused even to consider evidence to the contrary. With that same obstinacy, most of Israel, from New Testament times to the present, have refused even to consider the claims of the gospel. Consequently, they have failed to know God, Jesus Christ, and saving faith.

THE PREDICTIONS OF SCRIPTURE

But I say, surely Israel did not know, did they? At the first Moses says, "I will make you jealous by that which is not a nation, by a nation without understanding will I anger you." And Isaiah is very bold and says, "I was found by those who sought Me not, I became manifest to those who did not ask for Me." But as for Israel He says, "All the day long I have stretched out My hands to a disobedient and obstinate people." (10:19-21)

Finally, Paul points out that Israel was ignorant of the predictions of their own Scriptures, a truth implied throughout the previous part of this chapter. But ironically, the ignorance of **Israel** was not based on lack of truth; it was not because the people **did not know.** As already noted, God called Abraham and his descendants in order that "the whole earth shall be blessed" (Gen. 12:3) and He called those descendants (Israel) to be His witnesses before all His earth, "a kingdom of priests and a holy nation" (Ex. 19:5-6). They did know, and consequently had no excuse for not understanding and accepting God's universal parameters of salvation.

Quoting another part of the Pentateuch, Paul reminds his readers that **Moses says, "I will make you jealous by that which is not a nation, by a nation without understanding will I anger you"** (see Deut. 32:21). God's blessing of Gentiles who believe in Him would make His chosen people jealous and angry. Some fifteen hundred years before Paul wrote this letter, Moses declared that the salvation message was to reach Gentiles as well as Jews.

Jesus depicted that truth in the parable of the "landowner who planted a vineyard and put a wall around it and dug a wine press in it, and built a tower, and rented it out to vine-growers, and went on a journey" (Matt. 21:33). When the vine-growers beat, killed, or stoned two successive groups of slaves who came to reap the owner's produce and then killed the owner's son, the owner brought "those wretches to a wretched end" and rented "out the vineyard to other vine-growers, who [would] pay him the proceeds at the proper seasons" (vv. 34-41).

Quoting again from **Isaiah,** Paul finally reminds his readers that the prophet was **very bold** when the Lord said through him, **"I was found by those who sought Me not, I became manifest to those who did not ask for Me"** (cf. Isa. 65:1). Through **Moses,** who represented the law and through **Isaiah,** who represented the prophets, Paul firmly established that Israel's rejection of her Messiah came as no surprise to God. It was predicted that, because of that rejection, God would be **found by** Gentiles who had not **sought** Him and would **manifest** Himself to those Gentiles **who did not ask for Him.**

But as for Israel, God's chosen people, who ignored His Word and sought Him in their own way and on their own terms, the Lord said, **All the day long I have stretched out My hands to a disobedient and obstinate people.** *Apeitheō* **(disobedient)** literally means to contradict, to speak against. Throughout her history, **Israel** had, for the most part, contradicted and opposed the truth of the God who had lovingly called her and graciously and patiently **(all the day long) stretched out [His] hands** to her.

In another of Jesus' parables, a man gave a great banquet to which none of the originally invited guests came. When the slave reported the various excuses that were given, "the head of the household became angry and said to his slave, 'Go out at once into the streets and lanes of the city and bring in here the poor and crippled and blind and lame.' And the slave said, 'Master, what you commanded has been done, and still there is room.' And the master said to the slave, 'Go out into the highways and along the hedges, and compel them to come in, that my house may be filled. For I tell you, none of those men who were invited shall taste of my dinner'" (Luke 14:21-24).

Because of Israel's persistent rejection of Him, Jesus lamented, "O Jerusalem, Jerusalem, who kills the prophets and stones those who are sent to her! How often I wanted to gather your children together, the way a hen gathers her chicks under her wings, and you were unwilling" (Matt. 23:37).

What monumental and tragic failure! Unbelieving Jews misunderstood and rejected God, Jesus Christ, and saving faith because of their self-righteousness, and they misunderstood the extent of salvation because of their proud prejudice. They therefore failed as God's witness nation.

God Has Not Canceled His Promises to Israel —part 1 His Setting Aside of Israel Is Partial (Romans 11:1-10)

8

I say then, God has not rejected His people, has He? May it never be! For I too am an Israelite, a descendant of Abraham, of the tribe of Benjamin. God has not rejected His people whom He foreknew. Or do you not know what the Scripture says in the passage about Elijah, how he pleads with God against Israel? "Lord, they have killed Thy prophets, they have torn down Thine altars, and I alone am left, and they are seeking my life." But what is the divine response to him? "I have kept for Myself seven thousand men who have not bowed the knee to Baal." In the same way then, there has also come to be at the present time a remnant according to God's gracious choice. But if it is by grace, it is no longer on the basis of works, otherwise grace is no longer grace. What then? That which Israel is seeking for, it has not obtained, but those who were chosen obtained it, and the rest were hardened; just as it is written, "God gave them a spirit of stupor, eyes to see not and ears to hear not, down to this very day." And David says, "Let their table become a snare and a trap, and a stumbling block and a retribution to them. Let their eyes be darkened to see not, and bend their backs forever." (11:1-10)

No message of Scripture is clearer or repeated more often than the unqualified declaration that God can be trusted, that He is the very source and measure of truth. By definition, His divine Word is absolutely trustworthy. Whatever He says is true and whatever He promises comes to pass.

Shortly before his death, Joshua testified to Israel, "Now behold, today I am going the way of all the earth, and you know in all your hearts and in all your souls that not one word of all the good words which the Lord your God spoke concerning you has failed; all have been fulfilled for you, not one of them has failed" (Josh. 23:14; cf. 21:45). David praised and exalted the Lord as "the God of Truth" (Ps. 31:5). After Solomon prayed before the altar on behalf of his people, "he stood and blessed all the assembly of Israel with a loud voice, saying, 'Blessed be the Lord, who has given rest to His people Israel, according to all that He promised; not one word has failed of all His good promise, which He promised through Moses His servant'" (1 Kings 8:55-56).

In His high priestly prayer, Jesus prayed to His Father on behalf of His followers, "Sanctify them in the truth; Thy word is truth" (John 17:17). Paul reminded Titus that God cannot lie (Titus 1:2), and the writer of Hebrews declares that "He [God] who promised is faithful" (Heb. 10:23; cf. 6:17-18). God's promises never fail because everything He says is wholly true, without a trace of error.

No passage of Scripture articulates God's truthfulness and trustworthiness more eloquently than chapters 9-11 of Romans. As we have seen in an earlier chapter, Paul begins this remarkable section on the nation of Israel with the declaration that it is "Israelites, to whom belongs the adoption as sons and the glory and the covenants and the giving of the Law and the temple service and the promises" (Rom. 9:4).

God had made clear and specific promises to His chosen nation Israel. Some of those promises were conditional, dependent on Israel's obedience. But His greatest promises to His chosen people were unconditional and therefore were grounded solely in God's righteous integrity. Were God to fail in those promises, He would be less than righteous and just. He would be what God cannot be.

Contrary to what some sincere Christians maintain, God cannot be finished with the nation of Israel—for the obvious reason that all of His promises to her have not yet been fulfilled. If God were through with His chosen nation, His Word would be false and His integrity discredited. Among those who most strongly insist that God is through with the nation of Israel are those whose theology is commonly referred to as covenant theology. It is ironic that, because of a distorted view of Israel, covenant theology cannot escape the implication that God is not faithful in fully honoring His covenants.

God's first covenant with Israel was through Abraham, the father of the Hebrew people, who became the nation of Israel. Just before He commanded Abraham to proceed from Haran to Canaan, God promised, "I will make you a great nation, and I will bless you, and make your name great; and so you shall be a blessing; and I will bless those who bless you, and the one who curses you I will curse. And in you all the families of the earth shall be blessed" (Gen. 12:2-3). After Abraham (then called Abram) entered Canaan, "The Lord said to Abram, after Lot had separated from him, 'Now lift up your eyes and look from the place where you are, northward and southward and eastward and westward; for all the land which you see, I will give it to you and to your descendants forever. And I will make your descendants as the dust of the earth; so that if anyone can number the dust of the earth, then your descendants can also be numbered"' (Gen. 13:14-16). Some years later, God reiterated the promise, saying, "'Now look toward the heavens, and count the stars, if you are able to count them.' And He said to him, 'So shall your descendants be'" (Gen. 15:5).

On that occasion God instructed Abraham to cut certain prescribed animals in half, laying the two parts opposite each other. Except as an observer, Abraham did not participate in the confirmation of that covenant. Only the Lord passed between the pieces of the animals, signifying that He alone had dictated and would fulfill the covenant (see Gen. 15:8-21).

Although that covenant was for the benefit of Abraham and his descendants, and ultimately for the blessing of the entire earth, the terms of the covenant were unconditional, and it was sworn to and affirmed *by God with Himself.* He made an inviolable oath with Himself to keep His promises to Abraham. However faithful Abraham or his Israelite descendants might be, God would fulfill the covenant in every detail. This was a divine covenant founded on God's sovereign election of Israel as His chosen people (see Heb. 6:13-20).

Because of God's promises to Abraham and to his descendants through Isaac, the son of promise, the nation of Israel has always been and always will be divinely preserved. Otherwise God could not fulfill His irrevocable promises to her. He caused Israel to outlast all the nations who were contemporary with her, and He still preserves her today. In 1948 He brought her back into her own land as an independent and recognized state among the nations of the world.

God's character and integrity, His trustworthiness and faithfulness depend on His continued preservation of Israel. God has obligated Himself to ultimately redeem the nation of Israel and to establish her as a purified and glorious kingdom above all others in the world.

God has promised to bless all the peoples of the world through Abraham and his descendants, and the fulfillment of that promise culminated in the coming of the Messiah, Jesus Christ, the Savior of the world. He arose from Israel, but the redemption He offered was to Jew and Gentile alike. Early in His ministry, Jesus declared that "God so loved the world, that He gave His only begotten Son, that whoever believes in Him should not perish, but have eternal life" (John 3:16). Near the opening of this epistle, Paul assures his readers that "the gospel ... is the power of God for salvation to everyone who believes, to the Jew first and also to the Greek [Gentile]" (Rom. 1:16).

But because the Jews as a nation rejected their Messiah, God temporarily set that nation aside "until the fulness of the Gentiles has come in" (Rom. 11:25). At that time, with unfailing certainty, "all Israel will be saved" (v. 26). In addition to bringing His chosen people to salvation, God will fulfill His promises to restore her own kingdom in her own land, which will become a land of eternal blessing and peace.

Above all, God promised

> "a new covenant with the house of Israel and with the house of Judah, not like the covenant which I made with their fathers in the day I took them by the hand to bring them out of the land of Egypt, My covenant which they broke, although I was a husband to them," declares the Lord. "But this is the covenant which I will make with the house of Israel after those days," declares the Lord, "I will put My law within them, and on their heart I will write it; and I will be their God, and they shall be My people." (Jer. 31:31-33)

The Jews of Old Testament times understood that those divine promises would be fulfilled literally. But when their Messiah came, spiritual blindness prevented them from recognizing Him. "He came to His own, and those who were His own did not receive Him" (John 1:11). When Pilate mockingly asked the Jewish crowd, "Shall I crucify your King?" the chief priests, speaking for all of apostate Israel, declared with hypocritical vehemence, "We have no king but Caesar" (John 19:15).

Paul knew that most Jews were confused about Israel's true destiny in regard to her Messiah. They reasoned that, because Israel was God's chosen nation, it would be inconceivable that she would spurn her own Messiah, much less put Him to death. Regardless of how disobedient, rebellious, and spiritually blind Israel might become, surely she could not fail to recognize and receive her long-awaited Deliverer. Even if ordinary Jews failed to acknowledge and honor Him, the religious leaders were certain that they themselves could never make such an egregious error.

But Jesus prophesied that rejection in the parable of "a certain nobleman [who] went to a distant country to receive a kingdom for himself, and then return." Just as the citizens of that country declared, "We do not want this man to reign over us" (Luke 19:12-14), so the nation of Israel refused the reign of Jesus Christ over them. Shortly after Pentecost, Peter reminded his fellow Jews of that tragic rejection: "You disowned the Holy and Righteous One, and asked for a murderer to be granted to you, but put to death the Prince of life, the one whom God raised from the dead, a fact to which we are witnesses" (Acts 3:15).

Because Israel "stumbled over the stumbling stone," Jesus Christ, and would not believe in Him (Rom. 9:32-33), because Israel did not know "about God's righteousness, and [sought] to establish their own" (10:3), and because God had continually, "all the day long, …stretched out [His] hands to a disobedient and obstinate people" (10:21) who rejected Him, would not God be fully justified in forever rejecting them?

In itself, that wickedness would more than deserve God's complete and permanent condemnation. Paul makes clear, however, that Israel's rejection of Christ did not catch God by surprise but was, in fact, an integral part of His eternal plan of redemption. He makes equally clear that, despite its being part of that plan, Israel's rejection of Christ was by her own rebellious choice, for which the Lord holds her fully accountable.

Once again we see the remarkable and seemingly irreconcilable association of God's sovereignty and man's responsibility. It is perfectly evident from history as well as from Scripture that Israel rejected Jesus Christ and the gospel of salvation He offered. Scripture also makes certain that God consequently set His ancient and beloved people aside.

But Paul knew that neither Jew nor Gentile would place his trust in a God who did not keep His promises. And God's unqualified promises to Israel included the assurance that He would never completely forsake her. Because God's Word is grounded in His divine integrity and faithfulness, even His chosen people's rejection and crucifixion of His Son could not abrogate the ultimate fulfillment of His promises to them. It is that glorious truth that Paul explains and clarifies in Romans 11.

The apostle begins by stating the truth in the form of a rhetorical question, a question reflecting the confusion and misunderstanding he must have dealt with countless times: **I say then, God has not rejected His people, has He?**

Rejected is from *apōtheō,* which means to thrust away. In the New Testament this verb is always used in the middle voice, indicating a thrusting away from oneself. Paul is therefore not asking whether or not God has refused to *receive* His people to Himself but whether or not He has thrust away from Himself the people He long ago received as His own.

Paul immediately answers his own question, declaring what should have been obvious to his believing readers. For those who know God's character and understand His promises to Israel, there could be but one answer: **May it never be!** Impossible! That is the succinct thrust of Romans 11—It is totally inconceivable that God could renege on His unconditional promises to Israel.

The phrase *mē genoito* **(May it never be!)** was the strongest negative in the Greek language, translated idiomatically in the King James Version as "God forbid." Except for its use in one of Jesus' parables (Luke 20:16), the expression is used elsewhere in the New Testament only by Paul, who employs it fourteen times, ten times in Romans alone. As here, he employed it almost exclusively to repudiate an anticipated misunderstanding by his readers (see, e.g., Rom. 3:4, 6, 31; 6:2, 15; 1 Cor. 6:15; Gal. 2:17).

Despite Israel's being "disobedient and obstinate" (Rom. 10:21), Scripture is replete with the Lord's promises never to forsake His chosen people. "The Lord will not abandon His people on account of His great name, because the Lord has been pleased to make you a people for Himself" (1 Sam. 12:22). It is God's faithfulness to Israel that guarantees her ultimate redemption and restoration.

Through the psalmist the Lord declared of Israel,

> If they violate My statutes, and do not keep My commandments, then I will visit their transgression with the rod, and their iniquity with stripes. But I will not break off My lovingkindness from him, nor deal falsely in My faithfulness. My covenant I will not violate, nor will I alter the utterance of My lips. Once I have sworn by My holiness; I will not lie to David. His descendants shall endure forever, and his throne as the sun before Me. It shall be established forever like the moon, and the witness in the sky is faithful. (Ps. 89:31-37)

Through another psalmist God promised that "the Lord will not abandon His people, nor will He forsake His inheritance" (Ps. 94:14). In spite of Israel's continued unfaithfulness, God "looked upon their distress, when He heard their cry; and He remembered His covenant for their sake, and relented according to the greatness of His lovingkindness" (Ps. 106:44-45). God's grace always surpasses His people's sin.

Psalm 105 is devoted entirely to thanking and praising God for His unalterable and permanent covenant relationship with Israel. "He has remembered His covenant forever," the writer declares, "the word which He commanded to a thousand generations, the covenant which He made with Abraham, and His oath to Isaac. Then He confirmed it to Jacob for a statute, to Israel as an everlasting covenant" (Ps. 105:8-10).

After Israel returned from seventy years of captivity in Babylon, the Levites spoke to the Lord on behalf of a now penitent nation, acknowledging before Him the people's repeated cycles of going from wickedness to penitence to forgiveness to restoration and then reverting again to wickedness:

> They became disobedient and rebelled against Thee, and cast Thy law behind their backs and killed Thy prophets who had admonished them so that they might return to Thee, and they committed great blasphemies. Therefore Thou didst deliver them into the hand of their oppressors who oppressed them, but when they cried to Thee in the time of their distress, Thou didst hear from heaven, and according to Thy great compassion Thou didst give them deliverers who delivered them from the hand of their oppressors. (Neh. 9:26-27; cf. 28-30)

"Nevertheless, in Thy great compassion, Thou didst not make an end of them or forsake them," the Levites continued to pray, "for Thou art a gracious and compassionate God" (9:31). Although Israel deserved only God's damnation, His own promises to her would not permit it, because "the great, the mighty, and the awesome God, ... dost keep covenant and lovingkindness" (v. 32).

Through Jeremiah, the Lord assured His people:

> "Fear not, O Jacob My servant," declares the Lord, "and do not be dismayed, O Israel; for behold, I will save you from afar, and your offspring from the land of their captivity. And Jacob shall return, and shall be quiet and at ease, and no one shall make him afraid. For I am with you," declares the Lord, "to save you; for I will destroy completely all the nations where I have scattered you, only I will not destroy you completely." . . . He who scattered Israel will gather him, and keep him as a shepherd keeps his flock. (Jer. 30:10-11; 31:10)

Because of His covenant promises to Israel, that nation was never, and can never be, completely cast aside by the Lord.

In light of that truth, Paul affirms that God's present setting aside of Israel is only partial (11:1-10). He does so by pointing to himself as a believing Jew (v. 1-6), by pointing to the believing remnant whom God has always preserved in Israel (vv. 2-7*a*), and by pointing to God's revelation about unbelieving Israelites whose hearts are hardened to His grace (vv. 7*b*-10).

THE TRUTH ABOUT THE WRITER

For I too am an Israelite, a descendant of Abraham, of the tribe of Benjamin. (11:1*b*)

The first proof that God had not rejected His chosen people was that Paul, not only a believer in Christ but also an apostle (1:1), was himself **an Israelite.**

Although Paul does not mention it here, the vast majority of early Christians were Jews. It was for the very reason that so many of his fellow Jews had turned to Jesus as their Messiah that Paul, under his former name of Saul, had once fiercely persecuted the church (Acts 8:1-3; 9:1-2). Before his conversion, he had been the most fanatical Christ-hating and Christian-hating Jew in Israel. If such a Christ-rejecting Jew as himself could be brought to saving faith, the gospel had power to save *any* Jew.

More than that, however, Paul's own conversion made it obvious that God could not possibly have rejected all Israel. He was living proof that, just as God's promises to Israel do not include all individual Jews, so His judgment and rejection of Israel do not include all individual Jews. Paul would hardly devote the rest of his life, and many times risk his life, to preach a gospel from which he himself was excluded.

Paul was not a proselyte to Judaism, but was a Jew by birth, a genuine **Israelite, a descendent of Abraham.** Probably speaking of Judaizers, who were among the "false apostles, deceitful workers, [who were] disguising themselves as apostles of Christ," Paul asked the Corinthians, "Are they Hebrews? So am I. Are they Israelites? So am I. Are they descendants of Abraham? So am I" (2 Cor. 11:13,22).

Paul not only was **a descendent of Abraham** but a member **of the tribe of Benjamin,** "one of the most favoured tribes" of Israel according to theologian Charles Hodge. "Judah and Benjamin, especially after the exile, were the chief representatives of the theocractical people" (*Commentary on the Epistle to the Romans* [Grand Rapids: Eerdmans, 1950; orig. revised ed., 1886], 353).

Paul again mentioned that distinction in his letter to the church at Philippi, declaring, "If anyone else has a mind to put confidence in the flesh, I far more: circumcised the eighth day, of the nation of Israel, of the tribe of Benjamin, a Hebrew of Hebrews; as to the Law, a Pharisee; as to zeal, a persecutor of the church; as to the righteousness which is in the Law, found blameless" (Phil. 3:4-6). But being **of the tribe of Benjamin** was only an earthly distinction, which, like the others he names here, he counted as "loss in view of the surpassing value of knowing Christ Jesus my Lord, for whom I have suffered the loss of all things, and count them but rubbish in order that I may gain Christ" (v. 8).

THE TRUTH ABOUT THE REMNANT

God has not rejected His people whom He foreknew. Or do you not know what the Scripture says in the passage about Elijah, how he pleads with God against Israel? "Lord, they have killed Thy prophets, they have torn down Thine altars, and I alone am left, and they are seeking my life." But what is the divine response to him? "I have kept for Myself seven thousand men who have not bowed the knee to Baal." In the same way then, there has also come to be at the present time a remnant according to God's gracious choice. But if it is by grace, it is no longer on the basis of works, otherwise grace is no longer grace. What then? That which Israel is seeking for, it has not obtained, but those who were chosen obtained it, (11:2-7*a*)

The second proof that God's setting aside of Israel is only partial is that the Lord has always preserved a remnant for Himself. From Pentecost to the present day, Christ's church has never been without believing Jews.

Paul here gives a direct and emphatic answer to the rhetorical question with which he opened the chapter: **God has not rejected His people whom He foreknew.** As mentioned above in relation to verse 1*a*, the term **rejected** does not refer to *receiving* (as in rejecting an application) but to *not casting away from oneself* (rejecting what once had been received). It is not that God has never *received* **His people,** but that He will never completely and permanently cast away those **whom He foreknew** from eternity past and whom He long ago received to Himself through His covenant with Abraham.

Paul is not referring to individual regenerate Jews or Gentiles—although the basic promise would certainly apply to them—but to Israel as a nation, the corporate body of God's chosen people, who are the focus of Romans **9-11.** The **people** mentioned in **11:2** are the "disobedient and obstinate" nation of Israel, to whom the apostle has just referred (10:21).

In this context, **foreknew** (from *proginōskō*) does not simply mean to be aware of something beforehand but to determine that it will come to pass. In Scripture, "to know" often carries the idea of intimacy, such as that of a husband and wife, an intimacy characterized by devotion and love. God's foreknowledge is frequently used of His intimate, loving relationship with all those He called to Himself "before the foundation of the world" (Eph. 1:4). Speaking of Jesus Christ, Peter declared to those assembled at Pentecost, that "this Man, delivered up by the predetermined plan and foreknowledge of God, you nailed to a cross by the hands of godless men and put Him to death" (Acts 2:23). God's predetermined plan and His foreknowledge are equated. For God, to foreknow is to predetermine and preordain.

Peter speaks of believers as those "who are chosen according to the foreknowledge of God the Father" (1 Pet. 1:1-2). God's foreknowing those who will be saved is the same as His predestinating those who will be saved. "For whom [God] foreknew," Paul explains earlier in this epistle, "He also predestined to become conformed to the image of His Son, that He might be the First-born among many brethren; and whom He predestined, these He also called; and whom He called, these He also justified; and whom He justified, these He also glorified" (Rom. 8:29-30).

Israel is the only *nation* God has foreknown and predetermined to be His people and the recipients of His love and grace. "For you are a holy people to the Lord your God," Moses declared to Israel. "The Lord your God has chosen you to be a people for His own possession out of all the peoples who are on the face of the earth. The Lord did not set His love on you nor choose you because you were more in number than any of the peoples, for you were the fewest of all peoples, but because the Lord loved you and kept the oath which He swore to your forefathers" (Deut. 7:6-8).

Because God foreknew and predetermined before the foundation of the earth to set His special love upon Israel forever, He can never totally reject them. To do so would invalidate His divine promises, nullify His divine faithfulness, discredit His divine integrity, and compromise His divine love. One of the greatest evidences that God has not totally rejected Israel is the continual remnant of that people whom God has graciously preserved for Himself. From the day God called Abraham until the day Christ returns in glory and judgment, there has not been and will never be a time when the earth will be without believing Jews.

Paul reminds his readers about **what the Scripture says in the passage about Elijah, how he pleads with God against Israel? "Lord, they have killed Thy prophets, they have torn down Thine altars, and I alone am left, and they are seeking my life"** (cf. 1 Kings 19:10).

When his life was threatened by Jezebel, even the godly and normally fearless Elijah became fearful and despondent, thinking in self pity that he was the only believer left on earth. But **the divine response to him was, "I have kept for Myself seven thousand men who have not bowed the knee to Baal"** (cf. 1 Kings 19:18).

Chrēmatismos **(divine response)** carries the idea of divine oracle or revelation. Through His direct word, the Lord reassured Elijah that **seven thousand** others remained faithful to the true God and had **not bowed the knee to** the pagan god **Baal,** whom the wicked Jezebel and her priests had led most of Israel to worship (see 1 Kings 19:9-18).

When the Lord called Isaiah to preach, He warned the prophet that most of his hearers would not listen or repent and that only a small holy remnant would remain, like the stump left when a tree is felled (Isa. 6:9-13). That passage from Isaiah is the most quoted Old Testament text in the New Testament (see, e.g, Matt. 13:14-15; Mark 4:12; Luke 8:10; John 12:40; Acts 28:26)—used repeatedly to emphasize the truth that God has judicially blinded those of His chosen people who willfully blind themselves to Him.

While God's people were captives in Babylon, most of them refused to turn to God. But a few—the godly remnant that included Daniel, Ezekiel, Shadrach, Meshach, Abednego, Mordecai, and Esther—remained faithful to the Lord. Malachi assured such believers that their names were written in the Lord's "book of remembrance" (Mal. 3:16).

When Israel's Messiah, Jesus Christ, came to earth, the apostate nation rejected and crucified Him. But there was a godly remnant in Israel before Jesus was born—including Zacharias and Elizabeth, Mary and Joseph. There was a godly remnant—including Simeon, Anna, and the shepherds near Bethlehem—who received and worshiped Jesus when He was but an infant. During His ministry, a growing number of Jews turned to Him as Lord and Savior. Some 3,000 believers, mostly Jewish, were added at Pentecost (Acts 2:41), and another 5,000 a short while later (4:4). By the time of the events mentioned at the end of Acts 4, it is probable that there were at least 20,000 Jewish Christians in Jerusalem alone.

In the same way then, Paul goes on to say, **there has also come to be at the present time a remnant according to God's gracious choice.** By the time the apostle wrote those words, there were doubtless hundreds of thousands of Jewish Christians throughout the Roman empire and likely even beyond it.

Gracious choice translates *eklogēn charitos* and could be rendered "election by grace." As is true of all believers in all ages, the believing **remnant** of Jews during Paul's **time** were not elected by virtue of their spiritual worthiness or moral good works—and obviously not simply on the basis of their racial descent—but **according to God's** sovereign election, His **gracious choice.** Before the foundation of the world, God graciously predetermined His **choice** of those physical descendants of Abraham who also would become His spiritual descendants.

As a member of that elect remnant of Jews, Paul explains that "God has saved us, and called us with a holy calling, not according to our works, but according to His own purpose and grace which was granted us in Christ Jesus from all eternity" (2 Tim. 1:9).

As the apostle has already explained in some detail in Romans (see, e.g., 3:21-31; 4:1–11; 5:2, 20-21; 9:11), if God's salvation **is by**

grace, it is no longer on the basis of works, otherwise grace is no longer grace. The additional phrase in the King James Version ("otherwise work is no more work") may have been a copier's marginal note that found its way into the text.

Summing up what he has just emphasized, Paul asks, **What then?** Again answering his own question, he replies, **That which** unbelieving **Israel is seeking for, it has not obtained, but** only **those who were** graciously **chosen obtained it.**

The phrase **is seeking for** is from *epizēteō*, which indicates intense, diligent seeking. The Jews of Paul's day were fanatically religious, a condition the apostle acknowledged in the previous chapter: "For I bear them witness that they have a zeal for God, but not in accordance with knowledge" (Rom. 10:2). And because their zeal focused on their own false righteousness rather than on God's true righteousness, "they did not subject themselves to the righteousness of God" (v. 3). Consequently, they did not acknowledge or receive Jesus Christ, who "is the end of the law for righteousness to everyone who believes" (v. 4). But those whom God had **chosen** for Himself seek His righteousness and graciously **obtained it.**

In the end times, God will seal for Himself a special remnant of 144,000 Jews, who will be protected from Antichrist and who will be His witnesses during those increasingly degenerate and depraved days (Rev. 7:1-8; 14:1-5). Ultimately, Paul assures us later in this chapter, "All Israel will be saved" (Rom. 11:26).

The noted Christian scholar Charles Feinberg, like Paul a believing Jew, tells the following story that gives contemporary evidence that God will never be without a believing remnant of His chosen people Israel.

> Over a quarter of a century ago a Russian Jew of great learning named Joseph Rabbinowitz was sent to Palestine by the Jews to buy land for them. He went to Jerusalem. One day he went up on the Mount of Olives to rest. Someone had told him to take a New Testament as the best guidebook about Jerusalem. The Christ he had known was the Christ of the Greek and Roman churches, who were his persecutors and the persecutors of his people. But as he read the New Testament he became acquainted with the real Christ of whom the Old Testament Scriptures had foretold, and his heart grew warm. He looked off toward Calvary and thought: *Why is it that my people are persecuted and cast out?* And his conviction gave the answer: *It must be because we have put to death our Messiah.* He lifted his eyes to that Messiah and said: "My Lord and my God." He came down from the mount a disciple of the Lord Jesus Christ. He went home to Russia and erected a synagogue for the Jews, over the door of which was written: "Let all the house of Israel know that God hath made that same Jesus whom ye

have crucified, both Lord and Christ" [Acts 2:36]. He was one of the many present remnant of Israel, which proves conclusively and better than words that God has not cast away His people. *(Israel: At the Center of History and Revelation* [Portland, Ore.: Multnomah, 1980], 108)

THE TRUTH ABOUT THE REVELATION

and the rest were hardened; just as it is written, "God gave them a spirit of stupor, eyes to see not and ears to hear not, down to this very day." And David says, "Let their table become a snare and a trap, and a stumbling block and a retribution to them. Let their eyes be darkened to see not, and bend their backs forever." (11:7*b*-10)

The third proof that God's setting aside of Israel is only partial is that the Lord has hardened the hearts only of those Jews who refuse to believe.

Were hardened is passive, indicating that the hardening was caused by an outside power. That outside power was none other than God, who, **just as it is written, . . . gave them a spirit of stupor, eyes to see not and ears to hear not, down to this very day** (cf. Deut. 29:4; Isa. 29:10). Deuteronomy represents the law and Isaiah the prophets. Both the law and the prophets testify to God's sovereign and predetermined hardening of hearts. But that hardening is neither capricious nor unjust. God hardens only those hearts who, in rejecting His gracious offer of righteousness, harden themselves to His grace.

God judicially hardened Pharaoh's heart (see, e.g., Ex. 4:21; 9:12; 10:1), because Pharaoh willingly "hardened his [own] heart" against God (Ex. 8:15; cf. 8:32; 9:34; 10:20).

During the Lord's Supper, Jesus said, "Behold, the hand of the one betraying Me is with Me on the table. For indeed, the Son of Man is going as it has been determined; but woe to that man by whom He is betrayed!" (Luke 22:21-22). God's righteous predetermination of Judas's betrayal was inextricably connected to Judas's own unrighteous intentions, for which he was held eternally accountable. One of the great mysteries of Scripture is the coexistence of God's sovereign preordination and man's personal accountability. God's judicial hardening of a man's heart is never separate from that man's hardening of his own heart.

Citing the Old Testament again, Paul quotes **David,** who said, **"Let their table become a snare and a trap, and a stumbling block and a retribution to them. Let their eyes be darkened to**

see not, and bend their backs forever" (cf. Ps. 69:22-23). Psalm 69 is one of the most marvelous messianic passages in the Old Testament and one of the most quoted psalms in the New Testament. Like Psalm 22, it is a lament of the Messiah's suffering and grief. It is also imprecatory, pronouncing a curse on the enemies of God who caused that suffering and grief.

A person's **table** is generally thought of as a place of safety, feasting, and sustenance. But the **table** of the ungodly and self-righteous will **become a snare and a trap.** The Jews considered God's Word, in particular the Torah, to be their spiritual sustenance—which indeed it was. But because of their rebellious unbelief, that Word became a judgment on them, **a stumbling block and a retribution.**

One of the saddest commentaries of history is that so many people place their trust in the very thing that damns them. All false religions—pagan, cultic, unbiblical Christianity, and every other kind—present counterfeit means of salvation. The more their adherents feed on the falsehoods, the more immune they become to the true gospel of Jesus Christ, the living bread of life.

As she continued to reject God, Israel became progressively more spiritually blind—so blind that she could not recognize her own Messiah and Savior. Just as David had prayed in righteous indignation against the sins of his own people, Israel's **eyes** were **darkened to see not.** Because Israel refused to see the things of God, God judicially ratified her willing blindness. **Bend their backs** suggests the hunched over position in which blind people sometimes walk as they grope their way on a path they cannot see that leads to a destination they do not seek.

God Has Not Canceled His Promises to Israel —part 2 His Setting Israel Aside Is Passing (Romans 11:11-24)

9

I say then, they did not stumble so as to fall, did they? May it never be! But by their transgression salvation has come to the Gentiles, to make them jealous. Now if their transgression be riches for the world and their failure be riches for the Gentiles, how much more will their fulfillment be! But I am speaking to you who are Gentiles. Inasmuch then as I am an apostle of Gentiles, I magnify my ministry, if somehow I might move to jealousy my fellow countrymen and save some of them. For if their rejection be the reconciliation of the world, what will their acceptance be but life from the dead? And if the first piece of dough be holy, the lump is also; and if the root be holy, the branches are too. But if some of the branches were broken off, and you, being a wild olive, were grafted in among them and became partaker with them of the rich root of the olive tree, do not be arrogant toward the branches; but if you are arrogant, remember that it is not you who supports the root, but the root supports you. You will say then, "Branches were broken off so that I might be grafted in." Quite right, they were broken off for their unbelief, but you stand by your faith. Do not be conceited, but fear; for if God did not spare the natural branches, neither

will He spare you. Behold then the kindness and severity of God; to those who fell, severity, but to you, God's kindness, if you continue in His kindness; otherwise you also will be cut off. And they also, if they do not continue in their unbelief, will be grafted in; for God is able to graft them in again. For if you were cut off from what is by nature a wild olive tree, and were grafted contrary to nature into a cultivated olive tree, how much more shall these who are the natural branches be grafted into their own olive tree? (11:11-24)

The second major truth that Paul presents in Romans 11 is that God's act of setting Israel aside is passing, not permanent. This hopeful truth is seen in its definite purpose, its definite premonition, and its definite promise.

IT HAS A DEFINITE PURPOSE

I say then, they did not stumble so as to fall, did they? May it never be! But by their transgression salvation has come to the Gentiles, to make them jealous. Now if their transgression be riches for the world and their failure be riches for the Gentiles, how much more will their fulfillment be! But I am speaking to you who are Gentiles. Inasmuch then as I am an apostle of Gentiles, I magnify my ministry, if somehow I might move to jealousy my fellow countrymen and save some of them. For if their rejection be the reconciliation of the world, what will their acceptance be but life from the dead? (11:11-15)

First, God's temporarily setting Israel aside was not an after-thought or an outburst of emotional anger but had a definite purpose. Again (see **11:1**) Paul introduces his point by asking a rhetorical question and then giving the strongest negative answer possible: **I say then, they did not stumble so as to fall, did they? May it never be!** God has not allowed His chosen people Israel to fall into such unbelief and disobedience that they are unsalvageable. He has indeed given them "a spirit of stupor," and He "let their eyes be darkened to see not" (vv. 8, 10). For a divinely appointed time, He has let them wander about in spiritual blindness and darkness. Yet their blindness is not irreversible, and their darkness was never to be permanent.

The severe stumbling of which Paul speaks is, of course, Israel's rejection of her Messiah, Jesus Christ. But Israel's rejection of God's own Son and His kingdom did not thwart God's plan. On the contrary

(but), the Lord used that terrible **transgression** of His people to accomplish His own divine objective.

That vast objective is twofold: to bring salvation to the Gentiles and to the Jews.

GENTILE SALVATION

salvation has come to the Gentiles (11:11*b*)

Through the stumbling of Israel, God's gracious, far-reaching **salvation** was extended **to the Gentiles.** Israel's temporary loss was the Gentiles' permanent gain. "I say to you," Jesus promised, "that many [Gentiles] shall come from east and west, and recline at the table with Abraham, and Isaac, and Jacob, in the kingdom of heaven; but the sons of the kingdom [unbelieving Jews] shall be cast out into the outer darkness; in that place there shall be weeping and gnashing of teeth" (Matt. 8:11-12). The very people for whom the kingdom was intended and to whom the kingdom was offered will be shut out of the kingdom. Individual Jews who reject their Messiah will be banned and sent permanently "into the outer darkness," but the unbelieving nation shall one day believe and be restored. In the meanwhile, because of their rejection of the kingdom, God has offered the kingdom, and the **salvation** it represents, to a people called out from among **the Gentiles.**

On a later occasion, Jesus warned unbelieving Israel through a parable: "Therefore I say to you, the kingdom of God will be taken away from you, and be given to a nation producing the fruit of it" (Matt. 21:43). He proceeded to tell the enraged chief priests and Pharisees still another parable (22:1-14) that vividly portrayed their rejection of Him and His Father's rejection of them, while inviting into the kingdom the despised Gentiles to whom it had not originally been promised.

Although the widespread **salvation** of **Gentiles** came about because Israel as a nation refused her Savior, that extension of grace was not an afterthought with God. From His first calling of Abraham, it was God's intent that His chosen people should be the instruments of bringing salvation to the Gentiles. "In you," the Lord told Abraham, "all the families of the earth shall be blessed" (Gen. 12:3). In the covenant at Sinai God called Israel to be His witnesses, His spiritual ambassadors to the world as "a kingdom of priests and a holy nation" (Ex. 19:6). Like their Messiah, "the tribes of Jacob, and . . . the preserved ones of Israel" were to be "a light of the nations so that [God's] salvation may reach to the end of the earth" (Isa. 49:6).

Paul applied that same calling to himself and Barnabas. To the resentful and jealous Jews in Pisidian Antioch, and in the presence of many Gentiles, the two men declared, "It was necessary that the word of God should be spoken to you first; since you repudiate it, and judge yourselves unworthy of eternal life, behold, we are turning to the Gentiles. For thus the Lord has commanded us, 'I have placed You as a light for the Gentiles, that You should bring salvation to the end of the earth'" (Acts 13:46-47).

Some years later, while preaching to unbelieving and blasphemous Jews in Corinth, Paul "shook out his garments and said to them, 'Your blood be upon your own heads! I am clean. From now on I shall go to the Gentiles'" (Acts 18:6). In his last recorded words to his unbelieving "kinsmen according to the flesh" (Rom. 9:3), the apostle said,

> The Holy Spirit rightly spoke through Isaiah the prophet to your fathers, saying, "Go to this people and say, 'You will keep on hearing, but will not understand; and you will keep on seeing, but will not perceive; for the heart of this people has become dull, and with their ears they scarcely hear, and they have closed their eyes; lest they should see with their eyes, and hear with their ears, and understand with their heart and return, and I should heal them.'" Let it be known to you therefore, that this salvation of God has been sent to the Gentiles; they will also listen. (Acts 28:25-28)

Paul was uniquely called to be God's apostle to the Gentiles (Rom. 11:13; cf. Acts 9:15), as one to whom, "the very least of all saints, this grace was given, to preach to the Gentiles the unfathomable riches of Christ" (Eph. 3:8). Yet when he first came to a city, he invariably would go first to the synagogue or search out individual Jews if they were too few to have a synagogue. Some of those hearers would believe, but, for the most part, they resisted and rejected the gospel that was "spoken against everywhere" (Acts 28:22). At that point, Paul would turn his focus to the Gentiles. The church is the new people of God, called from among all nations.

JEWISH SALVATION

to make them jealous. Now if their transgression be riches for the world and their failure be riches for the Gentiles, how much more will their fulfillment be! But I am speaking to you who are Gentiles. Inasmuch then as I am an apostle of Gentiles, I magnify my ministry, if somehow I might move to jealousy my fellow countrymen and save some of them. For if their rejection be the reconciliation of the world, what will their acceptance be but life from the dead? (11:11c-15)

God's second objective in setting Israel aside was **to make her jealous** of Gentiles. **To make** translates a Greek infinitive with a preposition and carries the idea of purpose. And although jealousy is essentially a negative term, God's intention was for Israel's jealousy of Gentiles to be a positive stimulus to draw His people back to Himself. But Jews had long disdained Gentiles, whom they considered to be outside the boundaries of God's grace. To be told they had lost their special relationship to God was distressing enough, but to be told that God offered that forfeited relationship to Gentiles was a bitter pill indeed.

Paul already had reminded his Jewish readers of God's ancient revelation concerning His purpose for the Gentiles. Through Moses He said, "I will make you jealous by that which is not a nation, by a nation without understanding will I anger you," and through Isaiah said, "I was found by those who sought Me not, I became manifest to those who did not ask for Me" (Rom. 10:19-20).

But God's ultimate purpose in setting Israel aside was not to drive His people further away but to bring them back to Himself. He wanted to make them face their own sin and its consequences, to sense their alienation from Jehovah and to recognize their need for the salvation that He now offered the Gentiles. As Jews see the Lord pour out the kind of blessings on the Gentile church that once were reserved for Israel, some of them desire that blessing for themselves and come to Jesus Christ, their spurned Messiah, in repentance and faith. That happens with individual Jews throughout this age, and will one day happen to the whole nation.

One of the great ironies of history is the relationship of God's chosen people (the Jews) to the rest of humanity (the Gentiles). Anti-Semitism by Gentiles has often been paralleled by, and sometimes precipitated by, the anti-Gentile sentiments of Jews. It therefore was—and no doubt still is for many Jews—an enormous leap from a negative contempt of Gentiles to a positive jealousy of them. Yet that is precisely the leap the Lord intends for them to make as a first step in bringing them back to Him.

It should be the desire of every Christian to manifest the spiritual realities of a transformed life that would draw unbelieving Jews to belief in our Lord and their Messiah, a witness that would tap their divinely-inspired jealousy of Gentiles and be used to turn it to a divinely-desired faith in His Son.

Unfortunately, the Christianity that Jews see in many professed, and even some genuine, Christians reflects little of the love and righteousness of Christ and of the salvation He brings. When they see Gentile Christians who are dishonest and immoral, and especially those who are anti-Semitic in the name of Christ (who was the supremely perfect Jew), they are deeply and understandably offended and repulsed.

They are anything but **jealous** of such Gentiles, and they distance themselves still further from the Lord instead of drawing closer to Him.

A future time will come when the nation will recognize her Messiah, repent of killing Him, and be saved (Zech. 12:10).

God has used even the great **transgression** of Israel in rejecting her Messiah to accomplish His ultimate purpose of bringing spiritual **riches** to **the world,** that is, **the Gentiles,** just as He had declared to Abraham when He first called Israel to Himself: "In you all the families of the earth shall be blessed" (Gen. 12:3). Although Israel failed to witness to the world in righteousness, God caused her to witness to the world, as it were, in unrighteousness. Because the Lord could not use Israel's faithfulness to bring **riches** to **the Gentiles,** He instead used her **failure.**

But how much more will their [the Jews'] **fulfillment be!** Paul exults. That is, if the Lord has used Israel's great transgression of rejecting her Messiah to bless the Gentile world, how much more will He bless the world when Israel turns to Him in faith and the glorious millennial kingdom comes.

Earlier in the letter Paul had used another extreme contrast to portray the greatness of God's love and grace: "God demonstrates His own love toward us, in that while we were yet sinners, Christ died for us. Much more then, having now been justified by His blood, we shall be saved from the wrath of God through Him. For if while we were enemies, we were reconciled to God through the death of His Son, much more, having been reconciled, we shall be saved by His life" (Rom. 5:8-10). If a dead Savior could redeem us, how much more can a living Savior sustain us.

By the same logic, if a faithless Israel could bring salvation to the Gentiles, how much greater blessing will her faithfulness bring. The Lord promises that when Israel one day receives the Messiah she rejected, He "will pour out on the house of David and on the inhabitants of Jerusalem, the Spirit of grace and of supplication, so that they will look on Me whom they have pierced" (Zech. 12:10). "In that day a fountain will be opened for the house of David and for the inhabitants of Jerusalem, for sin and for impurity" (13:1). Following that, "the Lord will be king over all the earth; in that day the Lord will be the only one, and His name the only one....And there will be no more curse,...Then it will come about that any who are left of all the nations ... will go up from year to year to worship the King, the Lord of hosts" (14:9,11,16).

In that day the Lord Jesus Christ will establish His kingdom on earth, Israel will reign with Him, and her people will become the faithful witnesses and blessing to the world that God always intended them to be. And in that day when Israel turns to Christ, Satan will be bound, the heavens and earth will be renewed, justice will prevail on earth, and there will be worldwide righteousness and universal peace. That will be the **much more** blessing that Israel's faith will bring to the world.

As this spiritual revival of Israel begins during the Great Tribulation, the Lord will seal for Himself "one hundred and forty-four thousand ...from every tribe of the sons of Israel" (Rev. 7:4), and through their faithful witness "a great multitude [of Gentiles], which no one could count, from every nation and all tribes and peoples and tongues, [will stand] before the throne and before the Lamb, clothed in white robes, and palm branches [will be] in their hands" (v. 9). The fruit of Israel's faithful **fulfillment** will be worldwide salvation. That also will go on during the kingdom, as Jews lead Gentiles to the Lord Christ.

Paul reaches deeper into the evidence of his own genuine affection for Israel. **I am speaking to you who are Gentiles,** he says, and **inasmuch then as I am an apostle of Gentiles, I magnify my ministry.** In other words, he does not want to underplay his special calling to reach the Gentile world for Christ. He emphasized that calling wherever he ministered (see Acts 18:6; 22:21; 26:17-18; Eph. 3:8; 1 Tim. 2:7). But he also knew that "salvation is from the Jews" (John 4:22), and that "the gospel...is the power of God for salvation to everyone who believes, to the Jew first and also to the Greek" (Rom. 1:16). In addition to that knowledge, he had great personal love for his fellow Jews and "great sorrow and unceasing grief in [his] heart" because of their lostness. "For I could wish that I myself were accursed," he testified, "separated from Christ for the sake of my brethren, my kinsmen according to the flesh, who are Israelites" (Rom. 9:3-4). His constant "heart's desire and ...prayer to God [was] for ...their salvation" (10:1). His special calling to and love for the unsaved Gentile world in no way diminished his affection for unsaved fellow Jews and for unbelieving Israel as a people.

He therefore makes no apology for his own intention, which reflected his Lord's intention to bring **to jealousy [his] fellow countrymen and save some of them.** In addition to wanting to bring Gentiles to salvation for their own sakes, he also wanted their salvation to be God's instrument for redeeming Jews. And **if their rejection** can lead to **the reconciliation of the world,** he goes on to say, **what will their acceptance be but life from the dead?** The tragedy of **their rejection** will be surpassed by the glory of **their acceptance.**

In speaking of **life from the dead,** Paul was not referring to bodily resurrection. Regarding individual Jews, he was speaking of receiving spiritual life as a gracious gift to displace spiritual death, the wage of unbelief. Regarding Israel, he was speaking of its rebirth and the rebirth of the whole world in the glorified millennial kingdom of God (see, e.g., Isa. 11:1-9; Rev. 20). In that glorious day, even "the creation itself also will be set free from its slavery to corruption into the freedom of the glory of the children of God" (Rom. 8:21).

It Was a Definite Premonition

And if the first piece of dough be holy, the lump is also; and if the root be holy, the branches are too. But if some of the branches were broken off, and you, being a wild olive, were grafted in among them and became partaker with them of the rich root of the olive tree, do not be arrogant toward the branches; but if you are arrogant, remember that it is not you who supports the root, but the root supports you. You will say then, "Branches were broken off so that I might be grafted in." Quite right, they were broken off for their unbelief, but you stand by your faith. Do not be conceited, but fear; for if God did not spare the natural branches, neither will He spare you. Behold then the kindness and severity of God; to those who fell, severity, but to you, God's kindness, if you continue in His kindness; otherwise you also will be cut off. (11:16-22)

Second, God's temporarily setting Israel aside was a definite premonition. Paul here gives a stern warning to Gentiles about having the same kind of arrogant, presumptuous pride that caused unbelieving Israel's removal from blessing. God did not judge Israel and offer the gospel to Gentiles because Jews are inherently more unrighteous and unworthy or because Gentiles are inherently more righteous and worthy (cf. Rom. 2:14-15). That is the reverse of the view Jews had long had of Gentiles.

It did not take long for early Gentile Christians to be tempted to scorn the Jews because they had scorned Christ. That notion poured fuel on the fire of anti-Semitism that had existed in many Gentile nations and cultures for countless centuries. It is seen in Scripture in the enmity between Israel and her surrounding neighbors—such as Syria, Phoenicia, Moab, Edom, the Philistines, and other Canaanite peoples. It is seen in Israel's conquest and domination by Babylon, Assyria, Greece, and then Rome. And because many Gentile believers in the early church had been raised in the midst of pagan anti-Semitism, it was not difficult for Satan to tempt them to continued prejudice against Jews because of Israel's rejection and crucifixion of her own Messiah and Savior.

Some modern "Christian" cults are based on the notion of British Israelism. They hold the totally unscriptural and unhistorical notion that Anglo-Saxons comprise the ten so-called lost tribes of Israel—a name to which they believe Jews have long lost all claim, because God eternally rejected and condemned them for rejecting and putting Jesus Christ to death. Anti-Semitism is the very underpinning of such cults.

Less extreme prejudice, often hidden and usually denied, is also reflected in some Christian churches and organizations. It is not impossible even for true believers to become infected with that age-old spiritual disease which the Lord so intensely detests.

As always, Paul's logic is irrefutable. **If the first piece of dough be holy,** he points out, **the lump is also. First piece of dough** translates the single Greek word *aparchē,* which literally means a firstfruit (as in the KJV) offering of any kind, animal as well as grain. It refers to the first portion of an offering which was set aside specifically for the Lord.

Through Moses, God instructed His newly-delivered people: "When you eat of the food of the land, you shall lift up an offering to the Lord. Of the first of your dough you shall lift up a cake as an offering; as the offering of the threshing floor, so you shall lift it up. From the first of your dough you shall give to the Lord an offering throughout your generations" (Num. 15:19-21). Those cakes, or loaves, were given to feed the priests, who served—and thereby represented—the Lord in their unique ministry in the tabernacle and later in the temple. Therefore, before any bread would be eaten by a household, a special portion, **the first piece of dough,** was first consecrated and presented to the Lord.

Although only a portion of that special **piece of dough** represented the entire loaf **(the lump),** all of it was acknowledged as being from the Lord. In other words, they were giving back to the Lord a representation of all He had provided for them. It is for that reason that **the lump is also** holy ("set apart"). That idea is expressed in the lovely stanza sometimes sung in worship services just before or after the offering:

> We give Thee but Thine own,
> Whate'er the gift may be.
> All that we have is Thine alone,
> A trust, O Lord, from Thee.
>
> William W. How

Another, and somewhat reverse, analogy is given using the figure of a tree or vine. **And if the root be holy, the branches are too.** If the foundational part of a plant **(the root)** is **holy,** then that which it produces **(the branches)** must likewise **(too)** be holy.

But Paul's specific use of the analogy in this passage points up the truth that, if the firstfruits and root of Israel—perhaps symbolizing the first patriarchs (Abraham, Isaac, and Jacob)—were **holy,** consecrated to the Lord, so were all their descendants, the people of Israel. Therefore, for God to forsake Israel would be for Him to renege on His promises to those patriarchs—something His holy character will not allow.

Even John Murray, a leading amillennialist (one who does not believe in a literal, 1,000-year earthly kingdom promised to the Jews and ruled by Christ on the throne of David in Jerusalem, but who generally believes that God's dealing with the nation of Israel ended with their rejection of Jesus Christ), cannot resist the power of the marvelous truth that Paul stresses here. In his commentary on Romans, Murray amazingly observes that "there cannot be irremediable rejection of Israel. The holiness of the theocratic consecration is not abolished and will one day be vindicated in Israel's fulness and restoration" (*Epistle to the Romans* [Grand Rapids: Eerdmans, 1965], 85).

In order to be faithful to His own Word, the Lord must provide a future salvation for Israel. Israel has not yet completely fulfilled God's covenant promise to Abraham or His countless reiterations of that promise to redeem and restore Abraham's descendants. **If the root,** Abraham and the other patriarchs, is **holy,** then **the branches,** their descendants, **are** holy **too.** They were divinely called and set apart before the foundation of the world and God's work with those **branches** will not be complete until they bear the spiritual fruit He intends to produce in and through them, until the end of the age when they actually become the holy people they were destined to be.

"Listen to me, you who pursue righteousness," God said to Israel through Isaiah, "who seek the Lord: Look to the rock from which you were hewn, and to the quarry from which you were dug. Look to Abraham your father, and to Sarah who gave birth to you in pain; when he was one I called him, then I blessed him and multiplied him" (Isa. 51:1-2). God established His permanent relationship with Israel through His covenant with their forefather, Abraham. They were consecrated as a people in the consecration of Abraham.

Paul continues with the figure of a tree: **But if some of the branches were broken off, and you, being a wild olive, were grafted in among them and became partaker with them of the rich root of the olive tree.**

Here the apostle makes his point by referring to the familiar practice of grafting. Olive trees were an agricultural and commercial mainstay in ancient Palestine and much of the Near East and Mediterranean areas, and still support a valuable industry in most of those regions today. Olive trees can live for hundreds of years, but as they age, they become less and less productive, and in order to restore productivity, branches from younger trees are grafted to old ones. When a branch ceased to produce olives, a younger one was grafted in its place.

That is the figure Paul uses here. The old, unproductive **branches** of Israel **were broken off.** Centuries earlier God had warned His people of what their continued unbelief and idolatry would bring. "The Lord called your name, 'A green olive tree, beautiful in fruit and form'; with the noise of a great tumult He has kindled fire on it, and its branches are worthless. And the Lord of hosts, who planted you, has pronounced evil against you because of the evil of the house of Israel and of the house of Judah, which they have done to provoke Me by offering up sacrifices to Baal" (Jer. 11:16-17). Jesus Himself warned His own people Israel, "Therefore I say to you, the kingdom of God will be taken away from you, and be given to a nation [better, "a people" NIV] producing the fruit of it" (Matt. 21:43).

In place of the unfaithful, unproductive branches of Israel, those of **a wild olive,** the believing Gentiles, **were grafted in among them.** Those Gentile branches, people from all nations who believe in the Messiah, the Lord Jesus Christ, then **became partaker with them,** the believing descendants of Abraham, in **the rich root of the olive tree,** the **root** of divine blessing and of eternal relationship to God through salvation.

At the beginning of that verse, Paul makes clear that **some,** but not all, **of the branches were broken off.** That is also indicated by the phrase **among them.** There always had been a believing remnant in Israel, and many Jews believed in Christ during His earthly ministry and in the time of the early church. Probably until the end of the first century, most Christians, including all the apostles, were Jews. Those original Jewish branches remained attached to **the rich root of** God's **olive tree,** as have Jewish branches from then until now. Gentile believers are joint heirs with them and of Abraham, "the father of all who believe without being circumcised [without being or becoming Jews], that righteousness might be reckoned to them" (Rom. 4:11).

Now comes a command to the Gentiles based on that truth: **Do not be arrogant toward the branches,** that is, the unbelieving Jews who were cut off; **but if you are arrogant, remember that it is not you who supports the root** (the promise to Abraham that "in you all the families of the earth shall be blessed," Gen. 12:3), **but the root supports you.** The Gentiles themselves were not the source of blessing any more than believing Jews had been. Believing Gentiles are blessed by God because they are spiritual descendants of faithful Abraham. We are blessed because we have been grafted into the covenant of salvation that God made with Abraham and now graciously offers to all who believe in Abraham's God. As Paul had explained to the churches in Galatia a few years earlier,

> Even so Abraham believed God, and it was reckoned to him as righteousness. Therefore, be sure that it is those who are of faith who are sons of Abraham. And the Scripture, foreseeing that God would justify the Gentiles by faith, preached the gospel beforehand to Abraham, saying, "All the nations shall be blessed in you." So then those who are of faith are blessed with Abraham, the believer. (Gal. 3:6-9)

A few verses later in that same chapter of Galatians, the apostle explains further that "Christ redeemed us from the curse of the Law, having become a curse for us—for it is written, 'Cursed is everyone who hangs on a tree'—in order that in Christ Jesus the blessing of Abraham might come to the Gentiles, so that we might receive the promise of the Spirit through faith" (vv. 13-14). How ridiculous and presumptuous then, for believing Gentiles to be **arrogant toward the** natural **branches,** even those who were cut off in unbelief. **Remember,** he continues, **that it is not you who supports the root, but the root supports you.** The blessing of both Jewish and Gentile believers comes through the root of God's covenant promises and power.

It is tragic and lamentable that, throughout much of church history, Jewish converts to Christ have often been subjected to attitudes of Gentile superiority and been shunned or reluctantly accepted into Christian fellowship.

Paul anticipated that, in spite of this clear truth, some of his Gentile readers would continue to argue against him. **You will say then, "Branches were broken off so that I might be grafted in." Quite right,** he concedes, **they were broken off for their unbelief, but you stand by your faith.** In other words, the breaking off and grafting in were based on belief, not on any inherent racial or national inferiority or superiority. The issue is not worthiness and it is not racial, ethnic, social, intellectual, or even moral. The only issue is **faith.** The Jews **were broken off** because of that **unbelief,** and Gentiles who believed were **grafted in,** that is, made to **stand,** on the basis of their **faith** in the Lord Jesus Christ.

You therefore have no reason to **be conceited, but** very good reason to **fear,** Paul warns. He gave a similar warning to the church at Corinth: "Therefore let him who thinks he stands take heed lest he fall" (1 Cor. 10:12). **For if God did not spare the natural branches,** His covenant people Israel, **neither will He spare you** Gentiles, who are not a part of that covenant. If Israel's special calling and blessing from the Lord could not protect them from being broken off, then certainly the Gentiles' lack of that calling and blessing cannot protect them from being broken off for their unbelief. Therefore you would do well, Paul advises his Gentile readers, to have a righteous **fear** and to strongly resist any temptation to arrogance (v. 18) and conceit (v. 20).

Paul reminded believers at Ephesus, "Therefore remember, that formerly you, the Gentiles in the flesh, who are called 'Uncircumcision' by the so-called 'Circumcision,' which is performed in the flesh by human hands—remember that you were at that time separate from Christ, excluded from the commonwealth of Israel, and strangers to the covenants of promise, having no hope and without God in the world" (Eph.

2:11-12). If God cut off an apostate Israel because of her unbelief, how much more surely will He cut off an apostate church because of unbelief.

The visible church today is mostly Gentile, and that church encompasses a large percentage of apostates, heretics, and others who reject the absolute and inerrant authority of Scripture and deny its cardinal truths, including the deity of Christ. And the Lord's judgment will fall on the apostate Gentile church just as surely and swiftly as it did on apostate Israel. Jesus warned the church at Pergamum, "You also have some who in the same way hold the teaching of the Nicolaitans. Repent therefore; or else I am coming to you quickly, and I will make war against them with the sword of My mouth" (Rev. 2:15-16). And to the church at Laodicea, He promised that nominal, unbelieving Christians will be spit out of God's mouth in disgust (Rev. 3:16). Collectively, they are later referred to as the Babylonian harlot of the end times whom the Lord will cause to be brutally devastated by Antichrist and his ten-nation confederacy (Rev. 17:16).

The apostle had made clear earlier in this passage on Israel (chaps. 9-11), "What shall we say then? That Gentiles, who did not pursue righteousness, attained righteousness, even the righteousness which is by faith; but Israel, pursuing a law of righteousness, did not arrive at that law. Why? Because they did not pursue it by faith, but as though it were by works. They stumbled over the stumbling stone" (9:30-32). From the beginning and throughout the epistle, Paul repeats that foundational truth over and over. As far as man's part is concerned, salvation has always been and will always be by faith and faith alone. It is, of course, God's sovereign grace that makes faith possible, acceptable, and effective, but His grace will not save apart from faith.

Behold then the kindness and severity of God; to those who fell, severity, but to you, God's kindness, if you continue in His kindness; otherwise you also will be cut off. Severity translates *apotomia*, which has the root meaning of cutting right off, or cutting quickly, and corresponds to the verb *ekkoptō* **(cut off), with which** this verse ends. And in this context, *piptō* **(fell)** means to fall down so as to be completely ruined. Paul is therefore speaking of an extremely serious spiritual condition, in which people fell from spiritual opportunity into judgment.

That looks at the past. Paul then warns those in the present who have identified with the saving gospel that they must **continue in His kindness** or they, too, will be judged severely like those in the past who were near the blessing and fell. That is a familiar New Testament idea, which affirms the reality of true, saving faith by its continuity. That is the perseverance of the saints that evidences their genuine conversion (see John 8:31; 15:5-6; Col. 1:22-23; Heb. 3:12-14; 4:11; 1 John 2:19).

Because of God's blessing of ancient Israel as a nation, many Jewish unbelievers shared in that blessing. In the same way, because of God's blessing on the church, many unbelievers within the church taste that blessing. But if they fall away, God's patience will be exhausted and His offer of grace withdrawn, that blessing by association will be of no value when unbelievers face the living God in judgment and are eternally cut off from Him. Those who in unbelief refuse God's **kindness** in the offer of salvation are destined to be **cut off** by His **severity.**

It Has a Definite Promise

And they also, if they do not continue in their unbelief, will be grafted in; for God is able to graft them in again. For if you were cut off from what is by nature a wild olive tree, and were grafted contrary to nature into a cultivated olive tree, how much more shall these who are the natural branches be grafted into their own olive tree? (11:23-24)

Third, God's temporarily setting Israel aside has a marvelous and definite promise. Although the promise is given here with a condition (parallel to the condition of being judged for not continuing in belief)—**if they do not continue in their unbelief**—God had long beforehand assured His people that the condition would be met. Israel will at last see Jesus as her Messiah and will repent of her unbelief and lament her rejection of Him. Through Zechariah the Lord declared, "I will pour out on the house of David and on the inhabitants of Jerusalem, the Spirit of grace and of supplication, so that they will look on Me whom they have pierced; and they will mourn for Him, as one mourns for an only son, and they will weep bitterly over Him, like the bitter weeping over a first-born" (Zech. 12:10). **God is able to graft them in again,** and He will.

In the end times, during the Great Tribulation, the apostate Gentile church—which had been **cut off from what is by nature a wild olive tree, and [was] grafted contrary to nature into a cultivated olive tree**—will itself be cut off, just as Israel once was. And at that time Israel, **the natural branches,** will then **be grafted [back] into their own olive tree.** The natural descendants of Abraham will also become his spiritual descendants and once again be the Lord's chosen people of blessing.

One of the more interesting texts that promises the future restoration of Israel is found in Revelation 11.

> And there was given me a measuring rod like a staff; and someone said, "Rise and measure the temple of God, and the altar, and those who worship in it. And leave out the court which is outside the temple, and do not measure it, for it has been given to the nations; and they will tread under foot the holy city for forty-two months. And I will grant authority to my two witnesses, and they will prophesy for twelve hundred and sixty days, clothed in sackcloth. These are the two olive trees and the two lampstands that stand before the Lord of the earth." (vv. 1-4)

In that vision, the apostle John is told to take a measuring rod (cf. Ezek. 40:5) and measure the temple, the altar, and the worshipers. That act appears to define the extent of God's property (cf. Rev. 21:15). In other words, God commands John to mark off His divine possession for preservation.

Although at the time John wrote there no longer was a temple, the prophets had often spoken of a temple in the last days (Dan. 9:27; Amos 9:11; Mic. 4:1; Hag. 2:9; Zech. 6:12-13; Mal. 3:1; cf. Matt. 24:15; 2 Thess. 2:4).

During the time of the Great Tribulation, the Jews will be converted (cf. Zech. 12:8-14; 13:1-2) and be marked off by God as His own for protection during the Day of the Lord.

John's measuring of the temple therefore seems to symbolize that the Jews will be His people who will come to salvation and kingdom blessing. The Revelation scene is similar to that depicted in Zechariah 2:1-5, in which Jerusalem is measured for protection by the divine "wall of fire around her" and experiences God's "glory in her midst" (v. 5). As the city is measured to mark it out as God's possession, to be rebuilt in millennial glory, so the temple is measured to affirm that salvation is coming for Israel.

The Gentiles at this time are left out (Rev. 11:2). Most of them appear to oppose all that represents God, although some will receive Christ and be saved—but not as a whole people, as with Israel. Again, it is the future of Israel that is in view.

The identity of the two witnesses also speaks of Israel's coming salvation. They are called, "the two olive trees and the two lampstands" (11:4), terminology taken from Zechariah's vision. The prophet Zechariah lived between the times of Ezra and Nehemiah. The rebuilding of the temple had been approved in Ezra's time but had not begun. God therefore used Zechariah to encourage two men to lead in the restoration— Joshua, the high priest, and Zerubbabel, the governor of Jerusalem.

The Jews of that day knew they had sinned and feared they had no basis for God's favor. They knew He could not tolerate their faithless, evil hearts and felt He had forever forsaken them. But the vision recorded in Zechariah 3 graciously promised restoration.

> Then he showed me Joshua the high priest standing before the angel of the Lord, and Satan standing at his right hand to accuse him. And the Lord said to Satan, "The Lord rebuke you, Satan! Indeed, the Lord who has chosen Jerusalem rebuke you! Is this not a brand plucked from the fire?" Now Joshua was clothed with filthy garments and standing before the angel. And he spoke and said to those who were standing before him saying, "Remove the filthy garments from him." Again he said to him, "See, I have taken your iniquity away from you and will clothe you with festal robes." Then I said, "Let them put a clean turban on his head." So they put a clean turban on his head and clothed him with garments, while the angel of the Lord was standing by.
> And the angel of the Lord admonished Joshua saying, "Thus says the Lord of hosts, 'If you will walk in My ways, and if you will perform My service, then you will also govern My house and also have charge of My courts, and I will grant you free access among these who are standing here. Now listen, Joshua the high priest, you and your friends who are sitting in front of you—indeed they are men who are a symbol, for behold, I am going to bring in My servant the Branch. For behold, the stone that I have set before Joshua; on one stone are seven eyes. Behold, I will engrave an inscription on it,' declares the Lord of hosts, 'and I will remove the iniquity of that land in one day. In that day,' declares the Lord of hosts, 'every one of you will invite his neighbor to sit under his vine and under his fig tree.'" (vv. 1-10)

The high priest Joshua, the symbol of the nation of Israel and the representative of the people before God, is cleansed, forgiven, and restored to act as God's agent in the restoration of the nation. God reiterated His promise of salvation in the covenant, if the people would obey the conditions. When the people obey God, restoration will come. In verses 8-10 we look all the way to Messiah and His kingdom—the great, ultimate, final, and glorious restoration of holiness and peace.

God chose Joshua to stand before Him as the cleansed and forgiven representative of Israel, in a new temple to be built in a new Israel, returned from captivity to its land and its God. That was a taste, a small preview of the ultimate salvation and restoration that will be directed by Messiah at His second coming.

The second key figure, Zerubbabel, is presented next.

> Then the angel who was speaking with me returned, and roused me as a man who is awakened from his sleep. And he said to

me,"What do you see?" And I said,"I see, and behold, a lampstand all of gold with its bowl on the top of it, and its seven lamps on it with seven spouts belonging to each of the lamps which are on the top of it; also two olive trees by it, one on the right side of the bowl and the other on its left side." (Zech. 4:1-3)

The prophet then describes a spontaneous, automatic provision that is apart from any human agency:"Then I answered and said to the angel who was speaking with me saying,'What are these, my lord?' So the angel who was speaking with me answered and said to me,'Do you not know what these are?' And I said,'No, my lord.' Then he answered and said to me,'This is the word of the Lord to Zerubbabel saying,"Not by might nor by power, but by My Spirit," says the Lord of hosts'" (4:4-6).

The Holy Spirit alone has the power to restore Israel, but that power will flow through "two olive trees."

What are you, O great mountain? Before Zerubbabel you will become a plain; and he will bring forth the top stone with shouts of "Grace, grace to it!" Also the word of the Lord came to me saying,"The hands of Zerubbabel have laid the foundation of this house, and his hands will finish it. Then you will know that the Lord of hosts has sent me to you. For who has despised the day of small things? But these seven will be glad when they see the plumb line in the hand of Zerubbabel—these are eyes of the Lord which range to and fro throughout the earth. (4:7-10)

As seen earlier, Zerubbabel, along with Joshua, is one of the two olive trees God will use. Together, one a priest and one a ruler (governor), they were the human tools the Holy Spirit used to restore the nation.

But there was a final component of God's plan.

Then I answered and said to him,"What are these two olive trees on the right of the lampstand and on its left?" And I answered the second time and said to him,"What are the two olive branches which are beside the two golden pipes, which empty the golden oil from themselves?" So he answered me saying,"Do you not know what these are?" And I said,"No, my lord." Then he said,"These are the two anointed ones, who are standing by the Lord of the whole earth." (Zech. 4:11-14)

God used those two "anointed ones" to rebuild and restore ancient Israel. Therefore, when we read in Revelation that God has two witnesses who are "olive trees" and "lampstands" (11:3-4), we know what Zechariah's vision means. God is in the midst of renewal and restoration, only this time the new temple will be millennial, the new work will be national salvation, and the new worship will be of the Lord Jesus Christ.

Joshua and Zerubbabel were God's tools for the ancient physical restoration of Israel—the "golden pipes" through whom the Holy Spirit flowed. In a similar way the two witnesses of Revelation 11 will be future instruments of Israel's salvation. They are preaching in Jerusalem (v. 8) at the time they are killed, and their resurrection three and one half days later leads to the salvation of that city (v. 13). The phrase "gave glory to the God of heaven" is best taken to refer to salvation (cf. 14:6-7; 16:9; 19:7). After that salvation, the last trumpet will be blown, and "the kingdom of the world has become the kingdom of our Lord, and of His Christ; and He will reign forever and ever" (Rev. 11:15).

The destiny of Israel can and will be reversed. Her return to the Lord not only is possible but certain. To be true to His own promise, His chosen people cannot continue forever in unbelief. Quoting from Isaiah, Paul declares with absolute finality that "all Israel will be saved; just as it is written, 'The Deliverer will come from Zion, He will remove ungodliness from Jacob. And this is My covenant with them, when I take away their sins'" (vv. 26-27, emphasis added; cf. Isa. 59:20-21).

God Has Not Canceled His Promises to Israel —part 3 His Setting Israel Aside Is Purposeful: To Glorify God (Romans 11:25-36)

10

For I do not want you, brethren, to be uninformed of this mystery, lest you be wise in your own estimation, that a partial hardening has happened to Israel until the fulness of the Gentiles has come in; and thus all Israel will be saved; just as it is written, "The Deliverer will come from Zion, He will remove ungodliness from Jacob." "And this is My covenant with them, when I take away their sins." From the standpoint of the gospel they are enemies for your sake, but from the standpoint of God's choice they are beloved for the sake of the fathers; for the gifts and the calling of God are irrevocable. For just as you once were disobedient to God, but now have been shown mercy because of their disobedience, so these also now have been disobedient, in order that because of the mercy shown to you they also may now be shown mercy. For God has shut up all in disobedience that He might show mercy to all. Oh, the depth of the riches both of the wisdom and knowledge of God! How unsearchable are His judgments and unfathomable His ways! For who has known the mind of the Lord, or who became His counselor? Or who has first given to Him that it might be paid back to him again? For from Him

and through Him and to Him are all things. To Him be the glory forever. Amen. (11:25-36)

God's setting Israel aside not only is partial and passing but also purposeful. God temporarily set aside His chosen people in order to bring salvation to the Gentiles (11:11*b*), to make Israel jealous of them (v. 11*c*) so they would yearn to receive the blessings of the Messiah they had rejected, and thereby be used to bring blessing to the rest of the world (vv. 12-15). But God's ultimate, overriding purpose is to glorify Himself.

The doxology at the end of the present passage climaxes the doctrinal section of the epistle and focuses on the supreme purpose of everything God does—to glorify Himself.

The supreme benefit of God's redemptive plan, both for Jews and for Gentiles, is to bring them salvation and eternal life. But the supreme *purpose* of that plan is to glorify Himself. Even His purpose in judging the unrighteous is to glorify Himself. His preparation of heaven for the saved and of hell for the unsaved is to display His glory. The surpassing purpose of every created being and thing in the universe is to glorify God (cf. Ps. 19:1; Isa. 43:20; 1 Cor. 10:31). All other divine intentions are subservient to that supreme and ultimate goal. In the words of the Westminster Shorter Catechism, "The chief end of man is to glorify God and to enjoy Him forever."

There are two aspects of God's glory. The first is what might be called His intrinsic glory, the glory which is a part of His very being and nature. Glory is the very essence of God, the manifestation of who He is. It is that which He possesses in Himself and which cannot be given to Him or taken from Him. It is that radiant, essential glory which Moses longed to see. "I pray Thee," he pleaded, "show me Thy glory!" (Ex. 33:18). "Reveal Yourself to me," he was saying. It is that glory which one of the seraphim declared to another before the Lord in Isaiah's heavenly vision: "Holy, Holy, Holy, is the Lord of hosts, the whole earth is full of His glory" (Isa. 6:3). It is that glory which Stephen proclaimed before the Sanhedrin in Jerusalem: "Hear me, brethren and fathers! The God of glory appeared to our father Abraham" (Acts 7:2). It is that glory which was in Jesus, the glory of God's full "grace and truth" (John 1:14), and which was displayed in the transfiguration (Matt. 17:2).

The second aspect of God's glory is given to Him. It is the honor that men and angels render to the Lord who made them. That glory does not, of course, add the least bit to God's intrinsic glory, which is complete and perfect. It is rather the recognition and affirmation of the glory God has in Himself and the holy living and proclamation that displays His glory through the believer to the world.

It is this glory of which the priestly choir sang when David brought the Ark of the Covenant to Jerusalem: "Sing to the Lord, all the earth; proclaim good tidings of His salvation from day to day. Tell of His glory among the nations, His wonderful deeds among all the peoples... .Ascribe to the Lord, O families of the peoples, ascribe to the Lord glory and strength. Ascribe to the Lord the glory due His name" (1 Chron. 16:23-24, 28-29).

Because man's supreme purpose is to recognize and honor God for His glory and majesty, failure to glorify Him is the certain mark of spiritual rebellion and ungodliness. As Paul explains at the beginning of this epistle, there is no excuse for any person, living at any time or in any place, to fail or refuse to glorify God. "The wrath of God is revealed from heaven against all ungodliness and unrighteousness of men, who suppress the truth in unrighteousness, because that which is known about God is evident within them; for God made it evident to them. For since the creation of the world His invisible attributes, His eternal power and divine nature, have been clearly seen, being understood through what has been made, so that they are without excuse. For even though they knew God, they did not honor Him as God" (Rom. 1:18-21).

God chose His people Israel "that they might be for Me a people, for renown, for praise, and for glory" (Jer. 13:11). The prophet therefore implores his fellow Israelites to "give glory to the Lord your God, before He brings darkness and before your feet stumble on the dusky mountains, and while you are hoping for light He makes it into deep darkness, and turns it into gloom" (v. 16).

For a full year, Nebuchadnezzar refused to heed God's command to repent of his great pride and arrogance (Dan. 4:19-29). Then, one day as he was walking around the roof of his magnificent palace, reveling in his own power and glory, "while the word was in the king's mouth, a voice came from heaven, saying, 'King Nebuchadnezzar, to you it is declared: sovereignty has been removed from you.'... Immediately the word concerning Nebuchadnezzar was fulfilled; and he was driven away from mankind and began eating grass like cattle, and his body was drenched with the dew of heaven, until his hair had grown like eagles' feathers and his nails like birds' claws" (vv. 31,33). When that time of humiliation was over, the penitent king testified, "I, Nebuchadnezzar, raised my eyes toward heaven, and my reason returned to me, and I blessed the Most High and praised and honored Him who lives forever" (v. 34).

When the people of Tyre and Sidon flattered King Herod Agrippa, saying, "'The voice of a god and not of a man!'... immediately an angel of the Lord struck him because he did not give God the glory, and he was eaten by worms and died" (Acts 12:22-23). By contrast, when Cornelius met Peter "and fell at his feet and worshiped him," the apostle quickly "raised him up, saying, 'Stand up; I too am just a man'" (Acts 10:25-26). Similarly, after the pagans of Lystra heard Paul speak and witnessed the healing of the cripple, "they raised their voice, saying in the Lycaonian language, 'The gods have become like men and have come down to us.' And they began calling Barnabas, Zeus, and Paul, Hermes, because he was the chief speaker. ... But when the apostles, Barnabas and Paul, heard of it, they tore their robes and rushed out into the crowd, crying out and saying, 'Men, why are you doing these things? We are also men of the same nature as you'" (Acts 14:11-12, 14-15).

Throughout redemptive history, God has called men and women to give praise, honor, worship, and glory only to Him and to ascribe to Him His worth as the only infinitely holy and majestic Creator, Savior, and Lord. The purpose of all things—angels, men, other creatures, life, death, heaven, hell, the land and seas and heavens, the entire universe—is to display the majesty of the holy, sovereign Creator who made them and to lead all creatures to glorify Him.

With a far greater obligation and privilege than other men, believers can and should glorify God, because they have witnessed the glory of His saving grace. We therefore should continually proclaim with Paul, "To Him be the glory in the church and in Christ Jesus to all generations forever and ever. Amen" (Eph. 3:21).

The most certain reason that God will ultimately redeem Israel is that His word of promise must be fulfilled to the praise of His glory. Just as He sovereignly ordained, "The people [Israel] whom I formed for Myself, will [one day] declare My praise" (Isa. 43:21).

In the present passage—which climaxes Paul's focus on God's gracious dealing with Israel (chaps. 9-11)—we see God glorified in His sovereignty (vv. 25-26a), in His integrity (vv. 26b-29), in His generosity (vv. 30-32), and in His incomprehensibility (vv. 33-36).

To Glorify God's Sovereignty

For I do not want you, brethren, to be uninformed of this mystery, lest you be wise in your own estimation, that a partial hardening has happened to Israel until the fulness of the Gentiles has come in; and thus all Israel will be saved; (11:25-26a)

Paul had just warned Gentile believers about becoming proud and conceited because unbelieving Israel was cut off from blessing in order that it might be offered to Gentiles, explaining that "if God did not spare the natural branches [Israel], neither will He spare you [the Gentile church]" (Rom. 11:20-21). If in His sovereign grace He is now granting salvation to believing Gentiles, "how much more" will He bring His covenant nation Israel back to Himself in belief and for blessing and cut off the apostate Gentile church (v. 24). God is not finished with His ancient chosen people, and even during this time when Jews as a nation are severed from God's special blessing because of unbelief, anti-Semitism in any form is anathema to the Lord. Whoever harms God's chosen people "touches the apple [pupil] of His eye" (Zech. 2:8).

Doubtless with great joy and expectation, Paul tells believing Jews and Gentiles alike that he does not want them **to be uninformed of** a marvelous **mystery.** At the end of the epistle Paul defines **mystery** as being a revelation "which has been kept secret for long ages past, but now is manifested, and by the Scriptures of the prophets, according to the commandment of the eternal God" (Rom. 16:26; cf. Eph. 3:5-7).

Before Paul identifies and explains the particular **mystery** of which he is speaking here, he once again cautions Gentiles against pride, warning them to avoid construing the truths of that mystery as reasons for being **wise in** their **own estimation.**

The first component of this **mystery** is **that a partial** spiritual **hardening has happened to Israel. Partial** does not modify **mystery** but Israel. That is, those who are hardened—the great majority— are totally hardened, but not every Jew has been or will be hardened. As always through the ages of redemptive history, God sovereignly has preserved for Himself a believing remnant. That is the gracious truth Paul emphasizes in the first part of this chapter (11:1-10).

The second component of this **mystery** is that the **hardening** will remain only **until the fulness of the Gentiles has come in. Until** refers to time, **fulness** indicates completion, and together those terms denote impermanence. The **hardening** will last only for God's divinely-determined duration. It began when Israel rejected Jesus as her Messiah and Savior, and it will end when **the fulness of the Gentiles has come in.**

Has come in is from *eiserchomai,* a verb Jesus frequently used. He used it of entering the kingdom of heaven/God (Matt. 5:20; Mark 9:47; John 3:5; cf. Acts 14:22) and of entering eternal life (Mark 9:43, 45), both of which refer to receiving salvation. Israel's unbelief will last only until the complete number **of the Gentiles** chosen by God have come to salvation. Paul's special calling was "to be a minister of Christ Jesus to the Gentiles, ministering as a priest the gospel of God, that my offering of the Gentiles might become acceptable, sanctified by the Holy Spirit" (Rom. 15:16). In his letter to Titus, Paul refers to himself as "an apostle of Jesus Christ, for the faith of those chosen of God" (1:1). The mystery ends when the gathering of the elect is complete.

That, of course, is also the calling of the church. Although many Jews have been saved through the church's witness, the vast majority of converts have been, and will continue to be, **Gentiles**—until their number is complete. That will signal the beginning of events that lead to Israel's redemption, when **all Israel will be saved**—a truth that must have filled Paul's heart with great joy (cf. Rom. 9:1-3; 10:1).

All Israel must be taken to mean just that—the entire nation that survives God's judgment during the Great Tribulation. The common amillennial view that **all Israel** refers only to a remnant redeemed during the church age does injustice to the text. Paul's declaration about all Israel is set in clear contrast to what he has already said about the believing Jewish remnant which the Lord has always preserved for Himself. The fact, for instance, that only *some* of the branches (unbelieving Jews) were broken off (v. 17), plainly indicates that a remnant of believing Jews—those not broken off—will continually exist while the fulness of the Gentiles is being completed. These are Jews being redeemed who are *not* part of the spiritual hardening that has come upon Israel because of her rejection of her Messiah (v. 25).

Before **all Israel** is **saved,** its unbelieving, ungodly members will be separated out by God's inerrant hand of judgment. Ezekiel makes that truth vividly clear:

> "As I live," declares the Lord God, "surely with a mighty hand and with an outstretched arm and with wrath poured out, I shall be king over you. And I shall bring you out from the peoples and gather you from the lands where you are scattered, with a mighty hand and with an outstretched arm and with wrath poured out; and I shall bring you into the wilderness of the peoples, and there I shall enter into judgment with you face to face. As I entered into judgment with your fathers in the wilderness of the land of Egypt, so I will enter into judgment with you," declares the Lord God. "And I shall make you pass under the rod, and I shall bring you into the bond of the covenant; *and I shall purge from you the rebels and those who transgress against Me; I shall bring them out of the land where they sojourn, but they will not enter the land of Israel.* Thus you will know that I am the Lord." (Ezek. 20:33-38, emphasis added; cf. Dan. 12:10; Zech. 13:8-9)

Those who hear the preaching of the 144,000 (Rev. 7:1-8; 14:1-5), of other converts (7:9), of the two witnesses (11:3-13), and of the angel (14:6), and thus safely pass under God's rod of judgment will then comprise all Israel, which—in fulfillment of God's sovereign and irrevocable promise—will be *completely* a nation of believers who are ready for the kingdom of the Messiah Jesus.

"Behold, days are coming," declares the Lord, "when I will make a new covenant with the house of Israel and with the house of Judah, not like the covenant which I made with their fathers in the day I took them by the hand to bring them out of the land of Egypt, My covenant which they broke, although I was a husband to them," declares the Lord. "But this is the covenant which I will make with the house of Israel after those days," declares the Lord, "I will put My law within them, and on their heart I will write it; and I will be their God, and they shall be My people. And they shall not teach again, each man his neighbor and each man his brother, saying, 'Know the Lord,' for they shall all know Me, from the least of them to the greatest of them," declares the Lord, "for I will forgive their iniquity, and their sin I will remember no more." (Jer. 31:31-34; cf. 32:38)

God's control of history is irrefutable evidence of His sovereignty. And as surely as He cut off unbelieving Israel from His tree of salvation, just as surely will He graft believing Israel back in—a nation completely restored and completely saved.

It is helpful to note an additional truth that Paul does not mention at this point—namely, that, just as the fulness of the Gentiles will initiate the salvation of Israel, so the salvation of Israel will initiate the millennial kingdom of Jesus Christ.

That three-stage plan of God was predicted in the Old Testament and proclaimed in the New. In about A.D. 50, a council of "the apostles and the elders came together" in Jerusalem to discuss whether or not Gentiles had to submit to the Mosaic law, including circumcision, in order to be saved (Acts 15:1-6). After considerable debate, including statements by Peter, Paul, and Barnabas,

James answered, saying, "Brethren, listen to me. Simeon [Peter] has related how God first concerned Himself about taking from among the Gentiles a people for His name. And with this the words of the Prophets agree, just as it is written, 'After these things I will return, and I will rebuild the tabernacle of David which has fallen, and I will rebuild its ruins, and I will restore it, in order that the rest of mankind may seek the Lord, and all the Gentiles who are called by My name, says the Lord, who makes these things known from of old.'" (vv. 12-18)

After Israel is temporarily set aside, God will gather Gentile believers for Himself, then ("after these things") He will restore and reclaim His ancient people Israel (figuratively, "the tabernacle of David"), and finally He will establish His glorious kingdom on earth.

To Glorify God's Integrity

just as it is written, "The Deliverer will come from Zion, He will remove ungodliness from Jacob." "And this is My covenant with them, when I take away their sins." From the standpoint of the gospel they are enemies for your sake, but from the standpoint of God's choice they are beloved for the sake of the fathers; for the gifts and the calling of God are irrevocable. (11:26*b*- 29)

Scripture is replete with affirmations of God's utter truthfulness and trustworthiness. "God is not a man, that He should lie," Balaam informed Balak, "nor a son of man, that He should repent; has He said, and will He not do it? Or has He spoken, and will He not make it good?" (Num. 23:19). The writer of Hebrews gives the encouraging assurance, "Let us hold fast the confession of our hope without wavering, for He who promised is faithful" (Heb. 10:23). From Peter we have a similar affirmation: "The Lord is not slow about His promise, as some count slowness, but is patient toward you, not wishing for any to perish but for all to come to repentance" (2 Pet. 3:9). God's promises are certain and they are punctual. They will be fulfilled in exactly the way and at exactly the time that the Lord has determined and declared. Others *cannot* thwart God's promises, and He Himself *cannot* break them. In every form and to every degree, His Word is immutable.

As he nears the conclusion of this momentous section on God's dealing with Israel (chaps. 9-11), Paul emphasizes once again God's sovereignty and integrity. In saving "all Israel," the Lord will display Himself to the One who always keeps His promises and fulfills His covenants. **Just as it is written,** Paul says, **"The Deliverer** *will* **come from Zion, He** *will* **remove ungodliness from Jacob"** (emphasis added; cf. Isa. 59:20-21). Quoting again from Isaiah, he then says, **"And this is My covenant with them, when I take away their sins"** (cf. Isa. 27:9).

Salvation is the forgiveness and removal of sin, the eradication of that which separates fallen man from the holy God. The power of salvation is God's grace, and the condition of salvation is man's faith. But even that required faith is divinely provided. As Paul has already made clear, our calling to salvation, our justification, sanctification, and glorification all flow from God's sovereign grace, the fruit of His divine foreknowledge and predestination (Rom. 8:29-30).

The ultimate salvation of Israel is also assured by divine certainty. In order for "all Israel [to] be saved," all her sin must be forgiven and removed. And that is expressly what God promises to do: **remove ungodliness from Jacob** and **take away their sins.** The promise is unconditional. It will not depend on Israel's deciding on its own to come back to the Lord but on the Lord's sovereignly bringing Israel back to Himself.

Perhaps God's most dramatic promise of final, unconditional dealing with His chosen people Israel is seen in the mysterious and unique covenant He made with Abraham that is described in Genesis 15. In answer to the patriarch's question, "O Lord God, how may I know that I shall possess [the land]?" God directed him to take "a three year old heifer, and a three year old female goat, and a three year old ram" and to cut them in half (vv. 8-9). The parts of each animal were then laid out opposite each other, along with a turtledove and a pigeon. After causing Abraham to fall into a deep sleep, God alone passed between the pieces, thereby sealing several divine promises. Abraham would die peacefully in old age; after 400 years of oppression and enslavement, his descendants would be delivered from a foreign nation; and God's promise of the land was reiterated (vv. 10-21). But unlike other covenants, not only its terms but its ratification were wholly God's doing. Despite his being asleep, Abraham was aware of what God was doing and saying, but only as a silent onlooker. Abraham was not required so much as to acknowledge, much less agree to, this covenant. The promises were without condition. This covenant amounted to a divine and unalterable declaration, to which God bound Himself in the unique act described in this passage.

Paul continues to explain that, **from the standpoint of the gospel they [Israel] are enemies for your [the Gentile's] sake, but from the standpoint of God's choice they are beloved for the sake of the fathers.** As he has already explained at some length (vv. 11-24), because of Israel's transgression in rejecting her Messiah, she was set aside—becoming God's **enemies,** as it were—in order that salvation could come to the Gentiles. That was her temporary situation **from the standpoint of the gospel.** But from the permanent, eternal **standpoint of God's** sovereign **choice,** Israel is even now **(they are)** and forever will be **beloved for the sake of the fathers**—Abraham, Isaac, and Jacob.

When the Lord elected (by divine **choice)** the nation of Israel to be His own people, He bound Himself by His own promises to bring the Jews to salvation and to be forever His **beloved** and holy people. During this present age, Israel might be called the "beloved" enemies of God. Because of unbelief, they are, like all the unsaved, at enmity with God (Rom. 5:10; 8:7). But God's eternal election guarantees that their enmity is not permanent, **for the gifts and the calling of God are irrevocable. Gifts** translates *charismata,* which carries the fuller connotation of grace gifts, gifts flowing from the pure and wholly unmerited favor of God. **Calling** refers to God's divine election of Israel to be His holy people. God will not change His plan for Israel's spiritual regeneration.

Just as God's sovereign grace and election cannot be earned, neither can they be rejected or thwarted. They are **irrevocable** and unalterable. Nothing, therefore, can prevent Israel's being saved and restored—not even her own rebellion and unbelief, because, as Paul has just declared, her ungodliness will be sovereignly removed and her sins graciously taken away (vv. 26-27). What is true of elected believers is true of elected Israel: "Faithful is He who calls you, and He also will bring it to pass" (1 Thess. 5:24).

To Glorify God's Generosity

For just as you once were disobedient to God, but now have been shown mercy because of their disobedience, so these also now have been disobedient, in order that because of the mercy shown to you they also may now be shown mercy. For God has shut up all in disobedience that He might show mercy to all. (11:30-32)

Mercy is from *eleeō*, which carries the basic idea of having a compassion for those in need that leads to meeting their need. Because man's greatest need is to have his sins removed and be given spiritual life, God's **mercy** generously provides just that.

The psalmists declared, "Thou, Lord, art good, and ready to forgive, and abundant in lovingkindness [mercy] to all who call upon Thee" (Ps. 86:5), and "Give thanks to the Lord, for He is good; for His lovingkindness [mercy] is everlasting" (Ps. 136:1). Solomon testified before the Lord: "Thou hast shown great lovingkindness [mercy] to Thy servant David my father, according as he walked before Thee in truth and righteousness and uprightness of heart toward Thee; and Thou hast reserved for him this great lovingkindness [mercy], that Thou hast given him a son to sit on his throne, as it is this day" (1 Kings 3:6).

Filled with the Holy Spirit, Zacharias, the father of John the Baptist, exulted over the prophesied ministry of his newborn son, saying, "And you, child, will be called the prophet of the Most High; for you will go on before the Lord to prepare His ways; to give to His people the knowledge of salvation by the forgiveness of their sins, *because of the tender mercy of our God*, with which the Sunrise from on high shall visit us, to shine upon those who sit in darkness and the shadow of death, to guide our feet into the way of peace" (Luke 1:76-79, emphasis added).

In his first letter, Peter wrote, "Blessed be the God and Father of our Lord Jesus Christ, who *according to His great mercy* has caused us to be born again to a living hope through the resurrection of Jesus Christ from the dead" (1 Pet. 1:3, emphasis added; cf. Eph. 2:4-5). Just as He bestows forgiveness, which is *not* deserved, at the same time He rescinds His punishment, which is deserved.

Paul's explanation has gone full circle, as it were. Because of Israel's unbelief, the nation was partially and temporarily set aside and the gospel of salvation was extended to the Gentiles. And if God extended His grace to pagan Gentiles even while they were in unbelief, how much more surely will He extend His grace again to His chosen people Israel while *they* are in unbelief? Specifically, he says, if **you, as Gentiles, were disobedient to God, but now have been shown mercy because of** Israel's **disobedience,** how much more will Israel, **because of the mercy shown to you** Gentiles, **also . . . now be shown mercy.**

Whether for Gentile or for Jew, salvation is based on mercy, not merit. It is an expression of God's sovereign and generous grace. About his own gracious salvation, Paul testified: "I thank Christ Jesus our Lord, who has strengthened me, because He considered me faithful, putting me into service; even though I was formerly a blasphemer and a persecutor and a violent aggressor. And yet I was shown mercy, because I acted ignorantly in unbelief; and the grace of our Lord was more than abundant, with the faith and love which are found in Christ Jesus" (1 Tim. 1:12-14). In his second letter to Corinth the apostle calls the Lord "the Father of mercies" (2 Cor. 1:3).

Through the centuries, theologians have struggled with what is called theodicy, the explanation of God's righteousness and omnipotence in the light of evil. No doubt almost every believer has at some time wondered about where evil came from and why God allowed it to enter His perfect world. Although God's Word does not fully answer that question, Paul gives at least a partial explanation, declaring that **God has shut up all in disobedience that He might show mercy to all.**

Disobedience ("unbelief" KJV) is from *apeitheia,* which has the basic meaning of being unpersuadable. It denotes intentional and obstinate refusal to believe, acknowledge, or obey. In his letter to Ephesus, Paul twice refers to unrepentant sinners as "sons of disobedience" (Eph. 2:2; 5:6).

Man's sin, manifested in his willful **disobedience,** provides a means for God to demonstrate the magnitude and graciousness of His **mercy.** Were there no **disobedience,** there would be no need for and there could be no expression of God's **mercy.** To reveal Himself as merciful, He permitted sin. **He has shut up all**—the whole world, Jew and Gentile—**in disobedience** and unbelief in order that He **might show mercy to all** who repent of their sin and turn to Him for gracious salvation.

By His nature, God is a Savior, as seen in Paul's uses of the phrase "God and Savior" in 1 and 2 Timothy and Titus. He could not display that feature of His person without allowing for sin and hell.

In His sovereign omnipotence, God has allowed man intellectually, morally, and spiritually to fall into a state of sin to the extent that, on his own, he is unable to be convinced of God's truth, specifically the truth that he is lost and condemned and that he is powerless in himself to change his condition. God allowed man to fall into sin in order that his only hope would be divine **mercy.**

It must be noted that this saving mercy is shown **to all.** The perfect, satisfactory work of Jesus Christ in His death and resurrection has met the demands of the justice and holiness of God, and thereby has removed every barrier to forgiveness for **all,** and any person who seeks forgiveness and salvation will receive it. As John Brown observed, God's revelation of mercy in the gospels refers to men as sinners, not as *elect* sinners.

Christ died for the world and is reconciling the world to Himself because He loves the world.

As Paul explained earlier in this epistle, the Lord gave His law "that every mouth may be closed, and all the world may become accountable to God" (Rom. 3:19). Sin came to all mankind through the Fall, and knowledge of and accountability for sin came "to all the world" through the Law. "But now apart from the Law the righteousness of God has been manifested," he continues, "being witnessed by the Law and the Prophets, even the righteousness of God through faith in Jesus Christ for all those who believe; for there is no distinction; for all have sinned and fall short of the glory of God, being justified as a gift by His grace [expressed in His mercy] through the redemption which is in Christ Jesus" (vv. 21-24).

To Glorify God's Incomprehensibility

Oh, the depth of the riches both of the wisdom and knowledge of God! How unsearchable are His judgments and unfathomable His ways! For who has known the mind of the Lord, or who became His counselor? Or who has first given to Him that it might be paid back to him again? For from Him and through Him and to Him are all things. To Him be the glory forever. Amen. (11:33-36)

Paul bursts out with a marvelous doxology, in which he rejoices that God's temporarily setting Israel aside glorifies His incomprehensibility. The full wonder of God's gracious omnipotence is wholly beyond human understanding. It staggers even the most mature Christian mind, including the mind of the apostle himself.

Having completed his argument and affirmed God's sovereignty, integrity, and generosity, Paul has nothing more to add but a paean of praise for **the depth of the riches** of God's **wisdom and knowledge.** Further description and explanation are completely beyond the realm of human expression and comprehension. Like a mountain climber who has reached the summit of Mt. Everest, the apostle can only stand awestruck at God's beauty and majesty. Unable to further explain an infinite and holy God to finite and sinful men, he can only acknowledge that God's **judgments** are **unsearchable** and **His ways** are **unfathomable!**

Unfathomable translates *anexichniastos,* which literally refers to footprints that are untrackable, such as those of an animal that a hunter is unable to follow. It is the exact idea expressed by the psalmist in declaring of God: "Thy way was in the sea, and Thy paths in the mighty waters, and Thy footprints may not be known" (Ps. 77:19). Only God's own "Spirit searches all things, even the depths of God" (1 Cor. 2:10).

Scripture is God's divine revelation of Himself and of His will, and He has not given it to mock and confuse men but to enlighten them and bring them to Himself. The Lord has made certain that any person who genuinely seeks Him can know enough of His truth to be saved. Although "a natural man does not accept the things of the Spirit of God; for they are foolishness to him, and he cannot understand them, because they are spiritually appraised" (1 Cor. 2:14), God nevertheless gives the gracious assurance that "you will seek Me and find Me, when you search for Me with all your heart" (Jer. 29:13).

Believers who faithfully study God's Word can learn and have a certain understanding of His truth—all that is necessary "for teaching, for reproof, for correction, for training in righteousness," in order for us to "be adequate, equipped for every good work" (2 Tim. 3:16-17). Our gracious God gives us more than all the truth we need to know Him, trust Him, and serve Him. But no matter how diligently we may have studied His Word, we must confess with David that "such knowledge is too wonderful for me; it is too high, I cannot attain to it" (Ps. 139:6).

As his praise ascends in this doxology, Paul presents three rhetorical questions which serve to exalt God, the answer to each of which is obvious and the same. The first two questions, quoted from the Septuagint (Greek Old Testament), are: **For who has known the mind of**

the Lord, or who became His counselor? (cf. Isa. 40:13). The very asking shows both questions to have but one answer: No one. Men can ponder **the mind of the Lord,** but only **the Lord** Himself can know it. Among men, "in abundance of counselors there is victory," or safety (Prov. 11:14), but God's only **counselor** is Himself.

It is not the countless *unrevealed* things about God of which Paul is speaking, but the depths of the things which we *do* know through His self-revelation. Yet even these partially knowable truths conceal elements that are far beyond our comprehension (cf. Deut. 29:29).

Paul's third question is also taken from the Old Testament. Quoting Job, he asks, **Or who has first given to Him that it might be paid back to him again?** (cf. Job 41:11). Because no one was before God and none can give *to* God what has not first been received *from* Him, the answer here must also be: No one. God is sovereign, self-sufficient, and free from any obligation except those He places on Himself. He owes the Jew nothing and the Gentile nothing.

We stand in awe before our gracious Lord and rejoice that **from Him and through Him and to Him are all things.** With the twenty-four elders, who "will fall down before Him who sits on the throne, and will worship Him who lives forever and ever, and will cast their crowns before the throne," we proclaim, "Worthy art Thou, our Lord and our God, to receive glory and honor and power; for Thou didst create all things, and because of Thy will they existed, and were created" (Rev. 4:10-11; cf. 1 Cor. 15:24-28).

To Him be the glory forever. Amen.

That is the inspired apostle's culminating comment on the first eleven chapters of this magnificent epistle. After traversing all the great realities of salvation, Paul ends with an ascription of glory to his Lord. This simple doxology draws a clear line between the doctrinal section and the final five chapters on Christian duty.

The Believer's Supreme Act of Spiritual Worship (Romans 12:1-2)

11

I urge you therefore, brethren, by the mercies of God, to present your bodies a living and holy sacrifice, acceptable to God, which is your spiritual service of worship. And do not be conformed to this world, but be transformed by the renewing of your mind, that you may prove what the will of God is, that which is good and acceptable and perfect. (12:1-2)

Having concluded eleven chapters of profound and stirring teaching about what God has given believers, Paul now charges those believers with what they need to give God.

Some years ago, a tearful and obviously distraught young woman approached me at a conference where I was speaking. She told me a story I have heard many times. "I just can't seem to live the Christian life the way I should," she said. "I'm frustrated. I don't have spiritual victory or a sense of accomplishment. I struggle with the simplest forms of obedience, and I'm constantly defeated. Can you help me?"

I said, "What has been your approach to solving the problems yourself?" She replied, "I've tried everything. I've attended churches where they speak in tongues, have healings, and have all kinds of ex-

traordinary spiritual experiences. I've spoken in tongues myself, had
ecstatic experiences, been prophesied over, and experienced several
supposed miracles. I've been 'slain in the spirit.' But despite all of that, I'm
not pleased with my life and I know God isn't pleased. *I've tried to get
everything from Him that I can,* but I'm not satisfied. I'm still miserable
and want more."

"I think you have just put your finger on the problem," I said. "The
key to spiritual victory and true happiness is not in trying to get all we
can from God but in giving all that we are and have to Him."

Countless thousands of people today, including many genuine Christians, flock to various churches, seminars, and conferences in
search of personal benefits—practical, emotional, and spiritual—that
they hope to receive. They do just the opposite of what Paul so plainly
emphasizes in Romans 12:1-2. In this forceful and compassionate exhortation, the apostle does not focus on what more we need to receive
from God but on what we are to give Him. The key to a productive and
satisfying Christian life is not in getting more but in giving all.

Jesus said, "True worshipers shall worship the Father in spirit
and truth; for such people the Father seeks to be His worshipers" (John
4:23). God gave Himself for us in order that we might give ourselves to
Him. Paul defines Christians as those "who worship in the Spirit of God
and glory in Christ Jesus and put no confidence in the flesh" (Phil. 3:3).

Every Christian is like Melchizedek, "a priest of God Most High"
(Gen. 14:18). Together, we are a spiritual priesthood, as much so as the
Levitical and Aaronic priesthoods of the Old Covenant. The church is
"a holy priesthood," whose calling is "to offer up spiritual sacrifices acceptable to God through Jesus Christ.... [It is] a royal priesthood, a holy
nation, a people for God's own possession, that you may proclaim the
excellencies of Him who has called you out of darkness into His marvelous light" (1 Pet. 2:5, 9).

Our supreme calling is to serve God with all our being, first and
foremost in worship. Through Christ, the writer of Hebrews tells us, we
are to "continually offer up a sacrifice of praise to God, that is, the fruit
of lips that give thanks to His name" (Heb. 13:15).

True worship includes many things besides the obvious ones
of prayer, praise, and thanksgiving. It includes serving God by serving others in His name, especially fellow believers. Sacrificial worship
includes "doing good and sharing; for with such sacrifices God is
pleased" (Heb. 13:15-16; cf. Phil. 4:14). But above all else, our supreme
act of worship is to offer ourselves wholly and continually to the Lord
as living sacrifices.

Tragically, that is far from the approach that is so common today
by which believers seek the key to the abundant life. We are told that

victory in the Christian life is to have more of God and to have more *from* God—although "the God and Father of our Lord Jesus Christ, [already] has blessed us with *every spiritual blessing* in the heavenly places in Christ" (Eph. 1:3, emphasis added). And in Christ, we already have "all the treasures of wisdom and knowledge," so that in Him we "have been made complete" (Col. 2:3, 10). Peter said that in the true and saving knowledge of Christ, we have "everything pertaining to life and godliness" (2 Pet. 1:3). And we have the resident truth teacher, the Holy Spirit, whose anointing, John says, "teaches [us] about all things" (1 John 2:27).

In the deepest, eternal sense, therefore, we cannot have more of God or from God than we now possess. It is more than obvious, however, that most of us do not have the fulness of joy that this fulness of blessing should bring. The joy and satisfaction for which so many Christians are vainly striving can be had only by surrendering back to the Lord what He already has given to us, including our inmost being. The first and greatest commandment is what Jesus said it has always been: "You shall love the Lord your God with all your heart, and with all your soul, and with all your mind" (Matt. 22:37; cf. Deut. 6:5).

In the present text we discover four elements of presenting ourselves to God as a living, holy, and acceptable sacrifice—essentially the same four elements found in the first and greatest commandment. They are: offering God our souls, our bodies, our minds, and our wills. While recognizing that these four overlap, we still can see how they provide a useful outline for grasping this text.

THE SOUL HAS BEEN GIVEN TO GOD

I urge you therefore, brethren, by the mercies of God, (12:1*a*)

Urge is from *parakaleō,* which has the basic meaning of coming alongside in order to help or give aid. It later came to connote exhorting, admonishing, or encouraging. In His Upper Room discourse, shortly before His betrayal and arrest, Jesus referred to the Holy Spirit as the *Paraklētos,* our divine Helper (also translated Comforter, Counselor, Advocate). He would be "another Helper," who in this present life takes the place of the incarnate Lord (John 14:16; cf. v. 26; 15:26; 16:7).

Paul is speaking as a human helper or counselor to his Christian brethren in Rome. His admonition is a command that carries the full weight of his apostleship. It is not optional. Yet he also wanted to come alongside those **brethren** as a fellow believer, to lovingly encourage them to fulfill what already was the true inner desire and bent of their new hearts—to dedicate themselves without reservation to the Lord who had redeemed them. He reflects the same humble tenderness seen in his admonition to Philemon, to whom he wrote, "Though I have enough confidence in Christ to order you to do that which is proper, yet for love's sake I rather appeal to you" (Philem. 8-9).

The gentle command **[urge]** that Paul proceeds to give can only be obeyed by **brethren,** by those who already belong to God's family. No other offering is acceptable to God unless we have first offered Him our souls. For Christians, that first element of "a living and holy sacrifice" has already been presented to God.

The unregenerate person cannot give God his body, his mind, or his will, because he has not given God *himself.* Because he has no saving relationship to God, "a natural man does not accept the things of the Spirit of God; for they are foolishness to him, and he cannot understand them, because they are spiritually appraised" (1 Cor. 2:14). Only the redeemed can present a *living* sacrifice to God, because only the redeemed have spiritual *life.* And only believers are priests who can come before God with an offering.

"For what will a man be profited," Jesus said, "if he gains the whole world, and forfeits his soul? Or what will a man give in exchange for his soul?" (Matt. 16:26). The soul is the inner, invisible part of man that is the very essence of his being. Therefore, until a man's soul belongs to God, nothing else matters or has any spiritual significance.

The loving generosity of the Macedonian churches was made possible and was acceptable to God and praised by Paul because the believers in those churches "first gave themselves to the Lord and to us by the will of God" (2 Cor. 8:5). Before anything else worthwhile and acceptable can be given to God, the self must be given to Him in saving faith toward Jesus Christ for regeneration.

Earlier in the epistle Paul has made clear that "those who are in the flesh cannot please God" (Rom. 8:8). No matter what his personal feelings might be, the unredeemed person cannot worship God, cannot make an acceptable offering to God, cannot please God in any way with any offering. That is analogous to what Paul meant when he said, "And if I give all my possessions to feed the poor, and if I deliver my body to be burned, but do not have love, it profits me nothing" (1 Cor. 13:3). If a person does not possess the love of God, all of his offerings, no matter how costly, are worthless to Him.

Because an unbeliever's soul has not been offered to God, he cannot make any other sacrifice that is acceptable to Him. The unredeemed cannot present their bodies to God as living sacrifices because they have not presented themselves to God to receive spiritual life.

Therefore refers back to the glorious doxology just given in the previous four verses (11:33-36). It is because "from Him and through

Him and to Him are all things," that to Him belongs "the glory forever." We can only glorify the Lord—we can only *want* to glorify the Lord—if we have been saved **by the mercies of God.**

As noted above, God already "has blessed us with every spiritual blessing in the heavenly places in Christ" (Eph. 1:3). **The mercies of God** of which Paul speaks here include the many gracious blessings, or grace gifts (cf. 11:29), that he has discussed in the first eleven chapters of Romans.

Perhaps the two most precious **mercies of God** are His *love* and His *grace.* In Christ, we are the "beloved of God" (Rom. 1:7; cf. 5:5; 8:35, 39), and, like the apostle, we all "have received grace" through Jesus Christ our Lord (1:6-7; 3:24; 5:2, 20-21; 6:15). **The mercies of God** are reflected in His *power* of salvation (1:16) and in His great *kindness* toward those He saves (2:4; 11:22). His **mercies** in Christ bring us the *forgiveness* and *propitiation* of our sins (3:25; 4:7-8) and also *freedom* from them (6:18; 7:6). We have received *reconciliation* with Him (5:10), *justification* (2:13; 3:4; etc.) before Him, *conformation* to His Son (8:29), *glorification* (8:30) in His very likeness, *eternal life* (5:21; 6:22-23) in His very presence, and the *resurrection* of our bodies (8:11) to serve Him in His everlasting kingdom. We have received the **mercies** of *divine sonship* (8:14-17) and of the *Holy Spirit*—who personally indwells us (8:9, 11), who intercedes for us (8:26), and through whom "the love of God has been poured out within our hearts" (5:5). In Christ we also have received the **mercies** of (mentioned thirty times in Romans 1-11), *peace* (1:7; 2:10; 5:1; 8:6), *hope* (5:2; 20, 24). God's **mercies** include His shared *righteousness* (3:21-22; 4:6, 11, 13; 5:17, 19, 21; etc.) and even His shared *glory* (2:10; 5:2; 8:18; 9:23) and *honor* (2:10; cf. 9:21). And, of course, **the mercies of God** include His sovereign *mercy* (9:15-16,18; 11:30-32).

Such soul-saving **mercies** should motivate believers to complete dedication. The New Testament gives many warnings about God's chastisement of unfaithful and disobedient believers. "The one who sows to his own flesh shall from the flesh reap corruption" (Gal. 6:8), and "Those whom the Lord loves He disciplines, and He scourges every son whom He receives" (Heb. 12:6). One day "we must all appear before the judgment seat of Christ, that each one may be recompensed for his deeds in the body, according to what he has done, whether good or bad" (2 Cor. 5:10). But the most compelling motivation for faithful, obedient living should not be the threat of discipline or loss of reward but overflowing and unceasing gratitude for the marvelous **mercies of God.**

THE BODY MUST BE GIVEN TO GOD

to present your bodies a living and holy sacrifice, acceptable to God, which is your spiritual service of worship. (12:1*b*)

The second and consequent element of presenting ourselves to God is that of offering Him our **bodies.** After it is implied that believers have given their souls to God through faith in Jesus Christ, they are specifically called **to present** their **bodies** to Him as **a living and holy sacrifice.**

In the Septuagint (Greek Old Testament), *paristēmi* **(to present)** was often used as a technical term for a priest's placing an offering on the altar. It therefore carried the general idea of surrendering or yielding up. As members of God's present "holy priesthood" (1 Pet. 2:5), Christians are here exhorted to perform what is essentially a priestly act of worship. Because the verb is in the imperative, the exhortation carries the weight of a command.

The first thing we are commanded **to present** to God is our **bodies.** Because our souls belong to God through salvation, He already has the inner man. But He also wants the outer man, in which the inner man dwells.

Our **bodies,** however, are more than physical shells that house our souls. They are also where our old, unredeemed humanness resides. In fact, our humanness is a *part* of our **bodies,** whereas our souls are not. Our **bodies** incorporate our humanness, our humanness incorporates our flesh, and our flesh incorporates our sin, as Romans 6 and 7 so clearly explain.

Our **bodies** therefore encompass not only our physical being but also the evil longings of our mind, emotions, and will. "For while we were in the flesh," Paul informs us, "the sinful passions, which were aroused by the Law, were at work in the members of our body to bear fruit for death" (Rom. 7:5). Long after he was saved, however, the apostle confessed, "For I joyfully concur with the law of God in the inner man, but I see a different law in the members of my body, waging war against the law of my mind, and making me a prisoner of the law of sin which is in my members" (Rom. 7:22-23). In other words, the redeemed soul must reside in a body of flesh that is still the beachhead of sin, a place that can readily be given to unholy thoughts and longings. It is that powerful force within our "mortal bodies" that tempts and lures us to do evil. When they succumb to the impulses of the fleshly mind, our "mortal bodies" again become instruments of sin and unrighteousness.

It is a fearful thing to consider that, if we allow them to, our fallen and unredeemed bodies are still able to thwart the impulses of our redeemed and eternal souls. The body is still the center of sinful desires, emotional depression, and spiritual doubts. Paul gives insight into that sobering reality when he said, "I buffet my body and make it my slave, lest possibly, after I have preached to others, I myself should be disqualified" (1 Cor. 9:27). In order to maintain a holy life and testimony and to minister effectively, even the great apostle had to exert himself strongly and continually in order to control the human and sinful part of himself that persistently wanted to rule and corrupt his life and his work for the Lord. In Romans 8, we learned that he had to kill the flesh. Paul also said that God had given him a "thorn," or a stake, on which to impale his otherwise proud flesh (2 Cor. 12:7).

It is helpful to understand that dualistic Greek philosophy still dominated the Roman world in New Testament times. This pagan ideology considered the spirit, or soul, to be inherently good and the body to be inherently evil. And because the body was deemed worthless and would eventually die anyway, what was done to it or with it did not matter. For obvious reasons, that view opened the door to every sort of immorality. Tragically, many believers in the early church, who have many counterparts in the church today, found it easy to fall back into the immoral practices of their former lives, justifying their sin by the false and heretical idea that what the body did could not harm the soul and had no spiritual or eternal significance. Much as in our own day, because immorality was so pervasive, many Christians who did not themselves lead immoral lives became tolerant of sin in fellow believers, thinking it merely was the flesh doing what it naturally did, completely apart from the soul's influence or responsibility.

Yet Paul clearly taught that the body can be controlled by the redeemed soul. He told the sinful Corinthians that "the body is not for immorality, but for the Lord; and the Lord is for the body" (1 Cor. 6:11-13).

Scripture makes clear that God created the body as good (Genesis), and that, despite their continuing corruption by sin, the bodies of redeemed souls will also one day be redeemed and sanctified. Even now, our unredeemed bodies can and should be made slaves to the power of our redeemed souls.

As with our souls, the Lord created our bodies for Himself, and, in this life, He cannot work through us without in some way working through our bodies. If we speak for Him, it must be through our mouths. If we read His Word, it must be with our eyes (or hands for those who are blind). If we hear His Word it must be through our ears. If we go to do His work, we must use our feet, and if we help others in His name, it must be with our hands. And if we think for Him, it must be with our minds, which now reside in our bodies. There can be no sanctification, no holy living, apart from our bodies. That is why Paul prayed, "May the God of peace Himself sanctify you entirely; and may your spirit and soul and body be preserved complete, without blame at the coming of our Lord Jesus Christ" (1 Thess. 5:23).

It is because our **bodies** are yet unredeemed that they must be yielded continually to the Lord. It was also for that reason that Paul warned, "Therefore do not let sin reign in your mortal body that you should obey its lusts" (Rom. 6:12). Paul then gave a positive admonition similar to the one found in our text (12:1), preceded by its negative counterpart: "Do not go on presenting the members of your body to sin as instruments of unrighteousness; but present yourselves to God as those alive from the dead, and your members as instruments of righteousness to God" (Rom. 6:13). Under God's control, our unredeemed bodies can and should become instruments of righteousness.

Paul rhetorically asked the believers at Corinth, "Do you not know that your body is a temple of the Holy Spirit who is in you, whom you have from God, and that you are not your own?" (1 Cor. 6:19). In other words, our unredeemed bodies are temporarily the home of God! It is because our bodies are still mortal and sinful that, "having the first fruits of the Spirit, even we ourselves groan within ourselves, waiting eagerly for our adoption as sons, the redemption of our body" (Rom. 8:23). Our spiritual "citizenship is in heaven," Paul explained to the Philippians, "from which also we eagerly wait for a Savior, the Lord Jesus Christ; who will transform the body of our humble state into conformity with the body of His glory, by the exertion of the power that He has even to subject all things to Himself" (Phil. 3:20-21).

We cannot prevent the remnants of sin from persisting in our mortal bodies. But we are able, with the Lord's power, to keep that sin from ruling our bodies. Since we are given a new, Spirit-indwelt nature through Christ, sin *cannot* reign in our souls. And it *should not* reign in our bodies (Rom. 8:11). Sin *will not* reign "if by the Spirit [we] are putting to death the deeds of the body" (Rom. 8:13; cf. 6:16). (For a complete discussion of Romans 6-8, see the *Romans 1-8* volume in this commentary series.)

Paul admonishes us, by God's mercies, to offer our imperfect but useful bodies to the Lord as a **living and holy sacrifice.** As noted above, Paul uses the language of the Old Testament ritual offerings in the Tabernacle and Temple, the language of the Levitical priesthood. According to the Law, a Jew would bring his offering of an animal to the priest, who would take it, slay it, and place it on the altar in behalf of the person who brought it.

But the sacrifices required by the Law are no longer of any effect, not even symbolic effect, because, "When Christ appeared as a high priest of the good things to come, He entered through the greater and more perfect tabernacle, not made with hands, that is to say, not of this creation; and not through the blood of goats and calves, but through His own blood, He entered the holy place once for all, having obtained eternal redemption" (Heb. 9:11-12).

Sacrifices of dead animals are no longer acceptable to God. Because the Lamb of God was sacrificed in their place, the redeemed of the Lord are now to offer themselves, all that they are and have, as **living** sacrifices. The only acceptable worship under the New Covenant is the offering of oneself to God.

From the very beginning, God's first and most important requirement for acceptable worship has been a faithful and obedient heart. It was because of his faith, not because of his material offering, that "Abel offered to God a better sacrifice than Cain" (Heb. 11:4). It is because God's first desire is for a faithful and obedient heart that Samuel rebuked King Saul for not completely destroying the Amalekites and their animals and for allowing the Israelites to sacrifice some of those animals to the Lord at Gilgal. The prophet said, "Has the Lord as much delight in burnt offerings and sacrifices as in obeying the voice of the Lord? Behold, to obey is better than sacrifice, and to heed than the fat of rams" (1 Sam. 15:22).

David, Saul's successor to the throne, understood that truth. When confronted by the prophet Nathan concerning his adultery with Bathsheba, David did not offer an animal sacrifice but rather confessed, "The sacrifices of God are a broken spirit; a broken and a contrite heart, O God, Thou wilt not despise" (Ps. 51:17). David offered God his repentant heart as a living sacrifice—apart from outward, visible ceremony—and he was forgiven (2 Sam. 12:13).

A helpful illustration of the difference between a dead and a living sacrifice is the story of Abraham and Isaac. Isaac was the son of promise, the only heir through whom God's covenant with Abraham could be fulfilled. He was miraculously conceived after Sarah, Abraham's wife, was far past childbearing age. It could only be from Isaac that God's chosen nation, whose citizens would be as numberless as the stars in the sky and the grains of sand on the seashore (Gen. 15:5; 22:17), could descend. But when Isaac was a young man, probably in his late teens, God commanded Abraham, "Take now your son, your only son, whom you love, Isaac, and go to the land of Moriah; and offer him there as a burnt offering on one of the mountains of which I will tell you" (Gen. 22:2). Without question or hesitation, Abraham immediately began to obey. After reaching Moriah and having tied Isaac to the altar, Abraham was ready to plunge the knife into his beloved son's heart.

Had he carried out that sacrifice, Isaac would have been a dead offering, just like the sheep and rams that later would be offered on the Temple altar by the priests of Israel. Abraham would have been a living sacrifice, as it were, saying to God in effect, "I will obey You even if it means that I will live without my son, without my heir, without the hope of Your covenant promise being fulfilled." But Isaac, the son of promise, would have been a dead sacrifice.

Hebrews 11:19 makes clear that Abraham was willing to slay Isaac because he was certain that God could raise him from the dead if necessary to keep His promise. Abraham was willing to commit absolutely everything to God and to trust Him, no matter how great the demand and how devastating the sacrifice, because God would be faithful.

God did not require either father or son to carry out the intended sacrifice. Both men already had offered the real sacrifice that God wanted—their willingness to give to Him everything they held dear.

The living sacrifice we are to offer to the Lord who died for us is the willingness to surrender to Him all our hopes, plans, and everything that is precious to us, all that is humanly important to us, all that we find fulfilling. Like Paul, we should in that sense "die daily" (1 Cor. 15:31), because for us "to live is Christ" (Phil. 1:21). For the sake of his Lord and for the sake of those to whom he ministered, the apostle later testified, "Even if I am being poured out as a drink offering upon the sacrifice and service of your faith, I rejoice and share my joy with you all" (Phil. 2:17).

Because Jesus Christ has already made the only dead sacrifice the New Covenant requires—the only sacrifice that has power to save men from eternal death—all that remains for worshipers today is the presentation of themselves as living sacrifices.

The story is told of a Chinese Christian who was moved with compassion when many of his countrymen were taken to work as coolies in South African mines. In order to be able to witness to his fellow Chinese, this prominent man sold himself to the mining company to work as a coolie for five years. He died there, still a slave, but not until he had won more than 200 men to Christ. He was a living sacrifice in the fullest sense.

In the mid-seventeenth century, a somewhat well-known Englishman was captured by Algerian pirates and made a slave. While a slave, he founded a church. When his brother arranged his release, he refused freedom, having vowed to remain a slave until he died in order to continue serving the church he had founded. Today a plaque in an Algerian church bears his name.

David Livingstone, the renowned and noble missionary to Africa, wrote in his journal,

> People talk of the sacrifice I have made in spending so much of my life in Africa. Can that be called sacrifice which is simply paid back as a small part of the great debt owing to our God, which we can never repay? Is that a sacrifice which brings its own reward of healthful

activity, the consciousness of doing good, peace of mind, and bright hope of a glorious destiny hereafter?

. . . Away with such a word, such a view, and such a thought! It is emphatically no sacrifice. Say rather it is a privilege. Anxiety, sickness, suffering or danger now and then, with a foregoing of the common conveniences and charities of this life, may make us pause and cause the spirit to waver and sink; but let this only be for a moment. All these are nothing when compared with the glory which shall hereafter be revealed in and for us. I never made a sacrifice. Of this we ought not talk when we remember the great sacrifice which He made who left His Father's throne on high to give Himself for us. (*Private Journal: 1851-53*, ed. I. Schapera [London: Chatto & Windus, 1960], 108,132)

Like Livingstone, Christians who offer a living sacrifice of themselves usually do not consider it to be a sacrifice. And it is not a sacrifice in the common sense of losing something valuable. The only things we entirely give up for God—to be removed and destroyed—are sin and sinful things, which only bring us injury and death. But when we offer God the living sacrifice of ourselves, He does not destroy what we give Him but refines it and purifies it, not only for His glory but for our present and eternal good.

Our living sacrifice also is to be **holy.** *Hagios* **(holy)** has the literal sense of being set apart for a special purpose. In secular and pagan Greek society the word carried no idea of moral or spiritual purity. The man-made gods were as sinful and degraded as the men who made them, and there simply was no need for a word that represented righteousness. Like the Hebrew scholars who translated the Greek Old Testament (Septuagint), Christianity sanctified the term, using it to describe God, godly people, and godly things.

Under the Old Covenant, a sacrificial animal was to be without spot or blemish. That physical purity symbolized the spiritual and moral purity that God required of the offerer himself. Like that worshiper who was to come to God with "clean hands and a pure heart" (Ps. 24:4), the offering of a Christian's body not only should be **a living** but also a **holy sacrifice.**

Through Malachi, the Lord rebuked those who sacrificed animals that were blind and otherwise impaired. "When you present the blind for sacrifice, is it not evil? And when you present the lame and sick, is it not evil? Why not offer it to your governor? Would he be pleased with you? Or would he receive you kindly?" (Mal. 1:8). Those people were willing to give a second-rate offering to the Lord that they would not think of presenting as a gift or tax payment to a government official. They feared men more than God.

Although we have been counted righteous and are being made righteous because of salvation in Jesus Christ, we are not yet perfected in righteousness. It is therefore the Lord's purpose for His church to "sanctify her, having cleansed her by the washing of water with the word, that He might present to Himself the church in all her glory, having no spot or wrinkle or any such thing; but that she should be holy and blameless" (Eph. 5:25-27). That was also Paul's purpose for those to whom he ministered. "I am jealous for you with a godly jealousy," he told the Corinthian Christians; "for I betrothed you to one husband, that to Christ I might present you as a pure virgin" (2 Cor. 11:2).

Sadly, like those in Malachi's day, many people today are perfectly willing to give God second best, the leftovers that mean little to them—and mean even less to Him.

Only **a living and holy sacrifice,** the giving of ourselves and the giving of our best, is **acceptable to God.** Only in that way can we give Him our **spiritual service of worship.**

Logikos **(spiritual)** is the term from which we get *logic* and *logical.* Our offerings to God are certainly to be **spiritual,** but that is not what Paul is speaking about at this point. *Logikos* also can be translated *reasonable,* as in the King James Version. The apostle is saying that, in light of "the depth of the riches both of the wisdom and knowledge of God" and of His "unsearchable ... judgments and unfathomable ... ways"; and because "from Him and through Him and to Him are all things" (Rom. 11:33, 36), including His immeasurable "mercies" that we already have received (12:1*a*), our only *reasonable*—and by implication, **spiritual—service of worship** is to present God with all that we are and all that we have.

Service of worship translates the single Greek word *latreia,* which refers to **service** of any kind, the context giving it the added meaning of **worship.** Like *paristēmi* and *hagios* (mentioned above), *latreia* was used in the Greek Old Testament to speak of worshiping God according to the prescribed Levitical ceremonies, and it became part of the priestly, sacrificial language. The priestly **service** was an integral part of Old Testament **worship.** The writer of Hebrews uses *latreia* to describe the "divine worship" (9:6 NASB), or "service of God" (KJV), performed by Old Testament priests.

True worship does not consist of elaborate and impressive prayers, intricate liturgy, stained-glass windows, lighted candles, flowing robes, incense, and classical sacred music. It does not require great talent, skill, or leadership ability. Many of those things can be a part of the outward forms of genuine worship, but they are acceptable to God only if the heart and mind of the worshiper is focused on Him. The only **spiritual service of worship** that honors and pleases God is the sincere, loving, thoughtful, and heartfelt devotion and praise of His children.

During a conference in which I was preaching on the difference between true and false believers, a man came to me with tears running down his cheeks, lamenting, "I believe I'm a sham Christian." I replied, "Let me ask you something. What is the deepest desire of your heart? What weighs heaviest on your heart? What occupies your mind and thoughts more than anything else?" He answered, "My greatest desire is to give all I am and have to Jesus Christ." I said, "Friend, that is not the desire of a sham Christian. That is the Spirit-prompted desire of a redeemed soul to become a living sacrifice."

THE MIND MUST BE GIVEN TO GOD

And do not be conformed to this world, but be transformed by the renewing of your mind, (12:2*a*)

The third element of our priestly self-sacrifice is that of offering Him our minds.

It is in the **mind** that our new nature and our old humanness are intermixed. It is in the **mind** that we make choices as to whether we will express our new nature in holiness or allow our fleshly humanness to act in unholiness.

Be conformed is from *suschēmatizō*, which refers to an outward expression that does not reflect what is within. It is used of masquerading, or putting on an act, specifically by following a prescribed pattern or scheme *(schēma)*. It also carries the idea of being transitory, impermanent, and unstable. The negative *me* **(not)** makes the verb prohibitive. The verb itself is passive and imperative, the passive indicating that conformation is something we allow to be done *to us,* the imperative indicating a command, not a suggestion.

Paul's gentle but firm command is that we are **not** to allow ourselves to **be conformed to this world.** We are not to masquerade as a worldly person, for whatever the reason. J. B. Phillips translates this phrase as "Don't let the world around you squeeze you into its own mould." We must not pattern ourselves or allow ourselves to be patterned after the spirit of the age. We must not become victims of the world. We are to stop allowing ourselves to be fashioned after the present evil age in which we live.

New Testament scholar Kenneth Wuest paraphrased this clause: "Stop assuming an outward expression which is patterned after this world, an expression which does not come from, nor is representative of what you are in your inner being as a regenerated child of God" *(Wuest's Word Studies from the Greek New Testament* [Grand Rapids: Eerdmans, 1955], 1:206-7).

World translates *aiōn*, which is better rendered "age," referring to the present sinful age, the **world** system now dominated by Satan, "the god of this world *(aiōn)*" (2 Cor. 4:4). **World** here represents the sum of the demonic-human philosophy of life, it corresponds to the German *zeitgeist* (the spirit of the age) and has been well described as "that floating mass of thoughts, opinions, maxims, speculations, hopes, impulses, aims, aspirations, at any time current in the world, which it may be impossible to seize and accurately define, but which constitute a most real and effective power, being the moral, or immoral atmosphere which at every moment of our lives we inhale, again inevitably to exhale" (G. C. Trench, *Synonyms of the New Testament* [Grand Rapids: Eerdmans, 1973], 217-18).

It is not uncommon for unbelievers to mask themselves as Christians. Unfortunately, it also is not uncommon for Christians to wear the world's masks. They want to enjoy the world's entertainment, the world's fashions, the world's vocabulary, the world's music, and many of the world's attitudes—even when those things clearly do not conform to the standards of God's Word. That sort of living is wholly unacceptable to God.

The world is an instrument of Satan, and his ungodly influence is pandemic. This is seen in the prideful spirit of rebellion, lies, error, and in the rapid spread of false religions—especially those that promote self and come under the broad umbrella of "New Age." "We know that we are of God," John wrote nearly two thousand years ago, "and the whole world lies in the power of the evil one" (1 John 5:19). It clearly still does.

Instead, Paul goes on to say, you should rather **be transformed.** The Greek verb *(metamorphoō)* connotes change in outward appearance and is the term from which we get the English *metamorphosis.* Matthew used the word in describing Jesus' transfiguration. When "He was transfigured [*metamorphōtheē*] before them; and His face shone like the sun, and His garments became as white as light" (Matt. 17:2), Christ's inner divine nature and glory were, for a brief time and to a limited degree, manifested outwardly. Our inner redeemed nature also is to be manifested outwardly, but as completely and continually as possible, in our daily living.

Like the preceding verb **(be conformed), be transformed** is a passive imperative. Positively, we are commanded to allow ourselves to be changed outwardly into conformity to our redeemed inner natures. "We all," Paul assured the Corinthians believers, "with unveiled face beholding as in a mirror the glory of the Lord, are being transformed into the same image from glory to glory, just as from the Lord, the Spirit" (2 Cor. 3:18). Although we are to aspire to this outward change, it can be accomplished only by the Holy Spirit working in us, by our being "filled with the Spirit" (Eph. 5:18).

The Holy Spirit achieves this transformation **by the renewing of** the **mind,** an essential and repeated New Testament theme. The outward transformation is effected by an inner change in the mind, and the Spirit's means of transforming our minds is the Word. David testified, "Thy word I have treasured in my heart, that I may not sin against Thee" (Ps. 119:11). God's own Word is the instrument His own Holy Spirit uses to renew our minds, which, in turn, He uses to transform our living.

Paul repeatedly emphasized that truth in his letter to Colossae. As he proclaimed Christ, he was "admonishing every man and teaching every man with all wisdom, that we may present every man complete in Christ" (Col. 1:28). By receiving Christ as Lord and Savior, we "have put on the new self who is being renewed to a true knowledge according to the image of the One who created him" (3:10). Consequently, we are to "let the word of Christ richly dwell within [us], with all wisdom teaching and admonishing one another with psalms and hymns and spiritual songs, singing with thankfulness in [our] hearts to God" (3:16).

The transformed and renewed **mind** is the mind saturated with and controlled by the Word of God. It is the mind that spends as little time as possible even with the necessary things of earthly living and as much time as possible with the things of God. It is the mind that is set "on the things above, not on the things that are on earth" (Col. 3:2). Whether good or bad, when anything happens in our lives, our immediate, almost reflexive response should be biblical. During His incarnation, Jesus responded to Satan's temptations by hurling Scripture back into His adversary's face (Matt. 4:4, 7, 10). Only the mind that is constantly being renewed by God's Spirit working through God's Word is pleasing to God. Only such a mind is able to make our lives "a living and holy sacrifice, acceptable to God, which is [our] spiritual service of worship."

The Will Must Be Given to God

that you may prove what the will of God is, that which is good and acceptable and perfect. (12:2*b*)

An implied fourth element of presenting ourselves to God as a living, holy, and acceptable sacrifice is that of offering Him our wills, of allowing His Spirit through His Word to conform our wills to **the will of God.**

The Greek construction makes **that you may prove** a purpose/result phrase. That is to say, when a believer's mind is transformed, his thinking ability, moral reasoning, and spiritual understanding are able to properly assess everything, and to accept only what conforms to **the**

will of God. Our lives can prove what the will of God is only by doing those things that are good and acceptable and perfect to Him.

In using *euarestos* **(acceptable),** Paul again borrows from Old Testament sacrificial language to describe the kind of holy living that God approves, a "living sacrifice" that is morally and spiritually spotless and without blemish.

Perfect carries the idea of being complete, of something's being everything it should be. Our wills should desire only what God desires and lead us to do only what He wants us to do in the way He wants us to do it—according to His will and by His power. Our imperfect wills must always be subject to His **perfect** will.

A transformed mind produces a transformed will, by which we become eager and able, with the Spirit's help, to lay aside our own plans and to trustingly accept God's, no matter what the cost. This continued yielding involves the strong desire to know God better and to comprehend and follow His purpose for our lives.

The divine transformation of our minds and wills must be constant. Because we are still continuously tempted through our remaining humanness, our minds and wills must be continuously transformed through God's Word and by God's Spirit.

The product of a transformed mind is a life that does the things God has declared to be righteous, fitting, and complete. That is the goal of the supreme act of spiritual worship, and sets the stage for what Paul speaks of next—the ministry of our spiritual gifts.

The Ministry of Spiritual Gifts —part 1 (Romans 12:3-5)

For through the grace given to me I say to every man among you not to think more highly of himself than he ought to think; but to think so as to have sound judgment, as God has allotted to each a measure of faith. For just as we have many members in one body and all the members do not have the same function, so we, who are many, are one body in Christ, and individually members one of another. (12:3-5)

After World War II, a group of German students volunteered to help rebuild an English cathedral that had been severely damaged by German bombs. As work progressed, they became concerned about a large statue of Jesus, whose arms were outstretched and beneath which was the inscription: "Come unto Me." They had particular difficulty trying to restore the hands, which had been completely destroyed. After much discussion, they decided to let the hands remain missing and changed the inscription to: "Christ has no hands but ours."

It is the basic truth of that phrase that Paul emphasizes in Romans 12. The work of Jesus Christ in the world is in the hands of those who belong to Him. In that sense, He has no hands but our hands, no feet but our feet. The Lord commissioned His earthly ministry to His followers, saying, "Go therefore and make disciples of all the nations, baptizing them in the name of the Father and the Son and the Holy Spirit, teaching them to observe all that I commanded you" (Matt. 28:19-20). His present ministers to the world in His name are those described in the previous eleven chapters of Romans, who had been freed from the bondage of sin and become children of God and bond-servants of Jesus Christ. On the human side, it is upon their faithfulness, obedience, and usefulness that the work of His kingdom now depends.

As we have seen, the first obligation of the bond-servant of Christ is the supreme worship expressed in offering himself to his Lord as a living sacrifice (Rom. 12:1). That is God's fundamental requirement for every believer. Only as a living sacrifice can we be what He wants us to be, do what He wants us to do, and thereby "prove what the will of God is, that which is good and acceptable and perfect" (12:2). That act of spiritual worship marks the Christian's entrance into divine usefulness. God's order of obedience for His people has always been worship and then service.

But our present passage (Rom. 12:3-8) adds the marvelous truth that, although Christ sends forth His servants with a common commission to serve Him, He equips them for that responsibility with greatly diverse gifts. His divine plan for believers is unity in message and commitment but diversity in service. The primary purpose of these verses is to make clear that, although we must enter the place of usefulness for Christ with the same total self-sacrifice, we are equipped to fulfill that usefulness in uniquely distinct ways.

The purpose of offering ourselves to God as living sacrifices is not mystical or monastic but eminently practical. Devotion to the Lord and active, faithful ministry for Him are inseparable. We cannot be truly sacrificed to Him and be inactive in His work. And, on the other hand, we cannot be truly successful in His work without being genuinely devoted to Him. Service to God brings honor to Him and blessing for us only when it is the outflow of our worship in offering ourselves as living sacrifices. Such commitment naturally and inevitably produces effective ministry. There is no godly commitment without God-blessed ministry, and no God-blessed ministry without godly commitment.

This passage utterly destroys the notion that a Christian can be committed to Christ but be inactive in His service, that he can love the Lord but not obey the Lord, that he can be surrendered to the Lord but not minister for the Lord. True worship cannot be divorced from service.

Unfortunately, the church has always had members who piously claim closeness and devotion to the Lord but whose lives exhibit no service for Him. It also has always had those who are busily active in the work of the church but who exhibit little personal depth of devotion to the Lord of the church. Both are a shame to the Lord and are a hindrance to His work, because they thwart the spiritual maturity of the saved and the evangelism of the lost.

I received a letter from a man who expressed concern about what is surely a common problem. He wrote, "Please meet with me and pray with me. I've driven my wife away because I taught her by example how to be a Sunday saint and to live any way you want during the week. I've lived outwardly as a Christian and been active in the church, but the rest of the time I've lived a lie. When our relationship started to fall apart, I tried to get us into Bible reading and prayer, but she thought that was just another one of my facades and wanted nothing of it." Such situations are a familiar feature in the church today.

It is true, of course, that God can work even through unfaithful and disobedient believers. He may use the preaching and witness of a hypocrite to bring sinners to Himself. But in such cases it is the truth of the message that He blesses, not the hypocritical effort of the one who gives it. Hypocrites, although they cannot limit the power of the truth which transcends duplicity, accrue no blessing from God for what He may do through them, because their true motive is to serve their own ends and glory, not His. If we perform on the outside but are not devoted on the inside, our service is limited and our reward is forfeited. More importantly, the name of God is not honored and His work is limited and made less effective with a dirty vessel than with a clean one (cf. 2 Tim. 2:20-22).

But the unity of believers is not limited to their common commitment. Although our gifts are diverse, our obligation to use them in the Lord's service is not. The person with one seemingly insignificant gift is as much obligated to use that gift faithfully and fully as the one who has several prominent and seemingly more important gifts. Just as no believer is exempt from being a living sacrifice, no believer is exempt from using his divine giftedness, whatever it is. In this chapter Paul makes clear that he is admonishing "every man" (v. 3), that is, every believer. He also makes clear that, although we do not have the "same function" (v. 4) and although our gifts "differ according to the grace given to us" (v. 6*a*), we *all* have a function in Christ's church and we *all* have gifts from His Holy Spirit and the obligation to "exercise them" (v. 6*b*) in His behalf and in His power.

Total surrender to the Lord is also foundational to Christian service in another way. Without genuine, selfless commitment to Him, we not only will lose the desire and forfeit the power needed to serve Him effectively but also will never experience what God has intended for us to do when our gifts and calling are used to the fullest. God does not give His children gifts without letting them know what those gifts are. Therefore, if we are not sure of our gifts *from* God, it is most likely because we are not close *to* God. We come to know our gifts more fully as, through worship in spiritual truth, we come to know Him more fully. When our lives are on the altar of sacrifice, we will have no problem discovering or using our spiritual gifts. They cannot be recognized except as we use them. When a believer walks in holy obedience to the Lord, filled with the Holy Spirit and serving God, it will become apparent to him and to others what his gift is and how it blesses the body of Christ.

It is estimated that even the brightest people use only about eleven percent of their brain capacity—leaving nearly ninety percent unused. A similar ratio probably applies to most Christians' use of their spiritual gifts. When a believer has trouble understanding how the gifts mentioned in Romans 12:6-8 apply to him personally, it is not because he cannot figure out what his gift is but because he has not come to terms with the dedication and requirements of the preceding five verses. And, on the other hand, when a believer is used powerfully in the Lord's work, it is not because he has perfectly understood and analyzed his gift, but rather because his life is "a living and holy sacrifice," which is "acceptable to God" as a "spiritual service of worship" (v. 1), and God's Spirit is moving through him in serving power.

The noble American preacher and theologian Jonathan Edwards was so fearful that his personal mannerisms and inflections might interfere with the power of God's Word, that he not only read his sermons but often delivered them almost mechanically. Yet the Holy Spirit strongly used those messages, and listeners were sometimes so convicted of sin that they screamed for God's mercy and tightly gripped their pews for fear of falling immediately into hell. God was able to use him in such ways because he lived up to the following resolutions (abbreviated) that he made early in his ministry:

> Resolved, to live with all my might
>   while I do live.
> Resolved, never to lose one moment of time,
>   to improve it in the most profitable way I possibly can.
> Resolved, never to do anything which I should
>   despise or think meanly of in another.
> Resolved, never to do anything out of revenge.
> Resolved, never to do anything which I should be
>   afraid to do if it were the last hour of my life.
>
> *(See Iain H. Murray, Jonathan Edwards: A New Biography*
> [Carlisle, Penn.: Banner of Truth Trust, 1987], 43.)

The following beautiful prayer, used at the end of the communion services in the Church of England, accurately reflects the total dedication of which Paul speaks in Romans 12. It reads, "And here we offer and present unto Thee, O Lord, ourselves, our souls and bodies to be a reasonable holy and living sacrifice unto Thee."

Our absolute usefulness to the Lord depends on the three things Paul mentions in our present text: proper attitude (v. 3), proper relationship (vv. 4-5), and proper service (vv. 6-8).

THE PROPER ATTITUDE: TRUE HUMILITY

For through the grace given to me I say to every man among you not to think more highly of himself than he ought to think; but to think so as to have sound judgment, as God has allotted to each a measure of faith. (12:3)

For indicates a transition from what the apostle has just commanded, tying spiritual service to spiritual dedication, the bridge between them being spiritual attitude.

The Christian's proper attitude is humility, **not to think more highly of himself than he ought to think.** Lack of that foundational virtue causes many believers to stumble. No matter how well grounded we may be in God's Word, how theologically sound we may be, or how vigorously we may seek to serve Him, our gifts will not operate so that our lives can be spiritually productive until self is set aside. From self-denial in the spiritual worship of God flows self-surrender to the will of God, and from self-surrender flows selfless service in the work of God. No believer is exempt from this call to humility, because Paul is speaking **to every man among you**—a universal command to all who are Christ's.

The basis of everything worthwhile that a Christian has and does, from salvation to service, is **the grace given to** him by God. Just as we are saved only by God's grace, so we can serve Him only by that same grace. But the specific divine **grace** of which Paul speaks here is that from which he was ordained as God's apostle and authorized to reveal God's Word (Rom. 1:1-5; cf. 15:15; 1 Cor. 3:10; Gal. 2:9).

Yet in this passage on humility, it is not surprising that Paul appeals only indirectly to his apostolic rank, calling attention rather to the divine authority from which his own authority was derived. He is humble even in relationship to his own apostleship, which was conferred on him solely on the basis of God's **grace,** and on no merit or worth of his own. "I thank Christ Jesus our Lord, who has strengthened me," he informed Timothy, "because He considered me faithful, putting me into service; even though I was formerly a blasphemer and a persecutor and a violent aggressor. And yet I was shown mercy, because I acted ignorantly in unbelief; and *the grace of our Lord was more than abundant,* with the faith and love which are found in Christ Jesus" (1 Tim. 1:12-14, emphasis added). As an apostle of Jesus Christ, he calls for humility— the most basic Christian virtue, and the one that opens the door to love, power, and unity.

To emphasize the necessity of meekness, Paul uses a form of *phroneō* **(to think)** four times in verse 3. A Christian is not to overestimate himself, to **think more highly** (*huperphroneō*) **of himself than he ought to think,** but is to think of himself as he really is. He is not to overvalue his abilities, his gifts, or his worth but make an accurate estimate of himself. "For if anyone thinks he is something when he is nothing," Paul elsewhere cautions, "he deceives himself" (Gal. 6:3). And an honest estimate will be very low (cf. 1 Tim. 1:12-16).

Referring to self-examination and judgment of other Christians, Paul told the Corinthian church, "Now these things brethren, I have figuratively applied to myself and Apollos for your sakes, that in us you might learn not to exceed what is written, in order that no one of you might become arrogant in behalf of one against the other. For who regards you as superior? And what do you have that you did not receive? But if you did receive it, why do you boast as if you had not received it?" (1 Cor. 4:6-7; cf. 1-5). Peter admonished all elders in the church, young and old, to "clothe yourselves with humility toward one another, for God is opposed to the proud, but gives grace to the humble" (1 Pet. 5:5).

To have sound judgment translates a compound (*sōphroneō*) of that verb and has the basic meaning of "to think with a sound mind, to think soberly" (as the KJV). **To think** of ourselves with **sound judgment** leads us to recognize that, in ourselves, we are nothing at all, but that, in Christ, we can be used to the glory of God through the gift of the Spirit bestowed on us. We must realize that from ourselves, from our fleshly humanness, nothing eternal can be produced, but that in the power of the Spirit we can be used to build the kingdom and honor the King.

People do not suffer from low self-esteem. Rather, they are proud. That is the essential attitude of human nature. Selfish pride dominates the flesh. To be useful to our Lord, we must honestly recognize our limits as fallen men and women as well as our abilities as new creations in Christ, keeping both in proper perspective.

Such humility, which is essential for all spiritual matters, is not easily found or maintained. In New Testament times, some churches were characterized by members who desired to have the more showy and spectacular gifts, the church at Corinth being the chief offender. Paul therefore warns them rather to "earnestly desire the greater gifts. And I show you a still more excellent way," the way of humble love (1 Cor. 12:31; cf. 13:1-13). With a clearly-implied rebuke, the apostle John identifies a self-seeking believer by name, a man named Diotrephes, "who loves to be first" (3 John 9). Sadly, the church is still well-saturated with members who proudly seek personal preeminence and thereby forfeit the power of humility.

Modern society looks down on true humility. It is instead characterized by brash, and even exalted, self-centeredness, ego building, pampering the body, and striving to fulfill every personal lust and ambition, with little regard for who may be harmed. It is small wonder that depression and emotional chaos are so prevalent. In his book *Psychological Seduction, the Failure of Modern Psychology,* professor William K. Kilpatrick writes, "Extreme forms of mental illness are always extreme cases of self-absorption....The distinctive quality, the thing that literally sets paranoid people apart is hyper-self-consciousness. And the thing they prize most about themselves is autonomy. Their constant fear is that someone else is interfering with their will or trying to direct their lives" (Nashville: Nelson, 1983, 67).

Long before the advent of modern psychology, theologians confronted the devastating effects of self-love. In the early days of the church, Augustine wrote in his classic work *The City of God,* "Two cities have been formed by two loves; the earthly by the love of self, even to the contempt of God, the heavenly by the love of God even to the contempt of self. The former, in a word, glories in itself, the latter in the Lord" (*Civitas Dei,* XIV 28. Cited by John Warwick Montgomery, *The Shape of the Past* [Minneapolis: Bethany, 1975], 46).

The great Reformer John Calvin observed,

> For so blindly do we all rush in the direction of self-love that everyone thinks he has a good reason for exalting himself and despising all others in comparison....There is no other remedy than to pluck up by the roots those most noxious pests, self-love and love of victory....This the doctrine of Scripture does. For it teaches us to remember that the endowments which God has bestowed upon us are not our own, but His free gifts, and that those who plume themselves upon them betray their ingratitude. *(Institutes of the Christian Religion,* trans. Henry Beveridge, 2 vols. [Grand Rapids: Eerdmans, 1966], 2:10)

Addressing the problem in a positive way, the writer of Hebrews admonishes, "Let us consider how to stimulate one another to love and good deeds, not forsaking our own assembling together, as is the habit of some, but encouraging one another; and all the more, as you see the day drawing near" (Heb. 10:24-25).

Although they are not mentioned in the text, proud attitudes toward spiritual gifts can be placed into five categories. Several already have been mentioned. The first wrong attitude is that of using a prominent gift—or any other gift, for that matter—boastfully. As Paul admonished the Corinthian believers, "The eye cannot say to the hand, 'I have no need of you'; or again the head to the feet, 'I have no need of you'" (1 Cor. 12:21), which is what a Christian does by implication whenever he boasts of his own gifts and accomplishments.

A second wrong attitude is that of depreciating ourselves and our gifts in false humility (see 1 Cor. 12:11-12,19). Such an attitude is a poorly disguised effort to get praise. At the other end, when a person is clearly gifted above most Christians, it is tempting to feign humility when genuinely praised, thereby belittling what God has given to and is doing through him or her. All spiritual gifts are necessary and perfectly designed by God for His glorious purpose.

A third wrong attitude about spiritual gifts is that of claiming gifts, especially the more impressive ones, which we do not possess. Doing that not only is dishonest but denigrates God's wisdom and sovereignty in belittling by implication the gift or gifts that we do have from Him. "All are not apostles, are they?" Paul asks rhetorically. "All are not prophets, are they? All are not teachers, are they? All are not workers of miracles, are they? All do not have gifts of healings, do they? All do not speak with tongues, do they? All do not interpret, do they?" (1 Cor. 12:29-30). If God has not chosen to give us any of the more notable gifts, we should neither feign nor covet them.

A fourth wrong attitude is that of failing to use an inconspicuous gift out of jealousy, resentment, or shame. To purposely disregard and neglect a spiritual gift is to disdain God's sovereign grace. "If the foot should say, 'Because I am not a hand, I am not a part of the body,' it is not for this reason any the less a part of the body. And if the ear should say, 'Because I am not an eye, I am not a part of the body,' it is not for this reason any the less a part of the body" (1 Cor. 12:15-16). God has a plan for each of His children, and every plan is good, perfect, and appropriate.

A fifth wrong attitude is failing to use one's gifts at all, for whatever reason—whether out of neglect, bitterness, jealousy, shame, or simply indifference. Every spiritual gift of God is to be used to its fullest, because every gift is divinely ordained and meant to be divinely empowered and employed. Certainly Paul is concerned with this issue when, in verses 6-8, he urges that all gifts be used.

The humility that God requires and honors does not overestimate or underestimate His gifts but estimates them rightly and uses them rightly. Every Christian can attest, "God has gifted me. He has gifted me graciously and lovingly and will give me everything I need to use my gifts effectively to His glory. I thank Him and bless His name."

There also are certain right attitudes toward our spiritual gifts. First, we must correctly recognize them and acknowledge that the Lord Himself provides exactly what He wants for us and everything we need to serve Him according to His will, just **as [He] has allotted to each a measure of faith.** In this context, **a measure of faith** seems to refer to the correct measure of the spiritual gift and its operating features that God sovereignly bestows on every believer. Every believer receives the exact gift and resources best suited to fulfill his role in the body of Christ.

A fictitious article published some years ago in the Springfield, Oregon, public school newsletter illustrates this principle very well.

Once upon a time, the animals decided they should do something meaningful to meet the problems of the new world. So they organized a school.

They adopted an activity curriculum of running, climbing, swimming and flying. To make it easier to administer the curriculum, all the animals took all the subjects.

The duck was excellent in swimming; in fact, better than his instructor. But he made only passing grades in flying, and was very poor in running. Since he was slow in running, he had to drop swimming and stay after school to practice running. This caused his web feet to be badly worn, so that he [became] only average in swimming. But average was quite acceptable, so nobody worried about that—except the duck.

The rabbit started at the top of his class in running, but developed a nervous twitch in his leg muscles because of so much make-up work in swimming.

The squirrel was excellent in climbing, but he encountered constant frustration in flying class because his teacher made him start from the ground up instead of from the treetop down. He developed "charley horses" from overexertion, and so only got a C in climbing and a D in running.

The eagle was a problem child and was severely disciplined for being a non-conformist. In climbing classes he beat all the others to the top of the tree, but insisted on using his own way to get there. . . .

The point of the story is obvious. Like the animals, every person has his own special but limited set of capabilities. Trying to operate outside those capabilities produces frustration, discouragement, guilt feelings, mediocrity, and ultimate defeat. We fulfill our calling when we function according to God's sovereign design for us.

Paul is not here referring to *saving* faith, which believers already have exercised. He is speaking of faithful stewardship, the kind and quantity of **faith** required to exercise our own particular gift. It is the **faith** through which the Lord uses His measured gift in us to the fullest. It encompasses all the sensitivity, capacity, and understanding we need to rightly and fully use our uniquely-bestowed gift. Our heavenly Father does not burden us with gifts for which He does not provide every spiritual, intellectual, physical, and emotional resource we need to successfully exercise them.

Because every believer is perfectly gifted, no gift that God has not given should be sought and no gift He *has* given should be neglected or denigrated. "To each one is given the manifestation of the Spirit for the common good," Paul explains in his first letter to Corinth, and "one and the same Spirit works all these things, distributing to each one individually just as He wills" (1 Cor. 12:7,11).

Following are nine guidelines that can be helpful in fulfilling the purpose of our spiritual gifts. We should present ourselves as a living sacrifice (Rom. 12:1); recognize that all believers, including ourselves, are gifted (v. 3); pray for wisdom; seek for nothing (Acts 8:18,24); examine our heart's desire (1 Tim. 3:1); seek confirmation; look for the blessing of God; wholeheartedly serve Him; and cultivate the gift as it becomes obvious.

Even when all that is done, it still may be impossible to fully analyze and specifically identify our spiritual gift. It is often not possible to distinguish between God-given natural talent, God-given spiritual abilities, and Holy Spirit power. When a Christian's life is a living sacrifice to God and he is walking in the Spirit of God, he has no reason to make precise distinctions, because everything he is and has is committed to the Lord. Oversimplifying and overdefining spiritual gifts can cause great confusion, frustration, discouragement, and limitation of their usefulness. Focusing too much on the gifts themselves can hinder their faithful use in the Lord's service.

The New Testament does not promise that our gift will come neatly packaged and labeled. Nor does it precisely identify the specific gift of any New Testament believer, including the apostles. Believers in the early church were never classified by gifts. On the contrary, the New Testament makes clear that God endows His children with many combinations and degrees of giftedness. He mixes these gifts much as an artist mixes colors on his palette to create the exact shade he desires for a particular part of the painting.

Peter said, "As each one has received a special gift, employ it..." (1 Pet. 4:10*a*). He used the definite article (the), indicating a single gift for every believer. But clearly that single gift will be unique in the life of each believer, because it is a combination of the manifold and multicolored categories of speaking and serving giftedness (vv. 10*b*-11) from which the Spirit colors the believer, and which are then blended with the uniqueness of the mind, the training, the experience, and the effort of the individual—the result being that every Christian is like a snowflake, with no other having the same pattern.

The thrust of Romans 12 and 1 Corinthians 12, the two central passages on spiritual gifts, is not on a believer's precisely identifying his gifts but on his faithfully using them. It is also significant that each of these passages mentions gifts that the other does not. This leads us to believe that the categories are basic colors, as it were, from which the Lord mixes the unique hue of each of His children.

All of this must produce humility, because our spiritual usefulness is a purely sovereign work of God, none of which can be attributed to man. Our spiritual usefulness is in spite of and in contrast to our unworthiness and uselessness in the flesh, in which nothing dwells that is good or is capable of glorifying God.

THE PROPER RELATIONSHIP: UNITY IN DIVERSITY

For just as we have many members in one body and all the members do not have the same function, so we, who are many, are one body in Christ, and individually members one of another. (12:4-5)

In verse 1 Paul urges his fellow believers to present their physical bodies as "a living and holy sacrifice, acceptable to God, which is your spiritual service of worship." Now he uses the figure of the body to represent the church, the Body of Christ, of which every believer is a member. He focuses on its unity in diversity—**one body** (mentioned in both verses) representing its unity, and **many members** that **do not have the same function,** representing the diversity. Just as it is in nature, unified diversity in the church is a mark of God's sovereign and marvelous handiwork.

A football team may have forty to fifty men on the roster. If all of them decided to be the quarterback, the team would have no unity and no effectiveness. True unity arises when each team member is willing to play the specific position assigned to him.

Paul now focuses specifically on the diverse uniqueness and importance of each member to the body's proper performance. He points out the obvious truth that, although **we have many members in one body,** nevertheless **all the members do not have the same function.**

Function translates *praxis,* which has the basic meaning of a doing of something, that is, a deed. It later came to connote something that was ordinarily done or practiced, a normal **function.**

Spiritual gifts do not always correspond to what we commonly refer to as church offices—such as apostle, prophet, evangelist, pastor-teacher, or deacon—as the King James rendering suggests ("all members have not the same *office*," emphasis added). Most church members do not have a specific office or title. But every believer, from the youngest to the oldest and from the newest to the most mature, has a Spirit-given ability to minister to the body of Christ through some spiritual gift. It is the use of the gift that is his God-ordained **function** in the kingdom.

In the spiritual organism that is Christ's church, every constituent part—whether obvious and important, such as the arm, or hidden and unnoticed, such as the small blood vessels and glands—is critical to its proper functioning as a whole. **So we, who are many,** Paul explains, **are one body in Christ, and individually members one of another.** It is diversity working in unity and in harmony that enables Christ's Body to be and to do what He directs it to be and to do.

Because it is so normal and dependable, the great wonder of the proper operation of our bodies is seldom appreciated or even noticed. We have but to think, and our hands, feet, or eyes immediately do what we want them to do. Because we have trained them to respond in certain ways, they do many things almost automatically. Our most critical bodily functions—such as our hearts' beating and our lungs' breathing —require no thought at all. They simply do their jobs, performing their divinely-designed functions minute after minute, day after day, year after year. The interrelationship of the parts of our bodies is so unbelievably intricate that medical science continually discovers new functions and relationships. It is often only when our bodies cease to function properly that we appreciate how marvelously God has designed them.

In his book *Fearfully and Wonderfully Made,* the internationally renowned surgeon Dr. Paul Brand writes of the amazing diversity and interrelationship of the parts of the human body. Speaking of the body's cells, he says:

> I am first struck by their variety. Chemically my cells are almost alike, but visually and functionally they are as different as the animals in a zoo. Red blood cells, discs resembling Lifesaver candies, voyage through my blood loaded with oxygen to feed the other cells. Muscle cells, which absorb so much of that nourishment, are sleek and supple, full of coiled energy. Cartilage cells with shiny black nuclei look like bunches of black-eyed peas glued tightly together for strength. Fat cells seem lazy and leaden, like bulging white plastic garbage bags jammed together.
>
> Bone cells live in rigid structures that exude strength. Cut in cross section, bones resemble tree rings, overlapping strength with

strength, offering impliability and sturdiness. In contrast, skin cells form undulating patterns of softness and texture that rise and dip, giving shape and beauty to our bodies. They curve and jut at unpredictable angles so that every person's fingerprint—not to mention his or her face—is unique.

The aristocrats of the cellular world are the sex cells and nerve cells. A woman's contribution, the egg, is one of the largest cells in the human body, its ovoid shape just visible to the unaided eye. It seems fitting that all the other cells in the body should derive from this elegant and primordial structure. In great contrast to the egg's quiet repose, the male's tiny sperm cells are furiously flagellating tadpoles with distended heads and skinny tails. They scramble for position as if competitively aware that only one of billions will gain the honor of fertilization.

The king of cells, the one I have devoted much of my life to studying, is the nerve cell. It has an aura of wisdom and complexity about it. Spider-like, it branches out and unites the body with a computer network of dazzling sophistication. Its axons, "wires" carrying distant messages to and from the human brain, can reach a yard in length.

I never tire of viewing these varied specimens or thumbing through books which render cells. Individually they seem puny and oddly designed, but I know these invisible parts cooperate to lavish me with the phenomenon of life.....

My body employs a bewildering zoo of cells, none of which individually resembles the larger body. Just so, Christ's Body comprises an unlikely assortment of humans. Unlikely is precisely the right word, for we are decidedly unlike one another and the One we follow. From whose design come these comical human shapes which so faintly reflect the ideals of the Body as a whole?

The Body of Christ, like our own bodies, is composed of individual, unlike cells that are knit together to form one Body. He is the whole thing, and the joy of the Body increases as individual cells realize they can be diverse without becoming isolated outposts.

Dr. Brand also describes the unity of the seemingly endless diversity of the cells.

What moves cells to work together? What ushers in the higher specialized functions of movement, sight, and consciousness through the coordination of a hundred trillion cells?

The secret to membership lies locked away inside each cell nucleus, chemically coiled in a strand of DNA. Once the egg and sperm share their inheritance, the DNA chemical ladder splits down the center of every gene much as the teeth of a zipper pull apart. DNA re-forms itself each time the cell divides: 2, 4, 8, 16, 32 cells, each with

the identical DNA. Along the way cells specialize, but each carries
the entire instruction book of one hundred thousand genes. DNA is
estimated to contain instructions that, if written out, would fill a thousand six-hundred-page books. A nerve cell may operate according to
instructions from volume four and a kidney cell from volume twenty-five, but both carry the whole compendium. It provides each cell's
sealed credential of membership in the body. Every cell possesses a
genetic code so complete that the entire body could be reassembled
from information in any one of the body's cells. . . .

Just as the complete identity code of my body inheres in
each individual cell, so also the reality of God permeates every cell in
[Christ's] Body, linking us members with a true, organic bond. I sense
that bond when I meet strangers in India or Africa or California who
share my loyalty to the Head; instantly we become brothers and sisters, fellow cells in Christ's Body. I share the ecstasy of community in
a universal Body that includes every man and woman in whom God
resides. (Taken from *Fearfully and Wonderfully Made*, by Dr. Paul Brand
and Philip Yancy. Copyright © 1980 by Dr. Paul Brand and Philip Yancy.
Used by permission of Zondervan Publishing House.)

There are also rebellious cells, as it were, in the Body of Christ.
Some are benign, in the sense that they do not destroy the church. They
simply gorge themselves on blessings and benefits at the expense of the
rest of the body. They become fatter and fatter, always taking in, seldom
giving out. The focus of their whole existence is self-service. Their creed
is: "I will get all I can from God and all I can from the church." In their
unfaithfulness to the Lord and to His people, they sap the church of its
vitality and can so weaken it that it becomes emaciated and cannot
function normally.

The church also has "cells" that are mutinous to the point of
destruction. Through outright heresy and flagrant immorality, these ma-
lignant members openly attack the rest of the body, eating away at its
very life.

As believers, we are all interrelated in a spiritual unity. Christ
has designed us to work uniquely but harmoniously as His Body on
earth—to be His own hands, His own feet, His own voice. We share a
common life, a common ministry, a common power, and, above all, a
common Head. We are endowed in countless different combinations of
the specific gifts mentioned here and elsewhere in the New Testament.
But it is our Lord's design and desire that our diversity in spiritual gifts
be manifested in unity of spiritual service.

The Ministry of Spiritual Gifts —part 2 (Romans 12:6-8)

THE PROPER SERVICE: EXERCISING OUR GIFTS

And since we have gifts that differ according to the grace given to us, let each exercise them accordingly: if prophecy, according to the proportion of his faith; if service, in his serving; or he who teaches, in his teaching; or he who exhorts, in his exhortation; he who gives, with liberality; he who leads, with diligence; he who shows mercy, with cheerfulness. (12:6-8)

No gift or ability, spiritual or otherwise, is of value if it is not used. I read the account of a retired farmer in a small prairie town in Saskatchewan, Canada, who owns a large collection of rare and valuable violins. It is highly unlikely that anyone will play those marvelous instruments as long as they are simply stored, protected, and admired. But in the hands of accomplished musicians, those violins could be making beautiful music to inspire and bless countless thousands of hearers.

It is infinitely more tragic that many Christians keep their spiritual gifts stored, rather than using them to serve the Lord who gave them the gifts.

It has been remarked that American mothers often preserve their children's first shoes in bronze, perhaps to represent freedom and independence, whereas many Japanese mothers preserve a small part of the child's umbilical cord, to represent dependence and loyalty. *Dependence* and *loyalty* beautifully describe the interrelationship the Lord desires for the members of His Body, the church.

The spiritual gifts mentioned in the New Testament, primarily in Romans 12 and in I Corinthians 12, fall into three categories: sign, speaking, and serving. Before the New Testament was written, men had no standard for judging the truthfulness of someone who preached, taught, or witnessed in the name of Christ. The sign gifts authenticated the teaching of the apostles—which was the measure of all other teaching—and therefore ceased after the apostles died, probably even earlier. "The signs of a true apostle were performed among you with all perseverance," Paul explained to the Corinthian church, "by signs and wonders and miracles" (2 Cor. 12:12). The writer of Hebrews gives further revelation about the purpose of these special gifts: "After [the gospel] was at the first spoken through the Lord, it was confirmed to us by those who heard, God also bearing witness with them, both by signs and wonders and by various miracles and by gifts of the Holy Spirit according to His own will" (Heb. 2:3-4). Even during Jesus' earthly ministry, the apostles "went out and preached everywhere, while the Lord worked with them, and confirmed the word by the signs that followed" (Mark 16:20).

First Corinthians was written about A.D. 54 and Romans some four years later. It is important to note that none of the sign gifts mentioned in 1 Corinthians 12:9-10—namely, the gifts of healing, miracles, speaking in tongues, and interpreting tongues—is found in Romans 12. The other two New Testament passages that mention spiritual gifts (Eph. 4:7, 11; 1 Pet. 4:10-11) were written several years after Romans and, like that epistle, make no mention of sign gifts. Peter specifically mentions the categories of speaking and serving gifts ("whoever speaks" and "whoever serves," v. 11) but neither the category nor an example of the sign gifts.

It seems evident, therefore, that Paul did not mention the sign gifts in Romans because their place in the church was already coming to an end. They belonged to a unique era in the church's life and would have no permanent place in its ongoing ministry. It is significant, therefore, that the seven gifts mentioned in Romans 12:6-8 are all within the categories of speaking and serving.

It is also important to note that in 1 Corinthians 12, Paul uses the term *pneumatikos*(v. 1, lit., "spirituals") to describe the specific divinely-bestowed gifts mentioned in verses 8-10. He explains that "there are varieties of gifts, but the same Spirit" (v. 4), and that "the same Spirit works all these things, distributing to each one individually just as He wills" (v. 11).

But in Romans 12, the apostle uses the term *charisma* (gifts), which is from *charis* (grace). In First Corinthians, Paul emphasizes the nature and authority of the gifts—spiritual endowments empowered by the Holy Spirit. In Romans he simply emphasizes their source—the **grace** of God.

Paul introduces this list of gifts by referring back to the unity in diversity he has just pointed out in verses 4-5. **Since we have gifts that differ according to the grace given to us, let each exercise them accordingly. Differ** relates to the diversity, and **grace** to the unity. Under God's sovereign **grace,** which all believers share, **we have gifts that differ according to** the specific ways in which He individually endows us. Just as verse 3 does not refer to saving faith, verse 6 does not refer to saving **grace.** Paul is speaking to those who already have trusted in Christ and become children of God. To His children, the apostle explains, "God has allotted to each a measure of faith" (v. 3) and has bestowed on them **gifts that differ according to the grace given** to each one. Grace is God's favor, unmerited kindness on His part, which is the only source of all spiritual enablements. They are not earned or deserved, or they would not be by grace. And the grace is sovereign, in that God alone makes the choice as to what gift each of His children receives. Each believer, therefore, is to exercise his gifts accordingly.

Paul next lists some categories of giftedness as examples.

PROPHECY

if prophecy, according to the proportion of his faith; (12:6*b*)

The first spiritual gift in this list is **prophecy.** Some interpreters believe this was a special revelatory gift that belonged only to the apostles, and, like the sign gifts, ceased after those men died. While it certainly had a revelatory aspect during Old Testament and apostolic times, it was not limited to revelation. It was exercised when there was public proclamation of divine truth, old or new. In 1 Corinthians 12:10 it is linked with sign gifts, supernatural and revelatory. Here it is linked with speaking and serving gifts, leading to the conclusion that it had both revelatory and non-revelatory aspects. The Old Testament or New Testament prophet (or apostle) might speak direct revelation, but could and did also declare what had been revealed previously. The gift of prophecy does not pertain to the content but rather to the means of proclamation. In our day, it is active enablement to proclaim God's

Word already written in Scripture. Paul gives no distinction to this gift among the other six, which are clearly ongoing gifts in the church, thus not limiting it to revelation.

Prophēteia **(prophecy)** has the literal meaning of speaking forth, with no connotation of prediction or other supernatural or mystical significance. The gift of **prophecy** is simply the gift of preaching, of proclaiming the Word of God. God used many Old and New Testament prophets to foretell future events, but that was never an indispensable part of prophetic ministry. Paul gives perhaps the best definition of the prophetic gift in 1 Corinthians: "One who prophesies speaks to men for edification and exhortation and consolation" (1 Cor. 14:3). Peter's admonition also applies to that gift: "Whoever speaks, let him speak, as it were, the utterances of God; ... so that in all things God may be glorified through Jesus Christ, to whom belongs the glory and dominion forever and ever" (1 Pet. 4:11).

When God called Moses to deliver Israel out of Egypt, Moses gave the excuse, "Please, Lord, I have never been eloquent, neither recently nor in time past, nor since Thou hast spoken to Thy servant; for I am slow of speech and slow of tongue" (Ex. 4:10). Although angered at Moses' lack of trust, God said, "Is there not your brother Aaron the Levite? I know that he speaks fluently. ... You are to speak to him and put the words in his mouth; and I, even I, will be with your mouth and his mouth, and I will teach you what you are to do" (vv. 14-15).

The gift of prophecy is the gift of being God's public spokesman, primarily to God's own people—to instruct, admonish, warn, rebuke, correct, challenge, comfort, and encourage. God also uses His prophets to reach unbelievers. "If all prophesy," Paul explained to the Corinthians, "and an unbeliever or an ungifted man enters, he is convicted by all, he is called to account by all; the secrets of his heart are disclosed; and so he will fall on his face and worship God, declaring that God is certainly among you" (1 Cor. 14:24-25).

God used certain prophets at certain times to give new revelation and to predict future events, but He has used and continues to use all of His prophets to speak His truth in His behalf. They are God's instruments for proclaiming and making relevant His Word to His world. John Calvin said that, by prophesying, he understood not the gift of foretelling the future but of interpreting Scripture, so that a prophet is an interpreter of God's will.

In his commentary on this text, Calvin wrote:

> I prefer to follow those who extend this word wider, even to the peculiar gift of revelation, by which any one skillfully and wisely performed the office of an interpreter in explaining the will of God. Hence prophecy

at this day in the Christian Church is hardly anything else than the right understanding of the Scripture, and the peculiar faculty of explaining it, inasmuch as all the ancient prophecies and the oracles of God have been completed in Christ and in his gospel. For in this sense it is taken by Paul when he says, "I wish that you spoke in tongues, but rather that ye prophecy," (1 Cor. xiv. 5:) "In part we know and in part we prophecy," (1 Cor. xiii. 9). And it does not appear that Paul intended here to mention those miraculous graces by which Christ at first rendered illustrious his gospel; but, on the contrary, we find he refers only to ordinary gifts, such as were to continue perpetually in the Church. (*Calvin's Commentaries, axix,* "Romans" [Grand Rapids: Baker, 1991], 460)

In sixteenth-century Switzerland, pastors in Zurich came together every week for what they called "prophesying." They shared exegetical, expositional, and practical insights they had gleaned from Scripture that helped them more effectively minister to their people in that day.

The book of Acts speaks of many prophets besides the apostles. Agabus, part of a group of prophets (the others are unnamed) from Jerusalem, predicted a famine that would plague Judea during the reign of Emperor Claudius (Acts 11:27-28) and later foretold Paul's arrest and imprisonment (21:10-11). "Judas and Silas," on the other hand, "also being prophets themselves," gave no predictions or new revelation but simply "encouraged and strengthened the brethren with a lengthy message" after Paul and Barnabas had delivered the letter from the Jerusalem Council (Acts 15:32; cf. vv. 22-31). (For a fuller discussion of prophecy, see the relevant section on 12:10 in the author's commentary on 1 Corinthians in this series [Chicago: Moody Press, 1984].)

Whatever the form his message may take, the prophet is to minister it **according to the proportion of his faith.** Because the Greek includes the definite article, **faith** may here refer to *the* faith, that is, the full gospel message. In that case, **according to the proportion of his faith** would relate objectively to the prophet's being careful to preach in accordance with the gospel revealed through the apostles—"the faith which was once for all delivered to the saints" (Jude 3). It could also relate subjectively to the believer's personal understanding and insight concerning the gospel—to his speaking **according to the** individual **proportion of . . . faith** that God has sovereignly assigned to him for the operation of his gift.

Whether it relates to revelation, prediction, declaration, instruction, encouragement, or anything else, all **prophecy** was always to proclaim the Word of God and exalt the Son of God, because "the testimony of Jesus is the spirit of prophecy" (Rev. 19:10). Paul's specific charge to Timothy applies to all proclaimers of God's Word, including prophets: "Preach the word; be ready in season and out of season; reprove, rebuke, exhort, with great patience and instruction" (2 Tim. 4:2).

SERVICE

if service, in his serving; (12:7a)

The second spiritual gift is that of service, a general term for ministry. Service translates *diakonia,* from which we also get *deacon* and *deaconess*—those who serve. The first deacons in the early church were "men of good reputation, full of the Spirit and of wisdom" who were placed in charge of providing food for the widows in order to free the apostles to devote themselves "to prayer, and to the ministry of the word" (Acts 6:3-4).

Service is a simple, straightforward gift that is broad in its application. It seems to carry a meaning similar to that of the gift of helps mentioned in 1 Corinthians 12:28, although a different Greek term (*antilēpsis*) is used there. This gift certainly applies beyond the offices of deacon and deaconess and is the idea in Paul's charge to the Ephesian elders to "help the weak" (Acts 20:35). The gift of service is manifested in every sort of practical help that Christians can give one another in Jesus' name.

TEACHING

or he who teaches, in his teaching; (12:7b)

The third spiritual gift is that of **teaching.** Again, the meaning is simple and straightforward. *Didaskōn* **(teaches)** refers to the act of teaching, and *didaskalia* **(teaching)** can refer to what is taught as well as to the act of teaching it. Both of those meanings are appropriate to this gift.

The Christian **who teaches** is divinely gifted with special ability to interpret and present God's truth understandably. The primary difference between teaching and prophesying is not in content but in the distinction between the ability to proclaim and the ability to give systematic and regular instruction in God's Word. The gift of **teaching** could apply to a teacher in seminary, Christian college, Sunday school, or any other place, elementary or advanced, where God's truth is taught. The earliest church was characterized by regular teaching (Acts 2:42). The Great Commission includes the command, "Go therefore and make disciples of all the nations,...teaching them to observe all that I commanded you" (Matt. 28:19-20). Paul's spiritual gift included features of both preaching and teaching (2 Tim. 1:11).

Later in the epistle just cited, Paul charged Timothy:"And the things which you have heard from me in the presence of many witnesses, these entrust to faithful men, who will be able to teach others also" (2 Tim. 2:2).Barnabas had that gift and ministered it in Antioch beside Paul, where they were "teaching and preaching, with many others also, the word of the Lord" (Acts 15:35). Likewise "a certain Jew named Apollos, an Alexandrian by birth, an eloquent man,...had been instructed in the way of the Lord; and being fervent in spirit, he was speaking and teaching accurately the things concerning Jesus" (Acts 18:24-25).

Jesus, of course, was both the supreme Preacher and supreme Teacher. Even after His resurrection, He continued to teach. When He joined the two disciples on the road to Emmaus,"beginning with Moses and with all the prophets, He explained to them the things concerning Himself in all the Scriptures....And they said to one another,'Were not our hearts burning within us while He was speaking to us on the road, while He was explaining the Scriptures to us?'" (Luke 24:27, 32). Both *diermēneuō* ("explained," v. 27) and *dianoigō* ("explaining," lit. "opening up," v. 32) are synonyms of *didaskōn* **(teaches)** and *didaskalia* **(teaching)** in Romans 12:7.

Regular, systematic teaching of the Word of God is the primary function of the pastor-teacher. As an elder, he is required "to teach" (1 Tim. 3:2) and to hold "fast the faithful word which is in accordance with the teaching, that he may be able both to exhort in sound doctrine and to refute those who contradict" (Titus 1:9).Above all, Paul entreated Timothy,"pay close attention to yourself and to your teaching" (1 Tim. 4:16). Pastors are not the only ones the Lord calls and empowers to teach. But if a pastor's ministry is to be judged, among other things, on the soundness of his teaching—as the passages just cited indicate—then it seems reasonable to assume that, in some measure, he should have the gift of **teaching.**

EXHORTATION

or he who exhorts, in his exhortation; (12:8*a*)

As with the previous three gifts, the connotation of **exhortation** is broad. Both the verb *parakaleō* **(exhorts)** and the noun *paraklēsis* **(exhortation)** are compounds of the same two Greek words *(para* and *kaleō)* and have the literal meaning of calling someone to one's side.

They are closely related to *paraklētos* (advocate, comforter, helper), a title Jesus used both of Himself ("Helper," John 14:16) and of the Holy Spirit ("another Helper"; John 14:16, 26; 15:26; 16:7). In 1 John 2:1, this word is translated "Advocate," referring to Jesus Christ.

The gift of **exhortation,** therefore, encompasses the ideas of advising, pleading, encouraging, warning, strengthening, and comforting. At one time the gift may be used to persuade a believer to turn from a sin or bad habit and at a later time to encourage that same person to maintain his corrected behavior. The gift may be used to admonish the church as a whole to obedience to the Word. Like the gift of showing mercy (see below), **exhortation** may be exercised in comforting a brother or sister in the Lord who is facing trouble or is suffering physically or emotionally. One **who exhorts** may also be used of God to encourage and undergird a weak believer who is facing a difficult trial or persistent temptation. Sometimes he may use his gift simply to walk beside a friend who is grieving, discouraged, frustrated, or depressed, to give help in whatever way is needed. This gift may be exercised in helping someone carry a burden that is too heavy to bear alone.

Paul and Barnabas were exercising the ministry of **exhortation** when "they returned to Lystra and to Iconium and to Antioch, strengthening the souls of the disciples, encouraging them to continue in the faith, and saying, 'Through many tribulations we must enter the kingdom of God'" (Acts 14:21-22). This ministry is reflected in Paul's charge to Timothy to "reprove, rebuke, exhort, with great patience and instruction" (2 Tim. 4:2).

It is the ministry of **exhortation** of which the writer of Hebrews speaks as he admonishes believers to "consider how to stimulate one another to love and good deeds, not forsaking our own assembling together, as is the habit of some, but encouraging one another; and all the more, as you see the day drawing near" (Heb. 10:24-25). The sentiment that motivates this gift is also exhibited in the beautiful benediction with which that epistle closes: "Now the God of peace, who brought up from the dead the great Shepherd of the sheep through the blood of the eternal covenant, even Jesus our Lord, equip you in every good thing to do His will, working in us that which is pleasing in His sight, through Jesus Christ, to whom be the glory forever and ever. Amen" (13:20-21).

In summary, it might be said that, just as prophecy proclaims the truth and teaching systematizes and explains the truth, **exhortation** calls believers to obey and follow the truth, to live as Christians are supposed to live—consistent with God's revealed will. In many servants of Christ, all of these abilities are uniquely and beautifully blended.

GIVING

he who gives, with liberality; (12:8*b*)

The fifth category of giftedness is that of giving. The usual Greek verb for giving is *didōmi*, but the word here is the intensified *metadidōmi*, which carries the additional meanings of sharing and imparting that which is one's own. The one who exercises this gift **gives** sacrificially of himself.

When asked by the multitudes what they should do to "bring forth fruits in keeping with repentance," John the Baptist replied, "Let the man who has two tunics share *[metadidōi]* with him who has none; and let him who has food do likewise (Luke 3:8, 11).

In the opening of his letter to Rome, Paul expressed his desire to "impart *[metadidōi]* some spiritual gift to you, that you may be established" (Rom. 1:11). And in his letter to Ephesus he makes clear that, whether or not a believer has the gift of giving, he is to have the spirit of generosity that characterizes this gift. Every Christian should "labor, performing with his own hands what is good, in order that he may have something to share *[metadidōi]* with him who has need" (Eph. 4:28). It seems certain that Paul had elements of such generosity in his gift. And nowhere is it reflected more than in his service to the saints at Thessalonica. After having ministered to them for a relatively short time, he could say with perfect humility and sincerity that the gospel that he, Sylvanus, and Timothy brought them "did not come to you in word only, but also in power and in the Holy Spirit and with full conviction; just as you know what kind of men we proved to be among you for your sake" (1 Thess. 1:5; cf. 1:1). "Having thus a fond affection for you," he continued a few verses later, "we were well-pleased to impart *[metadidōi]* to you not only the gospel of God but also our own lives, because you had become very dear to us" (2:8).

Liberality translates *haplotēs,* which has the root meaning of singleness and came to connote simplicity (as in the KJV), singlemindedness, openheartedness, and then generosity. It carries the idea of sincere, heartfelt giving that is untainted by affectation or ulterior motive. The Christian **who gives with liberality** gives himself, not *for* himself. He does not give for thanks or recognition, but for the sake of the one who receives his help and for the glory of the Lord.

Those who give **with liberality** are the opposite of those who "sound a trumpet before [themselves], as the hypocrites do in the synagogues and in the streets, that they may be honored by men" (Matt. 6:2). Ananias and Sapphira were struck dead by God for lying to the Holy Spirit, and behind their lie was the selfish desire to hold back for themselves some of the proceeds from the sale of their property (Acts 5:1-10). In that tragic instance, failing to give **with liberality** cost the lives of the givers.

Ananias and Sapphira were exceptions in the early church, which was characterized by those who voluntarily possessed "all things in common; and [who] began selling their property and possessions, and were sharing them with all, as anyone might have need" (Acts 2:44-45). Because the inns could not begin to house all the Jews who came to Jerusalem at the feast of Pentecost, most of them stayed in homes of fellow Jews. But those who trusted in Christ immediately became unwelcome. Many wanted to stay within the community of believers in Jerusalem but had no place to stay. Some had difficulty buying food to eat. In that crisis, Christians who had the means spontaneously shared their homes, their food, and their money with fellow believers in need.

Many years later, the churches of Macedonia had an abundance of believers who exercised the gift of giving to its fullest. "In a great ordeal of affliction their abundance of joy and their deep poverty overflowed in the wealth of their liberality," Paul said. "For I testify that according to their ability, and beyond their ability they gave of their own accord, begging us with much entreaty for the favor of participation in the support of the saints, and this, not as we had expected, but they first gave themselves to the Lord and to us by the will of God" (2 Cor. 8:2-5). They gave **with** great **liberality,** believing that sowing bountifully meant reaping bountifully (2 Cor. 9:6).

LEADERSHIP

he who leads, with diligence; (12:8c)

Leads is from *proistēmi,* which has the basic meaning of "standing before" others and, hence, the idea of leadership. In the New Testament it is never used of governmental rulers but of headship in the family (1 Tim. 3:4, 5, 12) and in the church (1 Tim. 5:17). In 1 Corinthians 12:28, Paul refers to the same gift by a different name, "administrations" (*kubernēsis*), which means "to guide." In Acts 27:11 and Revelation 18:17, it is used of a pilot or helmsman, the person who steers, or **leads,** a ship.

Although it is not limited to those offices, the gift of church leadership clearly belongs to elders, deacons, and deaconesses. It is significant that Paul makes no mention of leaders in his first letter to Corinth. Lack of a functioning leadership would help explain its serious moral and spiritual problems, which certainly would have been exacerbated by that deficiency. "Free-for-all" democracy amounts to anarchy and is disastrous in any society, including the church. The absence of leaders results in everyone doing what is "right in his own eyes," as the Israelites did under the judges (Judg. 17:6; 21:25; cf. Deut. 12:8).

Effective leadership must be done **with diligence,** with earnestness and zeal. *Spoudē* **(diligence)** can also carry the idea of haste (see Mark 6:25; Luke 1:39). Proper leadership therefore precludes procrastination and idleness. Whether it is possessed by church officers or by members who direct such things as Sunday school, the youth group, the nursery, or a building program, the gift of leadership is to be exercised with carefulness, constancy, and consistency.

SHOWING MERCY

he who shows mercy, with cheerfulness. (12:8*d*)

The seventh and last spiritual category mentioned here is that of showing **mercy.** *Eleeō* **(shows mercy)** carries the joint idea of actively demonstrating sympathy for someone else and of having the necessary resources to successfully comfort and strengthen that person.

The gifted Christian **who shows mercy** is divinely endowed with special sensitivity to suffering and sorrow, with the ability to notice misery and distress that may go unnoticed by others, and with the desire and means to help alleviate such afflictions. This gift involves much more than sympathetic feeling. It is feeling put into action. The Christian with this gift always finds a way to express his feelings of concern in practical help. He **shows** his **mercy** by what he says to and what he does for the one in need.

The believer **who shows mercy** may exercise his gift in hospital visitation, jail ministry, or in service to the homeless, the poor, the handicapped, the suffering, and the sorrowing. This gift is closely related to that of exhortation, and it is not uncommon for believers to have a measure of both.

This enablement is not to be ministered grudgingly or merely out of a sense of duty, but **with cheerfulness.** As everyone knows who has had a time of suffering or special need, the attitude of a fellow believer can make the difference between his being a help or a hindrance. The counsel of Job's friends only drove him into deeper despair.

"He who despises his neighbor sins," the writer of Proverbs tells us, "but happy is he who is gracious to the poor" (Prov. 14:21); and "He who oppresses the poor reproaches his Maker, but he who is gracious to the needy honors Him" (Prov. 14:31). The keyword in those verses is *gracious*. The genuine helper always serves with gracious **cheerfulness,** and is never condescending or patronizing.

Reading from the book of Isaiah, Jesus testified of Himself that "the Spirit of the Lord is upon Me, because He anointed Me to preach the gospel to the poor. He has sent Me to proclaim release to the captives, and recovery of sight to the blind, to set free those who are downtrodden, to proclaim the favorable year of the Lord" (Luke 4:18-19). The very Son of God in His incarnation showed great mercy with gracious **cheerfulness.**

Would that all Christians with this gift not only would minister it cheerfully but also regularly and consistently. There would be far fewer needy who have to depend on a godless, impersonal government or social agency. And if Christ's people patterned their lives after His gracious example, far more people would hear and respond to the saving gospel that meets their deepest need.

In regard to that gift and every other, believers should "kindle afresh the gift of God which is in [them]" (2 Tim. 1:6).

The prolific Puritan John Owen wrote that spiritual gifts are that without which the church cannot subsist in the world, nor can believers be useful to one another and the rest of mankind to the glory of Christ as they ought to be. They are the powers of the world to come, those effectual operations of the power of Christ whereby His kingdom was erected and is preserved (see *The Holy Spirit* [Grand Rapids: Kregel, n.d.]).

Although we obviously must pay attention to our gift, we can never faithfully exercise it by focusing on the gift itself. They can be used fully of the Lord only as "with unveiled face beholding as in a mirror the glory of the Lord, [we] are being transformed into the same image from glory to glory, just as from the Lord, the Spirit" (2 Cor. 3:18). We can serve Christ only as we become like Christ, and we can exercise the Spirit's gifts only as we present ourselves as living sacrifices and submit to His continuing transformation and sanctification of our lives.

A. B. Simpson's beautiful hymn expresses what the true attitude about our spiritual gifts and all the rest of our lives should be:

> Once it was the blessing,
> Now it is the Lord.
> Once it was the feeling,
> Now it is His Word.
> Once His gifts I wanted,
> Now the Giver alone.
> Once I sought healing,
> Now Himself alone.

Supernatural Living —part 1 (Romans 12:9-13)

14

Let love be without hypocrisy. Abhor what is evil; cling to what is good. Be devoted to one another in brotherly love; give preference to one another in honor; not lagging behind in diligence, fervent in spirit, serving the Lord; rejoicing in hope, persevering in tribulation, devoted to prayer, contributing to the needs of the saints, practicing hospitality. (12:9-13)

Our society is obsessed with sports, recreation, entertainment, and emotional gratification, and it is paying the consequences of that unbalanced preoccupation. When such pursuits exceed their reasonable roles, they become conspicuous marks of the shallow, superficial, and often decadent society that cultivates them. "Bodily discipline is only of little profit," Paul cautions, "but godliness is profitable for all things, since it holds promise for the present life and also for the life to come" (1 Tim. 4:8).

Teddy Roosevelt once commented, "The things that will destroy America are prosperity at any price, peace at any price, safety first instead of duty first, the love of soft living and the get-rich theory of life." That observation is still valid.

The only productive life, as well as the only truly satisfying life, is the self-disciplined life. That is certainly true of the Christian life. Although our spiritual guidance and power come from the Lord, He can only work effectively through lives that are subjected to Him. "Everyone who competes in the games exercises self-control in all things," Paul reminded the church at Corinth. "They then do it to receive a perishable wreath, but we an imperishable. Therefore I run in such a way, as not without aim; I box in such a way, as not beating the air; but I buffet my body and make it my slave, lest possibly, after I have preached to others, I myself should be disqualified" (1 Cor. 9:25-27).

Only the disciplined mind can think clearly and be used of the Lord to properly understand and present His truth to the world. Only the disciplined mind can effectively evaluate and challenge the world's ideals and standards in the light of that truth. By the same token, only the disciplined Christian life can be a persuasive and effective example, both within the church and before the world.

In his book *The Disciplined Life,* Richard Shelley Taylor writes,

> Disciplined character belongs to the person who achieves balance by bringing all his faculties and powers under control. . . . He resolutely faces his duty. He is governed by a sense of responsibility. He has inward resources and personal reserves which are the wonder of weaker souls. He brings adversity under tribute, and compels it to serve him. When adversity becomes too overwhelming and blows fall which he cannot parry, he bows to them, but is not broken by them. His spirit still soars. The strong character of Madam Guyon [the early eighteenth-century French evangelical] enabled her, though imprisoned, to rise in spirit and sing:
>
> > My cage confines me round;
> >   Abroad I cannot fly.
> > But though my wing is closely bound,
> >   My heart's at liberty.
> > My prison walls cannot control
> >   The flight, the freedom of the soul.
>
> (Kansas City, Mo.: Beacon Hill, 1962, 22)

Simply put, self-discipline is the willingness to subordinate personal desires and objectives to those that are selfless and divine, to subordinate that which is attractive and easy to that which is right and necessary. For the Christian, self-discipline is obedience to the Word of God, the willingness to subordinate everything in our lives—physical, emotional, social, intellectual, moral, and spiritual—to God's will and control, and for God's glory.

It is as absurd as it is unbiblical to believe that anyone can live a faithful, fruitful Christian life on mere good intentions and warm feelings for the Lord and His work. The Christian life is an accountable life, and, by definition, accountability is based on specific principles and standards. For the Christian, they are the divinely-revealed principles and standards to which God holds each of His children. It is because we are accountable that the Lord disciplines us when we disobey His Word and ignore His will.

"You have forgotten the exhortation which is addressed to you as sons," the writer of Hebrews reminds us: "'My son, do not regard lightly the discipline of the Lord, nor faint when you are reproved by Him; for those whom the Lord loves He disciplines, and He scourges every son whom He receives.' It is for discipline that you endure; God deals with you as with sons; for what son is there whom his father does not discipline? . . . All discipline for the moment seems not to be joyful, but sorrowful; yet to those who have been trained by it, afterwards it yields the peaceful fruit of righteousness" (Heb. 12:5-7, 11; cf. Prov. 3:11-12).

The nineteenth-century Englishman Robert C. Chapman wrote, "Seeing that so many preach Christ and so few live Christ, I will aim to live Him." His good friend J. N. Darby said of him, "He lives what I teach."

It was said of the popular nineteenth-century English author William Arnot, "His preaching is good. His writing is better. His living is best of all." Would that it could be said of all Christians that their living is best of all.

A young man once asked me, "How can you know if you are truly a Christian? How can you know if your decision for Christ wasn't just an emotional experience?" I replied, "The only way to know if we have experienced justification, been made right with Him and been brought into His family, is by looking at our heart and our lives. If Christ is our Savior and Lord, the deepest desire of our hearts will be to serve and to please Him, and that desire will be expressed in a longing for holiness and a pattern of righteous living." It is not that our lives will have become perfect or that we will never waver in our commitment and obedience, but that the direction of our lives will be godward, that our supreme desire will be to become more and more like Christ.

Although he rejected both the Bible and God, Julian Huxley correctly noted that "it doesn't take much of a man to be a Christian, it just takes all of him." Henry Drummond, a close friend of D. L. Moody, said, "The entrance fee to God's kingdom is nothing, but the annual dues are everything."

A person who has been justified by God's grace, who has presented his body as "a living and holy sacrifice" (Rom. 12:1), and who is exercising the spiritual gifts the Lord has given him (vv. 3-8), will experience an outflowing of sanctified, spiritual living. In other words, a person who is truly saved will evidence his salvation by the way he lives. And because the obedient, disciplined, and productive Christian life is directed and empowered by God's own Spirit, Christian living is supernatural living. In that sense, it is abnormal, unnatural living—living that is not natural to and cannot be attained by the unregenerate man.

Supernatural living is conducted "in a manner worthy of the gospel of Christ" (Phil. 1:27). Supernatural living is "to have this attitude in [ourselves] which was also in Christ Jesus" (2:5) and humbly to "work out [our] salvation with fear and trembling" (2:12). But the working out of our salvation is no more accomplished in our own power than the new birth was accomplished in our own power. "It is God who is at work in [us], both to will and to work for His good pleasure" (2:13).

In short, supernatural living is conforming our outer lives to our inner lives, living out the redeemed, purified, and holy nature we have in Jesus Christ, becoming in practice what we are in position and new creation.

But supernatural living is not a mystical, undefined life based on elusive good impulses and sincere intentions. It is practical living that results from conscious obedience to God's standards of righteousness, a life lived within divinely-ordained parameters. It is thinking, speaking, and acting in daily conformity with God's Word and will.

Supernatural living is free in that it is no longer under the bondage of sin. But it also is enslaved, in that it is unalterably bound to the righteous will of God. "Thanks be to God," Paul has declared earlier in this letter, "that though [we] were slaves of sin, [we] became obedient from the heart to that form of teaching to which [we] were committed, and having been freed from sin, [we] became slaves of righteousness" (Rom. 6:17-18). With Martin Luther, every Christian should be able to say, "My conscience is captive to the Word of God."

Through Romans 12:8, Paul has laid the doctrinal foundation of the justified, sanctified, and dedicated Christian life. In the rest of the epistle, he focuses on specific ways in which believers must live their lives in obedience to God's Word and to the glory of His name. The call to practical, holy living is the climax of this rich epistle.

In 12:9-21, Paul gives a comprehensive, but not exhaustive, list of the basic characteristics of the supernatural Christian life. In essence, he is giving the same admonition he had given to Corinthian believers a year or so earlier: "Therefore, having these promises, beloved, let us cleanse ourselves from all defilement of flesh and spirit, perfecting holiness in the fear of God" (2 Cor. 7:1). It is because of all that God has done for us and all that He has equipped us with that we are to respond by faithful, obedient, Spirit-empowered living. We are God's "workmanship," Paul explained to the church at Ephesus, "created in Christ Jesus for good works, which God prepared beforehand, that we should walk in them" (Eph. 2:10). Salvation is designed to produce in us an unmistakable pattern of godly, righteous living. We will bear some fruit, but the Lord wants us to bear much fruit to His glory (John 15:8). All of these characteristics will be the desires of the inner new creation, and Paul urges believers to submit the flesh to these inner holy longings and to manifest these virtues as a regular pattern of life. These qualities are not foreign to our nature but to what we desire, so that, as our will submits to the Word and Spirit, the qualities become reality.

In the present text (12:9-21), Paul gives some twenty-five distinct but closely related exhortations. Any believer who honestly appraises his life by these standards cannot help being convicted of falling far short of the perfection the inner person desires. On the other hand, however, the believer who is walking in the Spirit will see the Spirit working out these precepts in his life to a greater and greater extent. An honest look at our lives in light of these precepts will bring conviction about our failure to keep some of them and confidence about our success in keeping others. Where we fall short, we should ask the Lord's help. Where we have been faithful, we should give Him thanks and praise.

The specific exhortations fall under four general categories or phases, which form an ever-increasing circle, as it were, that expands from personal attitudes to the widest social applications. They are: personal duties (v. 9); family duties (vv. 10-13); duty to other people in general (vv. 14-16); and duty to those who are avowed personal enemies (vv. 17-21).

PERSONAL DUTIES

Let love be without hypocrisy. Abhor what is evil; cling to what is good. (12:9)

In one of several triplets (see also vv. 11, 12, 16), Paul mentions three personal duties of supernatural living.

LOVE WITHOUT HYPOCRISY (12:9*a*)

The first duty is, **Let love be without hypocrisy.** The greatest virtue of the Christian life is love. The use of *agapē* **(love)** was rare in pagan Greek literature, doubtless because the concept it represented —unselfish, self-giving, willful devotion—was so uncommon in that culture it was even ridiculed and despised as a sign of weakness. But in the New Testament it is proclaimed as the supreme virtue, the virtue under which all others are subsumed. *Agapē* **love** centers on the needs and welfare of the one loved and will pay whatever personal price is necessary to meet those needs and foster that welfare.

God Himself "is love, and the one who abides in love abides in God, and God abides in him" (1 John 4:16). Jesus made unequivocally clear that in both the Old and New Testaments the two greatest commandments are: "You shall love the Lord your God with all your heart, and with all your soul, and with all your mind" and "You shall love your neighbor as yourself" (Matt. 22:37-39). In fact, He went on to say, "On these two commandments depend the whole Law and the Prophets" (v. 40). Echoing that same truth, Paul later admonishes in his letter to Rome, "Owe nothing to anyone except to love one another; for he who loves his neighbor has fulfilled the law" (13:8; cf. v. 10).

Love is more important to a Christian than any spiritual gift he may have. "But now abide faith, hope, love, these three," Paul explained to the Corinthian believers, "but the greatest of these is love" (1 Cor. 13:13; cf. 12:31). It is therefore not surprising that the first "fruit of the Spirit is love" (Gal. 5:22) and that it is by our love for our fellow believers that "all men will know that [we are Jesus'] disciples" (John 13:35). In behalf of the Thessalonian believers, Paul prayed, "May the Lord cause you to increase and abound in love for one another" (1 Thess. 3:12; cf. 1 John 3:18). Suffering "much endurance, in afflictions, in hardships, in distresses, in beatings, in imprisonments, in tumults, in labors, in sleeplessness, in hunger," Paul himself served the Lord's people "in the Holy Spirit, in genuine love" (2 Cor. 6:4-6).

It is that same unfeigned love of one another that Peter admonishes all believers to exhibit: "Since you have in obedience to the truth purified your souls for a sincere love of the brethren, fervently love one another from the heart" (1 Pet. 1:22). Later in the same letter, the apostle repeats the command: "Above all, keep fervent in your love for one another, because love covers a multitude of sins" (1 Pet. 4:8).

Genuine love is so integral to supernatural living that John declares, "We know that we have passed out of death into life, because we love the brethren. He who does not love abides in death" (1 John 3:14). In other words, a person who shows no evidence of *agapē* **love** has no claim on Christ or on eternal life.

A Jewish woman who lived near our church was refused marriage counseling by her synagogue because she had not paid her dues. She was upset and determined to go to the nearest religious institution to get help. As she walked past our church one Sunday morning, she soon found herself inside. As she explained later, she was drawn to her Messiah and Savior that day because she could sense the great love manifested by our members for each other.

The love of which Paul, Peter, and John speak is genuine love, the sincere and fervent love that is completely **without hypocrisy** and untainted by self-centeredness. Christian love is pure, guileless, and unaffected.

Hypocrisy is the antithesis of and completely incompatible with *agapē* **love.** The two cannot coexist. **Hypocrisy** is exceeded in evil only by unbelief. The consummate hypocrite in Scripture, Judas, was also the consummate egoist. He feigned devotion to Jesus to achieve his own selfish purposes. His hypocrisy was unmasked and his self-centeredness was made evident when he betrayed Jesus for the thirty pieces of silver. Commenting on this verse in Romans, the theologian John Murray writes, "If love is the sum of virtue and hypocrisy is the epitome of vice, what a contradiction to bring the two together."

HATE EVIL (12:9*b*)

The second longing of the new nature and personal duty of supernatural living is to **abhor what is evil.** Hatred of evil is the other side of love, which, by its very nature, cannot approve of or "rejoice in unrighteousness" (1 Cor. 13:6). **Evil** is the antithesis of holiness and therefore the antithesis of godliness. Just as "Fear of the Lord is the beginning of wisdom" (Prov. 9:10), "Fear of the Lord [also] is to hate evil" (Prov. 8:13). The child of God abhors evil because God abhors evil.

Evil is the enemy of God and the enemy of love, and it is to be as fervently abhorred as love is to be fervently coveted. It is for that reason the psalmist commands, "Hate evil, you who love the Lord" (Ps. 97:10). The Christian who genuinely loves will genuinely **abhor what is evil.** Because of his great love for God, David determined, "A perverse heart shall depart from me; I will know no evil" (Ps. 101:4). The faithful believer can strike no settlement with evil, every form and degree of which will be avoided.

Even the great apostle struggled against sin. Earlier in this letter to Rome, Paul confessed, "I am of flesh, sold into bondage to sin. For that which I am doing, I do not understand; for I am not practicing what I would like to do, but I am doing the very thing I hate.... For the good that I wish, I do not do; but I practice the very evil that I do not wish. But if I am doing the very thing I do not wish, I am no longer the one doing it, but sin which dwells in me. I find then the principle that evil is present in me, the one who wishes to do good" (Rom. 7:14-15, 19-21). In other words, when believers fall back into sin, their inner, godly self will resolutely disapprove.

Jude admonishes, "But you, beloved, building yourselves up on your most holy faith; praying in the Holy Spirit; keep yourselves in the love of God, waiting anxiously for the mercy of our Lord Jesus Christ to eternal life. And have mercy on some, who are doubting; save others, snatching them out of the fire; and on some have mercy with fear, hating even the garment polluted by the flesh" (Jude 20-21, 23). In other words, when we witness to the unsaved, we must be careful that in our zeal to win them we do not allow ourselves to be drawn into sins from which they need deliverance. Doctors and nurses are dedicated to helping those who are ill, even from the deadliest diseases, but they take every precaution to protect themselves from those diseases, lest they, too, become infected.

"Demas, having loved this present world, has deserted me," Paul sadly reported to Timothy (2 Tim. 4:10). Demas's love of sin was greater than his love for the Lord, the Lord's people, and the Lord's work.

Someone has said that the only security against sin is to be shocked by it. The constant bombardment of our senses through TV newspapers, magazines, movies, and books with the immoralities, violence, and perversions of modern society makes it difficult to be shocked by anything. Tragically, many Christians regularly entertain themselves with sheer ungodliness, perhaps rationalizing that, simply by being a Christian, they are somehow immune from sinful infection.

Genuine hatred of evil engenders avoidance of evil. In his *Essay on Man*, Alexander Pope wisely observed that,

> Vice is a monster of so frightful mien,
> As to be hated needs but to be seen;
> Yet seen too oft, familiar with her face,
> We first endure, then pity, then embrace.

That stanza reflects the progression found in the first Psalm: "How blessed is the man who does not walk in the counsel of the wicked, nor stand in the path of sinners, nor sit in the seat of scoffers!" (1:1). We cannot flirt with sin and escape falling into it. Refusing to be enticed even by the first, seemingly harmless attractions of sin, the righteous man delights "in the law of the Lord, and in His law he meditates day and night" (v. 2).

Even among pagans, Corinth was known as "sin city," and many believers in the church there had great difficulty giving up the ways of their old life. Paul warned that their only safe response to the allures of sexual immorality and idolatry was to "flee" from them (1 Cor. 6:18; 10:14). He warned Timothy that "the love of money is a root of all sorts of evil, and some by longing for it have wandered away from the faith, and pierced themselves with many a pang" (1 Tim. 6:10). Again his advice was simple and direct: "Flee from these things, you man of God; and pursue righteousness, godliness, faith, love, perseverance and gentleness" (v. 11). Paul repeated that counsel to Timothy in the second letter: "Flee from youthful lusts, and pursue righteousness, faith, love and peace, with those who call on the Lord from a pure heart" (2 Tim. 2:22). It is impossible to pursue righteousness while we tolerate evil.

"There are six things which the Lord hates, yes, seven which are an abomination to Him," the writer of Proverbs tells us. They are: "Haughty eyes, a lying tongue, and hands that shed innocent blood, a heart that devises wicked plans, feet that run rapidly to evil, a false witness who utters lies, and one who spreads strife among brothers" (Prov. 6:16-19). Obviously, that is not an exhaustive list, but a representative sampling of the countless sins that man has devised to disobey the Lord and reject His ways.

Greater exposure to evil should invoke greater resistance to it, no matter how often or how intensely we are confronted by it. We must "examine everything carefully; hold fast to that which is good [and] abstain from every form of evil" (1 Thess. 5:21-22). Because "we have the mind of Christ" (1 Cor. 2:16), we must, like Him, love righteousness and hate sin (Heb. 1:9). We are to love what He loves and hate what He hates.

HOLD ON TO THE GOOD (12:9c)

The third personal duty of supernatural living is to **cling to what is good.** The verb *kollaō* (to **cling**) is from *kolla* **(glue)** and came to be used of any bond—physical, emotional, or spiritual. As servants of Jesus Christ, we are to bind ourselves **to what is good** (*agathos*), that which is inherently right and worthy.

The **good** is "whatever is true, whatever is honorable, whatever is right, whatever is pure, whatever is lovely, whatever is of good repute." And "if there is any excellence and if anything worthy of praise," Paul continues, "let your mind dwell on [or **cling to**] these things" (Phil. 4:8).

In 1 Thessalonians 5:21-22, the apostle gives similar instruction: "Examine everything carefully; hold fast to that which is good; abstain from every form of evil." That is clearly a call to discernment, the thoughtful, careful evaluation of everything, so we can decide, judged against God's Word, what to reject and what to cling to.

As Paul has already explained, the key to finding and following **what is good** is in not being "conformed to this world, but [being] transformed by the renewing of [our] mind, that [we] may prove what the will of God is, that which is good and acceptable and perfect" (Rom. 12:2). As we separate ourselves from the things of the world and saturate ourselves with the Word of God, the things that are good will more and more replace the things that are evil.

DUTY TO THE FAMILY OF GOD

Be devoted to one another in brotherly love; give preference to one another in honor; not lagging behind in diligence, fervent in spirit, serving the Lord; rejoicing in hope, persevering in tribulation, devoted to prayer, contributing to the needs of the saints, practicing hospitality. (12:10-13)

The second phase of supernatural living concerns a wider dimension—largely pertaining to the believer's duty to fellow members in the family of God.

BE DEVOTED IN BROTHERLY LOVE (12:10*a*)

Paul's list of ten "family" obligations begins with the command: **Be devoted to one another in brotherly love.**

Be devoted to and **brotherly love** carry synonymous ideas. **Devoted** translates ***philostorgos,*** a compound of ***philos*** (friend, friendly; friendship love) and *storgē* (natural family love, which is not based on personal attraction or desirability). **Brotherly love** translates ***Philadelphia,*** another compound—*phileō*(to have tender affection) and ***adelphos*** (brother). We are to have a loving filial affection for **one another** in the family of God.

Devoted . . . brotherly love is one of the marks by which the world will know that we belong to Christ. "By this all men will know that you are My disciples, if you have love for one another" (John 13:35). This love is not optional for believers. It not only is required but is inescapable, because "whoever loves the Father loves the child born of Him" (1 John 5:1). In fact, as John has just declared, "If someone says, 'I love God,' and hates his brother, he is a liar; for the one who does not love his brother whom he has seen, cannot love God whom he has not seen" (4:20).

Brotherly love reflects the nature of Christians. That is why Paul could say, "Now as to the love of the brethren, you have no need for anyone to write to you, for you yourselves are taught by God to love one another" (1 Thess. 4:9). Being "taught by God," the true child of God knows intuitively that he is to love his spiritual brothers and sisters.

For the very reason that God is our common heavenly Father, love for each other should be as natural and normal as family members' affectionate love for each other.

The apostle John forcefully affirms that truth. "The one who says he is in the light and yet hates his brother is in the darkness until now. The one who loves his brother abides in the light and there is no cause for stumbling in him. But the one who hates his brother is in the darkness and walks in the darkness, and does not know where he is going because the darkness has blinded his eyes" (1 John 2:9-11). In the next chapter the apostle uses even stronger words: "By this the children of God and the children of the devil are obvious: anyone who does not practice righteousness is not of God, nor the one who does not love his brother....But whoever has the world's goods, and beholds his brother in need and closes his heart against him, how does the love of God abide in him? Little children, let us not love with word or with tongue, but in deed and truth. We shall know by this that we are of the truth, and shall assure our heart before Him" (1 John 3:10,17-19).

PREFER ONE ANOTHER IN HONOR (12:10*b*)

If we are truly "devoted to one another in brotherly love," it almost goes without saying that we will **give preference to one another in honor.** The virtue here is humility, not thinking more highly of ourselves than we ought to think (Rom. 12:3). It is doing "nothing from selfishness or empty conceit, but with humility of mind," regarding "one another as more important than" oneself (Phil. 2:3).

Proegēomai **(give preference)** has the basic meaning of going before, or leading. But the idea here is not that of putting ourselves before others in regard to importance or worth but the very opposite idea of giving **honor** to fellow believers by putting them first.

To **honor** is not to flatter, to give hypocritical praise in hope of having the compliment returned or of gaining favor with the one honored. Again, the very opposite is in mind. To **honor** is to show genuine appreciation and admiration for **one another** in the family of God. We are to be quick to show respect, quick to acknowledge the accomplishments of others, quick to demonstrate genuine love by *not* being jealous or envious, which have no part in love, whether *agapē* or *Philadelphia.*

DO NOT LAG IN DILIGENCE (12:11*a*)

Not lagging behind in diligence could be rendered, "not lazy in zeal and intensity." A few verses earlier, Paul declares that the Christian who has the gift of ruling, or leading, should exercise it with diligence (v. 8).

In the context of Romans 12, **diligence** refers to whatever believers do in their supernatural living. Whatever is worth doing in the Lord's service is worth doing with enthusiasm and care. Jesus told His disciples that He "must work the works of Him who sent Me, as long as it is day; night is coming, when no man can work" (John 9:4). The Lord knew His time of ministry was limited and that every moment in His Father's service on earth should count for the most possible. Paul admonished believers in the Galatian churches: "So then, while we have opportunity, let us do good to all men, and especially to those who are of the household of the faith" (Gal. 6:10; cf. 2 Thess. 3:13).

There is no room for sloth and indolence in the Lord's work. "Whatever your hand finds to do," Solomon counseled, "verily, do it with all your might; for there is no activity or planning or knowledge or wisdom in Sheol [the grave]" (Eccles. 9:10). Whatever we do for the Lord must be done in this present life.

Slothfulness in Christian living not only prevents good from being done but allows evil to prosper. "Therefore be careful how you walk," Paul charged the Ephesians, "not as unwise men, but as wise, making the most of your time, because the days are evil" (Eph. 5:15-16). "He also who is slack in his work is brother to him who destroys " (Prov. 18:9). For weeds to prosper, the gardener need only leave the garden alone.

The Lord rewards those who serve Him with **diligence.** "God is not unjust so as to forget your work and the love which you have shown toward His name, in having ministered and in still ministering to the saints. And we desire that each one of you show the same diligence so as to realize the full assurance of hope until the end, that you may not be sluggish, but imitators of those who through faith and patience inherit the promises" (Heb. 6:10-12).

BE FERVENT IN SPIRIT (12:11b)

Whereas diligence pertains mainly to action, being **fervent in spirit** pertains to attitude. Literally, *zeō* means to boil and metaphorically to be **fervent.** The idea here is not of being overheated to the point of boiling over and out of control but, like a steam engine, of having sufficient heat to produce the energy necessary to get the work done. That principle is reflected in the life of Henry Martyn, the tireless missionary to India, whose heart's desire was to "burn out for God."

One of the oldest blights on earth is lack of enthusiasm. Most people could make a sizable list of their failures that were simply casualties to indifference and lack of commitment. Fervency requires resolve and persistence, not mere good intention. "Let us not lose heart in doing good," Paul admonishes, "for in due time we shall reap if we do not grow weary" (Gal. 6:9).

Even before he had a full understanding of the gospel, Apollos was "fervent in spirit, . . . speaking and teaching accurately the things concerning Jesus" (Acts 18:25). But no believer in the early church was more **fervent in spirit,** more indefatigable in the work of the Lord than Paul himself. "Therefore I run in such a way, as not without aim," he said; "I box in such a way, as not beating the air" (1 Cor. 9:26); "And for this purpose also I labor" (Col. 1:29).

SERVE THE LORD (12:11*c*)

Like fervency in spirit, **serving the Lord** has to do with perspective and priority. Everything we do should, first of all, be consistent with God's Word and, second, be truly in His service and to His glory. Strict devotion to the Lord would eliminate a great deal of fruitless church activity.

Paul never lost sight of that foundational mission. He begins this letter with the affirmation that he served God "in [his] spirit in the preaching of the gospel of His Son" (Rom. 1:9).

In Romans 12, Paul uses three different words to describe Christian service. In verse 1 he uses *latreia,* which is translated, "service of worship," and emphasizes reverential awe. The second word is *konia,* which pertains to practical service. In verse 11, he uses *douleuō,* which refers to the service of a bond-slave, whose very reason for existence is to do his master's will.

Above all else, Paul considered himself a bond-slave of Jesus Christ. It is with that description that he first identifies himself in this letter (Rom. 1:1), as well as in Philippians (1:1) and Titus (1:1).

Yet we do not serve the Lord in our own power any more than we came to Him in our own power. Our supreme purpose is to serve the Lord Jesus Christ, and our power to fulfill that service is from Him. "For this purpose also I labor," Paul testified, "striving according to His power, which mightily works within me" (Col. 1:29).

REJOICE IN HOPE (12:12*a*)

Living the supernatural life inevitably brings opposition from the world and sometimes even sparks resentment by fellow Christians. Even after years of faithful service to the Lord, some see few, if any, apparent results from their labors. Without **hope** we could never survive. "For in hope we have been saved," Paul has already explained, "but hope that is seen is not hope; for why does one also hope for what he sees? But if we hope for what we do not see, with perseverance we wait eagerly for it" (Rom. 8:24-25).

Rejoicing in that **hope,** we know that, if we are "steadfast, immovable, always abounding in the work of the Lord," our "toil is not in vain" (1 Cor. 15:58). We can therefore look forward to one day hearing, "Well done, good and faithful servant" (Matt. 25:21). We know that "in the future there is laid up for [us] the crown of righteousness, which the Lord, the righteous Judge, will award to [us] on that day; and . . . to all who have loved His appearing" (2 Tim. 4:8).

PERSEVERE IN TRIBULATION (12:12*b*)

It is because we can rejoice in hope that we also can persevere **in tribulation,** whatever its form or severity. Because we have perfect assurance concerning the ultimate outcome of our lives, we are able to persist against any obstacle and endure any suffering. That is why Paul could declare with perfect confidence that "we exult in hope of the glory of God. And not only this, but we also exult in our tribulations, knowing that tribulation brings about perseverance; and perseverance, proven character; and proven character, hope; and hope does not disappoint, because the love of God has been poured out within our hearts through the Holy Spirit who was given to us" (Rom. 5:2-5).

BE DEVOTED TO PRAYER (12:12*c*)

Doubtless one of the reasons the Lord allows His children to go through tribulation is to drive them to Himself. The believer who has the strength to persevere in trials, afflictions, adversity, and misfortune— sometimes even deprivation and destitution—will pray more than occasionally. He will be **devoted to prayer,** in communion with his Lord as a constant part of his life. So should we all be, no matter what the circumstances of our lives.

Proskartereō **(devoted)** means literally to be strong toward something, and it also carries the ideas of steadfast and unwavering. It was with such **devoted . . . prayer** that early Christians worshiped, both before and after the descent of the Holy Spirit at Pentecost (Acts 1:14; 2:42). It was to enable the apostles to devote themselves "to prayer, and to the ministry of the word" (Acts 6:4) that deacons were first appointed in the church.

Devoted, steadfast **prayer** should be as continual a part of a Christian's spiritual life as breathing is a part of his physical life. The victorious Christian prays "with the spirit and ... with the mind" (1 Cor. 14:15). As he prays with his own spirit, he also prays "in the Holy Spirit" (Jude 20; cf. Eph. 6:18). He prays "without ceasing" (1 Thess. 5:17). Paul therefore admonished Timothy to have "the men in every place to pray, lifting up holy hands" (1 Tim. 2:8).

CONTRIBUTE TO THE NEEDS OF THE SAINTS (12:13*a*)

The next two principles Paul mentions in this list seem rather mundane. But they are qualities that the Lord personified during His earthly ministry and for which Paul himself was lovingly known. The flow of the supernatural life is outward, not inward, and meeting the needs of fellow believers is more important than meeting our own.

Contributing is from *koinōneō* which means to share in, or share with, and the noun *koinōnia* is often translated "fellowship" or "communion." The basic meaning is that of commonality or partnership, which involves mutual sharing. The spirit of sharing was immediately evident in the early church, as believers after Pentecost "were continually devoting themselves to the apostles' teaching and to fellowship *[koinōnia]*, to the breaking of bread and prayer. ... And all those who had believed were together, and had all things in common *[koina]*" (Acts 2:42, 44; cf. 4:32). Peter used that term in speaking of our sharing *[koinōneō]* in "the sufferings of Christ" (1 Pet. 4:13).

But because the emphasis in the present text is on the giving side of sharing, the term is here rendered **contributing.** Paul also used a form of that word in the same sense when he admonished Timothy to "instruct those who are rich in this present world ... to be generous and ready to share *[koinōnikos]*" (1 Tim. 6:17-18).

In the eyes of society, we rightfully own certain things, but before the Lord we own nothing. We are simply stewards of what He has blessed us with. And one of our most important responsibilities as His stewards is using our personal resources to contribute **to the needs of the saints,** our brothers and sisters in Christ.

In the parable of the Good Samaritan, Jesus made clear that we have a responsibility, to the best of our ability, to help anyone in need whom we encounter. But we have a still greater responsibility to serve fellow Christians. "So then, while we have opportunity," Paul says, "let us do good to all men, and especially to those who are of the household of the faith" (Gal. 6:10).

PRACTICE HOSPITALITY (12:13*b*)

The last responsibility to fellow believers that Paul mentions in this list is that of **practicing hospitality.** The literal meaning of that phrase in the Greek is, "pursuing the love of strangers." In other words, we not only are to meet the needs of those people, believers and unbelievers, who come across our paths but are to look for opportunities to help. "Do not neglect to show hospitality to strangers," the writer of Hebrews admonishes us, "for by this some have entertained angels without knowing it" (Heb. 13:2).

In our text, Paul is speaking to all believers, but he also makes clear that leaders in the church should set an example by their own hospitality. Elders are to be "hospitable, loving what is good, sensible, just, devout, self-controlled" (Titus 1:8).

As with all virtues, this one must be exercised without hypocrisy or self-interest. Jesus' admonition to His Pharisee host applies to all of His followers: "When you give a luncheon or a dinner, do not invite your friends or your brothers or your relatives or rich neighbors, lest they also invite you in return, and repayment come to you. But when you give a reception, invite the poor, the crippled, the lame, the blind, and you will be blessed, since they do not have the means to repay you; for you will be repaid at the resurrection of the righteous" (Luke 14:12-14).

Because inns in New Testament times were scarce, expensive, and often dangerous, Christian families commonly opened their homes to believers who passed through their towns. Unlike Paul, who insisted on paying for most of his own expenses, most itinerant preachers and teachers relied entirely on the support of fellow Christians. John commended Gaius for his generosity in this regard: "Beloved, you are acting faithfully in whatever you accomplish for the brethren, and especially when they are strangers; and they bear witness to your love before the church; and you will do well to send them on their way in a manner worthy of God. For they went out for the sake of the Name, accepting nothing from the Gentiles. Therefore we ought to support such men, that we may be fellow workers with the truth" (3 John 5-8).

We are to "be hospitable to one another without complaint," Peter admonishes (1 Pet. 4:9). That is, we should look upon our hospitality as a happy privilege, not a drudging duty. Onesiphorus demonstrated that sort of beneficence in ministering to Paul, about whom the apostle wrote, "He often refreshed me, and was not ashamed of my chains; but when he was in Rome, he eagerly searched for me, and found me—the Lord grant to him to find mercy from the Lord on that day—and you know very well what services he rendered at Ephesus" (2 Tim. 1:16-18).

Supernatural Living —part 2 (Romans 12:14-21)

15

OUR DUTY TO ALL PEOPLE

Bless those who persecute you; bless and curse not. Rejoice with those who rejoice, and weep with those who weep. Be of the same mind toward one another; do not be haughty in mind, but associate with the lowly. Do not be wise in your own estimation. Never pay back evil for evil to anyone. Respect what is right in the sight of all men. If possible, so far as it depends on you, be at peace with all men. Never take your own revenge, beloved, but leave room for the wrath of God, for it is written, "Vengeance is Mine, I will repay," says the Lord. "But if your enemy is hungry, feed him, and if he is thirsty, give him a drink; for in so doing you will heap burning coals upon his head." Do not be overcome by evil, but overcome evil with good. (12:14-21)

The third circle in Paul's list of basic characteristics of the supernatural Christian life widens broadly to include our duty to everyone in general, believers and unbelievers.

BLESS THOSE WHO PERSECUTE YOU (12:14*a*)

      This section begins with a very difficult admonition, one that is completely contrary to unredeemed human nature: **Bless those who persecute you.** The obedient Christian not only must resist hating and retaliating against those who harm him but is commanded to take the additional step of blessing them.

      Paul is essentially paraphrasing the Lord's own words: "I say to you who hear, love your enemies, do good to those who hate you, bless those who curse you, pray for those who mistreat you" (Luke 6:27-28; cf. Matt. 5:44). Jesus referred to the same self-giving, heartfelt, unhypo-critical, willing love *(agapē)* that Paul admonishes in Romans 12:9. Lest anyone think He was speaking simply of kind feelings, the Lord gave several specific illustrations of what genuine love does in response to mistreatment. "Whoever hits you on the cheek," He commands, "offer him the other also; and whoever takes away your coat, do not withhold your shirt from him either. Give to everyone who asks of you, and who-ever takes away what is yours, do not demand it back" (Luke 6:29-30). Commenting further about our attitude in such situations, He explains, "If you love those who love you, what credit is that to you? For even sinners love those who love them. And if you do good to those who do good to you, what credit is that to you? For even sinners do the same" (vv. 32-33). To truly **bless** those **who persecute** us is to treat them as if they were our friends.

      Some years ago, in the store where he was working, a nephew of mine was murdered by an addict looking for drug money. Although deeply grieved by this tragic loss, my brother-in-law has refused to be-come bitter or hateful. Instead, his continued desire and prayer has been for the salvation of the man who took his son's life. He even visited him in prison to give him the greatest blessing, the gospel. Such is the kind of dis-tinctive Christian love that seeks to bless those who do us terrible harm.

      As we would expect, the supreme example of blessing one's persecutors was given by our Lord Himself. As the sinless Son of God hung in great sin-bearing on the cross, He prayed with unimaginable mercy, "Father, forgive them; for they do not know what they are doing" (Luke 23:34). As he lay beneath the bloody stones that were crushing the life out of him, Stephen echoed those words of his Savior, saying, "Lord, do not hold this sin against them!" (Acts 7:60). "For you have been called for this purpose," Peter wrote many years later, "since Christ also suffered for you, leaving you an example for you to follow in His steps, who committed no sin, nor was any deceit found in His mouth; and while being reviled, He did not revile in return; while suffering, He uttered no threats, but kept entrusting Himself to Him who judges righteously" (1 Pet. 2:21-23).

BLESS AND DO NOT CURSE THEM (12:14*b*)

Although it should go without saying, Paul makes certain to explain that true blessing of those who persecute us is comprehensive and permanent. Not only are we to **bless them,** we are **not** at all or ever to **curse** them.

Because of the general tone of religious freedom in modern western society, physical or political persecution for one's Christian faith is rare. Our temptations to curse are more likely to be in reaction to hostility that does us no life-threatening harm but causes us inconvenience or embarrassment. Some studies have indicated that much high blood pressure and other anxiety-related disease is caused not by serious, long-term problems and life-threatening pressures but by persistent attitudes of resentment and hostility that eat at people who habitually react negatively to unpleasant situations and people. It is often a host of "little foxes" that do the most damage in our spiritual and emotional "vineyards" (cf. Song of Sol. 2:15).

REJOICE WITH THOSE WHO REJOICE (12:15*a*)

In a much more positive vein, Paul next counsels us to **rejoice with those who rejoice.** At first thought, that principle would seem easy to follow. But when another person's blessing and happiness is at our expense, or when their favored circumstances or notable accomplishments make ours seem barren and dull, the flesh does not lead us to rejoice but tempts us to resent.

The person "who rejoices at calamity" displeases God and "will not go unpunished" (Prov. 17:5). But it is distinctively Christian to rejoice in the blessings, honor, and welfare of others—especially fellow believers—no matter what may be our personal circumstances. As always, Paul followed his own counsel. Just as he had formerly told the Corinthian believers that "if one member is honored, all the members rejoice with it" (1 Cor. 12:26), he later assured them, "My joy would be the joy of you all" (2 Cor. 2:3).

WEEP WITH THOSE WHO WEEP (12:15*b*)

It is also distinctively Christian to be sensitive to the disappointments, hardships, and sorrows of others, to **weep with those who weep.** That is the duty of sympathy, empathy, entering into the suffering of others. Compassion has in the very word the idea of suffering with someone. God is called a compassionate God (Deut. 4:31; Neh. 9:17; Joel 2:13; Jonah 4:2). He is so compassionate, so tender toward His people, that "His compassions never fail" (Lam. 3:22). James speaks of Him as being "full of compassion" (James 5:11). We see this compassion, sympathy, and tenderheartedness of God in the tears of Jesus over the grave of Lazarus. He mingled His tears with those of Mary and Martha (John 11:35). Reminding us that we should reflect our Lord's character, Paul said, "So, as those who have been chosen of God, holy and beloved, put on a heart of compassion, kindness, humility, gentleness and patience" (Col. 3:12).

Surely one of the most touchingly profound testimonies to God's heart of tender sympathy toward His children who weep is found in Psalm 56, where the writer implores the Lord, "Put my tears in Thy bottle" (v. 8). The Lord stores up our tears as treasures. If we are to be like our Father and His Son, we, too, must enter into the sorrow of others.

A lovely illustration of that attitude is seen in a custom practiced in ancient Jerusalem. When the great temple built by Herod stood on the temple mount, it had only one entrance, located at the base of the southern wall, the remains of which are still recognizable today. Farther east on the same wall was the exit. The people would enter through the opening that allowed them to go through the wall, ascend the stairs to the temple area, and then exit by the other passage. Huge crowds flowed in and out in steady streams. There was one exception, however, to that pattern. One group of worshipers was to go the opposite way, entering by way of the exit and leaving through the entrance. As they bumped into and squeezed by each other, the two groups came face-to-face. The sad faces of those who were experiencing sorrow could be seen by those going the opposite direction, and, in those brief moments, the grief could be shared.

In addition to weeping for those who *do* **weep,** we should, like Jeremiah grieving for sinful Israel (Jer. 9:1-3) and Jesus looking out over unbelieving Jerusalem (Luke 19:41-44), also **weep** for **those who** *should* **weep** but do not.

DO NOT BE PARTIAL (12:16*a*)

The virtue expressed in the words **be of the same mind toward one another** is that of impartiality. Later in this epistle Paul repeats the admonition, saying, "Now may the God who gives perseverance and encouragement grant you to be of the same mind with one another according to Christ Jesus" (Rom. 15:5).

The most explicit New Testament teaching on impartiality is given by James. "My brethren, do not hold your faith in our glorious Lord

Jesus Christ with an attitude of personal favoritism," he warns. "For if a man comes into your assembly with a gold ring and dressed in fine clothes, and there also comes in a poor man in dirty clothes, and you pay special attention to the one who is wearing the fine clothes, and say, 'You sit here in a good place,' and you say to the poor man, 'You stand over there, or sit down by my footstool,' have you not made distinctions among yourselves, and become judges with evil motives? … But if you show partiality, you are committing sin and are convicted by the law as transgressors" (James 2:1-4,9).

Speaking about honoring and correcting elders, Paul told Timothy, "I solemnly charge you in the presence of God and of Christ Jesus and of His chosen angels, to maintain these principles without bias, doing nothing in a spirit of partiality" (1 Tim. 5:21).

If "there is no partiality with God" (Rom. 2:11; cf. Acts 10:34; 1 Pet. 1:17), shouldn't the same be true for us?

AVOID HAUGHTINESS AND ASSOCIATE WITH THE HUMBLE (12:16*b*)

Closely related to not being partial is not being **haughty in mind,** as James makes clear in the passage cited above.

Haughty in mind translates *hupsēla phronountes,* which literally means "minding high things." But the things to which Paul refers here are not lofty in the spiritual sense but in the sense of self-seeking pride.

As James also makes clear in the passage mentioned above, partiality is closely related to a reluctance to show respect for, or even to **associate with the lowly,** such as "a poor man in dirty clothes" (James 2:2). The idea is not that we should avoid associating with those in high positions of wealth or influence. But as far as our service to them is concerned, we typically have more obligation to **associate with the lowly,** not because they are more important but because they are more needy.

The point is that there is no aristocracy in the church, no place for an elite uppercrust. As mentioned in the previous commentary chapter in relation to hospitality (v. 13), the Lord beautifully and explicitly illustrated that truth. "When you give a luncheon or a dinner," He said, "do not invite your friends or your brothers or your relatives or rich neighbors, lest they also invite you in return, and repayment come to you. But when you give a reception, invite the poor, the crippled, the lame, the blind, and you will be blessed, since they do not have the means to repay you; for you will be repaid at the resurrection of the righteous" (Luke 14:12-14).

Jesus, of course, was not speaking about the act itself but the motive behind it. It is not sinful or unspiritual to invite family, friends, or the wealthy and influential to a meal at our house. The wrong comes in inviting them for a self-serving purpose, to be invited back, a wrong that is magnified by ignoring those who have no means for repaying us.

DO NOT BE WISE IN YOUR OWN EYES (12:16c)

A conceited, self-promoting Christian is a serious contradiction. Every believer should be humbly submissive to the will of God found in the Word of God, having no confidence in himself or in his own wisdom and talent. And sure as there should be no social aristocracy in the church, neither should there be intellectual aristocracy. There are no castes of any sort in the Body of Christ. We must **not be wise in** our **own estimation** in *any* regard, thinking we are in any way superior to fellow Christians.

In recent years, certain church growth professionals have advocated building churches on the basis of homogeneous units, each congregation being composed of members who are as alike in as many ways as possible. Because many churches have indeed grown and prospered on that basis, it is somehow assumed that the pattern is right and should be imitated. Apparently little, if any, consideration is given to the biblical soundness of such a philosophy or to the matter of whether the growth and prosperity are the result of spiritual faithfulness or of unspiritual worldliness.

A church that is seeking to faithfully serve Christ will pursue and eagerly accept all genuine believers into its fellowship and consider them all alike, regardless of superficial human distinctions. The only required common ground should be a saving relationship to Jesus Christ and unqualified submission to the Word of God.

Our Duty Toward Personal Enemies

Never pay back evil for evil to anyone. Respect what is right in the sight of all men. If possible, so far as it depends on you, be at peace with all men. Never take your own revenge, beloved, but leave room for the wrath of God, for it is written, "Vengeance is Mine, I will repay," says the Lord. "But if your enemy is hungry, feed him, and if he is thirsty, give him a drink; for in so doing you will heap burning coals upon his head." Do not be overcome by evil, but overcome evil with good. (12:17-21)

The fourth circle in Paul's list of basic characteristics of the supernatural Christian life widens again to include our responsibilities to personal enemies.

NEVER RETURN EVIL FOR EVIL (12:17*a*)

First, we are **never** to **pay back evil for evil to anyone,** reiterating and extending the second aspect of the principle taught in verse 14. We not only are to bless those who persecute us and *not* curse them, but certainly are never to move beyond a verbal curse to an act of revenge.

The Old Testament law of "eye for eye, tooth for tooth" (Ex. 21:24; cf. Lev. 24:20; Deut. 19:21) pertained to civil justice, not personal revenge. Not only that, but its major purpose was to prevent the severity of punishment from exceeding the severity of the offense. In other words, someone guilty of destroying another person's eye could not be punished with any greater penalty than that of forfeiting one of his own eyes.

A few verses later in this letter Paul declares that civil authority "is a minister of God to you for good. But if you do what is evil, be afraid; for it does not bear the sword for nothing; for it is a minister of God, an avenger who brings wrath upon the one who practices evil" (Rom. 13:4). But that very authority, which not only is divinely permitted but divinely mandated for civil government, is divinely forbidden for personal purposes.

"See that no one repays another with evil for evil," Paul warned the Thessalonian believers, "but always seek after that which is good for one another and for all men" (1 Thess. 5:15). Peter echoes the same truth in nearly the same words: "To sum up, let all be harmonious, sympathetic, brotherly, kindhearted, and humble in spirit; not returning evil for evil, or insult for insult, but giving a blessing instead; for you were called for the very purpose that you might inherit a blessing" (1 Pet. 3:8-9).

ALWAYS RESPECT WHAT IS RIGHT (12:17*b*)

A right attitude toward enemies involves **respect** of **what is right in the sight of all men.** If we genuinely **respect** others, including our enemies, we will have a "built-in" protection against angrily repaying them evil for evil and will be predisposed to doing **what is right** toward them.

Such **respect** will help us develop the self-discipline necessary to prepare ourselves beforehand for responding to evil with what is good instead of with what is bad. Believers should respond instinctively and spontaneously with what is pleasing to God and beneficial to others.

Kalos **(right)** refers to that which is intrinsically good, proper, and honest (as in the KJV of this verse). It also carries the idea of being visibly, obviously **right,** as emphasized in its being fitting and proper **in the sight of all men.** Paul is not speaking of hidden feelings but of outwardly expressed goodness. Our forgiving, gracious behavior toward our enemies should commend us to them and to others who witness that behavior. It will also "adorn the doctrine of God our Savior in every respect" (Titus 2:10).

LIVE IN PEACE WITH EVERYONE (12:18)

Fulfillment of the next characteristic is conditional, in that it partly depends on the attitudes and responses of our enemies. **If possible,** Paul therefore says, **so far as it depends on you, be at peace with all men.** Whether between nations or individuals, peace is two-way. By definition, a peaceful relationship cannot be one-sided. Our responsibility is to make sure that our side of the relationship is right, that our inner desire is genuinely to **be at peace with all men,** even the meanest and most undeserving. Short of compromising God's truth and standards, we should be willing to go to great lengths to build peaceful bridges to those who hate us and harm us. We must forsake any grudge or settled bitterness and fully forgive from the heart all who harm us. Having done that, we can seek reconciliation honestly.

NEVER AVENGE YOURSELF (12:19)

The last two characteristics Paul lists here are both reiterations. He again denounces returning evil for evil, declaring, **Never take your own revenge, beloved, but leave room for the wrath of God.** If a wrong has been done to us, no matter how serious and harmful it may have been, we are never qualified for or have a right to render punishment for the offense ourselves. We are to leave that to **the wrath of God.** Quoting from the Mosaic law (Deut. 32:35), the apostle reminds his readers that **it is written, "Vengeance is Mine, I will repay," says the Lord** (cf. 2 Sam. 22:48; Nah. 1:2; Heb. 10:30). In His divine time, the wrath of God will come (Col. 3:6), and just retribution awaits the unforgiven.

OVERCOME EVIL WITH GOOD (12:20-21)

But merely not returning evil for evil does not fulfill our responsibility. And sometimes the positive part is more difficult. To withhold vengeance is one thing. It requires only doing nothing. But to actually return good for evil is quite another.

Yet that was the obligation of the godly man even under the Old Covenant. Paul quotes from Proverbs 25:21-22, citing God's centuries-old injunction: **"But if your enemy is hungry, feed him, and if he is thirsty, give him a drink; for in so doing you will heap burning coals upon his head."**

The phrase **heap burning coals upon his head** referred to an ancient Egyptian custom. When a person wanted to demonstrate public contrition, he would carry on his head a pan of burning coals to represent the burning pain of his shame and guilt. The point here is that, when we love our enemy and genuinely seek to meet his needs, we shame him for his hatred.

The admonition **Do not be overcome by evil** has two meanings and applications. First, we must not allow the **evil** done to us by other people to **overcome** and overwhelm us. Second, and even more important, we must not allow ourselves to be **overcome** by our *own* **evil** responses. Our own evil is infinitely more detrimental to us than is the evil done to us by others.

In each case, it is the **evil** itself that must be **overcome,** and that can be accomplished only **with good.**

The Christian's Response to Government —part 1 Submitting to Government (Romans 13:1-5)

16

Let every person be in subjection to the governing authorities. For there is no authority except from God, and those which exist are established by God. Therefore he who resists authority has opposed the ordinance of God; and they who have opposed will receive condemnation upon themselves. For rulers are not a cause of fear for good behavior, but for evil. Do you want to have no fear of authority? Do what is good, and you will have praise from the same; for it is a minister of God to you for good. But if you do what is evil, be afraid; for it does not bear the sword for nothing; for it is a minister of God, an avenger who brings wrath upon the one who practices evil. Wherefore it is necessary to be in subjection, not only because of wrath, but also for conscience' sake. (13:1-5)

These seven verses contain the clearest and most specific New Testament teaching on the Christian's responsibility to civil authority. Every Christian, no matter what form of government he lives under, is under command from the Lord to maintain proper and useful submission to that government for the sake of leading a peaceful life and having an effective witness. This recurring theme of submission to society's controlling power is nowhere more forcefully dealt with than here.

The first eleven chapters of Romans (in particular chaps. 1-8) explain in marvelous detail what it means to be saved and how men become saved—by being justified by God's grace working through faith. That whole reality is summed up generally by Paul:"But now apart from the Law the righteousness of God has been manifested, being witnessed by the Law and the Prophets, even the righteousness of God through faith in Jesus Christ for all those who believe; for there is no distinction; for all have sinned and fall short of the glory of God, being justified as a gift by His grace through the redemption which is in Christ Jesus" (3:21-24).

The monumental miracle of salvation impacts every relationship associated with the believer's life. Paul upholds these implications as chapter 12 begins. First, and most important and obvious, is the effect on our relationship to God. When we are saved, our initial response should be to fully present our "bodies a living and holy sacrifice, acceptable to God, which is [our] spiritual service of worship" (12:1). The apostle's next concern is for our having a right relationship with our brothers and sisters in Christ (12:3-16) and with non-Christians, including even our enemies (vv. 17-21).

After dealing with those matters, the inspired writer focuses on the need to have a right relationship to the human governments under which we live (13:1-7).

Due to the religious freedom that most westerners have enjoyed for many generations, it is difficult for believers living in such countries to fully appreciate the struggle that many of their brothers and sisters in Christ face under regimes that restrict freedom and oppress Christianity.

"Holy wars," such as the Crusades, that are fought in the name of Christianity, are generally and rightly condemned. But historically, Christians have been involved, frequently in the name of their faith, in the forceful overthrow of oppressive and sometimes despotic governments. Democracy and political freedom are commonly identified with Christianity. For such reasons it is difficult for many Christians to be clear, or even objective and honest, about a passage so unambiguously restrictive as Romans 13:1-7.

Many evangelicals strongly believe that the American Revolution was wholly justified, not only politically but biblically. They believe that the rights to life, liberty, and the pursuit of happiness not only are divinely endowed but that their attainment and defense somehow is Christian and thereby justified at whatever cost, including that of armed rebellion when necessary. Obviously, such action is forbidden by God, and, judged in light of our present text, it is equally obvious that the United States was born out of violation of Scripture. That does not mean that, in His grace, God has not bestowed great blessing on America, which He unquestionably has. It does mean, however, that His blessings have been in spite of the disobedience to His Word which was involved in the revolution bringing the nation into being.

Believing that the end sometimes justifies the means, many evangelicals contend that nonviolent civil disobedience is justified when a cause, such as opposition to abortion, is clearly biblical. Some evangelicals even refuse to pay taxes because part of the money will be used for causes and activities that are unjust and immoral. Many evangelicals believe that Christians should become active in political causes, relying on social action and pressure tactics to change laws and government policies and practices that are plainly evil and to protect cherished religious rights that are being encroached upon. In the name of such concepts as co-belligerency, some evangelicals are joining forces with individuals and organizations that are unchristian, heretical, and even cultic. The reasoning is that it is sometimes permissible to join forces with one evil in order to combat what is considered to be a greater evil. This zeal for preservation of the Christian faith, both culturally and individually, often gets blended in with strong views about economics, taxation, social issues, and partisanship, so that the Bible gets wrapped in the flag.

Even social and political activities that are perfectly worthwhile can deplete the amount of a believer's time, energy, and money that is available for the central work of the gospel. The focus is shifted from the call to build the spiritual kingdom through the gospel to efforts to moralize culture—trying to change society from the outside rather than individuals from the inside. When the church is politicized, even in support of good causes, its spiritual power is vitiated and its moral influence diluted. And when such causes are supported in worldly ways and by worldly means, the tragedy is compounded. We are to be the conscience of the nation through faithful preaching and godly living, confronting it not with the political pressure of man's wisdom—including our own—but with the spiritual power of God's Word. Using legislation, adjudication, or intimidation to achieve a superficial, temporal "Christian morality" is not our calling—and has no eternal value.

In a message delivered at Oxford University in 1898, the British theologian Robert L. Ottley observed,

> The Old Testament may be studied . . . as an instructor in social righteousness. It exhibits the moral government of God as attested in his dealings with nations rather than with individuals; and it was their consciousness of the action and presence of God in history that made the prophets preachers, not merely to their countrymen, but to the world at large. . . . There is indeed significance in the fact that in spite of their ardent zeal for social reform they did not as a rule take part in political

life or demand political reforms. They desired ... not better institutions but better men. (*Aspects of the Old Testament,* The Bampton Lectures, 1897 [London: Longmans, 1898], 430-31)

Some evangelical pastors and other Christian leaders have turned from emphasizing the gospel to emphasizing politics, from emphasizing the Word of God to emphasizing coalitions to "impact culture." Some Christians expect the government to be not only the church's ally but its primary partner. But the state is temporal and affects only things that are temporal. It is a foolish and wasteful stewardship that devotes a great deal of time trying to bring people better morality—which at best is transient—but little time bringing them the gospel, which offers eternal life. It really does not matter whether people go to hell as policemen or prostitutes, judges or criminals, pro-life or pro-abortion. The moral will perish with the immoral. Our task is the proclamation of the gospel. Neglecting it is the spiritual equivalent of a skilled heart surgeon abandoning his profession to become a make-up artist, spending his time making people look better rather than saving lives. The mission of the church is not to change society—although that is often a beneficial by-product of faithful ministry and living—but to worship and serve the Lord and to bring others to saving faith in Him.

Much like liberal Christians at the turn of the century, many evangelicals have lost their focus on eternal values and become enamored of temporal issues, creating what amounts to a politically conservative version of social Christianity. Also like liberals who preach only a social message, evangelicals who emphasize social concerns above spiritual ones look more and more to government as a temporal, earthly ally or enemy. But even the absolute best of human governments do not participate in the work of the kingdom, and the worst of human societal systems cannot hinder the power of the Word and the Spirit. God instituted civil authority for an entirely different, temporal, and transient purpose.

It is not that Christians are not to be involved, sometimes directly, in civil government. It is certainly not that believers should avoid expressing their beliefs through voting for the best qualified political candidates and for sound legislation. That is part of doing good in our society (cf. Gal. 6:10; Titus 3:1-2). We should be grateful to God for civil freedom to worship, to preach and teach the gospel, and to live our lives almost without restriction. That is a nice privilege, but it is not necessary to the effectiveness of the gospel truth or to spiritual growth. We also should be grateful for, and, within reason, take advantage of our many legal and effective recourses for changing bad laws and bad governments and for promoting good ones. But that has nothing to do with the Christian's priority of proclaiming the gospel and living a holy life to demonstrate that God is a saving God.

Both the Old and New Testament present illustrations of believers whose earthly role placed them in civil service, and they were useful to God there. Joseph in Egypt and Daniel in Babylon are the two supreme Old Testament examples. After Jesus healed the centurion's servant, He did not advise him to leave the army (see Matt. 8:5-13). After Zaccheus was converted, he did not leave his civil profession but became an honest tax collector (see Luke 19:1-10). Cornelius, another Roman centurion, was saved through the ministry of Peter and continued to serve in the army (see Acts 10). And there is no reason to believe that the proconsul Sergius Paulus did not remain in his high civil office after he was saved (see Acts 13:4-12).

At issue is the matter of priority, of realizing that even the greatest earthly good we may be able to accomplish in the temporal world pales beside what the Lord is able to accomplish through us in the spiritual work of His kingdom. Like ancient Israel (Ex. 19:6), the church is called to be a kingdom of priests, not a kingdom of social activists. "But you are a chosen race, a royal priesthood, a holy nation, a people for God's own possession," Peter reminds us, *"that you may proclaim the excellencies of Him who has called you out of darkness into His marvelous light"* (1 Pet. 2:9, emphasis added).

Our Lord was born into a society where political corruption and autocratic rule were common. Merciless tyrants and murderous dictators were everywhere, along with human slavery—the antitheses of democracy. Those were almost unchallenged norms. By some estimates, the Roman empire of that day had three slaves for every free person. Although a vassal of Rome, the Idumean King Herod ruled most of Palestine, including Judea and Samaria, with autocratic cruelty. "When Herod saw that he had been tricked by the magi" regarding the whereabouts of the infant Jesus, "he became very enraged, and," with absolute impunity, "sent and slew all the male children who were in Bethlehem and in all its environs, from two years old and under" (Matt. 2:16). During that time, taxes were exorbitant and government-approved overcharging and extortion by tax collectors made the financial burden on the people immeasurably worse.

Like the other conquered peoples, the Jews of Palestine were little more than Roman chattel, an underprivileged and oppressed minority. They had no voice at any level of government and little legal recourse for injustices. Consequently, many reactionary Jews were in constant rebellion against Rome, some outwardly and some only inwardly. Some of the leaders refused to see the reality of the situation because it was so distasteful. They apparently refused to recognize the obvious. When Jesus declared "to those Jews who had believed Him,

'If you abide in My word, then you are truly disciples of Mine; and you shall know the truth, and the truth shall make you free'" (John 8:31-32), they strangely replied, "We are Abraham's offspring, and have never yet been enslaved to anyone; how is it that You say, 'You shall become free'?" (v. 33). For over fifty years they had been subject to Rome, and before that to Greece, Medo-Persia, Babylon, Assyria, and Egypt. It was certainly their point that they had never been conquered inwardly, that, whatever their knees had to do, their hearts had never bowed to any Gentile power.

Despite heavy restrictions, Rome permitted Jews a remarkable degree of religious freedom. At the time of Christ, they were not required to worship Caesar or any pagan deity. They were free to maintain their priesthood and temple and to support these religious institutions by offerings. The Romans safeguarded the Sabbath, the Mosaic ceremonial and dietary laws, and they upheld the Jews' wish to prohibit idols, including images of the emperor, with the exception of coins, which did offend the Jews. They even upheld the Jewish law that required execution of a Gentile who entered the inner court of the temple. Because the Romans generally considered Christianity to be a sect of Judaism, the early church was able to share many of the Jews' religious freedoms.

Most Jews, however, chafed under Roman domination, and fanatical nationalists, called Zealots, refused to pay taxes and engaged in terrorist attacks against their rulers. On the basis of Deuteronomy 17:15 ("You may not put a foreigner over yourselves who is not your countryman"), some Jews believed that merely recognizing a Gentile ruler was sinful. Many zealots became assassins, wreaking vengeance not only on Romans but even on their own countrymen whom they considered traitors. Even as the church was just getting started, Jewish insurrection was rapidly expanding and eventuated in the Jerusalem holocaust of A.D. 70, in which the city and its temple were utterly destroyed and some 1,100,000 inhabitants—including women, children, and priests—were massacred without mercy by the retaliating Romans.

Because most Jews of that day believed the Messiah would come as a political deliverer, many of Jesus' disciples expected Him to free them from the Roman yoke. But He made no call for political or social reform, even by peaceful means. He never attempted to capture the culture for biblical morality or to gain greater freedom. To the contrary, He declared unambiguously, "Render to Caesar the things that are Caesar's; and to God the things that are God's" (Matt. 22:21). On a later occasion He told His disciples, "The scribes and the Pharisees have seated themselves in the chair of Moses; therefore all that they tell you, do and observe, but do not do according to their deeds; for they say things, and do not do them" (Matt. 23:2-3). Those wicked leaders were not to be emulated, but they were to be obeyed. Changing the form of government or superficially moralizing it were not Jesus' goals. He sought to redeem individual souls.

When He was not preaching, He was demonstrating His great compassion for the pain and hardships of men in their personal lives. Even the most casual reading of the gospels reveals that His compassion was not merely emotional or idealistic. He not only empathized with sinners but healed countless thousands of every sort of disease and affliction, often at great personal sacrifice. Social morality and structure were never His concern.

But even meeting physical needs was not the goal of His life and ministry. Above all else, He came to meet a need that far surpasses all other needs, a need that only He could satisfy. He therefore spoke to the hearts and souls of individual men and women—never to their political, social, economic, or racial rights or physical pain and plights. He taught the saving gospel that had power to make their souls right with His Father and to grant them eternal life—in light of which, temporal rights and morals pale in importance. He did not come to proclaim or establish a new social or moral order but a new spiritual order, His church. He did not seek to make the old creation moral but to make the new creations holy. And He mandated His church to perpetuate His ministry in that same way and toward that same end, to "go into all the world and preach the gospel to all creation" (Mark 16:15).

No minority in the United States or in any other part of the western world has had their babies massacred while they slept. Many people on welfare today have amenities, conveniences, opportunities, and rights that even the wealthiest citizens of Jesus' day could not have imagined. Yet neither the Lord nor His apostles give any justification for political revolt, rebellion, or civil disobedience. There was no effort on His part to eliminate social or political injustice.

What, then, is the Christian's responsibility to society, and to government in particular, if we are to remain "aliens and strangers" in this world (1 Pet. 2:11) who have a platform to call people to salvation? How are we to live in the world but not be of it (John 17:11, 16)? In the present text, Paul presents the two basic principles that answer those questions. First: Be subject to government (v. 1); and second: Pay taxes (v. 6). Those commands summarize the Christian's civic duty. It is through fulfilling those two obligations that we "render to Caesar the things that are Caesar's; and to God the things that are God's" (Matt. 22:21).

THE STANDARD:
BE SUBJECT TO CIVIL AUTHORITY

Let every person be in subjection to the governing authorities. (13:1*a*)

The basic command is simple and succinct: **Let every person be in subjection to the governing authorities.** In the broadest sense, **every person** applies to every human being, because the principle stated here reflects God's universal plan for mankind. But Paul is speaking specifically to Christians, declaring, in effect, that Christianity and good citizenship should go together. And, as he will continue to explain, **subjection to the governing authorities** includes much more than simply obeying civil laws. It also includes genuine honor and respect for government officials as God's agents for maintaining order and justice in human society.

Because the apostle was writing to the church in Rome, the capital of the empire, some interpreters suggest that he was giving a unique warning to Christians there because of the greater danger to traitors and insurrectionists, real or imagined. Most people did not enjoy the legal protection of presumed innocence, especially in regard to crimes against the state. Long considered a sect of Judaism, with its rebellious inclinations, the church was especially suspect.

But Paul's arguments here, as well as similar teachings elsewhere in the New Testament, make clear that the principle of subjection to human authority applies to every believer, in whatever part of the world and under whatever form of government. Writing to believers who were "scattered throughout Pontus, Galatia, Cappadocia, Asia, and Bithynia" (1 Pet. 1:1), Peter said, "Submit yourselves for the Lord's sake to every human institution, whether to a king as the one in authority, or to governors as sent by him for the punishment of evildoers and the praise of those who do right. For such is the will of God that by doing right you may silence the ignorance of foolish men. Act as free men, and do not use your freedom as a covering for evil, but use it as bondslaves of God. Honor all men; love the brotherhood, fear God, honor the king" (1 Pet. 2:13-17).

As always, Paul followed his own instruction. After being falsely accused of breaking Roman law, he and Silas were brutally beaten, thrown in prison, and placed in stocks in Philippi. But instead of railing out against the ones who had mistreated them and demanding their rights from the authorities, they spent the first night in jail (until the Lord miraculously delivered them) "praying and singing hymns of praise to God" (Acts 16:25).

Georgi Vins is a Russian pastor who, for many years before the fall of Soviet communism, suffered, along with many others, great persecution for his faith. Yet he recounts that, however severe their repression and mistreatment became, pastors and other Christians determined to obey every law, just or unjust, with the exception of laws that would force them to cease worship or to disobey God's Word. Following Peter's admonition, they willingly suffered "for doing what is right," but not "for doing what is wrong" (1 Pet. 3:17). They would not "suffer as a murderer, or thief, or evildoer, or a troublesome meddler," but would gladly suffer "as a Christian" (4:15-16).

Believers are to be model citizens, known as law abiding not rabble-rousing, obedient rather than rebellious, respectful of government rather than demeaning of it. We must speak against sin, against injustice, against immorality and ungodliness with fearless dedication, but we must do it within the framework of civil law and with respect for civil authorities. We are to be a godly society, doing good and living peaceably within an ungodly society, manifesting our transformed lives so that the saving power of God is seen clearly.

In his significant book *Toward a Biblical View of Civil Government,* Robert D. Culver writes,

> Churchmen whose Christian activism has taken mainly to placarding, marching, protesting, and shouting might well observe the author of these verses [Rom. 13:1-7] and then they might observe him first at prayer, then in counsel with his friends, and, *after that,* preaching in the homes and marketplaces. When Paul came to be heard by the mighty, it was to defend his action as a preacher (albeit in the streets) of [the] way to heaven. ([Chicago: Moody Press, 1975], 262, emphasis in original)

Be in subjection to translates *hupotassō,* which was often used as a military term referring to soldiers who were ranked under and subject to the absolute authority of a superior officer. The verb here is a passive imperative, meaning first of all that the principle is a command, not an option, and second that the Christian is to willingly place himself under all **governing authorities,** whoever they may be.

Paul gives no qualification or condition. Every civil authority is to be submitted to willingly. In his first letter to Timothy, Paul teaches "that entreaties and prayers, petitions and thanksgivings, be made on behalf of all men, for kings and all who are in authority, in order that we may lead a tranquil and quiet life in all godliness and dignity" (1 Tim. 2:1-2), again with no exception related to the rulers' competence or incompetence, morality or immorality, cruelty or kindness, or even godliness or ungodliness. He gives the same instruction in his letter to Titus, to whom he wrote, "Remind them [believers under his care] to be subject to rulers, to authorities, to be obedient, to be ready for every good deed, to malign no one, to be uncontentious, gentle, showing every consideration for all men" (Titus 3:1-2). He admonished the Thessalonian Christians "to make it your ambition to lead a quiet life and attend to your own business and work with your hands, just as we commanded you; so that you may behave properly toward outsiders and not be in any need" (1 Thess. 4:11-12).

During the first several centuries of the church, many Christians were so little involved with the societies in which they lived that sometimes they were considered outsiders in their own communities. They were not unloving, uncaring, or insensitive to others, but they lived very distinct and separated lives. And although they were not pacifists or opposed to civil government, few Christians enlisted in military service or sought government office. The third-century Christian writer Tertullian commented that, under the pagan Roman Empire, Christians were not executed for inflammatory teaching or behavior but for presumed antisocial tendencies. Even though that view was biased, it nevertheless reflected the church's focus on the kingdom of God rather the kingdoms of man. Sadly, that focus does not characterize most of the church today. Even spiritual and moral battles are often fought by worldly, materialistic means. Many of the "weapons of our warfare are ... of the flesh" and ineffective, rather than spiritual and "divinely powerful for the destruction of fortresses" (2 Cor. 10:4).

The principle of civil obedience applied in the Old Testament as well. Even while His people were captive in the distant, pagan land of Babylon, the Lord commanded them, "Seek the welfare of the city where I have sent you into exile, and pray to the Lord on its behalf; for in its welfare you will have welfare" (Jer. 29:7).

As alluded to above, there is but one limitation to the believer's obligation under the Lord to willing and completely submit to civil authority: namely, any law or command that would require disobedience to God's Word.

When the pharaoh ordered the Jewish midwives Shiphrah and Puah to kill all male babies when they were born, they "feared God, and did not do as the king of Egypt had commanded them, but let the boys live" (Ex. 1:17). Because those women refused to disobey God by committing murder, God honored that civil disobedience and "was good to the midwives, and the people multiplied, and became very mighty" (v. 20). When the four young Jewish men named Daniel, Shadrach, Meshach, and Abednego were commanded to eat "from the king's choice food and from the wine which he drank," they respectfully refused, because it would have meant defiling themselves by breaking of the Mosaic dietary laws. In order to keep from offending the king, Daniel suggested to the commander that the four of them "'be given some vegetables to eat and water to drink. Then let our appearance be observed in your presence, and the appearance of the youths who are eating the king's choice food; and deal with your servants according to what you see.' So he listened to them in this matter and tested them for ten days." God honored and blessed that faithfulness, "and at the end of ten days their appearance seemed better and they were fatter than all the youths who had been eating the king's choice food" (Dan. 1:12-15).

It is important to note that, even while refusing to do what God had forbidden, those four faithful men of God showed respect for the human authority they had to disobey. Speaking for the other three as well as for himself, Daniel did not demand deference to their beliefs but respectfully *"sought permission* from the commander of the officials that he might not defile himself" (v. 8, emphasis added), and he referred to themselves as the commander's "servants" (vv. 12-13). In obeying God, they did not self-righteously or disrespectfully malign, contend with, or condemn civil authority.

Two other familiar accounts of justifiable civil disobedience are also recorded in that book. When King Nebuchadnezzar commanded Shadrach, Meshach and Abednego to worship his gods and the golden image he had erected, they "answered and said to the king, '0 Nebuchadnezzar, we do not need to give you an answer concerning this matter. If it be so, our God whom we serve is able to deliver us from the furnace of blazing fire; and He will deliver us out of your hand, O king. But even if He does not, let it be known to you, O king, that we are not going to serve your gods or worship the golden image that you have set up'" (Dan. 3:16-18). Again God blessed their faithfulness, to the extent that "the fire had no effect on the bodies of these men nor was the hair of their head singed, nor were their trousers damaged, nor had the smell of fire even come upon them" (v. 27).

At the instigation of his commissioners and satraps, who were jealous of Daniel's royal favor, a later Babylonian king, Darius, issued a decree "that anyone who makes a petition to any god or man besides you, O king, for thirty days, shall be cast into the lions' den" (Dan. 6:7). Daniel respectfully but firmly refused to obey the decree, and the king reluctantly had him thrown into the lions' den. Once again, God honored His servant's faithfulness. "Daniel was taken up out of the den, and no injury whatever was found on him, because he had trusted in his God" (v. 23). Again it is important to note Daniel's lack of malice and his genuine respect for the human authority his conscience forced him to disobey. After being released unharmed, he said "O king, live forever!" (v. 21).

When the Jewish leaders of Jerusalem warned Peter and John "not to speak or teach at all in the name of Jesus" (Acts 4:18), the apostles replied, "Whether it is right in the sight of God to give heed to you rather than to God, you be the judge; for we cannot stop speaking what we have seen and heard" (Acts 4:19-20). The Lord had commanded, "Go into all the world and preach the gospel to all creation" (Mark 16:15; Matt. 28:19-20), and therefore to obey those human rulers would mean to disobey their divine Ruler, which they would not do. When Peter and John persisted in their evangelization, the Jewish leaders warned them again, "saying, 'We gave you strict orders not to continue teaching in this name, and behold, you have filled Jerusalem with your teaching, and intend to bring this man's blood upon us.' But Peter and the apostles answered and said, 'We must obey God rather than men'" (Acts 5:28-29).

Like individual believers, a local church is obligated to observe civil laws such as zoning, building codes, fire safety regulations, and every other law and regulation that would not cause them to disobey God's Word. A church is only justified in disobeying an ordinance that, for example, would require acceptance of homosexuals into church membership or of hiring them to work on staff.

In most of the world today, even including many former communist lands, Christians seldom face the need to "obey God rather than men." By far our most common obligation, therefore, is to obey both God and men.

Some years ago, the tax department of the state of California issued a broadly-worded form that required all tax-exempt organizations, including churches, to attest that they did not and would not engage in political activities. A number of local congregations arched their backs, as it were, and refused to sign the affidavit, which resulted in their buildings being boarded up by state officials. Although he had no association with those churches and was not asked by them to intervene, a prominent Christian attorney talked with state officials on the churches' behalf. He explained that a Christian's conscience sometimes requires him to take certain positions on moral issues that relate to civil laws, but that those positions come from religious convictions that are based on Scripture, not on political ideology. Appreciating that explanation, the state officials reworded the form in a way that better protected religious rights. Conflicts do not, of course, always work out that favorably, but churches and individual believers should make every effort to explain carefully and respectfully their reasons for wanting a civil law or mandate to be changed that they believe would force them to disobey God.

In most matters we are to respect and obey civil laws and ordinances, and we are to do it ungrudgingly. Even when conscience leaves us no alternative but to disobey human authority, we do so with respect and with willingness to suffer whatever penalties or consequences may result.

Although He sends His own people "out as sheep in the midst of wolves," our Lord commands us to "be shrewd as serpents, and innocent as doves" (Matt. 10:16). We are to be alert, cautious, and concerned about what is going on around us and in the world. But that must not be the focus of our attention, and our living in the midst of it must be innocent—free of anxiety, ill will, rancor, and self-righteousness. Men "will deliver you up to the courts, and scourge you in their synagogues," Jesus continued to warn; "and you shall even be brought before governors and kings for My sake, as a testimony to them and to the Gentiles. But when they deliver you up, do not become anxious about how or what you will speak; for it shall be given you in that hour what you are to speak. For it is not you who speak, but it is the Spirit of your Father who speaks in you" (Matt. 10:18-20). Furthermore, "brother will deliver up brother to death, and a father his child; and children will rise up against parents, and cause them to be put to death. And you will be hated by all on account of My name, but it is the one who has endured to the end who will be saved" (vv. 21-22).

Persecution is not cause for rebellion but for patient endurance and righteousness. It is not that a Christian should seek persecution or should not try to escape it when possible. Persecution in itself has no spiritual value. Therefore, "whenever they persecute you in this city," Jesus went on to say, "flee to the next" (v. 23).

Regardless of the failures of government—many of them immoral, unjust, and ungodly—Christians are to pray and live peaceful lives that influence the world by godly, selfless living, not by protests, sit-ins, and marches, much less by rebellion. Like the prophets of the Old Testament, we have both the right and the obligation to confront and oppose the sins and evils of our society, but only in the Lord's way and power, not the world's. In this way, says Paul, our living is "good and profitable for men" (Titus 3:8), because it shows them the power of God in salvation. They see what a person saved from sin is like.

THE PURPOSE:
GOD'S REASONS FOR OUR SUBMITTING TO HUMAN AUTHORITY

For there is no authority except from God, and those which exist are established by God. Therefore he who resists authority has opposed the ordinance of God; and they who have opposed will receive condemnation upon themselves. For rulers are not a cause of fear for good behavior, but for evil. Do you want to have

no fear of authority? Do what is good, and you will have praise from the same; for it is a minister of God to you for good. But if you do what is evil, be afraid; for it does not bear the sword for nothing; for it is a minister of God, an avenger who brings wrath upon the one who practices evil. Wherefore it is necessary to be in subjection, not only because of wrath, but also for conscience' sake. (13:1*b*-5)

Paul next presents seven reasons why Christians are to submit to human government: Government is by divine decree (v. 1*b*); resistance to government is rebellion against an institution of God (v. 2*a*); those who resist will be punished (v. 2*b*); government serves to restrain evil (v. 3*a*); government serves to promote good (vv. 3*b*-4*a*); rulers are empowered by God to inflict punishment for disobedience (v. 4*b*); and government should be obeyed for conscience's sake (v. 5).

GOVERNMENT IS BY DIVINE DECREE

For there is no authority except from God, and those which exist are established by God. (13:1*b*)

First, Paul says, human government is ordained by God for the benefit of society. In whatever of the many forms it exists, civil authority derives directly from God. Like marriage, it is a universal institution of God, and, like marriage, it is valid regardless of place, circumstance, or any other consideration.

There is no civil **authority,** Paul says, **except from God.** No matter what form it takes, no human government at any time in history, at any place on earth, among any people on earth, at any level of society, has ever existed or will ever exist apart from the sovereign **authority of God,** because all "power belongs to God" (Ps. 62:11). The entire world, everything in heaven and earth, including Satan and his hosts, are subject to their Creator. God sovereignly created and absolutely controls the universe, with no exceptions or limitations. Also without exception, the power that any person, group, or society may possess is divinely delegated and circumscribed. How well or how poorly that power is used is another matter. Paul's point here is that this power has only *one source*—God.

Yet, in His sovereign wisdom, God has permitted Satan to have vast but limited power over the world and the affairs of men. Although Satan was not directly responsible for man's sin at the Fall, it was his seductive enticement that led Adam and Eve to disobey God and thereby commit the first sin, a sin which they bequeathed to all their posterity.

Satan does not have power to **make** men sin, but since that tragic day in the Garden of Eden, he has used every means at his disposal to entice men to indulge their sinful impulses and thereby express their defiance of God. Paul reminded the Ephesian believers that "you were dead in your trespasses and sins, in which you formerly walked according to the course of this world, according to the prince of the power of the air, of the spirit that is now working in the sons of disobedience" (Eph. 2:1-2). In other words, man's natural propensity to sin is exploited by Satan's evil wiles.

Consequently, "the whole world lies in the power of the evil one" (1 John 5:19), who is "now the ruler of this world" (John 12:31; 16:11; 14:30). At His temptation, Jesus did not question Satan's claim to "all the kingdoms of the world" or his ability to give Jesus "all this domain and its glory; for it has been handed over to me, and I give it to whomever I wish" (Luke 4:6).

From Daniel 10 it is evident that some, if not all, nations are under the charge of a specific demon, or perhaps a group of demons. The context makes clear that "the prince of the kingdom of Persia" (v. 13), who withstood the holy angel (vv. 5-6, 11-12) "for twenty-one days," was himself supernatural, not human. He was not defeated until "Michael, one of the chief princes" of the holy angels, came to help (v. 13). After predicting the death of the proud and blasphemous king of Babylon (Isa. 14:4), Isaiah addresses one who has "fallen from heaven," and calls him "star of the morning [Lucifer]" and "son of the dawn" (v. 12). The close association of the human king and the supernatural agent seems to indicate that Satan himself took special charge of that pagan nation.

Although addressed as "the king of Tyre," the being that Isaiah refers to as having "had the seal of perfection, full of wisdom and perfect in beauty," as being in "Eden, the garden of God," and whom he calls "the anointed cherub" (Ezek. 28:12-14) is clearly supernatural and could only be Satan.

In both the Isaiah and Ezekiel accounts, Satan is closely identified with the kings of the nations involved. It becomes clear that, although human government was instituted by God and fulfills, to some extent, His plan for maintaining order on earth, many governments, if not most, are under the influence of Satan and are a means of promoting and perpetuating satanic activity.

The autocratic, ruthless, and demonic regimes of Adolf Hitler, Joseph Stalin, and Mao Tse Tung were no exceptions to God's command to be subject to civil authority. The equally ruthless empires of ancient Assyria and Babylon were no exceptions. The Roman empire, sometimes ruled by caesars who proclaimed themselves to be gods, was no exception. The apostate and heretical "Christian" kingdoms of the Middle Ages were no exceptions. Shaman-ruled primitive and animistic tribes of South America are no exceptions. *There are no exceptions.*

That is part of the truth Paul declared before the pagan philosophers in Athens:"The God who made the world and all things in it, since He is Lord of heaven and earth, does not dwell in temples made with hands; neither is He served by human hands, as though He needed anything, since He Himself gives to all life and breath and all things; and He made from one, every nation of mankind to live on all the face of the earth, having determined their appointed times, and the boundaries of their habitation" (Acts 17:24-26).

That is the primary reason we are to submit to human government: it is instituted by the decree of God and is an integral part of His divine plan for fallen mankind.

RESISTANCE TO GOVERNMENT IS REBELLION AGAINST GOD

Therefore he who resists authority has opposed the ordinance of God; (13:2*a*)

The logical ramification is simple. Because civil government is an institution of God, to rebel against government is to rebel against the God who has established it. In his commentary on Romans, the nineteenth-century Scottish evangelist Robert Haldane wrote,"The people of God then ought to consider resistance to the government under which they live as a very awful crime, even as resistance to God Himself" *(An Exposition of Romans* [McLean, Va.: MacDonald Pub. Co., n.d.], 579).

The seriousness with which God takes rebellion is illustrated vividly in the book of Numbers. God had chosen Moses not only to be the human lawgiver but to be the human leader of Israel as He delivered her from Egypt and led her through the wilderness to the Promised Land. The Lord also had appointed Moses' brother Aaron to be high priest. During that journey, a group of some 250 malcontents, led by Korah, Dathan, Abiram, and On,"assembled together against Moses and Aaron, and said to them,'You have gone far enough, for all the congregation are holy, every one of them, and the Lord is in their midst; so why do you exalt yourselves above the assembly of the Lord? ... Is it not enough that you have brought us up out of a land flowing with milk and honey to have us die in the wilderness, but you would also lord it over us?'" (Num. 16:3,13).

The Lord was so angered by their insolence "that the ground that was under them split open; . . . Fire also came forth from the Lord and consumed the two hundred and fifty men who were offering the incense" (vv. 31-35). Incredibly, the people learned nothing from that awful judgment. Instead of drawing them back to God, it merely escalated their hatred of His chosen leaders. "On the next day all the congregation of the sons of Israel grumbled against Moses and Aaron, saying, 'You are the ones who have caused the death of the Lord's people'" (v. 41). In response to that defiant accusation, the Lord sent a deadly plague that instantly killed "14,700, besides those who died on account of Korah" (v. 49). Had not Aaron intervened by making atonement for the people, the entire congregation would have been annihilated (vv. 46-48).

THOSE WHO RESIST GOVERNMENT WILL BE PUNISHED

and they who have opposed will receive condemnation upon themselves. (13:2*b*)

Paul is doubtless not speaking about God's direct judgment on those **who have opposed** civil authority but rather the **condemnation** men suffer from the government itself as punishment for crime. As the apostle mentions a few verses later, civil authority "is a minister of God, an avenger who brings wrath upon the one who practices evil" (Rom. 13:4).

A graphic and striking illustration of this principle came from our Lord Himself. When He was being taken prisoner in the garden, to be unjustly accused and executed, Peter drew a sword to fight the soldiers (authorities) who came to take Him. If ever there was a just cause for revolt, that would seem to have been it. But Jesus said to Peter, "Put your sword back into its place; for all those who take up the sword shall perish by the sword" (Matt. 26:52). Jesus affirmed that, no matter how noble the cause, government has the right to execute a murderer.

The Mosaic law prescribed many kinds of punishment, all of which were appropriate to the offense committed. For theft, the punishment included restitution, returning that which was stolen or payment of equal value. If he had no money or property with which to repay, the thief was required to work out his debt.

Under Mosaic law, punishment was always public. The offender was shamed before his family, friends, and society as a means of deterrence. Punishment was also generally corporal. The lashes of the whip, for example, brought immediate physical and bodily pain. But with the obvious exception of execution, punishment was also short-term. And, once the penalty was paid, the offender was free to pursue his life again.

Under Old Testament law, punishment was to be without pity for the offender. "You shall not pity him [a murderer], but you shall purge the blood of the innocent from Israel, that it may go well with you" (Deut. 19:13). That policy is in stark contrast to what is found in many societies today, where often more pity is expressed for criminals than for their victims.

Punishment under Mosaic law had several objectives. First, it was administered as a matter of justice, of appropriate retribution for a crime or other evil committed: "life for life, eye for eye, tooth for tooth, hand for hand, foot for foot" (Deut. 19:21). But this well-known precept of "eye for eye"—much maligned in our day—was given by God as much to prevent over-punishment as under-punishment. It must also be noted that punishment was to be determined and administered by the proper civil authority, not by victims. Personal revenge was not involved.

Second, punishment was to be a deterrent to crime—to discourage the guilty person from committing further crime and to discourage others from following his unlawful example. "Then all the people will hear and be afraid, and will not act presumptuously again" (Deut. 17:13; cf. 13:11; 19:20).

Third, Mosaic law required impartiality. The guilty were to be punished, regardless of their wealth, social standing, or position in the community—even if they were members of one's own family, "your brother, your mother's son, or your son or daughter, or the wife you cherish, or your friend who is as your own soul" (Deut. 13:6).

Fourth, punishment was to be without delay. "If the wicked man deserves to be beaten, the judge shall then make him lie down and be beaten in his presence with the number of stripes according to his guilt" (Deut. 25:2). Most punishment was administered on the spot, immediately after the sentence was declared. The principle of speedy trial and punishment is found in the constitutions of most modern democracies, but unfortunately it is frequently acknowledged more by disregard than by observance. Apparently the principle was also sometimes disregarded in Israel, hence the warning in Ecclesiastes: "Because the sentence against an evil deed is not executed quickly, therefore the hearts of the sons of men among them are given fully to do evil" (Eccles. 8:11).

Fifth—again with the exception of execution—Old Testament law provided for pardon and rehabilitation. The guilty person could be beaten "forty times but no more, lest he beat him with many more stripes than these, and your brother be degraded in your eyes" (Deut. 25:3). Criminals were not to be permanently stigmatized. Once an offender paid his penalty, he was to be accepted back into society as a respectable citizen.

GOVERNMENT SERVES TO RESTRAIN EVIL

For rulers are not a cause of fear for good behavior, but for evil.
(13:3*a*)

We are to submit to civil authority because God has ordained it
as a means of restraining evil.

Paul was obviously speaking in general terms in saying that **rulers are not a cause of fear for good behavior, but for evil.** He had
himself suffered a great deal at the hands of **rulers** who abused him
for no other reason than his godly **good behavior.** But in that day, as
throughout history, even the most wicked regimes were a deterrent to
murder, theft, and many other crimes of the populace. Although the fact
far from justifies totalitarian government, frequently crime rates under
such systems are lower than those in the free world. Until recently, at
least, such violations as murder, robbery, and rape were all but nonex-
istent in some communist countries. In Muslim nations, severe punishment has been a formidable deterrent to such crimes.

When Adam and Eve sinned by eating the forbidden fruit, they
entered into a knowledge of good and evil (Gen. 2:17; 3:1-7), and that
knowledge has been passed down to all their descendants throughout
history. It is that knowledge that forms the basis for conscience, even the
conscience of the unsaved. "When Gentiles who do not have the Law do
instinctively the things of the Law," Paul explains, "these, not having the
Law, are a law to themselves, in that they show the work of the Law written in their hearts, their conscience bearing witness, and their thoughts
alternately accusing or else defending them" (Rom. 2:14-15). When men
sin, it is not because they do not know the difference between good and
evil but because they "suppress the truth in unrighteousness, because
that which is known about God is evident within them; for God made it
evident to them" (Rom. 1:18-19).

Therefore, through God's natural revelation in conscience and
reason and under His universal common grace, even unregenerate rulers instinctively know right from wrong and consequently know that
part of their duty is to punish evil behavior and to promote **good behavior.** Civil authorities also realize that basic morality is essential to
a workable society. No society can long survive wanton murder, theft,
dishonesty, sexual immorality, and violence. **Good behavior** is essential
for any nation's self-preservation. Without it, society self-destructs.

It certainly is not insignificant that, although prisons were common in the pagan lands of biblical times, there is little record of their
being used in ancient Israel. Criminals lost their lives or worked to pay
reparations. Merely incarcerating them served no good purpose. The

reference to imprisonment in Ezra 7:26 was made in the middle of the fifth century B.C., after God's people had spent seventy years as captives in Babylon, where imprisonment was common. But long-term incarceration was never an option under divinely-revealed Old Testament law.

And although prisons had been common in Europe for centuries, they did not appear in America until the late eighteenth century. Interestingly, the idea was introduced by Quakers, probably on the grounds that imprisonment was more humane than corporal punishment. But the United States now has the dual—and I believe related— distinctions of having the highest per capita number of prison inmates in the western world as well as the highest crime rate. Prisons are breeding grounds for crime, for homosexuality, and for brutality. Because inmates are not able to make restitution for their crimes, there is no restoration of their dignity. Though certainly not meant to be, they are, in effect, government-sponsored crime schools. The fact that an unbelievably large percentage of criminals are never punished or even indicted encourages crime still further. "Because the sentence against an evil deed is not executed quickly, therefore the hearts of the sons of men among them are given fully to do evil" (Eccles. 8:11). How much more are men "given fully to do evil" when punishment is not executed at all.

GOVERNMENT SERVES TO PROMOTE GOOD

Do you want to have no fear of authority? Do what is good, and you will have praise from the same; for it is a minister of God to you for good. (13:3b-4a)

God intends for civil government to promote public good. Generally speaking, peaceful and law-abiding citizens have been favorably treated by their governments throughout history. With notable exceptions, such people have **no fear of authority.** As long as they **do what is good,** they not only will not be mistreated but **will have praise from** their government.

It is not wrong for Christians to look to their governments for protection of life and property. Paul took advantage of the government's role in promoting **what is good** when he used his Roman citizenship to secure justice by appealing to Caesar (Acts 25:11). The apostle also experienced the protection of Roman law while he was in Ephesus on his third missionary journey. When a multitude was incited against him by Demetrius the silversmith, the town clerk took Paul into protective custody and warned the crowd against rioting, saying, "So then, if Demetrius and the craftsmen who are with him have a complaint against any man, the courts are in session and proconsuls are available; let them bring charges against one another. But if you want anything beyond this, it shall be settled in the lawful assembly" (Acts 19:38-39).

Because he represents the God-ordained institution of civil government, a civil official is actually **a minister of God,** regardless of his personal beliefs about or relation to God. He is doing the Lord's work whether he realizes it or not, by promoting peace and safety among men.

Robert Haldane comments that

> The institution of civil government is a dispensation of mercy, and its existence is so indispensable, that the moment it ceases under one form, it re-establishes itself in another. The world, ever since the fall, when the dominion of one part of the human race over another was immediately introduced (Gen. 3:16), has been in such a state of corruption and depravity, that without the powerful obstacle presented by civil government to the selfish and malignant passions of men, it would be better to live among the beasts of the forest than in human society. As soon as its restraints are removed, man shows himself in his real character. When there was no king in Israel, and every man did that which was right in his own eyes, we see in the last three chapters of the Book of Judges what were the dreadful consequences. *(An Exposition of Romans,* 581)

RULERS ARE EMPOWERED BY GOD
TO INFLICT PUNISHMENT FOR DISOBEDIENCE

But if you do what is evil, be afraid; for it does not bear the sword for nothing; for it is a minister of God, an avenger who brings wrath upon the one who practices evil. (13:4*b*)

In order to promote and protect the good in society, human government must punish the evil. Consequently, those who **do what is evil** have reason to **be afraid.**

Because the **sword** is an instrument of death, the weapon here symbolizes the right of civil government to inflict punishment, including the ultimate penalty of death for crimes that deserve it. In the earliest period of human existence, the Lord instituted capital punishment. "Whoever sheds man's blood, by man his blood shall be shed, for in the image of God He made man" (Gen. 9:6). When Jesus told Peter, "Put your sword back into its place; for all those who take up the sword shall perish by the sword" (Matt. 26:52), He was reminding His disciple that the penalty for his killing one of Jesus' enemies would be to perish himself through execution, which the Lord here acknowledges would be justified.

When Paul stood before the Roman governor Festus and made his appeal to Caesar, he said, "If then I am a wrongdoer, and have committed anything worthy of death, I do not refuse to die" (Acts 25:11). In saying that, he acknowledged that capital punishment was sometimes justified and that he would willingly accept it if he were to be found guilty of a capital crime.

Robert Culver again reminds us:

> What must not be lost sight of is that, unpleasant as is the task of the jailor and the use of the whip, the cell, the noose, the guillotine, these things stand behind the stability of civilized society, and they stand there necessarily, for God has declared it so, in harmony with reality, rather than with apostate sociological opinion. Government, with its coercive powers, is a social necessity, but one determined by the Creator, not by the statistical tables of some university social research staff! No society can successfully vote fines, imprisonment, corporal and capital punishment away permanently. The society which tries has lost touch with realities of man (his fallen sinful state), realities of the world, and the truth of divine revelation in nature, man's conscience, and the Bible. (*Toward a Biblical View of Civil Government*, 256)

When a society rejects capital punishment for even the most serious crimes, including murder, it comes under blood guiltiness from God. After Cain killed Abel, "The Lord said to Cain, 'Where is Abel your brother?' And he said, 'I do not know. Am I my brother's keeper?' And He said, 'What have you done? The voice of your brother's blood is crying to Me from the ground'" (Gen. 4:10). Like Satan, whom he unknowingly had come to serve, Cain was both a murderer and a liar (see John 8:44). Immediately after the Flood, God established the divine law of capital punishment for murder (Gen. 9:6). As part of the Mosaic law, God declared, "You shall not pollute the land in which you are; for blood pollutes the land and no expiation can be made for the land for the blood that is shed on it, except by the blood of him who shed it" (Num. 35:33).

Among other things, Israel was sent into Babylonian captivity because of the many bloody crimes in the nation that went unpunished. "Make the chain," God said, "for the land is full of bloody crimes, and the city is full of violence. Therefore, I shall bring the worst of the nations, and they will possess their houses. I shall also make the pride of the strong ones cease, and their holy places will be profaned" (Ezek. 7:23-24). When a nation does not administer justice, it eventually falls under God's justice.

Abortion is murder of unborn children, and a nation that permits and even encourages this ghastly execution of the most innocent and helpless of those created in God's image cannot possibly escape His judgment. The land cries out for the blood of the millions upon millions of massacred babies. God will answer.

GOVERNMENT SHOULD BE SUBMITTED TO FOR CONSCIENCE'S SAKE

Wherefore it is necessary to be in subjection, not only because of wrath, but also for conscience' sake. (13:5)

Christians are to submit to civil authority not only out of fear of punishment, **because of wrath, but also for** their own **conscience's sake**—which for the Christian is for the Lord's sake. "Submit yourselves for the Lord's sake to every human institution," Peter declares, "whether to a king as the one in authority, or to governors as sent by him for the punishment of evildoers and the praise of those who do right. For such is the will of God that by doing right you may silence the ignorance of foolish men" (1 Pet. 2:13-15). As God's own children, who are indwelt by the Holy Spirit, we should realize with spiritual instinctiveness that disobedience of and disrespect for government is wrong, whether or not those sins are punished, and that obedience of and respect for it are right, whether we are personally protected by it or not.

The Christian's Response to Government —part 2 Paying Taxes (Romans 13:6-7)

17

For because of this you also pay taxes, for rulers are servants of God, devoting themselves to this very thing. Render to all what is due them: tax to whom tax is due; custom to whom custom; fear to whom fear; honor to whom honor. (13:6-7)

No one enjoys paying taxes. But taxes are a part of everyday life. While it is appropriate for citizens, including Christians, to take advantage of deductions and other benefits that the law provides, no citizen, especially a Christian, is justified in circumventing payment of taxes by any means that is illegal or unethical.

Yet tax fraud is probably the most widespread crime in the United States. Some years ago, the Internal Revenue Service estimated that the gap between what was paid and what should have been paid in income taxes was $93 billion for the most recent year.

It goes without saying that all taxes are not just. The only completely just tax system the world has known was in the divinely-revealed Mosaic law of ancient Israel. But although their taxes were absolutely fair, the people soon discovered ways to cheat on them.

Many taxes that *are* justly levied are *not* justly spent by the government body that collects them. Yet, just as with submission to human government in general (Rom. 13:1-5), Paul makes no exception in verses 6-7 for a Christian's paying *all* taxes that he is assessed.

As noted in the previous chapter, the Roman government of New Testament times was pagan, despotic, and often merciless. Some of its emperors declared themselves to be gods and demanded worship from every person in the empire. Also as noted before, the empire had many more slaves than freemen. During its latter years, Rome degenerated into a giant welfare state, in which fewer and fewer people worked for a living and more and more became dependent on the government. As in many countries today, those who worked had to pay increasingly higher taxes in order to support the growing number who did not work. And of special concern to Jews and Christians was the fact that part of the Roman taxes were used to support pagan temples and other religious institutions throughout the empire.

In Israel, as in most other parts of the empire, nationals of the country were appointed (usually after paying a high fee) as tax collectors and were given specified amounts to collect for Rome each year. They were free to charge virtually any rate they wanted and to collect taxes almost as often as they wanted, under the protection of Roman soldiers. Whatever they collected over the prescribed amount for Rome, they could keep for themselves. As would be expected, abuse was rampant, and because most of them were fellow countrymen, tax collectors often were more hated than the Roman officials and soldiers. The gospels vividly reveal how much the tax collector was despised in Israel (see, e.g., Matt. 9:10-11).

Such was the backdrop for Paul's teaching about the Christian's obligation regarding taxes. In two short verses he presents the principle (v. 6*a*), the purpose (v. 6*b*), and the particulars (v. 7).

THE PRINCIPLE

For because of this you also pay taxes, (13:6*a*)

For because of this refers, of course, to the previous five verses, in which Paul has set forth the Christian's obligation to submit to human authority. The **also** indicates that paying taxes is part of that general obligation.

Phoros **(taxes)** most commonly was used of taxes paid by individuals, especially those paid by citizens of a subjugated nation to their foreign rulers. This levy probably was a combination income and property tax. The context, however, indicates that Paul used the term to represent **taxes** of all kinds, all of which the Christian is to **pay.**

Israel had long been familiar with oppressive and unjust taxation. While rebuilding Jerusalem under the leadership of Nehemiah, the people complained bitterly about their heavy taxation by Persia, by whose permission the temple and the city walls were being rebuilt:"We have borrowed money for the king's tax on our fields and our vineyards" (Neh. 5:4). Even their own kings sometimes overtaxed them. After the death of Solomon, the northern tribes petitioned his son and successor, Rehoboam, pleading,"Your father made our yoke hard; now therefore lighten the hard service of your father and his heavy yoke which he put on us, and we will serve you" (1 Kings 12:4). But their request was in vain, and their taxes were raised still more. Rehoboam "spoke to them according to the advice of the young men, saying,'My father made your yoke heavy, but I will add to your yoke'" (v. 14). It was largely because of that grossly unjust tax policy that the northern tribes revolted and became a separate Jewish kingdom (see vv. 16-20).

Sometimes Jews were taxed by their own king for the purpose of his paying tribute, a form of extortion, demanded by an overlord nation. Such was the case when King Jehoiakim of Judah "exacted the silver and gold from the people of the land, each according to his valuation, to give it to Pharaoh Neco" (2 Kings 23:35).

The first biblical reference to taxation is found in the account of the great famine in the Near East when Joseph was made prime minister of Egypt. Because of the pharaoh's dreams that symbolically depicted seven years of abundant crops followed by seven years of famine, Joseph ordered that, during the seven years of abundance, a fifth of the grain produced would be stored and kept in reserve,"so that the land may not perish during the famine" (Gen. 41:36, 48-49). Some years later, when another famine gripped that region, Joseph enacted a permanent law requiring that a fifth of the produce of the land henceforth be paid to the pharaoh each year (47:26). Because Joseph was so uniquely directed by God, it seems reasonable to assume that this standard of paying twenty percent tax to human government was at least divinely sanctioned, if not divinely authored.

As alluded to above, when God established the nation of Israel, He instituted a specific and detailed system of taxation for His chosen people. The first tax was a tithe, or tenth."Thus all the tithe of the land, of the seed of the land or of the fruit of the tree, is the Lord's; it is holy to the Lord" (Lev. 27:30). This tithe was devoted entirely to the support of the priestly tribe of Levi (see Num. 18:21-24), which had no land allocated to it and had no means of self-support. It was therefore sometimes referred to as the Levite's tithe.

In addition to being the spiritual leaders of Israel, the priests, in particular the chief priests and high priest, were also the nation's civil rulers. This tithe, therefore, was essentially a tax to support Israel's theocratic government.

Another divinely-instituted tax was the annual festival tithe, which was used for sacrifices, for supporting the tabernacle and then the temple, for cultivating social and cultural life, and for fostering national unity (see Deut. 12:10-19).

It was for failure to contribute their tithes that the Lord strongly rebuked His people through Malachi, declaring, "Will a man rob God? Yet you are robbing Me! But you say, 'How have we robbed Thee?' In tithes and offerings" (Mal. 3:8). He then gave the well-known promise: "'Bring the whole tithe into the storehouse, so that there may be food in My house, and test Me now in this,' says the Lord of hosts, 'if I will not open for you the windows of heaven, and pour out for you a blessing until it overflows'" (Mal. 3:10).

A third tax also was a tithe, but since it was levied only every third year, it amounted to 3.3 percent a year. The proceeds were used to help "the alien, the orphan and the widow who are in your town, [who] shall come and eat and be satisfied, in order that the Lord your God may bless you in all the work of your hand which you do" (Deut. 14:29).

The first tithe paid for government expenses, the second tithe was used for cultivating national life, and the triennial third tithe supported welfare services.

A fourth tax was used to support the tabernacle and temple. This annual half-shekel tax was levied on every male Israelite "twenty years old and over," and was "a contribution to the Lord" (Ex. 30:14).

The Mosaic law also provided for two other taxes that were somewhat indirect. At the end of every season, Jews were required to leave some of their crops unharvested, allowing the remainder to be gleaned by the poor. "Now when you reap the harvest of your land," the Lord instructed His people, "you shall not reap to the very corners of your field, neither shall you gather the gleanings of your harvest. Nor shall you glean your vineyard, nor shall you gather the fallen fruit of your vineyard; you shall leave them for the needy and for the stranger. I am the Lord your God" (Lev. 19:10).

The second indirect tax required that every seventh year cultivated land was to lie fallow. Whatever crops might come up on their own during that year were to be left for the poor, and what remained after that was left for livestock to eat.

The total of those six taxes, all of which were mandatory, amounted to perhaps 24 percent a year.

By New Testament times, the tax situation in Israel was, of course, vastly different, first of all because of the Exile and second because of their subsequent subjugation to Greece and then Rome. But the Romans did allow the nation to levy certain religious taxes. When the tax collectors in Capernaum demanded the two-drachma temple tax of Jesus, He willingly paid it. In that instance He provided the money miraculously, by having Peter cast a line into the Sea of Galilee and catch a fish in whose mouth was a stater—a coin worth four drachmas, the exact amount needed to pay Jesus' and Peter's taxes (Matt. 17:24-27).

The force of Jesus' example in this instance was especially compelling for His followers. He explained to Peter, in effect, that, as the Son of God, He had no obligation to pay a tax to support God's own house (v. 26), but that, as the Son of Man, He did so in order not to give offense to the civil authorities and to be an example to His disciples (v. 27). His action on that occasion is all the more poignant in that the contribution went to the coffers of the high priest and chief priests, who, a short while later, would put Him to death. The money, in fact, went into the treasury of the temple, which had become so corrupt that Jesus had already cleansed it once of its moneychangers and sacrifice sellers (John 2:14-16) and would do so again shortly before His arrest and crucifixion (Matt. 21:12-13). It was even out of the temple treasury that thirty pieces of silver would be taken to bribe Judas into betraying Christ. Knowing all of that, Jesus paid the tax without hesitation or reservation.

As just noted, because the temple was the house of God, and because He was the Son of God, Jesus had no obligation to pay the temple tax. In somewhat the same way, Christians are not under obligation to give a specified amount to the work of their heavenly Father. In none of their forms do the tithe or other Old Testament levies apply to Christians. As far as the amount we are to give to the Lord, Paul advises, "On the first day of every week let each one of you put aside and save, as he may prosper" (1 Cor. 16:2). And as for our *attitude* in giving, he says, "Let each one do just as he has purposed in his heart; not grudgingly or under compulsion; for God loves a cheerful giver" (2 Cor. 9:7).

In the week following Jesus' triumphal entry into Jerusalem, the Pharisees were determined to convict Him of a capital offense, and they "counseled together how they might trap Him in what He said. And they sent their disciples to Him, along with the Herodians." The group addressed Jesus with mock flattery, "saying, 'Teacher, we know that You are truthful and teach the way of God in truth, and defer to no one; for You are not partial to any. Tell us therefore, what do You think? Is it lawful to give a poll-tax to Caesar, or not?'" (Matt. 22:15-17).

Because Pharisees were fiercely nationalistic and hated the Romans, they knew that their bringing a charge of treason against Jesus would not likely be taken seriously by the Roman authorities. It was doubtless for that reason that they became coconspirators against Jesus with the Herodians, whom they normally had nothing to do with, because the Herodians were very much pro-Roman. And, as their name implies, the Herodians supported the Herod kings, who not only were

vassals of Rome but also were despised Idumeans. The Pharisees therefore believed that a charge of treason brought by the Herodians would
almost certainly result in Jesus' conviction and execution. "But Jesus
perceived their malice, and said, 'Why are you testing Me, you hypocrites? Show Me the coin used for the poll-tax.' And they brought Him a
denarius. And He said to them, 'Whose likeness and inscription is this?'
They said to Him, 'Caesar's.' Then He said to them, 'Then render to Caesar
the things that are Caesar's; and to God the things that are God's'" (Matt.
22:18-21).

Because Jesus knew His death was imminent, even the harshest
critic could not accuse Him of making that reply in order to protect His
well-being. He would have given the same answer at the beginning or
during any part of His ministry. He was stating unequivocally that paying
taxes to human government is a God-ordained obligation. The facts that
Rome was despotic, pagan, often unjust, and even the fact that the caesar depicted on that particular coin was Augustus—who called himself
the son of god—did not abrogate the obligation. Taxes are to be paid.

THE PURPOSE

**for rulers are servants of God, devoting themselves to this very
thing.** (13:6*b*)

Government authorities, here referred to collectively as **rulers,**
have a much greater responsibility than they and the rest of the unbelieving world realize. Regardless of their political rank, personal qualification, or even their morality, spirituality, or personal awareness, officials
who collect taxes **are servants of God.** Like every other civil officer,
the tax collector "is a minister of God . . . for good" (13:4), and it is for
that reason that we are to pay our taxes.

Servants does not translate *doulos,* the most common New
Testament term for servant, but *leitourgos,* which originally was used of
a person who served in a public office at his own expense, and it was
later used of all officials, much in the same sense that the term *public
servant* is used today. Elsewhere in the New Testament, however, this
word is sometimes rendered *minister,* and is used of angels (Christ's
"ministers," Heb. 1:7,14), of Paul himself ("a minister of Christ Jesus to the
Gentiles," Rom. 15:16), and even of Christ ("a minister in the sanctuary,
and in the true tabernacle, which the Lord pitched, not man," Heb. 8:2).
It is doubtless because *leitourgos* was used in the New Testament and
in the early church to represent a religious *servant,* a minister of God,
that it eventually came into the English language as *liturgy,* which refers
to a prescribed religious *service.*

Having been the most zealous of Pharisees (Phil. 3:5-6), Paul (then known as Saul) doubtless had chafed fiercely under the despised Roman rule and resented every denarius he was forced to pay for its support. But now that he was submissive to Christ as his Lord, he knew that he must also be submissive to the institution of government, which his Lord had ordained. His point in the present text, therefore, is that, because their authority is from God, all *civil* servants—from the least to the greatest, from the best to the worst—also are **servants of God.** Despite the fact that the great majority of civil leaders would reject the idea that they are **devoting themselves** to God's service, Paul makes clear that they nevertheless represent a divine institution as well as a human mission.

Near the end of the first century, no doubt thinking of the severe persecution by the emperor Nero, and more recently by Domitian, Clement of Rome (possibly the fellow worker Paul mentions in Philippians 4:3) prayed the following prayer:

> Guide our steps to walk in holiness and righteousness and singleness of heart, and to do those things that are good and acceptable in Thy sight, and in the sight of our rulers. Yes, Lord, cause Thy face to shine upon us in peace for our good, that we may be sheltered by Thy mighty hand and delivered from every sin by Thine outstretched arm. Deliver us from those who hate us wrongfully. Give concord and peace to us and to all who dwell on earth, as Thou didst to our fathers, when they called on Thee in faith and truth with holiness, while we render obedience to Thine almighty and most excellent name, and to our earthly rulers and governors.
>
> Thou, O Lord and Master, hast given them the power of sovereignty through Thine excellent and unspeakable might, that we, knowing the glory and honour which Thou hast given them, may submit ourselves to them, in nothing resisting Thy will. Grant them therefore, O Lord, health, peace, concord and stability, that they may without failure administer the government which Thou hast committed to them. For Thou, O heavenly Master, King of the ages, dost give to the sons of men glory and honour and power over all things that are in the earth. Do Thou, O Lord, direct their counsel according to what is good and acceptable in Thy sight, that they, administering in peace and gentleness with godliness the power which Thou hast committed to them, may obtain Thy favour. (*1 Clement* lx.2-lxi.2. Cited in F. F. Bruce, *The Epistle of Paul to the Romans* [London: Tyndale Press, 1967], 235)

Justin Martyr, the second-century theologian and church Father, wrote to the Roman emperor Antoninus Pius, "Everywhere we [Christians], more readily than all men, endeavour to pay to those appointed by you the taxes both ordinary and extraordinary, as we have been taught by [Jesus].... Whence to God alone we render worship, but in

other things we gladly serve you, acknowledging you as kings and rulers
of men, and praying that with your kingly power you be found to possess
also sound judgment" ("The First Apology of Justin," chapter 27 in *The
Ante-Nicene Fathers,* vol. 1, Alexander Roberts and James Donaldson, ed.
[Grand Rapids: Eerdmans, rep. 1973, 168).

During a time when Rome was especially hostile toward Christians, a later church Father, Tertullian, wrote, "Without ceasing, for all our
emperors we offer prayer. We pray for life prolonged; for security to the
empire; for protection to the imperial house; for brave armies, a faithful
senate, a virtuous people, the world at rest, whatever, as man or Caesar, an
emperor would wish" ("Apology," chapter 30 in *The Ante-Nicene Fathers,*
vol. 3, 42).

Such respect for human government was the norm in the early
church long before the Roman Empire was "Christianized."

As noted in the previous chapter, Christians have every right to
use whatever legal recourse may be available to contest a civil law or
policy, including what they consider to be wrongful tax assessments.
But when those appeals have been exhausted, we are obligated to pay
whatever final amount the government demands, even if it is unjust or
excessive.

It is important for Christians to remind their leaders that civil responsibilities are a divine trust, granted and superintended by God. We
should remind them of, and remember ourselves, the many declarations
in the Psalms of God's sovereign rule over the affairs of men. In Psalm
92:8, He is addressed with the words, "Thou, O Lord, art on high forever."
In 93:1-2 the psalmist speaks of God as the supreme and eternal Ruler:
"The Lord reigns, He is clothed with majesty; the Lord has clothed and
girded Himself with strength; indeed, the world is firmly established, it
will not be moved. Thy throne is established from of old; Thou art from
everlasting."

When King Nebuchadnezzar of Babylon boasted, "Is this not
Babylon the great, which I myself have built as a royal residence by the
might of my power and for the glory of my majesty?" the Lord brought
immediate judgment on his arrogant self-esteem. "While the word was
in the king's mouth, a voice came from heaven, saying, 'King Nebuchadnezzar, to you it is declared: sovereignty has been removed from you,
and you will be driven away from mankind, and your dwelling place
will be with the beasts of the field. You will be given grass to eat like
cattle, and seven periods of time will pass over you, until you recognize
that the Most High is ruler over the realm of mankind, and bestows it
on whomever He wishes'" (Dan. 4:30-32). The once proud monarch was
sincerely humbled and confessed, "I, Nebuchadnezzar, raised my eyes
toward heaven, and my reason returned to me, and I blessed the Most
High and praised and honored Him who lives forever; for His dominion

is an everlasting dominion, and His kingdom endures from generation to generation" (Dan. 4:34).

Christians need to affirm before the world that God is the ultimate and only Sovereign. We should respectfully remind our human leaders that the Lord "chastens the nations" (Ps. 94:10), and that "He is coming to judge the earth; [that] He will judge the world with righteousness, and the peoples with equity" (Ps. 98:9). As His people, we should "tell of His glory among the nations, His wonderful deeds among all the peoples. For great is the Lord, and greatly to be praised; He is to be feared above all gods. For all the gods of the peoples are idols, but the Lord made the heavens" (Ps. 96:3-5).

Robert Culver is correct in saying,

> Where theistic religion grows weak, [the concept of justice] will weaken. Crimes then are defined as antisocial activity, which in turn is then merely what the majority says it is. Then punishments seem to be the result of the majorities ganging up on the minority. This in turn seems inconsistent with democratic feelings. The result is a decline in uniform application of penalties for crime, resultant miscarriage of justice, trampling on the rights of law-abiding people, together with an increase in what ought to be called crime. *(Toward a Biblical View of Civil Government* [Chicago: Moody Press, 1974], 78-79)

Standards based on majority opinion are, by definition, subject to the changes and whims of the individuals who comprise the majority. What is considered a crime one day may be seen as satisfactory behavior the next, and vice versa.

The founding fathers of the United States were well aware of that danger, and the furthest thing from their minds was establishing a system of government that did not recognize God's Word as the basis of good civil law, not to mention a government that would exclude Him altogether. Whenever the principles of government are detached from God and are not seen as a reflection of His divine mind, justice suffers to the extent that He is disregarded.

Christians should choose government officials who are faithful to their civic responsibilities. It is certainly desirable to have genuine Christians in public office, but the mere fact of being a Christian does not qualify a person for any public position. In some cases, a non-Christian may be more qualified for public service than his Christian opponent.

As **servants of God,** civil authorities not only should realize that they serve by God's sovereign permission but that they are therefore held accountable by Him for serving responsibly on behalf of society.

The Lord requires humility in government leaders, perhaps the most uncommon characteristic found among them, especially among those who wield considerable power. God promises to "put an end to the arrogance of the proud, and abase the haughtiness of the ruthless" (Isa. 13:11).

The Lord also requires justice, mercy and compassion. Speaking of an unidentified king of Babylon, He declared, "How the oppressor has ceased, and how fury has ceased! The Lord has broken the staff of the wicked, the scepter of rulers which used to strike the peoples in fury with unceasing strokes, which subdued the nations in anger with unrestrained persecution. . . . Your pomp and the music of your harps have been brought down to Sheol" (Isa. 14:4-6,11).

Daniel rebuked Nebuchadnezzar for his pride (Dan. 4:25) and for his not "showing mercy to the poor" (v.27). He rebuked Belshazzar for his indolence, laziness, stupidity, blasphemy, sacrilege, drunkenness, pride, and for failing to glorify God (Dan. 5).

The Lord requires that rulers maintain order by just and firm enforcement of the law. The Old Testament repeatedly indicted kings, governors, and other officials for not doing so. When the people of Judah reneged on their covenant with the Lord to release all Jewish slaves after six years of service, they were not punished by King Zedekiah and the other civil authorities. God therefore declared a terrible judgment on those officials for their dereliction of duty as well as on the disobedient slave owners they failed to chastise (Jer. 34:12-22). Refusal to release such slaves was one of the sins for which God delivered Judah into the hand of King Nebuchadnezzar of Babylon, who at that very time was preparing to lay siege to Jerusalem (Jer. 34:1-3).

In addition to those standards, the Lord charges rulers not to seek their own welfare at the expense of their subjects. Through Isaiah, He warned the leaders of Judah, "Woe to those who enact evil statutes, and to those who constantly record unjust decisions, so as to deprive the needy of justice, and rob the poor of My people of their rights, in order that widows may be their spoil, and that they may plunder the orphans" (Isa. 10:1-2).

God warned the oppressive and unjust King Shallum of Judah:

> "Woe to him who builds his house without righteousness and his upper rooms without justice, who uses his neighbor's services without pay and does not give him his wages, who says, 'I will build myself a roomy house with spacious upper rooms, and cut out its windows, paneling it with cedar and painting it bright red.' Do you become a king because you are competing in cedar? Did not your father eat and drink, and do justice and righteousness? Then it was well with him. He pled the cause of the afflicted and needy; then it was well. Is not that what it means to know Me?" declares the Lord. "But your eyes and your heart

are intent only upon your own dishonest gain, and on shedding innocent blood and on practicing oppression and extortion." (Jer. 22:13-17)

Contrary to the practice of Shallum, rulers are to sympathize with the needs of their people and to show them kindness by relieving their suffering and want. They are to be like King Josiah, the father of Shallum, who "did justice and righteousness" and "pled the cause of the afflicted and needy" (vv. 15-16).

The Lord demands truthfulness from human rulers, and they are subject to His divine wrath when their lies lead the people astray (Amos 2:4).

Finally, civil authorities are accountable for enforcing public morality and decency. The Lord sent Jonah to Nineveh to "cry against it, for their wickedness has come up before Me" (Jonah 1:2).

Although Christians are to be submissive to civil leaders, they also are compelled, like those prophets, to speak out against authority that is unrighteous.

THE PARTICULARS

Render to all what is due them: tax to whom tax is due; custom to whom custom; fear to whom fear; honor to whom honor. (13:7)

In his final comment on the Christian's submission to human government, Paul mentions several particulars about paying taxes.

First, we are to **render to all what is due them.** *Apodidōmi* **(render)** carries the idea of paying back something that is owed, and that meaning is reinforced by the phrase **what is due them.** Taxes are not voluntary or optional offerings given for the support of government, and paying them is the unqualified obligation of every citizen. Christians not only have a moral but a spiritual responsibility to pay taxes, because they know, or should know, that God requires it of them. Cheating on taxes is a crime against government and a sin against God.

This **tax** *(phoros)* is the same term mentioned in verse 6, probably referring to a combination income and property tax paid by individuals to their foreign rulers, which made its payment particularly onerous. Yet the command is clear: Christians are to pay **tax to** everyone **to whom tax is due.**

The **custom** *(telos)* was a form of toll or goods tax, paid directly to Roman governors or procurators or to their vassals, such as King Herod. Assessments such as those are also to be paid unbegrudgingly **to whom** they are legally due.

The next two obligations mentioned in this verse do not relate to paying taxes but to a Christian's attitude toward public officials.

First, Paul says, we are to render **fear to whom fear** is due. *Phobos* **(fear)** was used to refer to everything from awe to abject terror. In this context, it probably means having sincere respect for civil authorities who collect taxes.

Second, we are to render honor to whom honor is due. *Time* **(honor)** refers to high esteem that is genuine, not feigned or merely pretended. The **honor** we render to those in authority, including those who collect taxes from us, should itself be honorable.

In his *Epistle to Diognetus,* an anonymous second-century Christian wrote the following beautiful description of believers who genuinely obey the divine commands of Romans 13:1-7:

> Christians are distinguished from other men neither by country, nor language, nor the customs which they observe. For they neither inhabit cities of their own, nor employ a peculiar form of speech, nor lead a life which is marked out by any singularity. The course of conduct which they follow has not been devised by any speculation or deliberation of inquisitive men; nor do they, like some, proclaim themselves the advocates of any merely human doctrines. But, inhabiting Greek as well as barbarian cities, according as the lot of each of them had determined, and following the customs of the natives in respect to clothing, food, and the rest of their ordinary conduct, they display to us their wonderful and confessedly striking method of life. They dwell in their own countries, but simply as sojourners. As citizens, they share in all things with others, and yet endure all things as if foreigners. Every foreign land is to them as their native country, and every land of their birth as a land of strangers. They marry, as do all [others]; they beget children; but they do not destroy their offspring. They have a common table, but not a common bed. They are in the flesh, but they do not live after the flesh. They pass their days on earth, but they are citizens of heaven. They obey the prescribed laws, and at the same time surpass the laws by their lives. They love all men, and are persecuted by all. They are unknown and condemned; they are put to death, and restored to life. They are poor, yet make many rich; they are in lack of all things, and yet abound in all; they are dishonoured, and yet in their very dishonour are glorified. They are evil spoken of, and yet are justified; they are reviled, and bless; they are insulted, and repay the insult with honour; they do good, yet are punished as evil-doers. When punished, they rejoice as if quickened into life; they are assailed by the Jews as foreigners, and are persecuted by the Greeks; yet those who hate them are unable to assign any reason for their hatred. (*The Ante-Nicene Fathers*, Alexander Roberts and James Donaldson, ed. [Grand Rapids: Eerdmans, rep. 1973], 26-27)

Love Fulfills the Law (Romans 13:8-10)

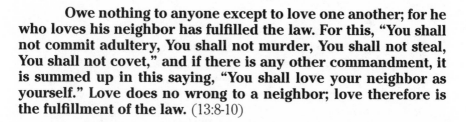

Owe nothing to anyone except to love one another; for he who loves his neighbor has fulfilled the law. For this, "You shall not commit adultery, You shall not murder, You shall not steal, You shall not covet," and if there is any other commandment, it is summed up in this saying, "You shall love your neighbor as yourself." Love does no wrong to a neighbor; love therefore is the fulfillment of the law. (13:8-10)

Enthusiasm is easier than obedience. That truth is especially appropriate to this text. It is much easier to commend love than to live by it, as it was even for Paul. Earlier in this epistle he confesses, "For we know that the Law is spiritual; but I am of flesh, sold into bondage to sin. For that which I am doing, I do not understand; for I am not practicing what I would like to do, but I am doing the very thing I hate," and that "the good that I wish, I do not do; but I practice the very evil that I do not wish" (Rom. 7:14-15,19). Every honest Christian knows that this sobering truth applies to his own life.

Yet obedience is the heart of faithful Christian living. It is through obedience to God that believers have blessing, joy, and spiritual power. Jesus warned, "Not everyone who says to Me, 'Lord, Lord,' will enter the kingdom of heaven; but he who does the will of My Father who is in heaven" (Matt. 7:21). On another occasion He said, "For whoever does the will of God, he is My brother and sister and mother" (Mark 3:35). Jesus also set the perfect example of obedience, the pattern for all believers to follow, saying, "My food is to do the will of Him who sent Me, and to accomplish His work" (John 4:34). The essence of His incarnation was to obey His heavenly Father. "I have come down from heaven," He said, "not to do My own will, but the will of Him who sent Me" (John 6:38). He also testified, "I can do nothing on My own initiative. As I hear, I judge; and My judgment is just, because I do not seek My own will, but the will of Him who sent Me" (John 5:30). During His intense agony in Gethsemane over the dreadful ordeal He knew just awaited Him, He nevertheless twice prayed that His Father's will be done. He first prayed, "My Father, if it is possible, let this cup pass from Me; yet not as I will, but as Thou wilt" (Matt. 26:39). A short while later, after finding the disciples asleep, "He went away again a second time and prayed, saying, 'My Father, if this cannot pass away unless I drink it, Thy will be done'" (v. 42).

Obedience demands the exercise of will under the prompting and the power of the Holy Spirit, just as in coming to the Lord for salvation. Such power is the source of all obedience, yet the Lord demands *obedience* for *living* the spiritual life just as He demands *faith* for *receiving* spiritual life. The popular admonition "Let go and let God" is valid if it is used in the sense of relying on God's wisdom and power instead of human resources. But it is not valid, and certainly not biblical, if it means putting the will into neutral, as it were, and expecting God to control everything apart from personal volition and effort. Otherwise, the countless commands and exhortations in Scripture, very much including the New Testament, would be meaningless. Why chasten the disobedient if they have no responsibility in themselves? For that matter, why reward them if they do obey?

Still, for obvious reasons, obedience has never been popular. From a child's earliest years, the idea of doing what his parents want him to do is disagreeable and frustrating, because it thwarts his own will and sense of independence. The notion of submitting personal will to the will of someone else, even God—or rather, especially God—has always been abhorrent to fallen human nature. It was Adam's and Eve's placing their own wills above God's that was the first sin, and it is that same spirit of disobedience that has been at the heart of every sin since that tragic day. Sin is lawlessness and rebellion in its very nature (cf. 1 John 3:4).

As the apostle explained early in this epistle, disobedience because of unbelief caused fallen mankind from the beginning to embrace "ungodliness and unrighteousness," to "suppress the truth in unrighteousness," to dishonor God, to become "futile in their speculations," to have their foolish hearts darkened, and to exchange "the glory of the incorruptible God for an image in the form of corruptible man and of birds and four-footed animals and crawling creatures" (see Rom. 1:18-23). And it was because of that disobedience that "God gave them over in the lusts of their hearts to impurity" (v. 24), "to degrading passions" (v. 26), and "to a depraved mind" (v. 28).

Because of the lingering old self (Eph. 4:22), obedience to God does not always come easy even for His own children. But because he is new in Jesus Christ and is indwelt by the Holy Spirit, the genuine Christian has a disposition that desires to do his Father's will—and that inner desire is a most reliable evidence of salvation. Every believer can rightly say with Paul, that, even though "I find then the principle that evil is present in me, the one who wishes to do good," nevertheless, "I joyfully concur with the law of God in the inner man" (Rom. 7:21-22). Even the most spiritual saint will disobey his Lord on occasion, but his conscience will not be free until he repents and becomes obedient, because his disobedience not only is contrary to God's will but contrary to his own deep longings.

For the believer, obedience to God's Word is lovely, encouraging, and hopeful. Nowhere is that truth more beautifully and majestically portrayed than in Psalm 119. Without question, this poem is the grandest series of statements made by a child of God expressing his inmost desire to submit to his Lord's will. The psalmist uses ten different words, most of them repeated numerous times, to represent the Word of God, which he loves and longs to obey. He tells the Lord (emphases added) of his desire to "learn Thy righteous *judgments*" (v. 7) and "never wander from Thy *commandments*" (v. 10). He declares, "I will meditate on Thy *precepts*, and regard Thy *ways*" (v. 15); "I shall delight in Thy *statutes*; I shall not forget Thy *word*" (v. 16); and, "If Thy *law* had not been my delight, then I would have perished in my affliction" (v. 92). He confesses, "My soul is crushed with longing after Thine *ordinances* at all times" (v. 20); "Thy *testimonies* also are my delight; they are my counselors" (v. 24); "Behold, I long for Thy *precepts·*, revive me through Thy righteousness" (v. 40); "The *law* of Thy mouth is better to me than thousands of gold and silver pieces" (v. 72); and "How sweet are Thy *words* to my taste! Yes, sweeter than honey to my mouth!" (v. 103). He implores the Lord, "Give me understanding, that I may observe Thy *law*, and keep it with all my heart" (v. 34); and "do not take the *word of truth* utterly out of my mouth, for I wait for Thine *ordinances*" (v. 43). And he exults, "Those who love Thy *law* have great peace, and nothing causes them to stumble" (v. 165). All these longings are embattled by remaining sin, as the psalmist concludes when he ends the psalm with,"I have gone astray like a lost sheep; seek Thy servant, for I do not forget Thy *commandments*"(v. 176).

A vital part of "the sanctifying work of the Spirit" is to enable us to "obey Jesus Christ" (1 Pet. 1:2). Paul admonished the Philippian saints, "So then, my beloved, just as you have always obeyed, not as in my presence only, but now much more in my absence, work out your salvation with fear and trembling" (Phil. 2:12). We "work out" our salvation on the outside by being obedient to the Lord Jesus Christ. Paul commended the Christians in Rome because their faithful obedience to Christ, often in the midst of persecution and hardship, was known throughout the churches (Rom. 16:19). The mark of any faithful Christian is a life of submission to God and to His Word, a life such as Paul's that joyfully concurs "with the law of God in the inner man" (Rom. 7:22). His consuming passion is to please his Lord in everything.

Paul has earlier made clear that, as far as its judgment and penalty are concerned, a Christian is free from the law. "There is therefore now no condemnation for those who are in Christ Jesus. For the law of the Spirit of life in Christ Jesus has set you free from the law of sin and of death" (Rom. 8:1-2). But immediately he goes on to explain that God "condemned sin in the flesh, in order that the requirement of the Law might be fulfilled in us, who do not walk according to the flesh, but according to the Spirit" (vv. 3-4). Because they reflect God's own eternal character and will, the moral and spiritual demands of the law are still valid. The difference for a Christian is not in "the requirement of the Law" but in the way that requirement is "fulfilled in us," namely, by our walking "according to the Spirit," whose righteousness and power work in and through us. For believers, the divine requirement is divinely fulfilled as Christ's Holy Spirit enables us to obey His holy Word.

I once talked to a recent convert who said, "Ever since I received Christ into my life, I seem to have a constant battle with sin. When will the struggle end?" I answered, "When you die or are raptured." When she expressed understandable distress, I assured her that her struggle with sin in her remaining humanness was a reliable sign of her salvation. The unsaved have no such intense struggle, because their sinful living is in harmony with their sinful desires. I also assured her that, the longer the battle is faithfully fought in obedience to God's Word and in the power of His Spirit, the more victorious our lives become.

In the practical section of the book of Romans, we have seen that Paul first deals with the believer's right relationship with God (12:1), then with his right relationship with the world (v. 1), with fellow believers (vv. 3-8), with everyone (vv. 9-21), and with human government (13:1-7). He now focuses again on our relationship to others, a relationship that is to be summarized by love (vv. 8-10). More than that, he points out, love is the key to *all* godly obedience, because love fulfills God's law (vv. 8, 10*b*).

In these three beautiful and challenging verses, the apostle relates the debt of love (v. 8), the discharge of love (vv. 9-10*a*), and the design of love (v. 10*b*).

THE DEBT OF LOVE

Owe nothing to anyone except to love one another; for he who loves his neighbor has fulfilled the law. (13:8)

Paul has just been speaking of paying taxes (vv. 6-7), and the admonition to **owe nothing to anyone** continues his focus on the Christian's financial obligations.

That phrase is sometimes interpreted to mean that a Christian is never justified in going into debt of any sort. But neither the Old nor New Testament categorically forbids borrowing or lending.

The Mosaic law did require that, "If you lend money to My people, to the poor among you, you are not to act as a creditor to him; you shall not charge him interest" (Ex. 22:25; cf. Ps. 15:5). It is obvious from this verse that if lending was permitted, so was borrowing. The moral issue involved charging interest (or "usury" KJV) to the poor. The principle of charging interest is stated more explicitly in Leviticus: "Now in case a countryman of yours becomes poor and his means with regard to you falter, then you are to sustain him, like a stranger or a sojourner, that he may live with you. Do not take *usurious interest* from him, but revere your God, that your countryman may live with you" (Lev. 25:35-36, emphasis added; cf. Neh. 5:7; Ezek. 22:12).

God also warned His people against refusing to give a loan to a fellow countryman because a sabbatical year was near, when all debts were canceled (Deut. 15:7-9). The Lord promised the unselfish and generous lender that "for this thing the Lord your God will bless you in all your work and in all your undertakings" (v. 10). He declared that "the righteous is gracious and gives....All day long he is gracious and lends; and his descendants are a blessing" (Ps. 37:21, 26), and that "He who is gracious to a poor man lends to the Lord, and He will repay him for his good deed" (Prov. 19:17). Whether or not a gracious lender is repaid by the borrower, he unquestionably will be repaid by the Lord.

From those passages and many others, it is obvious that lending, and therefore borrowing, were common and legitimate practices in ancient Israel. The Law carefully regulated lending by prohibiting charging interest to those who were destitute, but it did not forbid lending with honest and reasonable interest.

In the Sermon on the Mount, Jesus gives tacit approval of borrowing and commands potential lenders:"Give to him who asks of you, and do not turn away from him who wants to borrow from you" (Matt. 5:42). Augmenting the truth mentioned above regarding divine blessing of those who give graciously and generously, Jesus said,"Love your enemies, and do good, and lend, expecting nothing in return; and your reward will be great, and you will be sons of the Most High" (Luke 6:35). Again we are promised that, when we give out of genuine kindness to those in need, the Lord Himself will reward us in His own gracious way.

Both the old and new testaments, therefore, justify borrowing by those who are in serious need and have no other recourse, and both testaments command believers who are able to do so to lend to their needy brethren without taking advantage.

In the realm of business, apart from the needy, Jesus approved of financial borrowing for the purpose of investment. In the parable of the talents (Matt. 25:14-30), the master highly commended the two servants who had wisely invested his money, but he strongly rebuked the unfaithful servant who merely buried the money entrusted to him:"You ought to have put my money in the bank, and on my arrival I would have received my money back with interest" (v. 27).

Many businesses could not operate without borrowing money to invest in such things as buildings, equipment, and raw materials. Many farmers could not plant new crops without borrowing money for seed and fertilizer. Most families could never afford to buy a home without taking out a mortgage.

When borrowing is truly necessary, the money should be repaid as agreed upon with the lender, promptly and fully. But Scripture nowhere justifies borrowing for the purpose of buying unnecessary things, especially luxuries, that cannot be afforded. And whatever is owed must be paid on time and in full. Those financial principles are the essence of Paul's admonition to **owe nothing to anyone.**

The apostle then makes what appears at first glance to be a radical transition, declaring that all Christians have a type of perpetual indebtedness. Completely apart from financial considerations or situations, all believers have the constant obligation **to love one another.** It is a debt we are constantly to pay against but can never pay off. The early church Father, Origen said,"The debt of love remains with us permanently and never leaves us. This is a debt which we pay every day and forever owe." And by our Lord's gracious provision, it is a debt we will always have the resources to pay and which, the more we pay toward it, the more willing and joyous the payment will be.

Our **love** toward **one another** applies first of all to fellow believers, our brothers and sisters in Christ."A new commandment I give to you," Jesus said, "that you love one another, even as I have loved you, that you also love one another. By this all men will know that you are My disciples, if you have love for one another" (John 13:34-35). To serve other Christians is to serve Christ."I was hungry, and you gave Me something to eat," He said; "I was thirsty, and you gave Me drink; I was a stranger, and you invited Me in; naked, and you clothed Me; I was sick, and you visited Me; I was in prison, and you came to Me....Truly I say to you, to the extent that you did it to one of these brothers of Mine, even the least of them, you did it to Me" (Matt. 25:35-36, 40)."Ministering to the saints" not only demonstrates our love for them but also our love for God (Heb. 6:10).

Love is the theme of John's first letter. He tells us that "the one who loves his brother abides in the light and there is no cause for stumbling in him" (1 John 2:10). He reminds us that God commands "that we believe in the name of His Son Jesus Christ, and love one another, just as He commanded us" (3:23). He admonishes us, "Beloved, let us love one another, for love is from God; and everyone who loves is born of God and knows God" (4:7), and that "this commandment we have from Him, that the one who loves God should love his brother also" (4:21).

Paul also has much to say about loving fellow Christians. In his letter to Colossae, he wrote, "And so, as those who have been chosen of God, holy and beloved, put on a heart of compassion, kindness, humility, gentleness and patience; bearing with one another, and forgiving each other, whoever has a complaint against anyone; just as the Lord forgave you, so also should you. And beyond all these things put on love, which is the perfect bond of unity" (Col. 3:12-14). He counseled the often factious and worldly Corinthian believers to "pursue love" (1 Cor. 14:1), and he advised Timothy to encourage the godly women to "continue in faith and love and sanctity" (1 Tim. 2:15). He prayed that the love of believers in Philippi might "abound still more and more in real knowledge and all discernment" (Phil. 1:9).

The apostle Peter, who had found it so difficult to love in the way his Lord desired (see, e.g., John 21:15-22; Acts 10), wrote, "Since you have in obedience to the truth purified your souls for a sincere love of the brethren, fervently love one another from the heart" (1 Pet. 1:22).

But **one another** also applies to unbelievers—unbelievers, not just those who are likeable and friendly. Our Lord tells us, "You have heard that it was said, 'You shall love your neighbor, and hate your enemy.' But I say to you, love your enemies, and pray for those who persecute you" (Matt. 5:44). As we have seen in the previous chapter of Romans, Paul commands: "Bless those who persecute you; bless and curse not" (12:14), and, "If your enemy is hungry, feed him, and if he is thirsty, give him a drink" (v. 20). In his letter to the Galatian churches he admonishes, "So then, while we have opportunity, let us do good to *all* *men,* and especially to those who are of the household of the faith" (Gal. 6:10, emphasis added).

Righteous love is so immeasurably important that *he who loves his neighbor has fulfilled the law,* a truth that Paul reiterates in verse 10 and that will be discussed in detail in the study of that verse.

It is clear that righteous, godly love is much more than emotion or feeling. As seen in the Galatians passage just quoted, love begins with "a heart of compassion, kindness, humility, gentleness and patience." But it also and always finds ways to *"do"* to those whom we love, whether they seem to deserve it or not. Because of distance or other circumstances beyond our control, sometimes the only good we can do is to pray for them or forgive them. There are, of course, no greater things to do for anyone than to pray for them and forgive them, especially if we are praying for their salvation and if our forgiveness of them might lead them to seek God's. But, as noted above, "while we have opportunity," we are also commanded to demonstrate our love in direct and practical ways. Godly love includes ministering to the physical and financial needs of others, unbelievers as well as believers. That truth is the central point of Jesus' parable of the Good Samaritan (Luke 10:25-37).

There are many other ways to demonstrate godly love. Of supreme importance is to teach and to live God's truth. For unbelievers, by far the most important truth to convey is the gospel of salvation. Believers teach God's truth by living faithfully "in purity, in knowledge, in patience, in kindness, in the Holy Spirit, in genuine love, in the word of truth, in the power of God" (2 Cor. 6:6-7). Even when we find it necessary to warn or rebuke others, we are to speak "the truth in love" (Eph. 4:15).

Godly love never turns its "freedom into an opportunity for the flesh" (Gal. 5:13) and never rejoices in anything that is false or unrighteous (1 Cor. 13:6). Love refuses to do anything, even things that are not sinful in themselves, that might offend a brother's conscience and cause him to stumble morally or spiritually (Rom. 14:21). "Above all," Peter reminds us, "keep fervent in your love for one another, because love covers a multitude of sins" (1 Pet. 4:8).

Godly love is forgiving. We are to "be kind to one another, tender-hearted, forgiving each other, just as God in Christ also has forgiven [us]" (Eph. 4:32). The Lord's promise that "if you forgive men for their transgressions, your heavenly Father will also forgive you," is followed by the sober warning, "But if you do not forgive men, then your Father will not forgive your transgressions" (Matt. 6:14-15; cf. Luke 6:36-37).

Godly love is characterized by humility, gentleness, patience, and forbearance (Eph. 4:2). In his beautiful entreaty to the Corinthian church, which was *not* characterized by love, Paul said, "Love is patient, love is kind, and is not jealous; love does not brag and is not arrogant, does not act unbecomingly; it does not seek its own, is not provoked, does not take into account a wrong suffered, does not rejoice in unrighteousness, but rejoices with the truth; bears all things, believes all things, hopes all things, endures all things. Love never fails" (1 Cor. 13:4-8).

The greatest test of godly love is its willingness to sacrifice its own needs and welfare for the needs and welfare of others, even to the point of forfeiting life if necessary. "Greater love has no one than this," Jesus said, "that one lay down his life for his friends" (John 15:13). The supreme example of such love was the Lord Jesus Himself, "who, although He existed in the form of God, did not regard equality with God a thing to be grasped, but emptied Himself, taking the form of a bond-servant, and being made in the likeness of men. And being found in appearance as a man, He humbled Himself by becoming obedient to the point of death, even death on a cross" (Phil. 2:6-8). We are to be "imitators of God, as beloved children; and walk in love, just as Christ also loved [us], and gave Himself up for us, an offering and a sacrifice to God as a fragrant aroma" (Eph. 5:1-2). As John reminds us, "We know love by this, that He laid down His life for us; and we ought to lay down our lives for the brethren" (1 John 3:16).

But how, we ask, can we love in such a righteous and selfless way? First, we must keep in mind that our gracious heavenly Father provides His children every resource they need to obey His commands and to follow His example. We are divinely enabled to pay our great debt of love "because the love of God has been poured out within our hearts through the Holy Spirit who was given to us" (Rom. 5:5). God's own love is the inexhaustible well from which, as it were, we can draw the supernatural love He commands us to live by. Paul prayed for the Ephesians that, "being rooted and grounded in love, [you] may be able to comprehend with all the saints what is the breadth and length and height and depth, and to know the love of Christ which surpasses knowledge, that you may be filled up to all the fulness of God" (Eph. 3:17-19).

In order to love as God commands, Christians must submit to the Holy Spirit. In doing so, we must surrender all hatred, animosity, bitterness, revenge, or pride that stands between us and those we are called to love. "Now as to the love of the brethren," Paul says, "you have no need for anyone to write to you, for you yourselves are taught by God to love one another" (1 Thess. 4:9). Through His own Holy Spirit, God Himself teaches us to love! And because God Himself is love (1 John 4:16), it is hardly surprising that the first "fruit of the Spirit is love" (Gal. 5:22).

The love that God commands must be pure and genuine, because love cannot coexist with hypocrisy. Peter therefore admonishes, "Since you have in obedience to the truth purified your souls for a sincere love of the brethren, fervently love one another from the heart" (1 Pet. 1:22). Later in that same letter the apostle pleads for love with a sense of urgency:"The end of all things is at hand; therefore, be of sound judgment and sober spirit for the purpose of prayer. Above all, keep fervent in your love for one another, because love covers a multitude of sins" (4:7-8).

Godly love is a matter of choice, and nothing less than willing, voluntary love is pleasing to God or can energize and unify His people. "Beyond all these things put on love," Paul says, "which is the perfect bond of unity" (Col. 3:14). Our own godly love encourages other believers to love, and for that reason the writer of Hebrews calls us to "consider how to stimulate one another to love and good deeds" (Heb. 10:24). The best opportunity we have for inspiring love in others, the writer goes on to say, is by "not forsaking our own assembling together, as is the habit of some, but encouraging one another; and all the more, as you see the day drawing near" (v. 25). "If therefore there is any encouragement in Christ," Paul entreated the Philippians, "if there is any consolation of love, if there is any fellowship of the Spirit, if any affection and compassion, make my joy complete by being of the same mind, maintaining the same love, united in spirit, intent on one purpose" (Phil. 2:1-2).

And amazingly, in our Lord's infinite grace, righteous love is reciprocal love. We know that we are able to love God only "because He first loved us" (1 John 4:19). And yet our Lord promises that "he who loves Me shall be loved by My Father, and I will love him, and will disclose Myself to him.... And We will come to him, and make Our abode with him" (John 14:21,23).

THE DISCHARGE OF LOVE

For this, "You shall not commit adultery, You shall not murder, You shall not steal, You shall not covet," and if there is any other commandment, it is summed up in this saying, "You shall love your neighbor as yourself." Love does no wrong to a neighbor; (13:9-10*a*)

After declaring that love fulfills the law (v. 8) the apostle illustrates his point by quoting five specific Old Testament laws. The first four are from the Ten Commandments, although they are not in the exact order found in Exodus 20:13-17 and Deuteronomy 5:17-21. The fifth law is from Leviticus 19:18.

Godly love does **not commit adultery,** because such sinful defilement of a person shows disregard for another's purity. Love highly values the virtue of others and will do nothing that is morally defiling. Like every other form of sexual immorality, **adultery** comes from impure, sinful lust, never from pure love.

The same principle applies just as obviously to the person who would commit **murder** or who would **steal.** Love does not rob others of their lives or their property.

Because it does not always have an outward manifestation, when we **covet,** the Lord may be the only one, besides ourselves, who is aware of that sin. But again, if we are loving, we will not **covet,** because love has no part in any unrighteousness (1 Cor. 13:6).

Jesus made clear that *all* sin originates in the heart and in the will, whether or not it is expressed outwardly: "Out of the heart come evil thoughts, murders, adulteries, fornications, thefts, false witness, slanders" (Matt. 15:19). In the Sermon on the Mount He warned, "You have heard that the ancients were told, 'You shall not commit murder' and 'Whoever commits murder shall be liable to the court.' But I say to you that everyone who is angry with his brother shall be guilty before the court" (Matt. 5:21-22), and "You have heard that it was said, 'You shall not commit adultery'; but I say to you, that everyone who looks on a woman to lust for her has committed adultery with her already in his heart" (vv. 27-28).

The Christian who loves with God's love does not need to be concerned about breaking those or **any other commandment,** including the other two of the Ten Commandments that pertain to our relationship to other people, namely, honoring father and mother and not bearing false witness (Ex. 20:12, 16). *All* laws of God that concern human relationships are **summed up in this saying, "You shall love your neighbor as yourself."**

If we truly love others as ourselves, we will not want to do them any harm. This law that Paul quotes is taken from Leviticus 19:18, and Jesus declared it to be second only to the supreme commandment to "love the Lord your God with all your heart, and with all your soul, and with all your mind" (Matt. 22:37-39), which is taken from Deuteronomy 6:5.

The apostle does not mention the first and greatest commandment, or any other commandment relating directly to God, because he is here focusing on our relationships to other human beings, to whom he refers three times, once in each verse, as our **neighbor.** And, as noted above, Jesus made clear that a **neighbor** is anyone with whom we have contact, especially if he is in need (Luke 10:25-37).

The command to **love your neighbor as yourself** is not, as some interpreters today insist, a defense of the popular but totally unbiblical idea that we are to have a high psychological self-image. It rather assumes that, as fallen human beings, we already have a high view of ourselves and that we should, by God's grace, have the same affection for others. Elsewhere Paul admonishes that we are to care for others more than for ourselves. "Do nothing from selfishness or empty conceit," he says, "but with humility of mind let each of you regard one another *as more important than himself*, do not merely look out for your own personal interests, but also for the interests of others" (Phil. 2:3-4, emphasis added).

If believers have such selfless concern for the welfare of others, it clearly follows that genuine, godly **love does no wrong to a neighbor,** meaning it does no wrong to *anyone*.

Paul's point is that a Christian who allows God's love to rule his life is divinely protected from sin and inclined to righteousness. The loving Christian does not obey God's law because he fears the consequences of disobedience but because he loves God and seeks to please Him by loving others.

Fear is a legitimate reason for not sinning, as the Bible's countless warnings about sin and its consequences testify. It is always better not to sin than to sin, whatever the motive. But fear is not the noblest motive for not sinning, especially not for a Christian. Even unbelievers abstain from many visible vices because they are afraid of being caught and punished.

Many nominal Christians lead outwardly moral lives in the hope of pleasing God and making themselves acceptable to Him by their good behavior. But, as the Lord said of ancient Israel during the time of Isaiah, they "draw near with their words and honor Me with their lip service, but they remove their hearts far from Me, and their reverence for Me consists of tradition learned by rote" (Isa. 29:13).

God's Word is replete with promises of blessing and reward for His faithful children, although they are not always fulfilled in a way we would prefer or that is pleasing to the flesh. But even the gracious and marvelous prospect of His heavenly blessings is not the believer's highest and purest motive for obeying the Lord. Godly Christians reject evil and do good because those are the only things the indwelling love of their indwelling Lord will lead them to do. What God wants will be what we want. As someone has said, if we love God with all our heart and other people with all our heart, we can do as we please, because we will only want to do that which pleases God and benefits others.

THE DESIGN OF LOVE

love therefore is the fulfillment of the law. (13:10*b*)

Contrary to what many people think, living by **love** and living by **the law** are not mutually exclusive. They are, in fact, inseparably related. God's **law** cannot be truly obeyed apart from **love,** because love, and only love, as Paul has already explained (v.8*b*), is **the fulfillment of the law.**

Early in His ministry Jesus declared, "Do not think that I came to abolish the Law or the Prophets; I did not come to abolish, but *to fulfill.* For truly I say to you, until heaven and earth pass away not the smallest letter or stroke shall pass away from the Law, until all is accomplished. Whoever then annuls one of the least of these commandments, and so teaches others, shall be called least in the kingdom of heaven; but whoever keeps and teaches them, he shall be called great in the kingdom of heaven" (Matt. 5:17-19, emphasis added).

Later in the Sermon on the Mount, in what is commonly called the golden rule, He said, "Therefore, however you want people to treat you, so treat them, for this is the Law and the Prophets" (Matt. 7:12). James refers to loving our neighbors as ourselves as "fulfilling the royal law, according to the Scripture" (James 2:8). **Love** fulfills the Lord's *golden rule* and the Lord's *royal* **law.**

I have heard a beautiful analogy from the field of music that helps understand the greatness and completeness of love. The musical scale has only seven basic notes, which many children can learn in an hour or less. Yet great composers, such as Handel and Beethoven, could not exhaust those notes and their variations in an entire lifetime. Godly love is like that. It uses the basic, and sometimes seemingly insignificant, things in life to produce the greatest. Love controls temper and guides reason. It seeks to overcome the worst qualities and develop the best. Under the guidance and in the power of the Holy Spirit, it transforms redeemed men and women more and more into the likeness of Jesus Christ. There is no greatness of character to which love cannot elevate a person. In fact, no greatness of character is possible without it, because love is great character.

Some years ago the following paraphrase of 1 Corinthians 13 appeared:

> If I [know] the language perfectly and speak like a native, and have not [God's] love for them, I am nothing. If I have diplomas and degrees and know all the up-to-date methods, and have not His touch of understanding love, I am nothing. If I am able to argue successfully

against the religions of the people and make fools of them, and have not His wooing note, I am nothing. If I have all faith and great ideals and magnificent plans, and not His love that sweats and bleeds and weeps and prays and pleads, I am nothing. If I give my clothes and money to them, and have not His love for them, I am nothing.

If I surrender all prospects, leave home and friends, make the sacrifices of a missionary career, and turn sour and selfish amid the daily annoyances and slights of a missionary life, and have not the love that yields its rights, its leisures, its pet plans, I am nothing. Virtue has ceased to go out of me. If I can heal all manner of sickness and disease, but wound hearts and hurt feelings for want of His love that is kind, I am nothing. If I can write articles or publish books that win applause, but fail to transcribe the Word of the Cross into the language of His love, I am nothing. (Source unknown)

Put on the
Lord Jesus Christ
(Romans 13:11-14)

And this do, knowing the time, that it is already the hour for you to awaken from sleep; for now salvation is nearer to us than when we believed. The night is almost gone, and the day is at hand. Let us therefore lay aside the deeds of darkness and put on the armor of light. Let us behave properly as in the day, not in carousing and drunkenness, not in sexual promiscuity and sensuality, not in strife and jealousy. But put on the Lord Jesus Christ, and make no provision for the flesh in regard to its lusts. (13:11-14)

Following his declaration that godly love fulfills the law (13:8-10), Paul next focuses on the urgency of believers becoming more and more like their Savior and Lord, Jesus Christ, who is Himself the source and power of that divinely-required love. We are to "put on the Lord Jesus Christ" (v. 14a). That phrase summarizes sanctification (the theme of chapters 12-16), the continuing spiritual growth of those who have become children of God through faith in His Son, Jesus Christ. The faithful, obedient, loving Christian grows spiritually by becoming increasingly like Jesus Christ. As we clothe ourselves with Christ, His righteousness, truth, holiness, and love become more and more evident in our own lives. His character becomes reflected in us.

It is interesting that Gentile unbelievers in Antioch of Syria were the first to refer to Christ's followers mockingly as *Christians* (Acts 11:26), a name that carried the diminutive sense of "little Christs." *Christian* soon came to be used as a term of disdain by both Gentile and Jewish unbelievers during the time of the early church. When King Agrippa, an unbelieving Jew, "replied to Paul, 'In a short time you will persuade me to become a Christian'" (Acts 26:28), the obvious derision did not indicate that he considered the name to be one of honor and respect. The only other use of *Christian* in the New Testament is in Peter's first letter, in which he encourages fellow believers with the words, "If anyone suffers as a Christian, let him not feel ashamed, but in that name let him glorify God" (1 Pet. 4:16). He seems to be saying, in effect, "If your persecutors deride you with the name *Christian*, do not be ashamed, but rather accept 'that name' as a badge of honor, because it identifies you with God's Son and your Savior and thereby glorifies your heavenly Father. As Christians, you should *want* to be identified with Christ and be like Him."

The practical meaning of becoming like Christ can be understood through the simple imagery of putting on clothing. Sanctification is to be clothed with Christ. The figure of putting on clothing as symbolic of moral and spiritual behavior was used by the ancient rabbis, who spoke of true worshipers putting on the cloak of the Shekinah glory, meaning that they were to reflect and become like the God they worshiped. Jesus used the figure of clothing several times and it is found in numerous other places throughout the New Testament.

Paul admonished the Ephesians to "lay aside the old self, which is being corrupted in accordance with the lusts of deceit," and to "be renewed in the spirit of your mind, and *put on* the new self, which in the likeness of God has been created in righteousness and holiness of the truth" (Eph. 4:22-24, emphasis added). "As you therefore have received Christ Jesus the Lord," the apostle told the Colossians, "so walk in Him, having been firmly rooted and now being built up in Him and established in your faith" (Col. 2:6-7).

In some places, the figures of taking off and putting on are used in the past tense, indicating the time of conversion, when a believer is justified, accounted righteous because of his trust in Jesus Christ. The old nature dies and a new nature is created. Paul used the figure when he admonished the Christians at Colossae, "Do not lie to one another, since you laid aside the old self with its evil practices, and have put on the new self who is being renewed to a true knowledge according to the image of the One who created him" (Col. 3:9-10). "Laid aside" and "have put on" refer to what those believers already had experienced. "Is being renewed" refers to what was then happening in their lives. The first two phrases refer to justification, the aspect of salvation that occurs and is made permanent at the moment of belief. The third phrase refers to sanctification, the aspect of salvation that the Holy Spirit continues to achieve in believers' lives until glorification when their time on earth is ended, either by death or by rapture.

There is something that is already true about our spiritual life and something that *should be* true about it, an indicative and an imperative. There is a holiness that we already have and a holiness that we *should continue* to pursue. We have been made righteous, yet we strive to live righteously.

Speaking about the time of their conversion, the apostle reminded believers in Galatia that all who "were baptized into Christ have clothed yourselves with Christ" (Gal. 3:27). Earlier in his letter to Rome, Paul assures Christians that "the righteousness of God through faith in Jesus Christ" is bestowed on "all those who believe" (Rom. 3:22). He also declares that "to the one who does not work, but believes in Him who justifies the ungodly, his faith is reckoned as righteousness" (Rom. 4:5; cf. 5:17; 6:1-11; 2 Cor. 5:21; Matt. 22:11-12). By the grace of God the Father, we "are in Christ Jesus, who became to us wisdom from God, and righteousness and sanctification, and redemption" (1 Cor. 1:30).

Those passages, and many others in the New Testament, make clear that every true Christian *already has been clothed* with Christ and His righteousness. Long before the time of Christ, the prophet Isaiah exclaimed, "I will rejoice greatly in the Lord, my soul will exult in my God; for He has clothed me with garments of salvation, He has wrapped me with a robe of righteousness" (Isa. 61:10).

It is of great importance to distinguish between justification, which has been accomplished once and for all, and sanctification, which is a continuing process. Justification refers to declared and *positional* righteousness, sometimes called forensic righteousness. Sanctification refers to the lifelong process of growing in *practical* righteousness.

In the present passage (Rom. 13:11-14), Paul uses the figure of taking off and putting on clothing to represent sanctification, the Christian's forsaking the sins that remain in his remaining fallenness or flesh and embracing the righteousness of his new self, his new creation in Jesus Christ. But before the apostle presents that vital truth, he wants to have his readers' full attention and urges them to wake up from their spiritual lethargy and sin.

WAKE UP!

And this do, knowing the time, that it is already the hour for you to awaken from sleep; for now salvation is nearer to us

**than when we believed. The night is almost gone, and the day is
at hand.** (13:11-12*a*)

The phrases **it is already the hour . . . now salvation is
nearer . . . the night is almost gone . . . and the day is at hand**
all express urgency. Time is limited, opportunity is brief. The time to
heed and to obey is *now*. There is no time for apathy, complacency, or
indifference.

If that admonition was urgent during Paul's day, how much
more urgent is it today! It has always been urgent and will always continue to be urgent until the Lord returns, when our opportunities for
earthly faithfulness, obedience, and evangelism will end and judgment
will fall.

Every generation has had its share of skeptics who ask, "Where
is the promise of His coming? For ever since the fathers fell asleep, all
continues just as it was from the beginning of creation" (2 Pet. 3:4). No
believer who honestly holds God's Word to be inerrant could think that
Paul and Peter were simply overanxious about the imminency of Christ's
second coming. But the majority of Christians throughout most, if not all,
of church history have lived believing that was true.

And this do carries the idea of achieving something in addition to what Paul has just been stressing, especially in verses 8-10 regarding love. J. B. Phillips broadly paraphrases verse 11 as, "Why all this stress
on behaviour? Because, as I think you have realised, the present time
is of the highest importance." We are never to stop offering our "bodies
a living and holy sacrifice, acceptable to God, which is [our] spiritual
service of worship" (12:1). We are always to be properly related to unbelievers as well as believers, to civil leaders as well as church leaders, to
enemies as well as friends and neighbors—fulfilling God's law through
love (12:2-13:10).

Paul is not referring to chronological **time** (*chronos*) but to
kairos, **time** as an era, epoch, or age. This term and its Hebrew equivalent are frequently used in Scripture. During the reign of King David, "the
sons of Issachar" were described as "men who understood the times,
with knowledge of what Israel should do" (1 Chron. 12:32).

When a group of Pharisees and Sadducees tried to test Jesus'
authority, they demanded that He perform "a sign from heaven. But He
answered and said to them, 'When it is evening, you say, "It will be fair
weather, for the sky is red." And in the morning, "There will be a storm
today, for the sky is red and threatening." Do you know how to discern
the appearance of the sky, but cannot discern the signs of the times
[*kairos*]?'" (Matt. 16:1-3). Jesus was speaking about their understanding
of what God was then doing before their very eyes. The Messiah, the
divinely promised Redeemer, the incarnate Son of God, was standing

before them, yet they did not recognize Him or accept anything He taught or did. They were in the very midst of the season [*kairos*] of redemption, but their spiritual blindness prevented their seeing it.

Such distinct periods or epochs of special importance in God's redemptive history are referred to in many other New Testament passages (see, e.g., Matt. 26:18; Mark 1:15; Rom. 3:26; Rev. 1:3). The particular time of redemptive history of which Paul is speaking in the present text is that which precedes the parousia of Christ.

Because they are untaught or wrongly taught in God's Word or have little interest in spiritual things, many believers voluntarily share some of the spiritual blindness of unbelievers. Especially lamentable is their ignorance of and lack of interest in the return of their Lord. That spiritual malady plagued believers in the early church, obviously including some in Rome. It was for that reason that the apostle seems almost to shout: **It is already the hour for you to awaken from sleep.**

The *Encyclopedia Britannica* defines sleep as "a state of inactivity, with a loss of consciousness and a decrease in responsiveness to events taking place." Paul calls them **to awaken from** *spiritual* **sleep** —from unconsciousness, unresponsiveness, and inactivity concerning the things of God.

The apostle also cried out to certain believers in Ephesus, saying, "Awake, sleeper, and arise from the dead, and Christ will shine on you" (Eph. 5:14). He was not speaking to the unsaved, to those who were *spiritually* "dead," but to genuine believers whose spiritual *lethargy* and laziness made them appear and act as if they had no spiritual *life.* Such indolence is intolerable in light of the urgency of spiritual matters.

Paul both warned and appealed to believers at Corinth: "Become sober-minded as you ought, and stop sinning; for some have no knowledge of God. I speak this to your shame" (1 Cor. 15:34). As with the Ephesian believers just spoken of above, the apostle was not accusing those Corinthians of not knowing God as Savior but of being ignorant of God's Word. They were unaware of and unconcerned about what the Lord was then doing in the world and even less concerned about what He promised He would yet do—in particular the promise that Christ would come again to earth, not as a humble servant but as Conqueror, King, and Judge.

In declaring that **now salvation is nearer to us than when we believed,** Paul obviously is speaking about the *completion* of **salvation.** He is addressing Christians, those who already had **believed** and been converted. The **salvation** that is becoming **nearer** refers to the future and final dimension of redemption, namely, glorification. As mentioned above, justification refers to declared and positional righteousness that happens once and saves the believer from the penalty of sin. Sanctification refers to the lifelong process of the believer's growing spiritually in practical righteousness. Glorification refers to the believer's ultimate perfection as a child of God.

Earlier in this letter, the apostle has spoken of "waiting eagerly for our adoption as sons, the redemption of our body" (Rom. 8:23), referring to this third and final aspect of salvation, when the Lord takes us to be with Him for all eternity. That is the future aspect of **salvation** which he here says **is nearer to us than when we believed.**

It is to that eschatological motive, the hope of Christ's imminent return, to which the apostle appeals. Throughout the New Testament, Christians are called to holy living in anticipation of the return of Jesus Christ. That should be the utmost incentive for living according to His will and for His glory.

Paul reminds Titus that "the grace of God has appeared, bringing salvation to all men, instructing us to deny ungodliness and worldly desires and to live sensibly, righteously and godly in the present age, looking for the blessed hope and the appearing of the glory of our great God and Savior, Christ Jesus" (Titus 2:11-13). The writer of Hebrews admonishes believers to "consider how to stimulate one another to love and good deeds, not forsaking our own assembling together, as is the habit of some, but encouraging one another; and all the more, as you see the day drawing near" (Heb. 10:24-25). James counsels: "Be patient, therefore, brethren, until the coming of the Lord; . . . strengthen your hearts, for the coming of the Lord is at hand" (James 5:7-8). Peter warns: "The end of all things is at hand; therefore, be of sound judgment and sober spirit for the purpose of prayer. Above all, keep fervent in your love for one another, because love covers a multitude of sins" (1 Pet. 4:7-8). Paul reminds us that, even as believers, "we must all appear before the judgment seat of Christ, that each one may be recompensed for his deeds in the body, according to what he has done, whether good or bad" (2 Cor. 5:10).

We already are eternally freed from condemnation and punishment for our sins. Christ's taking upon Himself the sins of the world (John 1:29) became permanently effective for us the moment we received Him as Lord and Savior. But when He returns, there will be a judgment of our efforts on behalf of the kingdom, when He "will both bring to light the things hidden in the darkness and disclose the motives of men's hearts; and then each man's praise will come to him from God" (1 Cor. 4:5).

Near the end of his remarkably fruitful ministry, Paul rejoiced: "I have fought the good fight, I have finished the course, I have kept the faith; in the future there is laid up for me the crown of righteousness, which the Lord, the righteous Judge, will award to me on that day; and not only to me, but also to all who have loved His appearing" (2 Tim.

4:7-8).The Lord Himself promises His people:"Let the one who is righteous,still practice righteousness; and let the one who is holy,still keep himself holy. Behold, I am coming quickly, and My reward is with Me" (Rev. 22:1 1*b*-12*a*; cf. Rom. 14:10).

We do not know and cannot know the hour of Christ's coming. But we know that it is some 2,000 years closer than when Paul wrote his letter to Rome.We do not know how much sand remains in the top of the Lord's "hourglass" of human history as we know it, but there is abundant evidence that not much time is left.We know that we are nearer to the coming of our Lord "with power and great glory" (Matt. 24:30) than any other generation in history. Every day we live, we come one day closer to the coming of our Lord Jesus Christ, the final events in God's redemptive plan.

The promise of the two angels to the disciples immediately after Jesus' ascension should be the constant watchword and the continual hope of every Christian:"This Jesus,who has been taken up from you into heaven,will come in just the same way as you have watched Him go into heaven"(Acts 1:11).In the meanwhile,they were to obey the Lord's own last command to them:"It is not for you to know times or epochs which the Father has fixed by His own authority; but you shall receive power when the Holy Spirit has come upon you; and you shall be My witnesses both in Jerusalem,and in all Judea and Samaria,and even to the remotest part of the earth"(1:7-8).

Paul's declaration that **the night is almost gone, and the day is at hand** means that man's time of spiritual unbelief, rebellion, and sin is about to end and God's time of judgment,glory,and righteousness is about to begin.

In the New Testament,the term **day** is often used to signify the dawning, as it were, of Christ's imminent return, and is used here in contrast to the **night** of man's spiritual darkness,which is almost over.

Speaking of His return, Jesus warned,"Many will say to Me *on that day,* 'Lord, Lord, did we not prophesy in Your name, and in Your name cast out demons,and in Your name perform many miracles?' And then I will declare to them,'I never knew you; depart from Me,you who practice lawlessness'"(Matt. 7:22-23, emphasis added). Speaking of the rebellious "angels who did not keep their own domain,but abandoned their proper abode," Jude affirms that God "has kept [them] in eternal bonds under darkness for the judgment of *the great day*" (Jude 6, emphasis added).

From the human perspective,it sometimes seems that the **night** of man's depravity is interminable and that Satan's dominion over man is becoming stronger and more unalterable.The world as a whole is certainly not becoming more godly and peaceful but more ungodly and violent (cf. 2 Tim. 3:13). Every day, the news of man's inhumanity to man becomes more dreadful and his repudiation of God more blasphemous and presumptuous.

But this increasing degeneracy was not unforseen by God, nor should His people be surprised by it. Through Peter, the Lord long ago declared:

> Know this first of all, that in the last days mockers will come with their mocking, following after their own lusts, and saying, "Where is the promise of His coming? For ever since the fathers fell asleep, all continues just as it was from the beginning of creation." For when they maintain this, it escapes their notice that by the word of God the heavens existed long ago and the earth was formed out of water and by water, through which the world at that time was destroyed, being flooded with water. But the present heavens and earth by His word are being reserved for fire, kept for the day of judgment and destruction of ungodly men. (2 Pet. 3:3-7)

In a word of great encouragement to believers, the apostle goes on to say, "But do not let this one fact escape your notice, beloved, that with the Lord one day is as a thousand years, and a thousand years as one day. The Lord is not slow about His promise, as some count slowness, but is patient toward you, not wishing for any to perish but for all to come to repentance" (vv. 8-9).

The writer of Hebrews consoled the believers to whom he wrote, saying, "Do not throw away your confidence, which has a great reward. For you have need of endurance, so that when you have done the will of God, you may receive what was promised. For yet in a very little while, He who is coming will come, and will not delay" (Heb. 10:35-37).

Throughout the New Testament, the Lord encourages the saved and warns the unsaved that the return of Christ is near. Paul gives that combination of assurance and warning in his second letter to persecuted believers in Thessalonica. Their suffering for Christ's sake was

> a plain indication of God's righteous judgment so that you may be considered worthy of the kingdom of God, for which indeed you are suffering. For after all it is only just for God to repay with affliction those who afflict you, and to give relief to you who are afflicted and to us as well when the Lord Jesus shall be revealed from heaven with His mighty angels in flaming fire, dealing out retribution to those who do not know God and to those who do not obey the gospel of our Lord Jesus. (2 Thess. 1:5-8)

In his first letter, Peter admonished believers that "the end of all things is at hand; therefore, be of sound judgment and sober spirit for the purpose of prayer" (1 Pet. 4:7). James wrote, "Be patient; strengthen your hearts, for the coming of the Lord is at hand" (James 5:8).

The nighttime of world history will soon give way to the daylight of Christ's glorious kingdom. And in that day, "loud voices in heaven" will proclaim, "The kingdom of the world has become the kingdom of our Lord, and of His Christ; and He will reign forever and ever" (Rev. 11:15). As for our expectation of and preparation for that great day, Paul tells us:

> Now as to the times and the epochs, brethren, you have no need of anything to be written to you. For you yourselves know full well that the day of the Lord will come just like a thief in the night. While they are saying, "Peace and safety!" then destruction will come upon them suddenly like birth pangs upon a woman with child; and they shall not escape. But you, brethren, are not in darkness, that the day should overtake you like a thief; for you are all sons of light and sons of day. We are not of night nor of darkness; so then let us not sleep as others do, but let us be alert and sober. For those who sleep do their sleeping at night, and those who get drunk get drunk at night. But since we are of the day, let us be sober, having put on the breastplate of faith and love, and as a helmet, the hope of salvation. (1 Thess. 5:1-8)

THROW OFF!

Let us therefore lay aside the deeds of darkness and put on the armor of light. Let us behave properly as in the day, not in carousing and drunkenness, not in sexual promiscuity and sensuality, not in strife and jealousy. (13:12*b*-13)

The imagery here pictures a soldier who has been engaged in a night orgy and drinking bout and, still clad in the garments of his sin, has fallen into a drunken sleep. But the dawn is approaching and the battle is at hand. It is time to wake up, throw off the clothes of night, and put on the battle gear.

Lay aside here carries the idea of forsaking, or renouncing, and in this context obviously refers to repentance from **the deeds of darkness,** a general term that includes all sins in which a believer may indulge. The Lord is grieved by all sin, but the sins of His own children bring special grief to "the Holy Spirit of God, by whom [we] were sealed for the day of redemption" (Eph. 4:30).

David spoke of a man who "clothed himself with cursing as with his garment" (Ps. 109:18). We sin by choice, voluntarily clothing ourselves with its evil. In the Spirit's power we can reverse that decision and **lay aside** sin, disrobe ourselves of it. Paul uses the same figure in admonishing believers at Ephesus to "lay aside the old self, which is being corrupted in accordance with the lusts of deceit" (Eph. 4:22). He told believers in Colossae to put away "anger, wrath, malice, slander, and abusive speech from your mouth. Do not lie to one another, since you laid aside the old self with its evil practices" (Col. 3:8-9). As noted above, when we received Christ, all of our sin was removed before God. We were justified, counted to be perfectly righteous before God because He applied Christ's own righteousness to our spiritual account. Paul was telling the Colossians to *keep on laying aside,* to continually cast off particular sins—in this case, "anger, wrath, malice, slander, and abusive speech"—the dirty, unspiritual clothes they kept putting back on.

Through the writer of Hebrews, the Lord tells us to "lay aside every encumbrance, and the sin which so easily entangles us" (Heb. 12:1). Through Peter He tells us to put "aside all malice and all guile and hypocrisy and envy and all slander" (1 Pet. 2:1). And through James He tells us to put "aside all filthiness and all that remains of wickedness, [and] in humility receive the word implanted, which is able to save your souls" (James 1:21).

Scripture frequently uses the figure of darkness to represent sin, here described as **deeds of darkness.** Crimes are frequently committed at night, the time of **darkness,** because they can more easily go unnoticed. Job spoke of "those who rebel against the light; they do not want to know its ways, nor abide in its paths. The murderer arises at dawn; he kills the poor and the needy, and at night he is as a thief. And the eye of the adulterer waits for the twilight, saying, 'No eye will see me.' And he disguises his face. In the dark they dig into houses, they shut themselves up by day; they do not know the light. For the morning is the same to him as thick darkness, for he is familiar with the terrors of thick darkness" (Job 24:13-17).

Paul next moves from the negative to the positive, from emphasizing confession and genuine repentance in the laying aside of the destructive darkness of sin to putting on the protective **light** of righteousness.

Paul uses the imagery of a soldier who had dressed himself in party clothes and spent the night in reveling. As the day dawns, the commander orders him to wake up, take off his night clothes, and **put on the armor** he needs to fight the day's battle. **Armor** is made for warfare, and its purpose is to protect the one who wears it. By the indwelling Spirit working through our new nature in Christ, we not only have every resource necessary to forsake the deeds of darkness but also every resource we need to **put on the armor of light.** God's own **light** provides divine protection in our battle against Satan's supernatural powers of darkness as well as against the natural darkness of human sin, to which, even as believers, we still are so prone.

The armor of light is "the full armor of God," which we are to put on in order "to stand firm against the schemes of the devil. For our struggle is not against flesh and blood, but against the rulers, against the powers, against the world forces of this darkness, against the spiritual forces of wickedness in the heavenly places" (Eph. 6:11-12). We cannot be spiritually and morally safe in anything less than "the full armor of God," in order to "be able to resist in the evil day, and having done everything, to stand firm" (v. 13). God's full **armor of light** includes the girdle of "truth, . . . the breastplate of righteousness," feet shod "with the preparation of the gospel of peace,...the shield of faith with which [we] will be able to extinguish all the flaming missiles of the evil one," and "the sword of the Spirit, which is the word of God" (vv. 14-17).

In his gospel account, John describes Jesus as "the true light which, coming into the world, enlightens every man" (John 1:9), and in his first letter he proclaims that "God is light, and in Him there is no darkness at all" (1 John 1:5). He goes on to say that those who truly belong to God are also characterized by the light of divine righteousness. "If we say that we have fellowship with Him and yet walk in the darkness, we lie and do not practice the truth; but if we walk in the light as He Himself is in the light, we have fellowship with one another, and the blood of Jesus His Son cleanses us from all sin" (vv. 6-7; cf. 2:6). Sin and righteousness are as incompatible and mutually exclusive as darkness and light.

Paul admonished Ephesian believers to "be renewed in the spirit of your mind, and put on the new self, which in the likeness of God has been created in righteousness and holiness of the truth" (Eph. 4:23-24), reminding them a few verses later, "You were formerly darkness, but now you are light in the Lord; walk as children of light" (5:8). The Christian's spiritual **armor** is the **light** of God's own holiness and purity, with which He desires His children to be constantly clothed. It is the clothing of spiritual purity and integrity, a reflection of our Lord's holiness that—whether they recognize it or not—all the world can see.

Therefore, because we are children of light and have available the Lord's own **armor of light,** we should **behave properly as in the day.**

To **behave properly** is to live in a way that pleases God. It is to live honestly before our Lord and before men, to live an outward life that is consistent with our inner nature in Christ, to live a sanctified life that reflects our justified life. It is to live a life that has "no spot or wrinkle or any such thing" (Eph. 5:27), and it is "to be found by Him in peace, spotless and blameless" (2 Pet. 3:14).

The Christian who is not living a holy and obedient life is a Christian who does not comprehend the significance of the Lord's return. On the other hand, the believer who understands the coming judgment and is daily looking for his Lord to appear is a believer whose overriding purpose is to please and honor his Lord by consistent holy living. The Christian who longs for Christ's coming is characterized by "holy conduct and godliness," because he is "looking for and hastening the coming of the day of God,... looking for new heavens and a new earth, in which righteousness dwells" (2 Pet. 3:11-13).

After Paul admonished Colossian believers to consider themselves dead to the various sins to which they were prone and to "put them all aside" (Col. 3:5-9a), he reminds them that, when they were saved, they had "laid aside the old self with its evil practices, and [had] put on the new self who is being renewed to a true knowledge according to the image of the One who created him" (vv. 3:9b-10). And, "as those who have been chosen of God, holy and beloved," they were to devote themselves to righteousness, putting "on a heart of compassion, kindness, humility, gentleness and patience; bearing with one another, and forgiving each other, whoever has a complaint against anyone; just as the Lord forgave you, so also should you. And beyond all these things put on love, which is the perfect bond of unity" (vv. 12-14).

We are to **behave properly as in the day,** because, as children of God, "we are *of the day*" and therefore should "be sober, having put on the breastplate of faith and love, and as a helmet, the hope of salvation. For God has not destined us for wrath, but for obtaining salvation through our Lord Jesus Christ" (1 Thess. 5:8-9, emphasis added).

Returning again to the negative, Paul, as he often does, mentions a number of specific sins, characteristics of our lives that reflect spiritual darkness rather than light, the night of unrighteousness rather than the day of righteousness.

First on the list is **carousing,** which translates *kōmos,* a term often used of a military or athletic victory celebration. Because such revelry frequently turned into drunken and immoral disorder, *kōmos* came to be used of any wild partying, sexual orgies, brawls, and sometimes even rioting (as in the King James of this verse), especially when associated with **drunkenness,** the second sin mentioned here. *Methē* **(drunkenness)** most often was used of intentional and habitual intoxication. It is interesting that in Galatians 5:21 and 1 Peter 4:3 carousing and drunkenness are also found side-by-side.

The next two sins mentioned here, **sexual promiscuity and sensuality,** also are closely associated. **Sexual promiscuity** does not translate *porneia,* the most common Greek term for sexual immorality, but rather *koitē,* which literally refers to a bed or bedroom. But it came to have the same connotation that the phrase "going to bed" with someone of the opposite sex carries today. In the New Testament the word is used both of the honored marriage bed (Heb. 13:4) and of illicit **sexual promiscuity,** as here.

Sensuality translates *aselgeia,* which has the basic meaning of shameless excess and the absence of restraint. Like *koitē,* it was used almost exclusively of especially lewd sexual immorality, of uninhibited and unabashed lasciviousness. It refers to the kind of sexual debauchery and abandonment that characterizes much of modern society and that is often flaunted almost as a badge of distinction.

Strife (*eris*) refers to persistent contention, bickering, petty disagreement, and enmity. It reflects a spirit of antagonistic competitiveness that fights to have its own way, regardless of cost to itself or of harm to others. It is produced by a deep desire to prevail over others, to gain the highest prestige, prominence, and recognition possible. **Strife** is characterized by self-indulgence and egoism. It has no place even for simple tolerance, much less for humility or love.

Zēlos **(jealousy)** is the term from which we get the English *zeal* and *zealous,* which often carry a positive connotation. It is also sometimes used positively in the New Testament. Earlier in this letter, Paul spoke of certain unsaved Jews who had an untaught and misdirected "zeal for God" (Rom. 10:2). And in his second letter to the church at Corinth, he expressed deep appreciation for their zeal *(zēlos)* for him (2 Cor. 7:7). But in the present passage, this word is properly translated in the very negative sense of **jealousy** ("envying," KJV). James twice connects "jealousy" with "selfish ambition" (James 3:14, 16).

Strife and **jealousy** were the two specific fleshly sins that caused the deep, partisan divisions in the church at Corinth (1 Cor. 3:3). And, except for *koitē,* all of the sins mentioned in Romans 13:13 are specifically listed among the "deeds of the flesh" mentioned by Paul in Galatians 5:19-21. And the basic evil connoted by *koitē* is covered in that list by "immorality" and "impurity" (v. 19).

Paul never lost sight of the fact that he himself was once the foremost of sinners (1 Tim. 1:15). He reminded Titus,

> For we also once were foolish ourselves, disobedient, deceived, enslaved to various lusts and pleasures, spending our life in malice and envy, hateful, hating one another. But when the kindness of God our Savior and His love for mankind appeared, He saved us, not on the basis of deeds which we have done in righteousness, but according to His mercy, by the washing of regeneration and renewing by the Holy Spirit, whom He poured out upon us richly through Jesus Christ our Savior, that being justified by His grace we might be made heirs according to the hope of eternal life. (Titus 3:3-7)

PUT ON!

But put on the Lord Jesus Christ, and make no provision for the flesh in regard to its lusts. (13:14)

As mentioned at the beginning of this chapter, to **put on the Lord Jesus Christ** represents the continuing spiritual growth of those who have become children of God through faith in His Son, Jesus Christ. "Having been firmly rooted" in Christ, we are "now being built up in Him" (Col. 2:7). And as we grow in Christ, the old clothing of sinful thoughts and habits is continually being discarded, and *His* divine clothing of righteousness, truth, holiness, and love is being put on. As the process of sanctification progresses, the Lord's character becomes more and more our own character. In that sense, the single purpose of a Christian is to continually **put on the Lord Jesus Christ.** This is what Paul had in mind when he said he had only "one thing" to do—pursue the goal of Christlikeness, which will be the prize in glory (Phil. 3:13-14).

"Beloved, now we are children of God," John tells us, "and it has not appeared as yet what we shall be. We know that, when He appears, we shall be like Him, because we shall see Him just as He is. And everyone who has this hope fixed on Him purifies himself, just as He is pure" (1 John 3:2-3). Looking for Christ's coming with loving expectation purifies our lives, because to long for Him is to want to please Him, and to want to please Him is to want to be like Him. Paul told the Galatian believers that he would not be content, that he would remain "in labor," as it were, "until Christ is formed in you" (Gal. 4:19). Christ already is formed in us in the sense that He indwells us and has given us His own nature. But, like John, we should look forward to the glorious day when "we shall be like Him, because we shall see Him just as He is" (1 John 3:2). We rejoice that "we all, with unveiled face beholding as in a mirror the glory of the Lord, are being transformed into the same image from glory to glory, just as from the Lord, the Spirit" (2 Cor. 3:18).

We grow from one level of Christ's glory to another as we faithfully study and meditate on His Word, as we commune with Him in prayer, as we rely on His Holy Spirit, and as we "stimulate one another to love and good deeds, not forsaking our own assembling together, as is the habit of some, but encouraging one another; and all the more, as you see the day drawing near" (Heb. 10:24-25).

An athlete may don the uniform and take the name of a championship team, but it is his performance, not his team's uniform or name, that determines his own value as a player. A judge may put on the appropriate robe of his office, but it is his judicial knowledge and wisdom that determine his own merit as a judge. In a much deeper, but somewhat similar way, the person who receives Christ as Savior takes on the name of Christian. But the quality of his Christianity is determined by his own spiritual faithfulness.

Once again, Paul uses contrast to make his point, this time in reverse order from that of verse 12. Here the order is first to put on Christ and His righteousness and then to put off sin, by making **no provision for the flesh in regard to its lusts.**

Pronoia **(provision)** has the basic meaning of forethought, of planning ahead. More often than not, the sins we commit develop from wrong ideas and lustful desires that we have allowed to linger in our minds (cf. James 1:14-15). The longer we permit them to stay, the more **provision** we make **for the flesh** to bring them to fruition.

David understood that "transgression speaks to the ungodly within his heart; there is no fear of God before his eyes. . . . He plans wickedness upon his bed; he sets himself on a path that is not good; he does not despise evil" (Ps. 36:1, 4). To one degree or another, most wickedness is planned. The ungodly person does not stumble into sin but "plans to do evil" (Prov. 24:8).

The devout Puritan preacher Thomas Manton wrote, "Every corruption has a voice," meaning that every sort of sin finds a way to bring itself to man's mind and heart. To feel the desire to sin is evidence of the presence of sin in us. To fulfill that desire is evidence of the power of sin over us. As long as we are in our mortal bodies we will experience the presence of sin within us. But at no time does a Christian have to yield to sin's power. Because we have the provision of Christ's own nature and Spirit within us, we do not have to make **provision for the flesh** by fulfilling **its lusts.**

The flesh does not refer primarily to our physical bodies but to our remaining humanness, our lingering proclivity to sin, which finds expression through our bodies. It is for that reason that, "having the first fruits of the Spirit, even we ourselves groan within ourselves, waiting eagerly for our adoption as sons, the redemption of our body" (Rom. 8:23). The **provision** for sin originates in our hearts, minds, emotions, and will, which are still influenced powerfully by **the flesh.** It is only as we "walk by the Spirit" that we "will not carry out the desire of the flesh" (Gal. 5:16). And to walk by the Spirit is to live by the Word.

The urgency of obeying this command to put on Christ was expressed some years ago in a poem which beautifully communicates the sentiment of many Christians:

> When I stand at the judgment seat of Christ,
>   and He shows me His plan for me,
> The plan of my life as it might have been,
>   and I see how I blocked Him here

And checked Him there,
   and would not yield my will.
Will there be grief in my Savior's eyes,
   grief though He loves me still?
He would have me rich,
   but I stand there poor,
Stripped of all but His grace,
   while memory runs like a haunted thing
Down a path I can't retrace;
   then my desolate heart
Will well nigh break
   with tears I cannot shed.
I will cover my face with my empty hands,
   I will bow my uncrowned head.
O Lord, of the years that are left to me,
   I give them to Thy hand.
Take me and break me and mold me
   to the pattern Thou hast planned.

The Unity of Strong and Weak Christians
—part 1
Receive One Another with Understanding
(Romans 14:1-12)

20

Now accept the one who is weak in faith, but not for the purpose of passing judgment on his opinions. One man has faith that he may eat all things, but he who is weak eats vegetables only. Let not him who eats regard with contempt him who does not eat, and let not him who does not eat judge him who eats, for God has accepted him. Who are you to judge the servant of another? To his own master he stands or falls; and stand he will, for the Lord is able to make him stand. One man regards one day above another, another regards every day alike. Let each man be fully convinced in his own mind. He who observes the day, observes it for the Lord, and he who eats, does so for the Lord, for he gives thanks to God; and he who eats not, for the Lord he does not eat, and gives thanks to God. For not one of us lives for himself, and not one dies for himself; for if we live, we live for the Lord, or if we die, we die for the Lord; therefore whether we live or die, we are the Lord's. For to this end Christ died and lived again, that He might be Lord both of the dead and of the living. But you, why do you judge your brother? Or you again, why do you regard your brother with contempt? For we shall all stand before the judgment seat of God. For it is written, "As I live, says the Lord,

**every knee shall bow to Me, and every tongue shall give praise
to God." So then each one of us shall give account of himself to
God.** (14:1-12)

A major theme of the New Testament is that of sin's power to
destroy the spiritual and moral health of the church as well as of the
individuals who commit the sins. The epistles are filled with commands
and injunctions regarding the need to continually eradicate sin in the
church. That is the purpose of both church discipline and self-discipline.
Regular celebration of the Lord's Supper not only helps us remember
Jesus' sacrifice on our behalf but is a time for each Christian to "examine
himself" (1 Cor. 11:28), to take stock of his life and to confess, renounce,
and ask forgiveness for his sin.

Jesus commanded, "If your brother sins, go and reprove him in
private; if he listens to you, you have won your brother. But if he does
not listen to you, take one or two more with you, so that by the mouth
of two or three witnesses every fact may be confirmed. And if he refuses
to listen to them, tell it to the church; and if he refuses to listen even
to the church, let him be to you as a Gentile and a tax-gatherer" (Matt.
18:15-17).

Paul gave similar counsel to the church at Corinth regarding
self-discipline: "Clean out the old leaven [of sin], that you may be a new
lump, just as you are in fact unleavened. For Christ our Passover also
has been sacrificed. Let us therefore celebrate the feast, not with old
leaven, nor with the leaven of malice and wickedness, but with the unleavened bread of sincerity and truth" (1 Cor. 5:7-8). In his second letter
to that church he pled, "Therefore, having these promises, beloved, let
us cleanse ourselves from all defilement of flesh and spirit, perfecting
holiness in the fear of God" (2 Cor. 7:1).

But outright sin is not the only danger to a church's spiritual
health and unity. Although they are not sin in themselves, certain attitudes and behavior can destroy fellowship and fruitfulness and have
crippled the work, the witness, and the unity of countless congregations
throughout church history. These problems are caused by differences
between Christians over matters that are neither commanded nor forbidden in Scripture. They are matters of personal preference and his-
toric tradition, which, when imposed on others, inevitably cause confusion, strife, ill will, abused consciences, and disharmony.

Even in small churches, there often are considerable differences
in age, education, maturity, personalities, and cultural and religious back-
grounds. Some members may come from a long line of evangelicals.
Some of those families may have a heritage of strict legalism, while
others have one of considerable openness and freedom. Some members may have been accustomed to highly liturgical worship, others to

worship that is largely unstructured and spontaneous. Some may have heard the gospel and been exposed to biblical teaching for many years, while others may have heard the true gospel only recently and understand only its bare essentials. Some may have been converted out of paganism, a cult, liberal Protestantism, Roman Catholicism, Judaism, atheistic humanism, or simply religious indifference.

As mentioned in an earlier chapter of this commentary volume, contrary to what some church growth leaders maintain, such diversity can strengthen a local congregation, reminding the church itself and witnessing to the world around them of the power of Jesus Christ to bind together dissimilar people in a fellowship of genuine and profound unity. The Lord did not plan for His church to be divided into a hundred varieties, based on distinctives of personal preference and traditions that have no ground in Scripture. But for obvious reasons, diversity within a congregation can easily be used by the unredeemed flesh and by Satan to create division and discord, even hatred and animosity.

It was Paul's abiding concern that every Christian have a deep desire for preserving "the unity of the Spirit in the bond of peace" (Eph. 4:3) and for putting "on love, which is the perfect bond of unity" (Col. 3:14). Our Lord expressed that same desire in His "new commandment . . . that you love one another, even as I have loved you, that you also love one another. By this all men will know that you are My disciples, if you have love for one another" (John 13:34-35). It is the concern He voiced in His high priestly prayer to His Father on behalf of those who belong to Him by faith, "that they may all be one; even as Thou, Father, art in Me, and I in Thee, that they also may be in Us; that the world may believe that Thou didst send Me" (John 17:20-21).

The particular danger to unity that Paul addresses in Romans 14:1-15:13 is the conflict that easily arises between those to whom he refers as strong and weak believers, those who are mature in the faith and those who are immature, those who understand and enjoy freedom in Christ and those who still feel either shackled or threatened by certain religious and cultural taboos and practices that were deeply ingrained parts of their lives before coming to Christ.

In the early church, many Jews who came to faith in Christ could not bring themselves to discard the ceremonial laws and practices in which they had been steeped since early childhood, especially the rites and prohibitions the Lord Himself had instituted under the Old Covenant. They still felt compelled, for example, to comply with Mosaic dietary laws, to strictly observe the Sabbath, and even to offer sacrifices in the Temple because they were given by the true God.

On the other hand, many converted Gentiles had been just as strongly steeped in pagan rituals and customs from false gods, and they felt repulsed by anything remotely connected with such evils. Many

Gentiles, for example, could not bring themselves to eat meat that had been offered to a pagan deity and then was sold in the marketplace.

Other believers, both Jewish and Gentile, understood and exercised their freedom in Christ. Mature Jewish believers realized that, under the New Covenant in Christ, the ceremonial requirements of the Mosaic law were no longer valid. Mature believing Gentiles understood that idolatry was a spiritual evil and had no effect on anything physical, such as meat, that may have been used in idolatrous worship.

Those who were still strongly influenced, favorably or unfavorably, by their former religious beliefs and practices were weak in the faith because they did not understand their freedom in Christ.

I once met an Amish farmer in Pennsylvania who was a recent convert to Christ. Contrary to the Amish tradition of not using modern appliances and motor-powered vehicles, this man owned a radio, which he secretly listened to, and an automobile, which he kept hidden in the barn most of the time and rarely drove in the daytime. He knew in his mind that using these things was not sinful or unbiblical, but he still had difficulty expressing this freedom openly, especially before his Amish friends and neighbors.

On the other hand, those who are strong are often faced with the temptation to push their freedom in Christ to the limits, to live on the outer edge of moral propriety, to see how far they can go without actually committing a sin. Those who are weak are tempted in the opposite way. They are so afraid of committing some religious offense that they surround themselves with self-imposed restrictions.

The liberated believer is tempted to look upon his legalistic brother as being too rigid and restricted to be of any use to the Lord. The legalist, on the other hand, is tempted to think of his liberated brother as being too free-wheeling and undisciplined to serve Christ effectively. This is the root of the disunity.

In the present passage (Rom. 14:1-12), the apostle speaks to both types of believers and both attitudes, but his first counsel is directed to strong believers, for the very reason that they are stronger in the faith. Of the two groups, they are the better equipped both to understand and to be understanding. He therefore says to them, **Accept the one who is weak in faith.**

Proslambanō **(accept)** is a compound verb, the prefix *pros* being a preposition that intensifies the basic verb, making it a command. In other words, Paul was not simply suggesting, but commanding, that strong believers **accept** weak believers.

In the New Testament, *proslambanō* is always used in the Greek middle voice, which gives it the connotation of personal and willing acceptance of another person. This meaning is clearly seen in Acts 28:2, where Paul uses the verb to describe the gracious hospitality of the Malta natives, who "kindled a fire and *received* us all" (emphasis added). This meaning is also clear in Romans 15:7, where Paul uses the verb twice, first regarding Christians' accepting one another and then of Christ's accepting "us [that is, all believers] to the glory of God."

Is weak translates a Greek present participle, suggesting a temporary condition. The Greek text also has the definite article *(the)* before **faith,** indicating that Paul was not speaking of spiritual trust or faithfulness but of understanding the full truth of the gospel message. A better rendering, therefore, might be: **one who is weak in** *the* **faith.** That is clearly the apostle's meaning when he admonished the Colossians to "continue in *the faith* firmly established and steadfast" (Col. 1:23, emphasis added; cf. Titus 1:4).

As noted above, Paul was not speaking of doctrinal or moral compromise. In that regard, he sternly warned the Galatians that "even though we, or an angel from heaven, should preach to you a gospel contrary to that which we have preached to you, let him be accursed" (Gal. 1:8). He was not speaking, for example, about Judaizers, Jews who infiltrated the church and then insisted that a Gentile could not come to Christ without being circumcised and that both Jewish and Gentile believers had to observe the Mosaic law (see Acts 15:5). He was speaking of believers, Jew or Gentile, who are **weak in** their understanding of and living out their true **faith** in Jesus Christ.

Such believers are to be fully and lovingly accepted by those who are spiritually mature. It is not that the believer's freedom in Christ should never be discussed with Christians who are still under bondage to some type of religious compulsion or restraint, but that such discussion should never be **for the purpose of passing judgment on** undeveloped but sincere **opinions.**

One of Jesus' most somber warnings was against anyone who "causes one of these little ones who believe in Me to stumble." It would be "better for him that a heavy millstone be hung around his neck, and that he be drowned in the depth of the sea. Woe to the world because of its stumbling blocks! For it is inevitable that stumbling blocks come; but woe to that man through whom the stumbling block comes!" (Matt. 18:6-7). The Lord noted that opposition ("stumbling blocks") from the world against God's people is inevitable and to be expected. But on that occasion, Jesus was speaking largely, if not entirely, of and to "the disciples" (v. 1), probably only the Twelve (see Mark 9:30-50; Luke 9:43-48). In verse 14 He calls His hearers sons "of your Father who is in heaven." In the following verses (15-17), He plainly is speaking about church discipline, giving instruction for dealing with a "brother," that is, a fellow believer, who sins. The Lord is therefore speaking both to and about genuine Christians when He says in the intervening verses,

> If your hand or your foot causes you to stumble, cut it off and throw it from you; it is better for you to enter life crippled or lame, than having two hands or two feet, to be cast into the eternal fire. And if your eye causes you to stumble, pluck it out, and throw it from you. It is better for you to enter life with one eye, than having two eyes, to be cast into the fiery hell. See that you do not despise one of these little ones, for I say to you, that their angels in heaven continually behold the face of My Father who is in heaven. (Matt. 18:8-10)

This hyperbolic truism was meant to say that sin must be dealt with severely, in the case of an unbeliever who faced hell. But the principle still applies to a believer who has been delivered from hell. Sin is serious and calls for whatever action is necessary to stop it.

Paul warned the churches in Galatia, which had experienced considerable trouble from legalistic Judaizers, "You were called to freedom, brethren; only do not turn your freedom into an opportunity for the flesh, but through love serve one another. For the whole Law is fulfilled in one word, in the statement, 'You shall love your neighbor as yourself.' But if you bite and devour one another, take care lest you be consumed by one another" (Gal. 5:13-15).

The apostle reminded the elders from Ephesus: "In everything I showed you that by working hard in this manner you must help the weak and remember the words of the Lord Jesus, that He Himself said, 'It is more blessed to give than to receive'" (Acts 20:35). To mature believers in the churches of Galatia he gave an admonition and a caution. The admonition was, "Brethren, even if a man is caught in any trespass, you who are spiritual [the strong], restore such a one [the weak] in a spirit of gentleness." The caution was, "each one [look] to yourself, lest you too be tempted" (Gal. 6:1). In other words, those who are presently strong are not invulnerable to attitudes that can make them weak. In slightly different words, he gave the same advice to believers in Corinth: "Let him who thinks he stands take heed lest he fall" (1 Cor. 10:12).

Whatever spiritual strength we have, we have in and from the Lord. And when we become proud and self-satisfied, the Lord may see fit to withdraw some of His strength and blessing in order to remind us of how weak *every* believer is in himself.

The apostle urged the church at Thessalonica on the one hand to "admonish the unruly," that is, to warn believers who think they are strong and who continually take their freedom to its limits, not in order to serve and please the Lord but to serve and please themselves. In the same verse he then urges those who are genuinely strong to "encourage the fainthearted, help the weak, be patient with all men" (1 Thess. 5:14), that is, to use their freedom to serve the Lord by serving His people who are in special need of help.

Spiritual maturity is a continuum of growth that is meant to progress until the Lord takes us to be with Himself. In his first letter, John commends believers at various levels of spiritual maturity, referring to them as fathers, young men, and children. He reminds all of them that their spiritual strength comes from their knowing God and from His Word abiding in them (1 John 2:13-14).

It is important to note that the interchangeable use of titles and names of God in this passage present one of the clearest teachings of the deity of Christ. In verse 3 Paul speaks of God in verse 4 of *the Lord*, in verse 6 of both *the Lord* (three times) and *God* (twice), in verse 8 of *the Lord* (three times), and in verse 9, nine specifically of *Christ* as being *Lord*.

In Romans 14:2-12, Paul gives four reasons why all believers (both strong and weak) should receive all other believers. They should receive each other because God receives them (vv. 2-3), because the Lord sustains each believer (v. 4), because the Lord is sovereign to each believer (vv. 5-9), and because the Lord alone will judge each believer (vv. 10-12).

GOD RECEIVES THEM

One man has faith that he may eat all things, but he who is weak eats vegetables only. Let not him who eats regard with contempt him who does not eat, and let not him who does not eat judge him who eats, for God has accepted him. (14:1-3)

The first reason all believers should receive all other believers is that God receives them.

The **one man** who **has faith that he may eat all things** obviously refers to the stronger, more mature Christian who appreciates and exercises his freedom in Christ. The first example of freedom is that of the Christian's right to **eat all things.**

The gospel of the New Covenant in Jesus Christ includes no ceremonial or dietary restrictions, Mosaic or otherwise. In his first letter to Timothy, the apostle writes, "The Spirit explicitly says that in later times some will fall away from the faith, paying attention to deceitful spirits and doctrines of demons, by means of the hypocrisy of liars seared in their own conscience as with a branding iron, men who forbid marriage and advocate abstaining from foods, which God has created to be gratefully shared in by those who believe and know the truth" (1 Tim. 4:1-3).

Several years after he began his apostolic ministry, Peter was still afraid to eat animals that were declared ceremonially unclean under Old Testament law. It took three repeated declarations by the Lord in a vision to convince Peter that "What God has cleansed, no longer consider unholy" (Acts 10:15-16). The greater teaching of the vision was that Peter "should not call any man [that is, Gentiles] unholy or unclean" (v. 28).

As noted earlier, some Gentile believers, like some Jews, were troubled by the eating of certain foods, but for different reasons. Because of the idolatry and immorality related to their former religions, they could not bring themselves to eat meat or any other food that had been used as an offering to a pagan deity. Like Peter, they were still spiritually **weak** in regard to such things. Consequently, some Christian Jews and Gentiles would eat **vegetables only,** taking no chance of eating meat they considered to be defiled by idols.

Although Paul mentions only eating in verses 2-3 and 6, his comments in verses 17 and 21 suggest that some believers had similar concerns about drinking. If so, the reference probably applied primarily to Gentiles who had participated in or were familiar with pagan festivals such as the Roman bacchanalia, which were characterized by sexual orgies and drunkenness.

In verse 3 Paul gives a double injunction. The first is to the strong, to whom he says, **Let not him who eats regard with contempt him [the weak] who does not eat.** *Exoutheneō* **(regard with contempt)** is a strong term that carries the idea of looking on someone as totally worthless, as being nothing or less than nothing. It does not connote simply dislike or disrespect, but utter disdain and abhorrence. Many Jews of that day regarded all Gentiles **with contempt,** and many Greeks and Romans had the similar regard for those they referred to as barbarians.

It seems unlikely that many genuine Christians in the early church, at Rome or elsewhere, looked down on certain other believers **with contempt** in its most extreme sense. But it takes only one extremist to damage an entire congregation. Throughout the ages, churches have been plagued by those who proudly consider themselves to be spiritually superior.

Paul's next injunction is to the weak: **and let not him who does not eat judge him who eats.** Like **regard with contempt,** the term **judge** translates a strong Greek verb (*krinō*), which has the basic meaning of separating and isolating. In a legal sense it referred to finding an accused person guilty of a crime.

In this verse, **regard with contempt** and **judge** are essentially synonymous. In both cases, one type of person disdains the other, and both are wrong. The strong member contemptibly considers the weak member to be legalistic and self-righteous, and the weak member judges the strong member to be irresponsible at best and profligate at worst.

Although the phrase **God has accepted him** directly follows **him who eats** (the strong), the context makes clear that divine acceptance applies both to the strong and to the weak, to the one who eats freely and to the one who does not. Paul's point is that, if God Himself does not make an issue of such things, what right does one of His children have to do so? If the strong and the weak have equal acceptance by and fellowship with the Lord, it is sinful arrogance for those two kinds of believers not to accept each other.

THE LORD SUSTAINS EACH BELIEVER

Who are you to judge the servant of another? To his own master he stands or falls; and stand he will, for the Lord is able to make him stand. (14:4)

The second reason every Christian should accept every other Christian is that the Lord sustains them all. A believer who is "strong" about matters that are not doctrinal or moral, and that are neither commanded nor forbidden in Scripture, is just as much in need of God's strength as the one who is "weak." We are weak in the sense that everything good and righteous we possess is a gift of God, never the product of our own wisdom or efforts.

But the remaining influence of the flesh often tempts liberated believers to think legalists are so rigid and self-righteous that they sacrifice not only much personal joy but also limit their usefulness to the Lord. On the other hand, the same fleshly influence tempts legalists to believe that liberated believers are self-centered and loose-living and therefore cannot serve the Lord effectively.

Being well aware of those tendencies, Paul confronts both groups with the stinging rhetorical question, **Who are you to judge the servant of another?** What right do any of you, mature or immature, well taught or poorly taught, have **to judge the servant of another,** especially a fellow **servant** of Jesus Christ? A believer's personal assessment of other believers does not in the least affect their standing before the Lord.

Perhaps referring to critics in the church at Corinth, Paul wrote, "To me it is a very small thing that I should be examined by you, or by any human court; in fact, I do not even examine myself. For I am conscious of nothing against myself, yet I am not by this acquitted; but the one who examines me is the Lord. Therefore do not go on passing judgment before the time, but wait until the Lord comes who will both bring to light the things hidden in the darkness and disclose the motives of men's hearts; and then each man's praise will come to him from God" (1 Cor. 4:3-5).

It is **to his own master,** namely, Jesus Christ, that each believer **stands or falls.** And as far as matters of religious tradition and preference are concerned, *every* believer, strong and weak, will pass divine judgment, because the Lord does not take such things into account. **Stand he will,** Paul says of every believer, because **the Lord is able,** and obviously willing, **to make him stand.**

Earlier in the letter Paul posed a similar rhetorical question. "Who will bring a charge against God's elect?" he asks. "God is the one who justifies; who is the one who condemns? Christ Jesus is He who died, yes, rather who was raised, who is at the right hand of God, who also intercedes for us" (Rom. 8:33-34). "For I am convinced," he continues a few verses later, "that neither death, nor life, nor angels, nor principalities, nor things present, nor things to come, nor powers, nor height, nor depth, nor any other created thing, shall be able to separate us from the love of God, which is in Christ Jesus our Lord" (vv. 38-39).

Jesus Himself assures those who belong to Him: "I give eternal life to them, and they shall never perish; and no one shall snatch them out of My hand" (John 10:27-28). The closing benediction of Jude's brief epistle reflects that promise, reminding believers of "Him who is able to keep you from stumbling, and to make you stand in the presence of His glory blameless with great joy" (Jude 24).

The writer of Hebrews confirms that Christ "is able to save forever those who draw near to God through Him, since He always lives to make intercession for them (Heb. 7:25). Paul proclaimed his confidence "that He who began a good work in you will perfect it until the day of Christ Jesus" (Phil. 1:6), and Peter his assurance that we "are protected by the power of God through faith" (1 Pet. 1:5).

Many centuries before the coming of Christ, the Messiah, the psalmist declared with equal confidence that "He who dwells in the shelter of the Most High will abide in the shadow of the Almighty," that "He will cover you with His pinions, and under His wings you may seek refuge; His faithfulness is a shield and bulwark," and that "He will give His angels charge concerning you, to guard you in all your ways" (Ps. 91:1,4,11). Truly, the Lord sustains His own.

THE LORD IS SOVEREIGN TO EACH BELIEVER

One man regards one day above another, another regards every day alike. Let each man be fully convinced in his own mind. He who observes the day, observes it for the Lord, and he who eats, does so for the Lord, for he gives thanks to God; and he who eats

not, for the Lord he does not eat, and gives thanks to God. For not one of us lives for himself, and not one dies for himself; for if we live, we live for the Lord, or if we die, we die for the Lord; therefore whether we live or die, we are the Lord's. For to this end Christ died and lived again, that He might be Lord both of the dead and of the living. (14:5-9)

The third reason every Christian should accept every other Christian is that the Lord Jesus Christ is sovereign to each believer. Whether strong or weak, a sincere believer feels free or not free to do certain things out of the same motive: to please his Lord. Neither one is more or less spiritual or faithful because of his convictions about practices such as those discussed above. Being "strong" in this sense is not synonymous with being spiritual, and being "weak" is not synonymous with being carnal. The problem in the church at Rome, as in many churches since that day, was that some believers of both persuasions thought themselves to be more spiritual and the others to be more carnal. Paul's whole purpose in these verses, and in the larger context of 14:1-15:13, was to disabuse believers of those false, divisive, and destructive notions.

His first example has to do with the religious significance and observance of certain days. He continues to address both strong and weak believers, noting that **one man** (the weak) **regards one day above another,** whereas **another** (the strong) **regards every day alike.**

For Jews, the Sabbath referred not only to the seventh day of the week, the day of rest and worship, but to a number of other days and periods that were venerated and specially observed. Some pagan religions also venerated certain days or seasons.

As with the eating of certain foods, the weak Jewish Christian remained strongly attached to the special days of Judaism and felt compelled to observe them. The weak Gentile, on the other hand, wanted to separate himself as far as possible from the special days of his former paganism because of their idolatrous and immoral character.

Paul admonished believers in Colossae: "Let no one act as your judge in regard to food or drink or in respect to a festival or a new moon or a Sabbath day" (Col. 2:16). He did not advise either the forsaking or the following of such customs, but rather reminded his readers of their unimportance. Those were "things which are a mere shadow of what is to come; but the substance belongs to Christ" (Col. 2:17).

The apostle's words to the Galatian churches in that regard was much harsher, because some believers were returning to customs and rituals from which they had once considered themselves liberated. "How is it," he asked, "that you turn back again to the weak and worthless elemental things, to which you desire to be enslaved all over again? You observe days and months and seasons and years" (Gal. 4:9-10).

"There remains therefore a Sabbath rest for the people of God," Gentiles as well as Jews, the writer of Hebrews assures us (Heb. 4:9). But it is a future Sabbath, which we will enjoy and celebrate only when we are in heaven. As far as our present earthly life is concerned, Paul insists that **each man be fully convinced in his own mind** about observing or not observing the Sabbath or any other day.

In this context, **mind** obviously includes the heart and conscience, our deepest convictions and motives. Before God, it is not a matter of observance or nonobservance but of intent. The sincere weaker brother **who observes the day, observes it for the Lord.** The sincere stronger brother **who eats, does so for the Lord, for he gives thanks to God.** And again, the weaker believer **who eats not, for the Lord he does not eat, and gives thanks to God.**

In matters that are not specifically commanded or forbidden in Scripture, it is always wrong to go against conscience, because our conscience represents what we actually believe to be right. To go against our conscience, therefore, is to do that which we believe is wrong. And although an act or practice in itself may not be sinful, it is treated as sinful for those who are convinced in their own minds that it is wrong, and produces guilt.

It is also sinful, however, to try to impose our personal convictions on others, because, in doing so, we are tempting them to go against their own consciences. Paul is therefore giving a two-fold command: Do not compromise your own conscience in order to conform to the conscience of another believer and do not attempt to lead another believer to compromise his conscience to conform to yours.

As already noted, the greater responsibility is on the strong believer, for the very reason that he is better informed in the Word and more mature in his understanding. Paul therefore sternly warns the strong Christian: "Take care lest this liberty of yours somehow become a stumbling block to the weak. For if someone sees you, who have knowledge, dining in an idol's temple, will not his conscience, if he is weak, be strengthened to eat things sacrificed to idols? For through your knowledge he who is weak is ruined, the brother for whose sake Christ died. And thus, by sinning against the brethren and wounding their conscience when it is weak, you sin against Christ" (1 Cor. 8:9-12). Speaking for himself, he continues, "Therefore, if food causes my brother to stumble, I will never eat meat again, that I might not cause my brother to stumble" (1 Cor. 8:13).

Standing before the Sanhedrin, the supreme Jewish council in Jerusalem, Paul declared, "Brethren, I have lived my life with a perfectly good conscience before God up to this day" (Acts 23:1). In light of the passage from 1 Corinthians just cited, and of many others he had written, Paul not only was confessing that he was guiltless of compromising his own conscience but that he also was guiltless of having caused other believers to compromise their consciences.

That is the principle he emphasizes next in our present text: **For not one of us lives for himself, and not one dies for himself; for if we live, we live for the Lord, or if we die, we die for the Lord; therefore whether we live or die, we are the Lord's.** In all of Scripture, there is no greater call for holy living and for submission to the sovereign and unconditional lordship of Jesus Christ.

Neither the strong nor the weak **lives for himself** or **dies for himself,** and for the same reason—both of them **live for the Lord** and both of them **die for the Lord.** What we do for other believers, we do not only for their sakes but for our Lord's sake, because, **whether we live or die, we are the Lord's.** Christ is our mutual **Lord,** our mutual sovereign; and therefore everything we do, even in our dying, should be to please and to glorify our sovereign Savior and Lord.

We belong wholly to Christ because we "have been bought with a price" (1 Cor. 6:20; cf. 7:23) that He Himself paid with His own blood for our redemption (Eph. 1:7; Col. 1:14). Paul charged the Ephesian elders to "be on guard for yourselves and for all the flock, among which the Holy Spirit has made you overseers, to shepherd the church of God which He purchased with His own blood" (Acts 20:28).

We are the Lord's in the fullest possible sense, and **to this end Christ died and lived again,** Paul declares unequivocally, **that He might be Lord both of the dead and of the living.** To deny the lordship of Jesus Christ in the life of *any* believer is to subvert the full work, power, and purpose of His crucifixion and resurrection.

It seems inconceivable that genuine believers who love and serve the Lord and are well taught in His Word can maintain, as some do, that it is possible for a person to receive Jesus Christ as Savior but not as Lord. He died not only to save us but to own us, not only to free us from sin but to enslave us to Himself. Although the early church fully appreciated and praised Christ for His saviorhood, their earliest and most common confession was, "Jesus is Lord."

"Thanks be to God that though you were slaves of sin, you became obedient from the heart to that form of teaching to which you were committed," Paul already has exulted in and declared in this letter, "and having been freed from sin, you became slaves of righteousness. ...But now having been freed from sin and *enslaved to God,* you derive your benefit, resulting in sanctification, and the outcome, eternal life" (Rom. 6:17-18, 22, emphasis added).

Only when He returns will Christ be universally acknowledged as sovereign Lord, at which time "every tongue [will] confess that Jesus

Christ is Lord" (Phil. 2:11; cf. Rev. 17:14; 19:16). But He will not *become* Lord at that time. He already *is* "the blessed and only Sovereign, the King of kings and Lord of lords" (1 Tim. 6:15), and His people recognize Him as such.

THE LORD ALONE WILL JUDGE EACH BELIEVER

But you, why do you judge your brother? Or you again, why do you regard your brother with contempt? For we shall all stand before the judgment seat of God. For it is written, "As I live, says the Lord, every knee shall bow to Me, and every tongue shall give praise to God." So then each one of us shall give account of himself to God. (14:10-12)

The fourth reason Paul gives for every Christian's accepting every other Christian is that the Lord alone will judge each believer. If each believer belongs to the Lord alone, and if "Christ died and lived again, that He might be Lord both of the dead and of the living" (vv. 8-9), Paul asks, **why do you** (the weak, see v. *3b)* **judge your brother? Or you again, why do you** (the strong, see v. *3a)* **regard your brother with contempt?**

It is a terrible thing for men "to play God," as it is often phrased. It is particularly inexcusable for God's own people to intimate that presumption by judging and despising each other.

The work of Christians is to serve the Lord, not to usurp His lordship by self-righteously judging fellow believers. Our concern, rather, should be for being judged ourselves by the Lord, **For we shall all stand before the judgment seat of God.**

When we, along with all other believers, stand before the Lord on His **judgment seat,** His divine *bēma,* "each man's work will become evident, for the day will show it, because it is to be revealed with fire; and the fire itself will test the quality of each man's work. If any man's work which he has built upon it remains, he shall receive a reward. If any man's work is burned up, he shall suffer loss; but he himself shall be saved, yet so as through fire" (1 Cor. 3:13-15).

As cited earlier, the apostle said of himself,

> Let a man regard us in this manner, as servants of Christ, and stewards of the mysteries of God. In this case, moreover, it is required of stewards that one be found trustworthy. But to me it is a very small thing that I should be examined by you, or by any human court; in fact, I do not even examine myself. For I am conscious of nothing against myself, yet I am not by this acquitted; but the one who examines me is the

Lord. Therefore do not go on passing judgment before the time, but wait until the Lord comes who will both bring to light the things hidden in the darkness and disclose the motives of men's hearts; and then each man's praise will come to him from God. (1 Cor. 4:1-5)

Reinforcing his argument for believer's judgment with a quotation from Isaiah 45:23, Paul reminds his readers that **it is written, "As I live, says the Lord, every knee shall bow to Me, and every tongue shall give praise to God"** (cf. Phil. 2:10-11).

Our responsibility is not to judge, to despise, to criticize, or in any way to belittle our brothers and sisters in Christ. We will not be called on by our Lord to give an account of the sins and shortcomings of others, but rather **each one of us shall give account of himself to God.**

The Unity of Strong and Weak Christians

21

—part 2
Build Up One Another Without Offending
(Romans 14:13-23)

Therefore let us not judge one another anymore, but rather determine this—not to put an obstacle or a stumbling block in a brother's way. I know and am convinced in the Lord Jesus that nothing is unclean in itself; but to him who thinks anything to be unclean, to him it is unclean. For if because of food your brother is hurt, you are no longer walking according to love. Do not destroy with your food him for whom Christ died. Therefore do not let what is for you a good thing be spoken of as evil; for the kingdom of God is not eating and drinking, but righteousness and peace and joy in the Holy Spirit. For he who in this way serves Christ is acceptable to God and approved by men. So then let us pursue the things which make for peace and the building up of one another. Do not tear down the work of God for the sake of food. All things indeed are clean, but they are evil for the man who eats and gives offense. It is good not to eat meat or to drink wine, or to do anything by which your brother stumbles. The faith which you have, have as your own conviction before God. Happy is he who does not condemn himself in what he approves. But he who doubts is condemned if he eats, because his eating is not from faith; and whatever is not from faith is sin. (14:13-23)

In His New Covenant, our Lord Jesus Christ has granted marvelous freedom to those who belong to Him by faith. Most importantly, we are freed from the penalty of sin, from spiritual death and eternal damnation. But Christians also are freed from the encumbrances of the ceremonial law and dietary restrictions of the Old Covenant. Apart from sin, we are completely free to enjoy all the good gifts that God has so graciously bestowed on those who trust in His beloved Son, Jesus Christ.

But although we are permitted to enjoy that freedom, we are not commanded to do so. We are not obligated to exercise every freedom we have in Christ. In fact, the greater our love and spiritual maturity, the less important those freedoms will be to us and the more willing we will be to relinquish them for the sake of best serving the Lord and others, especially other believers. Most especially, our concern should be for fellow Christians whom Paul describes as weak, those who are still shackled in some way by the external requirements and restrictions under which they formerly lived. The issue for the strong, mature Christian is not whether or not he possesses freedom but how he should exercise or waive that freedom on the basis of how it will affect others.

But as Paul emphasizes throughout 14:1-15:13, and as was discussed in the previous chapter, all responsibility does not fall on the stronger brother. Strong and weak believers have a mutual responsibility to love and fellowship with each other and to refrain from judging the other's convictions in regard to issues that the New Testament neither commands nor condemns.

Most churches include dedicated, faithful believers whose consciences do not allow them to participate in or approve of certain practices. When stronger believers, out of love for those brothers and sisters in the Lord, voluntarily restrict their own lives to conform to the stricter standards of the weaker believers, they build closer relationships with each other and the church as a whole is strengthened and unified. And in that loving environment, the weaker believers are helped to become stronger.

Our Christian liberty is vertical, before the Lord. But the exercise of that liberty is horizontal, because it is seen by and affects others. To rightly understand and use our freedom in Christ brings great satisfaction. But that satisfaction is multiplied when we willingly surrender the exercise of a liberty for the sake of other believers. More importantly, it greatly pleases our Lord and promotes harmony in His church.

The New Testament places considerable restraints on the use of our liberty in Christ. It is not, for example, to be used self-deceptively to justify an evil or excess in our life. "Act as free men," Peter declares, "and do not use your freedom as a covering for evil, but use it as bond-slaves of God" (1 Pet. 2:16).

Nor does the Lord grant us liberty to cause self-destruction or self-bondage. What Paul said of himself should be true of every believer. "All things are lawful for me, but not all things are profitable. All things are lawful for me, but I will not be mastered by anything" (1 Cor. 6:12). Later in the same epistle, he added, "All things are lawful, but not all things edify" (10:23). A habit or practice that may not be sinful in itself can easily become sinful by gaining control over and injuring the person who engages in it. What is begun as an exercise of legitimate freedom can turn into a form of bondage and self-destruction. Careless and selfish exercise of a God-given freedom often results in loss of freedom, in our becoming "mastered," as Paul said, by the very thing we are freely using—a danger the apostle himself was determined to avoid. Instead of serving and honoring the One who gives it, freedom that is carelessly used can undermine the work of God, dishonor His name, and wreak havoc among His people.

Christian liberty is not meant to bring spiritual self-retardation, as its misuse invariably does. Far more than any other age in history, ours is besieged with a seemingly limitless array of things that can consume our time, energy, and finances. Many of those things are flagrantly immoral and ungodly. But even inherently innocent things are so pervasive and accessible that they easily can undermine our devotion to the Lord and to His people, retard our spiritual growth, and reduce our spiritual usefulness.

Paul's supreme purpose was to "do all things for the sake of the gospel" (1 Cor. 9:23). To illustrate his pursuit of that purpose he used the figure of the Isthmian games, which were held at Corinth and therefore well-known to Paul's readers. Those games were one of the two famous Greek athletic festivals, the other being the Olympics. "Do you not know that those who run in a race all run, but only one receives the prize?" Paul asks. Therefore, "run in such a way that you may win. And everyone who competes in the games exercises self-control in all things. They then do it to receive a perishable wreath, but we an imperishable. Therefore I run in such a way, as not without aim; I box in such a way, as not beating the air; but I buffet my body and make it my slave, lest possibly, after I have preached to others, I myself should be disqualified" (1 Cor. 9:24-27).

Paul used his Christian liberty, and every other gift and blessing he possessed, for but one purpose: to attain the righteousness "which is through faith in Christ, the righteousness which comes from God on the basis of faith, that I may know Him, and the power of His resurrection and the fellowship of His sufferings, being conformed to His death; in order that I may attain to the resurrection from the dead" (Phil. 3:9-11). He went on to confess with humility: "Not that I have already obtained it, or have already become perfect, but I press on in order that I may lay hold of that for which also I was laid hold of by Christ Jesus. Brethren, I do not regard myself as having laid hold of it yet; but one thing I do: forgetting what lies behind and reaching forward to what lies ahead, I press on toward the goal for the prize of the upward call of God in Christ Jesus" (Phil. 3:11-14).

In Romans 14:13-23 Paul continues his teaching about Christian liberty and the mutual obligation of strong and weak believers to accept each other in Christ without being judgmental or causing offense. In these eleven verses, the apostle mentions a number of principles, each given in negative form, that serve as guidelines for all Christians. The principles are closely related and sometimes overlap, but they seem to fall into six general categories: Our liberty should never cause a brother to stumble (v. 13), to grieve (vv. 14-15*a*), or to be devastated (v. 15*b*); and it should never forfeit our witness for Christ (vv. 16-19), tear down His work (vv. 20-21), or be either denounced or flaunted (vv. 22-23).

DON'T CAUSE YOUR BROTHER TO STUMBLE

Therefore let us not judge one another anymore, but rather determine this—not to put an obstacle or a stumbling block in a brother's way. (14:13)

Therefore refers back to verses 10-12, in which Paul reminds his readers that God alone is qualified and has the authority to judge the minds and hearts of His people, who will all stand before His judgment seat (v. 10) and give account of themselves to Him (v. 12; cf. 2 Cor. 5:10). Judgment is God's exclusive prerogative.

Consequently, we must **not judge one another** (cf. Matt. 7:1-5). It is the unloving attitude of contemptuous superiority by strong believers and the equally unloving attitude of self-righteousness by weak believers (v. 3) by which they **judge one another.** From Paul's day to ours, those wrongful judgments have been major causes of disrespect, disharmony, and disunity in the church.

As reflected in the text of the *New American Standard Bible* (used here), Paul uses the same Greek verb *(krinō)* with two different connotations in verse 13. In the first phrase, **let us not judge one another,** the verb carries the idea of condemnation, as it does in verses 3, 4, and 10. But in the following phrase, the same verb is translated **determine,** which refers to making a decision. Those two connotations are also found in the English word *judge.* "Being judgmental" carries the negative idea of denunciation, whereas "using your best judgment" refers to making a careful decision, with no negative connotation.

Paul's play on words demands that we should never be judgmental of fellow believers but instead should use our best judgment to help them. In relation to the second meaning, we should **determine . . . not to put an obstacle or a stumbling block in a brother's way.** He gives the same warning in his first letter to Corinth, saying, "Take care lest this liberty of yours [the strong] somehow become a stumbling block to the weak" (1 Cor. 8:9). This carries the idea of stumbling into sin.

For example, although the New Testament does not forbid the drinking of alcoholic beverages, there are many good reasons for Christians to abstain. One of the most important is the detrimental effect it can have on a former alcoholic. Our drinking, even in moderation, could easily place **a stumbling block** in that **brother's way** and cause him to fall back into his former addiction.

The same principle applies to any activity or practice that is not inherently sinful. Problem areas vary from society to society and from person to person, but the principle never changes. The loving, caring, strong Christian will determine in his mind and heart to be sensitive to *any* weakness in a fellow believer and avoid doing *anything,* including what is innocent in itself and otherwise permissible, that might cause him to morally or spiritually stumble.

Don't Grieve Your Brother

I know and am convinced in the Lord Jesus that nothing is unclean in itself; but to him who thinks anything to be unclean, to him it is unclean. For if because of food your brother is hurt, you are no longer walking according to love. (14:14-15*a*)

A second way to build up fellow believers without offending them is to be careful not to say or do anything that might cause them to be spiritually grieved or hurt.

As far as nonsinful things are concerned, the apostle says, **I know and am convinced in the Lord Jesus that nothing is unclean in itself.** He was not stating a personal opinion or preference about such things but was **convinced in the Lord Jesus;** that is, he knew by divine revelation.

Having been a Pharisee, Paul doubtless had been extremely careful about what he ate and did not eat. But he now understood with absolute certainty the truth which the Lord declared to Peter three times in a vision: "What God has cleansed, no longer consider unholy" (Acts 10:15). That divine cleansing referred directly to the multitude of animals Peter was commanded to eat that were ceremonially unclean according to Mosaic law (vv. 12-13). Indirectly, and in an even more important way, it referred to God's full and impartial acceptance of believing Gentiles into the church (vv. 28, 34).

Jesus declared that "there is nothing outside the man which going into him can defile him" (Mark 7:15). Paul assured Timothy that "God has created [all foods] to be gratefully shared in by those who believe and know the truth. For everything created by God is good, and nothing is to be rejected, if it is received with gratitude; for it is sanctified by means of the word of God and prayer" (1 Tim. 4:3-5). He informed Titus that "to the pure, all things are pure" (Titus 1:15).

The strong Christian is therefore entirely right in his conviction that he is at liberty to enjoy anything the Lord does not declare to be sinful. The weak Christian, on the other hand, is wrong in his understanding about some of those things. But he is not wrong in the sense of being heretical or immoral. He is wrong in the sense of not having complete and mature understanding, which causes his conscience to be unnecessarily sensitive. For that reason, **to him who thinks anything to be unclean, to him it is unclean** in his mind.

Concerning the same problem, Paul gave the following explanation to the church at Corinth:

> Therefore concerning the eating of things sacrificed to idols, we know that there is no such thing as an idol in the world, and that there is no God but one. For even if there are so-called gods whether in heaven or on earth, as indeed there are many gods and many lords, yet for us there is but one God, the Father, from whom are all things, and we exist for Him; and one Lord, Jesus Christ, by whom are all things, and we exist through Him. However not all men have this knowledge; but some, being accustomed to the idol until now, eat food as if it were sacrificed to an idol; and their conscience being weak is defiled. (1 Cor. 8:4-7)

It is likely that every Christian has a weak spot of some sort in his conscience. Paul himself probably had one or more. He did not claim to be free of every spiritual deficiency, but he testified before the Roman governor that he did his "best to maintain always a blameless conscience both before God and before men" (Acts 24:16).

For various reasons, there are certain things that we know are not sinful but that we do not feel comfortable in doing or even being near. And as long as we feel discomfort about any such thing, we should avoid doing it—even if it would not cause offense to other believers. If we ourselves consider **anything to be unclean,** then *to us* **it is unclean.** And if we persist in violating our conscience, that conscience will become more and more insensitive until it is "seared ... as with a branding iron" (1 Tim. 4:2). It then is no longer as sensitive as it needs to be to protect us from sin.

But Paul's major emphasis in this passage is on how our words and actions affect the spiritual welfare of fellow Christians. Therefore, **if because of food,** or any other issue, our **brother is hurt,** we **are no longer walking according to love.**

Is hurt translates *lupeō,* which has the basic meaning of causing pain, distress, or grief. It is used by John to describe Peter's reaction when Jesus asked "him the third time, 'Simon, son of John, do you love Me?'" and "Peter was grieved" (John 21:17). It is even used of the Holy Spirit, who is grieved when we sin (Eph. 4:30).

It is lamentable when Christians are harmed by unbelievers. But it is tragic when Christians **hurt** a **brother** Christian, particularly over matters that are not inherently wrong. A weak Christian can be **hurt** or distressed from watching another Christian say or do something he considers sinful. The hurt is deeper if the offending believer is admired and respected by the weaker one. A weak Christian also can be **hurt** when, by word or example, he is led by a stronger brother to go against the convictions of his own conscience. That is by far the greater offense. Being upset over what another Christian does can certainly **hurt,** but that hurt is not nearly so severe and damaging as the **hurt** of a believer's conscience over what he himself has done. He suffers feelings of guilt, and forfeits much of his peace of mind, his joy, his witness, and perhaps even his assurance of salvation. A Christian whose careless use of his liberty causes such **hurt** to other believers is **no longer walking according to love.**

After the caution cited above from 1 Corinthians 8, Paul goes on to say that a strong believer who causes a weaker brother to stumble by going against his conscience not only is unloving but commits sin against that brother and against the Lord Himself. "Food will not commend us to God; we are neither the worse if we do not eat, nor the better if we do eat. But take care," he warns, "lest this liberty of yours somehow become a stumbling block to the weak. For if someone sees you, who have knowledge, dining in an idol's temple, will not his conscience, if he is weak, be strengthened to eat things sacrificed to idols? For through your knowledge he who is weak is ruined, the brother for whose sake Christ died. And thus, by sinning against the brethren and wounding their conscience when it is weak, you sin against Christ" (1 Cor. 8:8-12).

Paul is not, of course, speaking of "ruined" in the sense of damnation, because that is what believers are eternally saved from. He is speaking of the loss of such things as those already mentioned—peace of mind, joy, witness, and assurance of salvation. The best safeguard against grieving another believer's conscience is to determine to do the opposite of what the insensitive and unloving person does: to always walk **according to love.**

DON'T DEVASTATE YOUR BROTHER

Do not destroy with your food him for whom Christ died. (14:15*b*)

A third principle for building up rather than harming weaker believers is not to spiritually devastate them. As mentioned in the beginning of this chapter, the six principles or guidelines in verses 13-23 overlap and are not completely distinct or separable. While this third warning is much like the second, it is considerably stronger.

Apollumi **(destroy)** refers to utter devastation. But as the noted Greek scholar W. E. Vine explains, "The idea is not extinction but ruin, loss, not of being, but of well-being" *(An Expository Dictionary of New Testament Words* [Westwood, N.J.: Revel, 1940]). The term is often used in the New Testament to indicate eternal damnation (see, e.g., Matt. 10:28; Luke 13:3; John 3:16; Rom. 2:12), which applies to unbelievers. But even with that meaning the word does not connote extinction, as annihilationists claim, but rather spiritual calamity that will continue forever.

To destroy . . . him for whom Christ died, is not to cause his damnation but to seriously devastate his spiritual growth. When Jesus said, "It is not the will of your Father who is in heaven that one of these little ones perish *[apollumi]* " (Matt. 18:14), the context makes clear that "these little ones" are believers. They have been "converted and become like children" (v. 3) and "believe in Me" (v. 6). Jesus was not concerned about their loss of salvation but about their loss of spiritual well-being, which, although not an eternal loss, is an injury the Lord considers to be extremely grave. Even to "despise one of those little ones" (v. 10) **for whom Christ died** is a great offense to God.

It is also important to note that the phrase **for whom Christ died** is here used to describe believers. This is commonly called limited atonement, or particular redemption, the idea that Christ sacrificed His life on the cross only on behalf of the elect who come to faith.

Certainly the atonement in its ultimate and full sense is limited to the elect, but the New Testament is replete with declarations that Christ's sacrifice was sufficient to cover the sin of every human being. In the following quotations, italics have been added for emphasis of that truth. John the Baptist proclaimed Jesus to be "the Lamb of God who takes away the sin of *the world!*" (John 1:29). Jesus said of Himself "that *whoever believes* may in Him [the Son of Man] have eternal life," and that

"God so loved the world, that He gave His only begotten Son, that *whoever believes* in Him should not perish, but have eternal life" (John 3:15-16). "I am the living bread that came down out of heaven," Jesus said; and "if *anyone* eats of this bread, he shall live forever; and the bread also which I shall give for *the life of the world* is My flesh" (John 6:51).

Paul already has made clear in Romans that "*Whoever* will call upon the name of the Lord will be saved" (10:13). Elsewhere he says with equal unambiguity, that "the love of Christ controls us, having concluded this, that one died *for all,* therefore all died" (2 Cor. 5:14), "God our Savior,… desires *all men to be saved* and to come to the knowledge of the truth. For there is one God, and one mediator also between God and men, the man Christ Jesus, who gave Himself as a ransom *for all,* the testimony borne at the proper time" (1 Tim. 2:3-6), and that "we have fixed our hope on the living God, who is the Savior of *all men,* especially of believers" (1 Tim. 4:10).

Peter warned against "false teachers among you, who will secretly introduce destructive heresies, even denying the Master *who bought them,* bringing swift destruction upon themselves" (2 Pet. 2:1). In other words, the Lord paid a price sufficient to save even those unbelievers who corrupt His Word and blaspheme His name.

In his first letter, John wrote that "we have an Advocate with the Father, Jesus Christ the righteous; and He Himself is the propitiation for our sins; and not for ours only, but also *for those of the whole world*" (1 John 2:1-2), and that "we have beheld and bear witness that the Father has sent the Son to be *the Savior of the world*" (4:14).

God's provision of an atonement without limit is prefigured in the Old Testament. When the high priest once a year made a sacrifice on the Day of Atonement, Yom Kippur, he made it on behalf of "all the people of the assembly," that is, all Israelites (Lev. 16:33). The scope of the sacrifice was unlimited in its sufficiency, but limited in its application. That act did not cleanse the sins even of believing Jews, but it prefigured God's future offering of atonement by the supreme High Priest, Jesus Christ, who would sacrifice Himself for the sins of the entire world and apply it to the elect.

DON'T FORFEIT YOUR WITNESS

Therefore do not let what is for you a good thing be spoken of as evil; for the kingdom of God is not eating and drinking, but righteousness and peace and joy in the Holy Spirit. For he who in this way serves Christ is acceptable to God and approved by men. So then let us pursue the things which make for peace and the building up of one another. (14:16-19)

A fourth purpose for building up rather than injuring weaker believers is to avoid forfeiting our witness before the rest of the world.

It is possible to so abuse our liberty in Christ in regard to fellow believers that we create conflicts within the church that give the world cause to criticize and condemn those who claim to hold brotherly love in such high esteem. **Therefore,** Paul says, **do not let what is for you a good thing be spoken of as evil.**

Although it brings much blessing and enjoyment to those who understand and exercise it properly, Christian liberty is not simply for our own benefit and certainly not for our selfish abuse. It is a gracious gift from God and a wonderfully **good thing.** But like every other divine blessing, it can be misused in ways that are outside of, and often contrary to, God's purposes. This **good thing** of liberty is to be used carefully, with loving concern for our weaker brethren and with concern for its witness to the unbelieving world. It should not cause those brothers to stumble, be grieved, or harmed in any way; and it should never give the watching world an excuse for it to **be spoken of as evil.**

As reported in Acts 15, the Jerusalem Council strongly denounced the Judaizers' insistence that "It is necessary to circumcise [Gentile believers], and to direct them to observe the Law of Moses" (v. 5). But it also was decided that care should be taken not to offend the consciences either of Jewish or Gentile believers who were weak. Consequently, the group sent a letter to the churches advising "that you abstain from things sacrificed to idols and from blood and from things strangled and from fornication; if you keep yourselves free from such things, you will do well" (Acts 15:29). Fornication apparently was a moral problem in many of the churches and was forbidden because it is outright sin. But the other three prohibitions had to do with religious law and ceremony, both Jewish and pagan.

As mentioned before, many Gentile believers could not bring themselves to eat meat that had been used in a pagan ritual. Paul carefully dealt with that problem in his first letter to Corinth, which, as one would imagine, included many Gentile converts who continued to have social contact with unbelieving Gentiles as well as with fellow believers. The apostle therefore advised them:

> All things are lawful, but not all things are profitable. All things are lawful, but not all things edify. Let no one seek his own good, but that of his neighbor. Eat anything that is sold in the meat market, without asking questions for conscience' sake; for the earth is the Lord's, and all it contains. If one of the unbelievers invites you, and you wish to go, eat anything that is set before you, without asking questions for conscience' sake. But if anyone should say to you, "This is meat sacrificed to idols," do not eat it, for the sake of the one who informed you, and

for conscience' sake; I mean not your own conscience, but the other man's; for why is my freedom judged by another's conscience? If I partake with thankfulness, why am I slandered concerning that for which I give thanks? Whether, then, you eat or drink or whatever you do, do all to the glory of God. Give no offense either to Jews or to Greeks or to the church of God. (1 Cor. 10:23-32)

The situation was this: A strong and a weak Christian sometimes would go to dinner at the house of an unbelieving Gentile. When the host served the meal, he might mention that the meat had been used in a pagan sacrifice. The weak believer would be immediately disturbed and tell the other believer that he could not in good conscience eat such meat. Out of love for his weaker brother, the strong Christian would join in refusing to eat the meat, understanding that it is better to offend an unbeliever than a fellow believer. Although that unusual and selfless act of love might temporarily offend the unbelieving host, it might also be used of the Spirit to show the depth of Christian love and draw him to the gospel.

Paul's dual message was, in effect, "Don't apologize for or renounce your freedom in Christ, and don't let your own conscience be bothered. Take advantage of your liberty with joy and gratitude, because it is a precious gift from God. But, on the other hand, be willing at any time to forfeit the exercise of your freedom if it might cause spiritual harm to a believer or become an unnecessary offense to an unbeliever. Before the church and before the world, it is much more important to demonstrate our love than our freedom." He told the Corinthian church, "For though I am free from all men, I have made myself a slave to all, that I might win the more" (1 Cor. 9:19).

Many Jewish Christians, because of the Mosaic restrictions under which they had been raised, could not bring themselves to eat meat that still contained blood nor could they eat meat from an animal that had been killed by strangulation. When a weak Jewish believer found himself at a meal where such meat was being served, any stronger believer who was present should, out of love for his brother, also refuse to eat it.

Such careful exercise of Christian liberty is vital to the unity of the church and to the church's witness before and to the unbelieving world. Forsaking a freedom is a small concession to make for the sake of both believers and potential believers, **for the kingdom of God is not eating and drinking, but righteousness and peace and joy in the Holy Spirit.**

When those three attributes characterize individual Christians and the local church in which they worship and through which they serve, the work of Christ is advanced and blessed **in the Holy Spirit.**

Righteousness in our daily living should always be more precious to us than the exercise of our liberties. Even though those liberties are God-given, we should seek continually to be "filled with the fruit of righteousness which comes through Jesus Christ, to the glory and praise of God" (Phil. 1:11) and to always be wearing "the breastplate of righteousness" (Eph. 6:14).

Peace in the church—the loving, tranquil relationship of believers who are more interested in serving others than in pleasing themselves—is also more important than individual liberties and is a powerful witness to the unbelieving world. It is a fruit of the Spirit (Gal. 5:22). God's people are called to "be devoted to one another in brotherly love; give preference to one another in honor; not lagging behind in diligence, fervent in spirit, serving the Lord; rejoicing in hope, persevering in tribulation, devoted to prayer, contributing to the needs of the saints, practicing hospitality" (Rom. 12:10-13; cf. James 3:17). Those are marks of genuine **peace.**

Like **peace,** the **joy** of believers is a product of **righteousness.** It is both a mystery and a strong attraction to the world and is often used by the Holy Spirit to draw men and women to Christ. Also like **peace, joy** is a fruit of the Spirit. Even in the midst of hardship and persecution, we are able to have, and should always seek, "the joy of the Holy Spirit" (1 Thess. 1:6).

The loving and selfless Christian **who in this way serves Christ is acceptable to God and approved by men.** *Dokimos* **(approved)** refers to acceptance after careful examination, as when a jeweler carefully inspects a gem under a magnifying glass to determine its genuineness and value. When we serve Christ selflessly, we prove ourselves "to be blameless and innocent, children of God above reproach in the midst of a crooked and perverse generation, among whom you appear as lights in the world" (Phil. 2:15).

Paul himself exemplified the selfless principles he commends in this passage. He acknowledged, for example, his right to have a wife and to be paid for his ministry (1 Cor. 9:5-6). Nevertheless, "we did not use this right," he explained, "but we endure all things, that we may cause no hindrance to the gospel of Christ" (v. 12).

So then, Paul continues, **let us pursue the things which make for peace and the building up of one another.** Humility, selfless love, and compassion for the needs of others are among **the things which make for peace.** In the closing remarks of his second letter to Corinth, Paul said, "Finally, brethren, rejoice, be made complete, be comforted, be like-minded, live in peace; and the God of love and peace shall be with you" (2 Cor. 13:11). An indispensable part of faithful witnessing is "being diligent to preserve the unity of the Spirit in the bond of peace" (Eph. 4:3). Those virtues, along with the willingness to forsake our liberties for the sake of fellow believers, also assure **the build ing up of one another** in Christian fellowship.

Don't Pull Down the Work of God

Do not tear down the work of God for the sake of food. All things indeed are clean, but they are evil for the man who eats and gives offense. It is good not to eat meat or to drink wine, or to do anything by which your brother stumbles. (14:20-21)

A fifth reason for building up rather than injuring weaker believers is **not** to **tear down the work of God for the sake of food.**

Do not tear down translates the present imperative of *kataluō*, suggesting that Paul was commanding certain believers in Rome to discontinue something they were already doing.

As we have seen, in the days of the early church many offenses against the consciences of weak brothers involved **food.** For Jews it related to eating **food** that was declared ceremonially unclean under the Mosaic law. For Gentiles, it related to eating food, most commonly meat, that had been used in a pagan sacrifice. But in the broader context of Romans 14 and 15, Paul's warnings about food and drink relate to *anything* not sinful in itself that might be said or done that would cause a weaker Christian to be offended and spiritually harmed.

Also in this context, **the work of God** clearly refers to believers, all of whom "are His workmanship, created in Christ Jesus" (Eph. 2:10). It is therefore not only a serious offense against a weaker brother to cause him to stumble but a serious offense against the purposes of God.

We would consider it an appalling crime for someone to deface a Rembrandt painting, to shatter a sculpture by Michelangelo, or to smash a Stradivarius violin. How infinitely worse it is to **tear down** a **work of God,** a man "for whom Christ died" (Rom. 14:15).

"By sinning against the brethren and wounding their conscience when it is weak, you sin against Christ," Paul wrote as he chastised the immature and self-indulgent believers at Corinth. "Therefore, if food causes my brother to stumble," he said of himself, "I will never eat meat again, that I might not cause my brother to stumble" (1 Cor. 8:12-13).

The apostle reminds us again that he is not speaking about sinful and unholy things, but about discretionary liberties that are good gifts from God. **All** such **things indeed are clean** and good in themselves (cf. w. 14, 16). The danger is that, when they are exercised selfishly and carelessly by strong Christians, those very blessings can become **evil for the man who eats and gives offense.**

Therefore, **it is good not to eat meat or to drink wine,** which are in themselves good, or **to do anything** else that is good in itself, **by which your brother stumbles,** because such stumbling hinders the work of God in and through that believer. God is endeavoring to build that believer up (Eph. 4:11-15) while we are tearing him down. That is unthinkable!

As noted previously, Paul is not prohibiting all drinking of alcoholic beverages, which neither the Old nor New Testament forbids. It should also be noted that the common wine drunk by Jews of that day was highly diluted with water and had a low alcohol content. But, if Paul considered the drinking of **wine** to be sinful in itself, it would not make sense to use it as an illustration of discretionary, nonsinful practices. (For a more detailed discussion of this matter, see the author's *Ephesians* in this commentary series, 229-44.)

The issue concerns doing **anything** at all **by which your brother stumbles.** The pleasure of eating offensive food or drink, or the pleasure of doing anything else our liberty allows us to do, is absolutely trivial compared to the spiritual welfare of a brother or sister in Christ. It is worse than trivial. It becomes actually sinful if we have reason to believe it might cause one of the little ones for whom Christ died to stumble.

Don't Denounce or Flaunt Your Liberty

The faith which you have, have as your own conviction before God. Happy is he who does not condemn himself in what he approves. But he who doubts is condemned if he eats, because his eating is not from faith; and whatever is not from faith is sin. (14:22-23)

The sixth and final reason for exercising our liberty with great care is that we can harm even ourselves when we do not view our liberty from God's perspective. We lose that divine perspective when we denounce or belittle good things He has given us or when, at the other extreme, we lovelessly flaunt our liberty without caring about how we affect others.

Verse 22 obviously is directed to the strong Christian, the one who understands and appreciates his freedom. Paul's counsel to him is simple and direct: **The faith which you have, have as your own conviction before God. Happy is he who does not condemn himself in what he approves.** When by sincere **faith** and a correct understanding of Scripture we have a **conviction before God** that a custom, a practice, or an activity is worthwhile and good, we dare not denounce it as sinful. Nor should we allow our conscience to **condemn** us for exercising it—with Paul's repeated stipulation that we gladly relinquish that freedom for the sake of a brother or sister in Christ.

Verse 23 just as obviously is directed to the weak Christian, the one whose conscience is still offended by certain religious carryovers from his former life. And the apostle's counsel to him is just as simple and direct: **He who doubts is condemned if he eats, because his eating is not from faith; and whatever is not from faith is sin.** The corresponding stipulation is that, just as the strong believer commits sin by causing a weak brother to go against his own conscience, the weak brother sins, **is condemned,** when, contrary to the convictions of his own faith, he succumbs to that which his conscience condemns.

The Unity of Strong and Weak Christians —part 3 Please One Another as Christ Did (Romans 15:1-6)

22

Now we who are strong ought to bear the weaknesses of those without strength and not just please ourselves. Let each of us please his neighbor for his good, to his edification. For even Christ did not please Himself; but as it is written, "The reproaches of those who reproached Thee fell upon Me." For whatever was written in earlier times was written for our instruction, that through perseverance and the encouragement of the Scriptures we might have hope. Now may the God who gives perseverance and encouragement grant you to be of the same mind with one another according to Christ Jesus; that with one accord you may with one voice glorify the God and Father of our Lord Jesus Christ. (15:1-6)

God has always been deeply concerned about the unity of His people. By salvation, He has effected a real spiritual oneness. He has created a commonness based on sharing the same eternal life. This reality of conversion should impact the life of the church by being the impetus for practical unity. Scripture emphasizes both aspects.

Through David, the Lord proclaimed, "Behold, how good and how pleasant it is for brothers to dwell together in unity!" (Ps. 133:1).

Speaking specifically of His chosen people Israel, He prophesied through Jeremiah that one day,"They shall be My people, and I will be their God; and I will give them one heart and one way, that they may fear Me always, for their own good, and for the good of their children after them" (Jer. 32:38-39). In one of Ezekiel's visions, the Lord instructed the prophet,"Son of man, take for yourself one stick and write on it,'For Judah and for the sons of Israel, his companions'; then take another stick and write on it,'For Joseph, the stick of Ephraim and all the house of Israel, his companions.' Then join them for yourself one to another into one stick, that they may become one in your hand, ... and they will be one in My hand" (Ezek. 37:16-17,19; cf. Hos. 1:11).

Speaking of the whole world, Jew and Gentile alike, God predicted that in the end times,"I will give to the peoples purified lips, that all of them may call on the name of the Lord, to serve Him shoulder to shoulder" (Zeph. 3:9), that is, side by side, as brothers."The Lord will be king over all the earth; in that day the Lord will be the only one, and His name the only one" (14:9).

The unity of believers is also the concern of God the Son. Speaking on one occasion before a largely Jewish audience, Jesus said,"I have other sheep [Gentiles], which are not of this fold [Israel]; I must bring them also, and they shall hear My voice; and they shall become one flock with one shepherd" (John 10:16). In other words, God's eternal plan is that all who believe in Him will become outwardly what they already are inwardly—unified in Him through faith in His Son."When all things are subjected to Him [Christ],"Paul says,"then the Son Himself also will be subjected to the One who subjected all things to Him, that God may be all in all" (1 Cor. 15:28). Ultimately, everyone who belongs to the Lord will be united in a great and glorious fellowship with Him and with each other.

While exiled on the island of Patmos, the apostle John wrote,

I saw a new heaven and a new earth; for the first heaven and the first earth passed away, and there is no longer any sea. And I saw the holy city, new Jerusalem, coming down out of heaven from God, made ready as a bride adorned for her husband. And I heard a loud voice from the throne, saying,"Behold, the tabernacle of God is among men, and He shall dwell among them, and they shall be His people, and God Himself shall be among them, and He shall wipe away every tear from their eyes; and there shall no longer be any death; there shall no longer be any mourning, or crying, or pain; the first things have passed away." (Rev. 21:1-4)

Even for now, however, despite the limitations of the remaining old garments of the sinful flesh, it is the Lord's absolute and unconditional will that His people be in harmony with Him and with each other.

The unity of His people was one of the desires our Savior expressed in His high priestly prayer:"I am no more in the world; and yet they themselves are in the world, and I come to Thee. Holy Father, keep them in Thy name, the name which Thou hast given Me, that they may be one, even as We are" (John 17:11).

The unity of the church is also, of course, the concern of God the Holy Spirit. At Pentecost, the Spirit dramatically came upon and indwelt the apostles (Acts 2:4), who then were miraculously enabled to speak "of the mighty deeds of God" in the native languages of the multitude of Jews from various parts of the world who had come to Jerusalem for the Feast of Pentecost (vv. 7-12). After Peter preached before the great crowd, "they were pierced to the heart, and said to Peter and the rest of the apostles, 'Brethren, what shall we do?' And Peter said to them, 'Repent, and let each of you be baptized in the name of Jesus Christ for the forgiveness of your sins; and you shall receive the gift of the Holy Spirit'" (vv. 37-38).

With the indwelling of the Spirit came a spiritual unity among believers that immediately was expressed in selfless service to one another. The some "three thousand souls" who believed the gospel and were saved that day "were continually devoting themselves to the apostles' teaching and to fellowship, to the breaking of bread and to prayer. ...And all those who had believed were together, and had all things in common; and they began selling their property and possessions, and were sharing them with all, as anyone might have need. And day by day continuing with one mind in the temple, and breaking bread from house to house, they were taking their meals together with gladness and sincerity of heart, praising God, and having favor with all the people. And the Lord was adding to their number day by day those who were being saved" (vv. 41-42, 44-47).

In the days following, as the apostles, especially Peter and John, continued to preach, "the congregation of those who believed were of one heart and soul; and not one of them claimed that anything belonging to him was his own; but all things were common property to them.... For there was not a needy person among them, for all who were owners of land or houses would sell them and bring the proceeds of the sales, and lay them at the apostles' feet; and they would be distributed to each, as any had need" (Acts 4:32, 34-35).

There is no evidence that this practice of the infant church in Jerusalem became the standard for other churches of that time or that it continued indefinitely even in Jerusalem. But the spiritual unity and selflessness of those early believers should characterize every Christian and every congregation in every age.

In his letter to Ephesus, Paul declared that, "with all humility and gentleness, with patience," we should show "forbearance to one another in love, being diligent to preserve the unity of the Spirit in the bond of peace" (4:2-3). He then specifically mentions the participation of each Person of the Trinity in the spiritual welfare and unity of the church. "There is one body and *one*; . . . *one Lord* [Christ, the Son], one faith, one baptism, *one God and Father* of all who is over all and through all and in all" (vv. 4-6, emphasis added).

To the factious, discordant church at Corinth, Paul wrote: "Now I exhort you, brethren, by the name of our Lord Jesus Christ, that you all agree, and there be no divisions among you, but you be made complete in the same mind and in the same judgment" (1 Cor. 1:10). Later in the same letter, he reminded them that, "even as the body is one and yet has many members, and all the members of the body, though they are many, are one body, so also is Christ. For by one Spirit we were all baptized into one body, whether Jews or Greeks, whether slaves or free, and we were all made to drink of one Spirit" (12:12-13).

The apostle reminded believers in the Galatian churches that "you are all sons of God through faith in Christ Jesus. For all of you who were baptized into Christ have clothed yourselves with Christ. There is neither Jew nor Greek, there is neither slave nor free man, there is neither male nor female; for you are all one in Christ Jesus" (Gal. 3:26-28). He admonished believers in Philippi: "Conduct yourselves in a manner worthy of the gospel of Christ; so that whether I come and see you or remain absent, I may hear of you that you are standing firm in one spirit, with one mind striving together for the faith of the gospel" (Phil. 1:27). They would make his "joy complete by being of the same mind, maintaining the same love, united in spirit, intent on one purpose" (2:2).

In the church of Christ, "there is no distinction between Greek and Jew, circumcised and uncircumcised, barbarian, Scythian, slave and freeman, but Christ is all, and in all" (Col. 3:11). Among the characteristics that make for unity and harmony in the church are "a heart of compassion, kindness, humility, gentleness and patience; bearing with one another, and forgiving each other" (vv. 12-13). "And beyond all these things," Paul continues, "put on love, which is the perfect bond of unity" (v. 14).

Peter admonishes Christians to "be harmonious, sympathetic, brotherly, kindhearted, and humble in spirit" (1 Pet. 3:8). In his first letter, John emphasizes the relationship between spiritual unity and the divine light of God's Word: "If we walk in the light as He Himself is in the light, we have fellowship with one another" (1 John 1:7). He also emphasizes the relationship between unity and love—God's love for us and our love for God and for each other."We know love by this," he says, "that He laid down His life for us; and we ought to lay down our lives for the brethren. But whoever has the world's goods, and beholds his brother in need and closes his heart against him, how does the love of God abide in him? Little children, let us not love with word or with tongue, but in deed and truth" (1 John 3:16-18; cf. 4:11,20-21).

Apart from outright sin, nothing shatters the fellowship, the spiritual growth, and the witness of a congregation so much as disharmony among its members. Romans 15 continues Paul's teaching on the vital importance of unity in the church, adding two more principles for achieving that objective. The first is pleasing one another, following the example of our Lord (vv. 1-6), and the second, discussed in the following chapter, is rejoicing with one another in God's eternal plan of redemption (vv. 7-13).

In the first of these heartfelt appeals, Paul calls believers to please one another, using Christ Himself as our model. He mentions six spiritual characteristics that should lead us to please one another: regard for others (15:1a), disregard of self (vv. 1b-2), conformity to Christ (v. 3), submission to Scripture (v. 4), dependence on divine power (v. 5), and giving glory to God (v. 6).

REGARD FOR OTHERS

Now we who are strong ought to bear the weaknesses of those without strength (15:1a)

As with the principles of receiving one another with understanding (14:1-12) and of building up one another without offending (vv. 13-23), responsibility for pleasing one another falls on all believers, but especially on those **who are strong.** Consequently, they **ought to bear the weaknesses of those without strength.**

Opheilō **(ought)** has the basic meaning of owing a debt or having a strong obligation. It is used in Hebrews 5:3 to refer to the unique responsibility of the high priest in ancient Israel, who was "*obligated* to offer sacrifices for sins, as for the people, so also for himself" (Heb. 5:3, emphasis added). In his first letter, John uses the term three times to indicate our obligation to follow God's example."The one who says he abides in Him [Christ] *ought* himself to walk in the same manner as He walked"; because Christ"laid down His life for us, ... we *ought* to lay down our lives for the brethren"; and, "if God so loved us, we also *ought* to love one another" (1 John 2:6; 3:16; 4:11, emphasis added).

Bastazō **(to bear)** refers to picking up and carrying a burden. It is used literally of "carrying a pitcher of water" (Mark 14:13) and of carrying a man (Acts 21:35), and figuratively of bearing a yoke of obligation (Acts 15:10).

Therefore, **to bear the weaknesses** of fellow believers is not simply to tolerate those **weaknesses** but to help carry them—by not being critical or condescending and by showing respect for sincere views or practices that we may not agree with. It is to "do nothing from selfishness or empty conceit, but with humility of mind ... [to] regard one another as more important than" ourselves, not merely looking "out for [our] own personal interests, but also for the interests of others" (Phil. 2:3-4).

The idea is that of showing genuine, loving, and practical consideration for other believers. We are not to argue about minor issues or be critical of those who may still be sensitive about a former religious practice or taboo. The injunction is for mature believers to voluntarily and lovingly refrain from exercising their liberty in ways that might needlessly offend the consciences of less mature brothers and sisters in Christ, those who are **without strength.**

Paul was referring to that attitude when he testified:

> Though I am free from all men, I have made myself a slave to all, that I might win the more. And to the Jews I became as a Jew, that I might win Jews; to those who are under the Law, as under the Law, though not being myself under the Law, that I might win those who are under the Law; to those who are without law, as without law, though not being without the law of God but under the law of Christ, that I might win those who are without law. To the weak I became weak, that I might win the weak; I have become all things to all men, that I may by all means save some. (1 Cor. 9:19-22)

He was not speaking of compromising the gospel or godly standards of living in order to gain acceptance and approval by the world, a sin he strongly condemned. "Am I now seeking the favor of men, or of God?" he asked the Galatians. "Or am I striving to please men? If I were still trying to please men, I would not be a bond-servant of Christ" (Gal. 1:10). On the contrary, he was speaking of relinquishing personal liberties and advantages for the sake of fellow believers—even for the sake of unbelievers, if doing so might be instrumental in leading them to Christ.

DISREGARD FOR SELF

and not just please ourselves. Let each of us please his neighbor for his good, to his edification. (15:1b-2)

The right use of Christian liberty, which the strong believer understands and appreciates, often involves self-sacrifice. When our true motivation is to please Christ by helping "to bear the weaknesses of those without strength" (v. 1a), we can expect to forfeit certain legitimate liberties, when exercising them would harm a weaker brother or sister.

The Lord designs that a relationship with Him be from the heart and so graciously grants us freedom for our own sakes, to liberate us from the shackles of religious superstitions and even from certain ceremonial externals and restrictions that He Himself had instituted as symbols, but which, in the New Covenant, He has declared to be no longer valid. Apart from that which in itself is sinful, we are divinely freed to do much as we **please.**

But the Lord does not grant those freedoms **just** so we can selfishly **please ourselves.** He grants them for the benefit of His entire church. Every believer has the same liberty in Christ as every other believer, but because believers vary greatly in spiritual knowledge and maturity, the careless exercise of a liberty by one member can do great harm to the conscience and spiritual well-being of another member and even to the well-being of an entire congregation.

Paul grieved over the Philippian church when he heard that some members there, apparently in positions of leadership and influence, sought "after their own interests, not those of Christ Jesus" (Phil. 2:21). It was not that they were teaching wrong doctrine or living immoral lives, but that they had great concern for their own interests and little concern for the interests of fellow believers. And for that reason, Paul declared, they had little genuine concern for the interests "of Christ Jesus" Himself or for His church.

Obviously, the church at Rome also had such members, and the apostle appealed to them, **Let each of us please his neighbor.** Paul did not exclude himself from the exhortation. **Let each of us** expresses all-inclusive responsibility and allows no exemptions, even for an apostle.

The objective of pleasing our **neighbor** is to promote **his good** and **his edification,** even if it requires the sacrifice of some of our own welfare and pleasure, which it often does. It is essentially the same appeal Paul had made earlier in this letter, again not exempting himself: "Let *us* pursue the things which make for peace and the building up of one another" (Rom. 14:19, emphasis added).

To do **good** for our **neighbor** and to promote **his edification** is to be "of the same mind" as our brothers and sisters in Christ, "maintaining the same love, united in spirit, intent on one purpose," doing "nothing from selfishness or empty conceit, but with humility of mind" regarding "one another as more important than [oneself]; . . . not merely [looking] out for [our] own personal interests, but also for the interests of others." It is to "have this attitude in [ourselves] which was also in Christ Jesus" (Phil. 2:2-5).

CONFORMITY TO CHRIST

For even Christ did not please Himself; but as it is written, "The reproaches of those who reproached Thee fell upon Me." (15:3)

The "attitude . . . in Christ Jesus" just referred to was **not** to **please Himself.** It is the attitude Paul goes on to explain in his letter to Philippi. During His incarnation, "although He existed in the form of God," our Lord "did not regard equality with God a thing to be grasped, but emptied Himself, taking the form of a bond-servant, and being made in the likeness of men. And being found in appearance as a man, He humbled Himself by becoming obedient to the point of death, even death on a cross" (Phil. 2:6-8). Despite His perfectly righteous and sinless life, Jesus could say with David, but with infinitely greater significance, **The reproaches of those who reproached Thee fell upon Me** (cf. Ps. 69:9).

Had Jesus wanted to please Himself instead of His Father, He would not have divested Himself of His glory and become a man, certainly not a bond-servant. Yet, with great longing He prayed, "Glorify Thou Me together with Thyself, Father, with the glory which I had with Thee before the world was" (John 17:5). Moments before He was arrested in the Garden of Gethsemane, He entreated His Father, "If it is possible, let this cup pass from Me," referring to His taking the sins of the world upon Himself by His crucifixion. But He had not come to earth to **please Himself,** and therefore added, "yet not as I will, but as Thou wilt" (Matt. 26:39; cf. Heb. 5:7).

That Jesus' supreme purpose was to please His Father and to accomplish His Father's will is evident in all four gospels, but His selfless resolve is seen most explicitly in the record of John. Jesus told the Twelve, "My food is to do the will of Him who sent Me, and to accomplish His work" (John 4:34). To a group of unbelieving Jews in the Temple—who already were incensed by His "calling God His own Father, making Himself equal with God"—Jesus testified, "I can do nothing on My own initiative. As I hear, I judge; and My judgment is just, because I do not seek My own will, but the will of Him who sent Me" (John 5:18, 30). To a multitude near Capernaum, He said, "For I have come down from heaven, not to do My own will, but the will of Him who sent Me" (John 6:38). To another group of Jews in the Temple treasury, who asked Him, "Who are You?" and who "did not realize that

He had been speaking to them about the Father, Jesus therefore said, 'When you lift up the Son of Man, then you will know that I am He, and I do nothing on My own initiative, but I speak these things as the Father taught Me. And He who sent Me is with Me; He has not left Me alone, for I always do the things that are pleasing to Him'" (John 8:25, 27-29; cf. 14:31). He came into the world to fulfill the wonderful plan of God to gather the redeemed to glory.

The writer of Hebrews pointedly makes clear that "Jesus, the Apostle and High Priest of our confession...was faithful to Him who appointed Him" (Heb. 3:1-2).

Yet Jesus' heavenly Father did not force His Son to become incarnate and to die for the world's sins. "I and the Father are one" (John 10:30), Jesus declared. Therefore, when the Father "gave His only begotten Son, that whoever believes in Him should not perish, but have eternal life" (John 3:16), the Son was as fully willing to go as His Father was to send Him. Not only that, but Jesus said, "I lay down My life that I may take it again. No one has taken it away from Me, but I lay it down on My own initiative. I have authority to lay it down, and I have authority to take it up again" (John 10:17-18).

Unlike our Lord, we do not have the power to lay down and take up again our own lives. But, as already noted, we are able, with the Spirit's power, to be conformed to Christ in having the selfless "attitude in [ourselves) which was also in Christ Jesus" (Phil. 2:5). By that same power of the Spirit, we are able to be conformed to Christ in His willingness to please God at any cost. Therefore, that willingness to please the Lord despite misunderstanding, ridicule, slander, deprivation, persecution, and even death should characterize every believer. It characterizes every believer whose life is conformed to Christ and who desires to please another brother.

SUBMISSION TO SCRIPTURE

For whatever was written in earlier times was written for our instruction, that through perseverance and the encouragement of the Scriptures we might have hope. (15:4)

A fourth characteristic that will lead us to please one another as Christ did is our willing and unreserved submission to God's Word.

Whatever was written in earlier times obviously refers to the divinely-revealed truths we now call the Old Testament. They were written for the **times** in which they were recorded but also for **our instruction,** for God's people in the present age.

As we have seen, beginning with Romans 14:1, Paul emphasizes that the ceremonial requirements of the Old Covenant are no longer binding on believers, Jews or Gentiles. But even though we are not bound to obey all of the commands of that covenant, every part of God's revelation **written in earlier times** is still valuable for **our instruction.** Knowledge of *all* Scripture had spiritual benefit for Christians in Paul's day and still has benefit for Christians for all time.

With few exceptions (Rom. 16:26; 2 Pet. 3:16), New Testament references to Scripture signify the Old Testament. Paul's well-known statement that "all Scripture is inspired by God and profitable for teaching, for reproof, for correction, for training in righteousness; that the man of God may be adequate, equipped for every good work" (2 Tim. 3:16-17) certainly applies to the New Testament. But in the minds of the initial readers, it referred to "the sacred writings" (v. 15) of the Old Testament. That same understanding was in the minds of those to whom Peter wrote, saying "that no prophecy of Scripture is a matter of one's own interpretation, for no prophecy was ever made by an act of human will, but men moved by the Holy Spirit spoke from God" (2 Pet. 1:20-21).

Paul reminded believers in Corinth that the events of the Exodus under Moses "happened as examples for us, that we should not crave evil things, as they also craved. . . . Now these things happened to them as an example, and they were written for our instruction, upon whom the ends of the ages have come" (1 Cor. 10:6,11).

Our part in this blessing is **perseverance,** which is closely related to patience. In regard to the Lord's return, James admonishes us to "be patient, therefore, brethren, until the coming of the Lord. Behold, the farmer waits for the precious produce of the soil, being patient about it, until it gets the early and late rains. You too be patient; strengthen your hearts, for the coming of the Lord is at hand" (James 5:7-8). Like saving faith, **perseverance** is both commanded of us and given to us by God, as Paul assures us in the next verse of our present passage (Rom. 15:5). It is continuing faithfulness to the Lord through all circumstances. Revelation 14:12 identifies **perseverance** with sustained faith and obedience. Second Thessalonians 1:4 says that **perseverance** is faith that does not fail "in the midst of all your persecutions and afflictions which you endure." The clearest exhortation to **perseverance** is given in Colossians 1:22-23: "Yet He has now reconciled you in His fleshly body through death, in order to present you before Him holy and blameless and beyond reproach—if indeed you continue in the faith firmly established and steadfast, and not moved away from the hope of the gospel that you have heard, which was proclaimed in all creation under heaven" (cf. Matt. 24:13; Heb. 3:12-14; 4:11).

God also gives us **encouragement** to persevere. He provides this impetus by means of **the Scriptures,** which chronicle all the reasons to keep believing. They give us reason to sustain **hope** for our glorious future.

Jeremiah speaks of God, the author of Scripture, as the "Hope of Israel, its Savior in time of distress" (Jer. 14:8; cf. 17:7). The psalmists repeatedly speak of their hope in the Lord. "Why are you in despair, O my soul?" one writer asks himself. "And why have you become disturbed within me?" Giving answer to his own question, he says, "Hope in God, for I shall again praise Him for the help of His presence" (Ps. 42:5). Another psalmist advises himself, "My soul, wait in silence for God only, for my hope is from Him" (Ps. 62:5). In the great psalm that so majestically exalts God's Word, the writer calls on the Lord to "remember the word to Thy servant, in which Thou hast made me hope" (Ps. 119:49), and pleads, "Sustain me according to Thy word, that I may live; and do not let me be ashamed of my hope" (v. 116), and testifies, "I hope for Thy salvation, O Lord, and do Thy commandments" (v. 166). Another psalmist affirms, "I wait for the Lord, my soul does wait, and in His word do I hope" (Ps. 130:5).

We read in the book of Job that "the hope of the godless will perish" (Job 8:13)—unlike Job himself, of whom James writes, "Behold, we count those blessed who endured. You have heard of the endurance of Job and have seen the outcome of the Lord's dealings, that the Lord is full of compassion and is merciful" (James 5:11). It was his certain **hope** in the Lord's righteousness and justice that gave Job the unimaginable perseverance to endure the torments with which God permitted Satan to afflict His "blameless and upright" servant (Job 1:8).

Paul reminded Gentile believers in Ephesus that before their conversion they "were at that time separate from Christ, excluded from the commonwealth of Israel, and strangers to the covenants of promise, having no hope and without God in the world" (Eph. 2:12; cf. 4:17-18). "The covenants of promise" were part of the Old Testament, God's revealed Word to His chosen people Israel.

From those passages and many others in both testaments, it is clear that, as far as the believer's **hope** is concerned, God and His Word are inseparable. We know that God's Word, His Son "Christ Jesus,... is our hope" (1 Tim. 1:1) because that glorious truth is made known to us in God's *written* Word.

DEPENDENCE ON DIVINE POWER

Now may the God who gives perseverance and encouragement grant you to be of the same mind with one another according to Christ Jesus; (15:5)

As mentioned above, even the things that God *demands* of us He *gives* to us by His sovereign grace. Paradoxically, it is **God who gives** the **perseverance** He requires as well as the **encouragement.** Just as verse 4 is essentially a call to rely on God's power through His Word, verse 5 is essentially a call to rely on His power through prayer.

In this benediction, Paul prays that the Lord would **grant** his fellow believers in Rome **to be of the same mind with one another according to Christ Jesus.** As with perseverance and encouragement, the harmony God requires, He will also provide.

In his call for believers **to be of the same mind with one another according to Christ Jesus,** the apostle is speaking of unity in regard to matters on which the Bible is silent or which are no longer valid. It is disagreement about nonessential issues that causes the conflict between strong and weak believers. Paul therefore continues to call on believers, despite their differing views, to be in loving, spiritual, and brotherly harmony **with one another according to** their common Savior and Lord, **Christ Jesus.** The fulfillment of this command is by God's power.

GIVING GLORY TO GOD

that with one accord you may with one voice glorify the God and Father of our Lord Jesus Christ. (15:6)

The consummate purpose of Christian unity, however, is not to please other believers, as essential as that is, but to please the Lord, both inwardly and outwardly and both individually and corporately. It is only when His people are in **one accord** and worship Him **with one voice** that they truly and fully **glorify the God and Father of our Lord Jesus Christ.**

Except for His plea on the cross—when He was temporarily separated from the Father as He took the full burden of mankind's sin upon Himself and cried out, "My God, My God, why hast Thou forsaken Me?" (Matt. 27:46)—Jesus *always* referred to God as His Father. It was for that reason, among others, that the Jewish leaders denounced Jesus as a blasphemer, because He called "God His own Father, making Himself equal with God" (John 5:18).

In calling believers to **glorify the God and Father of our Lord Jesus Christ,** Paul was emphasizing Jesus' deity. Jesus is not an adopted son of God, as are those who believe in Him (Rom. 8:14-17; Gal. 4:5; Eph. 1:5). He is the unique and "only begotten from the Father," who was *in Himself,* "full of grace and truth" (John 1:14; cf. v. 18; 3:16). He is the promised Messiah, the **Christ,** and is **our Lord,** completely equal to **God** the **Father** in deity.

The New Testament repeatedly speaks of this unique and unfathomable relationship of God the Father and God the Son. Immediately after his greeting to the church at Ephesus, Paul exults, "Blessed be the God and Father of our Lord Jesus Christ, who has blessed us with every spiritual blessing in the heavenly places in Christ" (Eph. 1:3; cf. 2 Cor. 1:3), and later in that first chapter he speaks of "the God of our Lord Jesus Christ, the Father of glory" (v. 17). In his letter to Philippi, the apostle prophesies that one day, "at the name of Jesus every knee [shall] bow, of those who are in heaven, and on earth, and under the earth, and that every tongue [shall] confess that Jesus Christ is Lord, to the glory of God the Father" (Phil. 2:10-11).

Using words identical to Paul's, Peter declared, "Blessed be the God and Father of our Lord Jesus Christ," adding, "who according to His great mercy has caused us to be born again to a living hope through the resurrection of Jesus Christ from the dead" (1 Pet. 1:3). John greeted the readers of his second letter with these words: "Grace, mercy and peace will be with us, from God the Father and from Jesus Christ, the Son of the Father, in truth and love" (2 John 3), clearly testifying that divine grace, mercy, and peace are equally from God the Father and God the Son.

Through grace far beyond our comprehension, **our Lord Jesus Christ** prayed to His **Father** on our behalf,

> that they may all be one; even as Thou, Father, art in Me, and I in Thee, that they also may be in Us; that the world may believe that Thou didst send Me. And the glory which Thou hast given Me I have given to them; that they may be one, just as We are one; I in them, and Thou in Me, that they may be perfected in unity, that the world may know that Thou didst send Me, and didst love them, even as Thou didst love Me. (John 17:21-23)

The Unity of Strong and Weak Christians

23

—part 4 Rejoice with One Another in God's Plan of Redemption (Romans 15:7-13)

Wherefore, accept one another, just as Christ also accepted us to the glory of God. For I say that Christ has become a servant to the circumcision on behalf of the truth of God to confirm the promises given to the fathers, and for the Gentiles to glorify God for His mercy; as it is written, "Therefore I will give praise to Thee among the Gentiles, and I will sing to Thy name." And again he says, "Rejoice, O Gentiles, with His people." And again, "Praise the Lord all you Gentiles, and let all the peoples praise Him." And again Isaiah says, "There shall come the root of Jesse, and He who arises to rule over the Gentiles, in Him shall the Gentiles hope." Now may the God of hope fill you with all joy and peace in believing, that you may abound in hope by the power of the Holy Spirit. (15:7-13)

In this passage, which closes the major theological section of his letter to Rome, Paul discusses the fourth major principle for promoting unity in the church: corporate rejoicing because of the common sharing in God's eternal plan of redemption.

This principle is presented in a more positive form and does not focus directly on the negatives of conflicts between strong and weak believers, as do the first three. The emphasis here is on the mutual responsibilities of *all* believers for each other, which encompasses three features: the basic instruction (v. 7), biblical illustrations (vv. 8-12), and a benedictory prayer of intercession (v. 13).

THE BASIC INSTRUCTION

Wherefore, accept one another, just as Christ also accepted us to the glory of God. (15:7)

This verse, in effect, summarizes the previous two, which also focus on our accepting **one another, just as Christ also accepted us** and on giving **glory to God.**

Proslambanō **(accept)** is an intensified form of *lambanō* and carries the meaning of receiving something or someone to oneself with special concern. It can have a negative connotation, as when Peter presumptuously "took [Jesus] aside *[proslambanō]* and began to rebuke Him" (Mark 8:32).

But the connotation in Romans 15:7 is positive and is illustrated several times in the book of Acts. When Apollos "began to speak out boldly in the synagogue," Priscilla and Aquila lovingly "took him aside *[proslambanō]* and explained to him the way of God more accurately" (Acts 18:26). After Paul's ship was wrecked just off the coast of Malta, "the natives showed us *extraordinary kindness*; for because of the rain that had set in and because of the cold, they kindled a fire and received *[proslambano]* us all" (Acts 28:2, emphasis added). It is the word Paul uses in imploring Philemon to lovingly take back his runaway slave Onesimus, to "accept *[proslambano]* him as you would me" (Philem. 17).

In the present text, the apostle gives an infinitely greater illustration of the way in which Christians are to receive each other. He has used the word twice in Romans 14, each time (vv. 1, 3) referring, as here, to believers accepting one another with love and without reservation or judgment. And in 14:3, as here, believers are commanded to **accept one another** in the same gracious way that **Christ** has **accepted us.** Although He used a different verb, Jesus declared that "He who receives you receives Me, and he who receives Me receives Him who sent Me" (Matt. 10:40). Therefore, to **accept one another** is to accept **Christ** Himself.

Paul does not mention specific types of believers in this verse. He is speaking to the strong and to the weak, to Gentiles and to Jews. *All* believers are called to **accept one another.** He is not simply speaking of accepting new believers into our church fellowship, although that would certainly be included in this admonition. He is calling on all

Christians to **accept one another** in the fullest and deepest sense, to treat each other with love and understanding, **just as Christ also accepted us.** If the perfect, sinless Son of God has accepted us into God's divine family, how much more should we be willing to accept each other, despite the fact that we all still carry sinful trappings from our old, unredeemed flesh. The self-righteous, hypocritical scribes and Pharisees criticized Jesus because He "receives sinners and eats with them" (Luke 15:2). All of those sinners may not have become saved, but before salvation, every person whom Christ accepts is just like those sinners.

Jesus Christ Himself is our pattern for accepting one another. As He reminded the Twelve, "A disciple is not above his teacher, nor a slave above his master" (Matt. 10:24). In saying, "Take My yoke upon you, and learn from Me, for I am gentle and humble in heart" (Matt. 11:29), Jesus commands us to learn from His example the virtues of kindness, gentleness, and humility. Paul admonished the Ephesians to "be kind to one another, tender-hearted, forgiving each other, just as God in Christ also has forgiven you. Therefore be imitators of God, as beloved children; and walk in love, just as Christ also loved you, and gave Himself up for us, an offering and a sacrifice to God as a fragrant aroma" (Eph. 4:32-5:2).

To **accept one another, just as Christ also accepted us,** is a sure mark of godliness, and failure to do so is just as surely a mark of carnality. Failure to **accept one another** in love and compassion is an affront to the Savior who **accepted us.** A congregation that is divisive, quarrelsome, contentious, and judgmental gives the world reason to ridicule Christ's church and to reject the One who is their only hope of salvation.

There are at least four characteristics of Christ's accepting sinners. First, He accepts them joyously. In the passage cited above from Luke 15, Jesus told His critics and the rest of the crowd a parable,

> saying, "What man among you, if he has a hundred sheep and has lost one of them, does not leave the ninety-nine in the open pasture, and go after the one which is lost, until he finds it? And when he has found it, he lays it on his shoulders, rejoicing. And when he comes home, he calls together his friends and his neighbors, saying to them, 'Rejoice with me, for I have found my sheep which was lost!' I tell you that in the same way, there will be more joy in heaven over one sinner who repents, than over ninety-nine righteous persons who need no repentance." (Luke 15:3-7)

Jesus graciously entreats all men: "Come to Me, *all* who are weary and heavy-laden, and I will give you rest" (Matt. 11:28), and "If *any* man is thirsty, let him come to Me and drink" (John 7:37, emphasis added). In great sorrow, He looked out over the holy city and lamented, "O Jerusalem, Jerusalem, who kills the prophets and stones those who are sent to her! How often I wanted to gather your children together, the way a hen gathers her chicks under her wings, and you were unwilling" (Matt. 23:37). From the cross, He expressed His willingness to forgive and to save even those who were then putting Him to death, "saying, 'Father, forgive them; for they do not know what they are doing' " (Luke 23:34).

Some years ago I was visiting in a city and drove by a church that had a prominent sign in front that proclaimed Jesus' invitation mentioned above: "Come unto Me all ye that labor and are heavy laden and I will give you rest." I later learned that a former pastor of that church had witnessed to and was discipling a man of another race. The people of the church and community strongly discouraged his doing that, and when he continued, he was virtually ostracized. He was not able to buy gas at the service station or groceries at the supermarket. His insurance was canceled and his children were continually harassed. The pastor became so distraught that he had a nervous breakdown and had to be hospitalized. A few days after being admitted, he committed suicide. His desperate state of mind and sinful act were, in some measure, impelled by the utter failure of that church to live up to the message it publicly proclaimed.

Jesus also has a message for believers who presumptuously oppress and mistreat His children: "Whoever causes one of these little ones who believe in Me to stumble, it is better for him that a heavy millstone be hung around his neck, and that he be drowned in the depth of the sea" (Matt. 18:6).

Second, Jesus accepts sinners for salvation in spite of their sin. Otherwise, no person could be saved, because no person can cleanse his own sin. "God demonstrates His own love toward us," Paul has said earlier in this letter, "in that while we were yet sinners, Christ died for us" (Rom. 5:8). In his first letter to Timothy, he testified, "It is a trustworthy statement, deserving full acceptance, that Christ Jesus came into the world to save sinners, among whom I am foremost of all" (1 Tim. 1:15).

One day, as Jesus "was reclining at the table in the house, behold many tax-gatherers and sinners came and were dining with Jesus and His disciples. And when the Pharisees saw this, they said to His disciples, 'Why is your Teacher eating with the tax-gatherers and sinners?' But when He heard this, He said, 'It is not those who are healthy who need a physician, but those who are sick. But go and learn what this means, "I desire compassion, and not sacrifice," for I did not come to call the righteous, but sinners'" (Matt. 9:10-13). On another occasion, "the Pharisees and their scribes began grumbling at His disciples, saying, 'Why do you eat and drink with the tax-gatherers and sinners?' And

Jesus answered and said to them, 'It is not those who are well who need a physician, but those who are sick'" (Luke 5:30-31; cf. 6:32-36).

On still another occasion, Jesus

> told this parable to certain ones who trusted in themselves that they were righteous, and viewed others with contempt: "Two men went up into the temple to pray, one a Pharisee, and the other a tax-gatherer. The Pharisee stood and was praying thus to himself, 'God, I thank Thee that I am not like other people: swindlers, unjust, adulterers, or even like this tax-gatherer. I fast twice a week; I pay tithes of all that I get.' But the tax-gatherer, standing some distance away, was even unwilling to lift up his eyes to heaven, but was beating his breast, saying, 'God, be merciful to me, the sinner!' I tell you, this man went down to his house justified rather than the other; for everyone who exalts himself shall be humbled, but he who humbles himself shall be exalted." (Luke 18:9-14)

Third, Jesus accepts sinners impartially. His promise is unequivocal: "All that the Father gives Me shall come to Me, and the one who comes to Me I will certainly not cast out" (John 6:37). The Lord has bound Himself by His own word that He will accept any person, without qualification, who receives Him by faith. Early in this letter, Paul declared that there absolutely "is no partiality with God" (Rom. 2:11). It was a difficult truth for Peter to accept, but he finally confessed, "I most certainly understand now that God is not one to show partiality, but in every nation the man who fears Him and does what is right, is welcome to Him" (Acts 10:34-35).

James vividly emphasized that truth. "My brethren," he wrote,

> do not hold your faith in our glorious Lord Jesus Christ with an attitude of personal favoritism. For if a man comes into your assembly with a gold ring and dressed in fine clothes, and there also comes in a poor man in dirty clothes, and you pay special attention to the one who is wearing the fine clothes, and say, "You sit here in a good place," and you say to the poor man, "You stand over there, or sit down by my footstool," have you not made distinctions among yourselves, and become judges with evil motives? ... If, however, you are fulfilling the royal law, according to the Scripture, "You shall love your neighbor as yourself," you are doing well. But if you show partiality, you are committing sin and are convicted by the law as transgressors. (James 2:1-4, 8-9)

Fourth, Jesus accepts sinners to the glory of God, as Paul states explicitly in our text: **Christ also accepted us to the glory of God.** God established His eternal plan of redemption to glorify Himself.

Everything He does is to His glory, and everything His children do *should be* to His glory.

God "predestined us to adoption as sons through Jesus Christ to Himself, according to the kind intention of His will, to the praise of the glory of His grace, which He freely bestowed on us in the Beloved," Paul declares (Eph. 1:5-6). In a benediction later in that letter he said, "Now to Him who is able to do exceeding abundantly beyond all that we ask or think, according to the power that works within us, to Him be the glory in the church and in Christ Jesus to all generations forever and ever. Amen" (3:20-21). "God highly exalted [Christ], and bestowed on Him the name which is above every name," in order that, when He comes again, "at the name of Jesus every knee should bow, of those who are in heaven, and on earth, and under the earth, and that every tongue should confess that Jesus Christ is Lord, to the glory of God the Father" (Phil. 2:9-11).

Therefore, when we follow our Lord's example in receiving each other in love and without judgment or condescension, we do so as He did, **to the glory of God.** And keep in mind, Jesus said, "Whoever receives one such child in My name receives *Me*" (Matt. 18:5, emphasis added)!

THE BIBLICAL ILLUSTRATIONS

For I say that Christ has become a servant to the circumcision on behalf of the truth of God to confirm the promises given to the fathers, and for the Gentiles to glorify God for His mercy; as it is written, "Therefore I will give praise to Thee among the Gentiles, and I will sing to Thy name." And again he says, "Rejoice, O Gentiles, with His people." And again, "Praise the Lord all you Gentiles, and let all the peoples praise Him." And again Isaiah says, "There shall come the root of Jesse, and He who arises to rule over the Gentiles, in Him shall the Gentiles hope." (15:8-12)

To illustrate that it has always been God's plan to bring Gentile and Jew alike into His kingdom, Paul cites passages from the Old Testament. They obviously were given to soften the prejudice of Christian Jews against Christian Gentiles by demonstrating from their own Scriptures that the inclusion of Gentiles was neither a divine nor a human afterthought.

Throughout the epistle, Paul has emphasized that truth. At the beginning he made clear that Christ "was declared the Son of God with power by the resurrection from the dead, according to the Spirit of holiness, Jesus Christ our Lord, through whom we have received grace and apostleship to bring about the obedience of faith among all the Gentiles, for His name's sake" (1:4-5). He also explained in his opening comments, "I do not want you to be unaware, brethren, that often I have planned to come to you (and have been prevented thus far) in order that I might obtain some fruit among you also, even as among the rest of the Gentiles. I am under obligation both to Greeks and to barbarians, both to the wise and to the foolish....For I am not ashamed of the gospel, for it is the power of God for salvation to everyone who believes, to the Jew first and also to the Greek" (Rom. 1:13-14,16).

Quoting from Isaiah 52:5, Paul chastised self-righteous Jews in the congregation, reminding them that for centuries, "'The name of God is blasphemed among the Gentiles because of you,' just as it is written" (Rom. 2:24). Instead of being like their Messiah, "a light of the nations so that My salvation may reach to the end of the earth" (Isa. 49:6), they self-righteously separated themselves from the Gentiles and treated them with disdain (cf. Acts 13:47). The apostle later asks rhetorically, "Is God the God of Jews only? Is He not the God of Gentiles also?" and then answers his own question, "Yes, of Gentiles also" (Rom. 3:29).

In Romans 9-11, which focuses specifically on Israel, he declares, "There is no distinction between Jew and Greek; for the same Lord is Lord of all, abounding in riches for all who call upon Him; for," as the prophet Joel proclaimed, "'*Whoever* will call upon the name of the Lord will be saved'" (Rom. 10:12-13, emphasis added; cf. Joel 2:32). He informed them that, "by their [the Jews'] transgression salvation has come to the Gentiles, to make them jealous. Now if their transgression be riches for the world and their failure be riches for the Gentiles, how much more will their fulfillment be! ... For I do not want you, brethren, to be uninformed of this mystery, lest you be wise in your own estimation, that a partial hardening has happened to Israel until the fulness of the Gentiles has come in" (11:11-12,25). The book of Romans is a declaration of the sovereign plan and effort of God to save both Jew and Gentile.

Jesus **Christ,** of course, was born a Jew and became **a servant to the circumcision [the Jews] on behalf of the truth of God to confirm the promises given to the fathers,** that is, to the patriarchs Abraham, Isaac, and Jacob. God the Son became incarnate as a Jew to fulfill and to verify God's Word. Although He came to bring a New Covenant, He did not come "to abolish the Law or the Prophets ... but to fulfill" them (Matt. 5:17). He fulfilled the law by upholding its sacredness and reestablishing its truth. He fulfilled the law by keeping it perfectly. He fulfilled the law in every other possible way, and Paul's point here is that Christ came to verify the whole revealed truth of God. He came to save sinful man and to bring glory to His Father by fulfilling His Father's promises in both "the Law [and] the Prophets."

Christ confirmed those **promises to the fathers** in order **to glorify God for His mercy.** Paul himself ministered to Jews by more fully explaining to them the truth of God and by showing Gentiles the mercy of God. The saved Jew primarily praises God for His truth, which

He verified in Christ. The saved Gentile primarily praises God for His mercy, which He provided in Christ.

Quoting David in Psalm 18:49 (cf. 2 Sam. 22:50), Paul goes on to explain, **as it is written, "Therefore I will give praise to Thee among the Gentiles, and I will sing to Thy name."** Quoting Deuteronomy 32:43, he points out that **again he says, "Rejoice, O Gentiles, with His people."** Although he here refers to the human author, Moses, it is the divine Author whose truth is being declared and praised.

In verse 11 Paul quotes from Psalm 117:1, continuing to remind his Jewish readers of the testimony of their own Scriptures: **"Praise the Lord all you Gentiles, and let all the peoples praise Him."** Still **again Isaiah says, "There shall come the root of Jesse, and He who arises to rule over the Gentiles, in Him shall the Gentiles hope"** (see Isa. 11:10). The Messiah, who comes from **the root of Jesse,** the father of David, not only will rule over His ancient people Israel but also **over the Gentiles,** and **in Him shall the Gentiles hope,** just as the Jews.

In light of the magnificent, gracious, and sovereign plan of God—disclosed in part in His ancient revelation to Israel—Jews can have no grudge against Gentiles, because their calling, their very purpose for existing, was to reach Gentiles for the glory of the Lord. The Gentiles can have no grudge against Jews, because it was through the Jews that God brought them salvation.

THE BENEDICTORY INTERCESSION

Now may the God of hope fill you with all joy and peace in believing, that you may abound in hope by the power of the Holy Spirit. (15:13)

Paul closes this passage with a beautiful benediction of intercession for all the people of God, not mentioning Jew or Gentile, but addressing the entire, unified Body of Jesus Christ. He petitions **the God of hope** to graciously fill His people with His divine **joy and peace** and **hope.** It expresses the apostle's deep desire for all believers to have total spiritual satisfaction in their beloved Savior and Lord.

It is essentially the same benediction with which Paul blessed the church at Philippi:"And the peace of God, which surpasses all comprehension, shall guard your hearts and your minds in Christ Jesus" (Phil. 4:7; cf. 1 Pet. 1:3, 8). It is a prayer for satisfied souls in Christ to know and experience the peace, the hope, the love, the victory, the joy, and the power of the indwelling Spirit of God, who makes them one in Jesus Christ their Lord.

In Defense of
Boldness
(Romans 15:14-21)

24

And concerning you, my brethren, I myself also am convinced that you yourselves are full of goodness, filled with all
knowledge, and able also to admonish one another. But I have
written very boldly to you on some points, so as to remind you
again, because of the grace that was given me from God, to be a
minister of Christ Jesus to the Gentiles, ministering as a priest
the gospel of God, that my offering of the Gentiles might become
acceptable, sanctified by the Holy Spirit. Therefore in Christ
Jesus I have found reason for boasting in things pertaining to
God. For I will not presume to speak of anything except what
Christ has accomplished through me, resulting in the obedience
of the Gentiles by word and deed, in the power of signs and
wonders, in the power of the Spirit; so that from Jerusalem and
round about as far as Illyricum I have fully preached the gospel
of Christ. And thus I aspired to preach the gospel, not where
Christ was already named, that I might not build upon another
man's foundation; but as it is written, "They who had no news of
Him shall see, and they who have not heard shall understand."
(15:14-21)

After completing the major doctrinal treatise of this letter (1:18-15:13), Paul now begins what amounts to an epilogue, which comprises comments about his ministry (15:14-21), his plans for future service (vv. 22-33), personal greetings from himself and others (16:1-24), and a closing benediction (vv. 25-27).

In the present text, Paul gives a defense of his ministry, especially of his boldness in writing this letter to a church he did not found and had never visited. Except for a few individuals he had met elsewhere, he did not know the Christians in Rome. Yet he addresses them both warmly and forthrightly, as if they were close friends. He confronts them with boldness on many crucial issues, including that of the relationship of stronger and weaker believers, which he has dealt with in the long section (14:1-15:13) just concluded. Having set forth his divinely-revealed doctrine, he now once again (see 1:8-16) bares his own heart and soul.

Because he has spoken so forcefully, Paul did not want to jeopardize his relationship with the church at Rome by seeming insensitive, presumptuous, or unloving. He had long hoped to visit them in person, in order to minister to them and to share mutual encouragement, "each of us by the other's faith, both yours and mine" (see 1:10-15). Now, at last, it seemed this desire soon would be fulfilled, during his expected stay in Rome on the way to Spain (15:24).

PAUL THE PARTNER IN FAITH

And concerning you, my brethren, I myself also am convinced that you yourselves are full of goodness, filled with all knowledge, and able also to admonish one another. But I have written very boldly to you on some points, so as to remind you again, because of the grace that was given me from God, (15:14-15)

Paul wrote this letter with full apostolic authority (1:1). But, as just noted above in regard to 1:10-15, he also knew that, in himself, he had the same personal needs and limitations that are common to all Christians.

In this context, Paul's addressing his readers as **my brethren** not only indicates his recognition of their salvation but also their maturity. At the beginning of the letter, he thanked God for their faithfulness, which was "being proclaimed throughout the whole world" (1:8).

The apostle now acknowledges again that, completely apart from his influence, the Roman believers **are full of goodness, filled with all knowledge, and able to admonish one another.** He is saying, in effect: "In spite of all that I have written to you in this letter—with strong reminders that you were saved solely by God's grace, made effective by your faith in His Son, with the admonitions for obedience to the Lord, for mortifying the flesh, for holy living, for exercising your spiritual gifts, for serving each other in love and humility, and all the other teachings—I am fully aware of your spiritual maturity and moral virtue, and I commend you for it." The only other church he praised so highly was the one in Thessalonica (see 1 Thess. 1:2-10).

The first commendation was for their **goodness,** their high moral character and living. As Paul makes clear in Galatians 5:22-23, all virtue is the fruit of the Holy Spirit. But the Spirit can bear fruit only in the lives of believers, such as those in Rome, who are submissive to His divine will and power. They were not perfect, but neither were they spiritually deficient. In this letter Paul makes no reference to particular problems in the church, either individual or corporate. Those believers genuinely hated evil and loved righteousness, and they lived accordingly. They were obedient to the Lord and were kind, generous, and humble. By their moral **goodness,** they gave abundant evidence of their spiritual transformation and of the good works in which God ordains all believers to walk (Eph. 2:10). The apostle could say of them what he said of the Colossians:

> We give thanks to God, the Father of our Lord Jesus Christ, praying always for you, since we heard of your faith in Christ Jesus and the love which you have for all the saints; because of the hope laid up for you in heaven, of which you previously heard in the word of truth, the gospel, which has come to you, just as in all the world also it is constantly bearing fruit and increasing, even as it has been doing in you also since the day you heard of it and understood the grace of God in truth. (Col. 1:3-6)

Second, Paul commended the church at Rome for being **filled with knowledge.** He is not, of course, speaking of broad human knowledge but of the deep **knowledge** of God's truth in the gospel of Jesus Christ. Believers in this church were doctrinally sound. They were well on their way to "attaining to all the wealth that comes from the full assurance of understanding, resulting in a true knowledge of God's mystery, that is, Christ Himself, in whom are hidden all the treasures of wisdom and knowledge" (Col. 2:2-3).

Virtue and truth, here referred to as **goodness** and **knowledge,** are inseparable. Paul could have described those believers as having "a pure heart and a good conscience and a sincere faith" (1 Tim. 1:5; cf. v. 19). They knew God, they knew His truth, and, by the power of His Spirit, they were committed to living holy lives.

Such goodness and knowledge are possible for all believers to possess and live by. The Holy Spirit, who indwells every believer, also works to teach and purify every believer. As Paul has already declared, "From [Christ] and through Him and to Him are all things" (Rom. 11:36). It is by the Lord's doing that we "are in Christ Jesus, who became to us wisdom from God, and righteousness and sanctification, and redemption" (1 Cor. 1:30; cf. Eph. 1:8-9).

The third virtue for which Paul commends believers in Rome is a product of the first two. Christians who are **full of goodness** and **filled with all knowledge** are **able also to admonish one another.**

Noutheteō **(to admonish)** carries the ideas of encouraging, warning, and advising. It is a comprehensive term for counseling. In this context, it refers to coming alongside other Christians for spiritual and moral counseling. Paul is not referring to a special gift of counseling, but of the duty and responsibility that every believer has for encouraging and strengthening other believers.

Tragically, many Christians today have been convinced that competent counseling can only be accomplished by a person who is trained in the principles of secular psychology—despite the fact that the various schools of psychology are, for the most part, at extreme odds with God's Word and frequently with each other. Although they may profess that "all Scripture is inspired by God and profitable for teaching, for reproof, for correction, for training in righteousness" (2 Tim. 3:16), many evangelicals—both those who give and those who receive counseling—do not rely on the full sufficiency of God's Word.

There is no such thing as a psychological problem. All personal problems are either spiritual or physical. Anyone who suggests that so-called psychological problems can exist apart from or between those two realms of human existence does not understand either the nature of man and the power of sin or the nature and power of God's Word and Spirit.

It is obvious that some Christians are uniquely gifted for giving encouraging counsel, just as some have special gifts and abilities in other areas of ministry. Paul has earlier made clear that, "since we have gifts that differ according to the grace given to us, [we should] each exercise them accordingly" (Rom. 12:6). His broader point in 15:14c is that, through His Word and His Holy Spirit, God had provided the church at Rome—and will provide every godly congregation of believers—with everything needed to live faithfully, effectively, and joyfully for Him. His specific point is that, apart from particular gifts of the Spirit, faithful Christians are divinely equipped **to admonish one another** as needs and opportunities arise among them. The Romans had set an example for others in this.

Paul emphasized the same general truth in his letter to Colossae, of which J. B. Phillips's paraphrase is especially helpful.

> As, therefore, God's picked representatives of the new human-ity, purified and beloved of God Himself, be merciful in action, kindly in heart, humble in mind. Accept life, and be most patient and toler-ant with one another, always ready to forgive if you have a difference with anyone. Forgive as freely as Christ has forgiven you. And, above everything else, be truly loving, for love is the golden chain of all the virtues. Let the harmony of God reign in your hearts, remembering that as members of the same body you are called to live in harmony, and never forget to be thankful for what God has done for you.
> Let Christ's teaching live in your hearts, making you rich in the true wisdom. Teach and help one another along the right road with your psalms and hymns and Christian songs, singing God's praises with joyful hearts. And whatever work you may have to do, do everything in the Name of the Lord Jesus, thanking God the Father through Him. (Col. 3:12-17)

When God's Word rules our hearts, His Holy Spirit makes us "rich in the true wisdom" and prepares us **to admonish one another,** to "teach and help one another along the right road."

The place for Christians to counsel and be counseled is in the church. That is not, of course, to say that it must be done in a church building, but that it be Christian counseling Christian. That principle applies to general admonitions among fellow believers, as Paul men-tions in this text, as well as to counseling regarding more serious and prolonged problems confronted by a biblically oriented and spiritually gifted Christian minister.

After that brief but touching commendation, Paul begins the defense of his boldness in writing the letter, which some readers might have considered to be presumptuous. I **have written very boldly to you on some points,** he explains, **so as to remind you again, be-cause of the grace that was given me from God.**

Paul was characterized by boldness and courage. Luke reports that, "at Damascus," Paul "had spoken out boldly in the name of Jesus" (Acts 9:27), as he also did in the cities of Galatia (13:46; 14:3) and in the synagogue at Ephesus, "reasoning and persuading them about the kingdom of God" (19:8).

As already noted, unlike some of Paul's other letters, the book of Romans contains no rebukes or reprimands. But it does include some serious cautions. He admonished believers in Rome to "consider your-selves dead to sin, but alive to God in Christ Jesus" and not to "let sin reign in your mortal body that you should obey its lusts, and do not go on presenting the members of your body to sin as instruments of unrighteousness; but present yourselves to God as those alive from the dead, and your members as instruments of righteousness to God" (6:11-13). He reminded them, "You are not in the flesh but in the Spirit, if indeed the Spirit of God dwells in you. But if anyone does not have the Spirit of Christ, he does not belong to Him" (8:9). He cautioned Gentiles in the church against being proud because they were now fully accepted into God's New Covenant:

> If you were cut off from what is by nature a wild olive tree, and were grafted contrary to nature into a cultivated olive tree, how much more shall these who are the natural branches [Jews] be grafted into their own olive tree? For I do not want you, brethren, to be uninformed of this mystery, lest you be wise in your own estimation, that a partial hardening has happened to Israel until the fulness of the Gentiles has come in; and thus all Israel will be saved. (11:24-25)

Paul warned every believer in the church "not to think more highly of himself than he ought to think" (12:3), to "be in subjection to the government authorities," all of whom "are established by God" (13:1), to pay taxes and customs that are assessed, and to have proper respect for those to whom it is due (v. 8).

He gave the church many other commands and admonitions too numerous to repeat here, but all of them were given in a spirit of love as well as boldness, **so as to remind** them **again.** He was not teaching them things they had never heard but was reminding them of truths they did know. He did not speak forcefully because those believers were untaught and immature but, to the contrary, because they were spiritually strong and well-equipped. He was not bold because they were carnal and vacillating but because they were uncompromising and steadfast.

A good teacher must keep in mind the opposing problems of familiarity and forgetfulness. Even for the best of minds with the sincerest devotion, that which is not kept familiar eventually will be forgotten.

Paul instructed his beloved Timothy to keep reminding the brethren under his care of the truths of the gospel, in order that Timothy himself, as well as those fellow believers, would be "constantly nourished on the words of the faith and of the sound doctrine which you have been following" (1 Tim. 4:6). In his second letter to this young protege, Paul again admonished him to continually remind his flock of the central truths of the gospel (2 Tim. 2:8-14). He advised Titus to remind those under his care "to be subject to rulers, to authorities, to be obedient, to be ready for every good deed (Titus 3:1). In his second letter, Peter assured his readers that he would always be ready to remind them of the important truths of the gospel that they already knew (2 Pet. 1:12) and explained that the very purpose of that epistle was to stir up their sincere minds "by way of reminder" (3:1). A major responsibility of every pastor is to keep teaching his people truths they already know in ways that refresh and reinforce.

Because of the grace that was given to him **by God** enabling him to do so, Paul boldly reminded the Roman Christians of truths they had long known and accepted. He was not speaking of God's saving or sustaining **grace,** but of the **grace** of his divinely-bestowed apostolic mandate and authority to proclaim the Word. He did not write this epistle to express his own beliefs and wisdom or to fulfill a personal desire or plan. He wrote under divine orders to teach divine truths. Paul was "a bond-servant of Christ Jesus, called as an apostle, set apart for the gospel of God," from whom and for whom he had "received grace and apostleship" (Rom. 1:1, 5). He explained to the church at Corinth that, although he considered himself to be "the least of the apostles, who am not fit to be called an apostle," he nevertheless could say that "by the grace of God I am what I am, and His grace toward me did not prove vain" (1 Cor. 15:9-10).

In less specific ways but just as certainly, every believer, whatever his spiritual gifts may be, is under divine compulsion to obey and serve the Lord "according to the grace given to [him]" (Rom. 12:6).

Having reintroduced, as it were, the subject of his divine calling as an apostle, Paul now defines his three-fold role in fulfilling that office—as priest (v. 16), as preacher (vv. 17-19), and as pioneer (vv. 20-21).

PAUL THE PRIEST

to be a minister of Christ Jesus to the Gentiles, ministering as a priest the gospel of God, that my offering of the Gentiles might become acceptable, sanctified by the Holy Spirit. (15:16)

Under the New Covenant, Jesus Christ is our perfect and eternal High Priest (Heb. 2:17; 3:1), and there no longer is a human, earthly institution of priesthood as under the Old Covenant. There is but "one mediator also between God and men, the man Christ Jesus" (1 Tim. 2:5).

Yet all believers are priests. "As living stones, [we] are being built up as a spiritual house for a holy priesthood, to offer up spiritual sacrifices acceptable to God through Jesus Christ" (1 Pet. 2:5). We "are a chosen race," Peter later adds, "a royal priesthood, a holy nation, a people for God's own possession, that [we] may proclaim the excellencies of Him who has called [us] out of darkness into His marvelous light" (v. 9). Christ "has made us to be a kingdom, priests to His God and Father" (Rev. 1:6). Those who have "a part in the first resurrection," that is, believers, "will be priests of God and of Christ and will reign with Him for a thousand years" (Rev. 20:6). In that sense, the entire church is a priesthood of believers. We do not have to go through a human mediator to reach God. He is our own heavenly Father, with whom we are able to have direct fellowship and communion. And we engage in a priestly role by bringing others into God's presence.

Paul did not inherit a priestly *office* by birth. He was a priest in the same way that all Christians are priests, except in a larger way. During his missionary travels, Paul typically began his ministry in a city or town by preaching and teaching in a synagogue or among an informal group of Jews, such as the women who were praying by a riverside (Acts 16:13). He would be used by God to bring some of them to Christ. But his special calling was **to be a minister of Christ Jesus to the Gentiles** in a priestly way.

Leitourgos **(minister)** was a general Greek term used of public officials. Earlier in this letter, Paul used it of government officials in general, who are, whether they realize it or not, "servants [*leitourgos*] of God" (13:6). But in the New Testament, the word is used most often of those who serve God in some form of public worship. It is used of the levitical priest Zacharias, the father of John the Baptist, and is translated "priestly service" in Luke 1:23. It is used in the same sense of worship ministry in Philippians 2:17 (cf. Heb. 9:21; 10:11). It is used of ministering angels (Heb. 1:7, 14), and even of Christ's heavenly ministry as our eternal High Priest (Heb. 8:1-2, 6).

As Paul ministered figuratively **as a priest the gospel of God** to the Gentiles, he did so in order that his **offering** of believing **Gentiles** to God, as it were, **might become acceptable** to Him, being **sanctified by the Holy Spirit.** In faithful fulfillment of his unique apostolic calling, Paul's supreme **offering** to God was a multitude of **Gentiles,** who by virtue of the Holy Spirit's power had been sanctified and thus made **acceptable** for fellowship with the Father.

Like Paul, every believer who is instrumental in winning a soul to Jesus Christ presents that convert, whether Jew or Gentile, as a priestly offering to the Lord.

PAUL THE PREACHER

Therefore in Christ Jesus I have found reason for boasting in things pertaining to God. For I will not presume to speak of anything except what Christ has accomplished through me, resulting in the obedience of the Gentiles by word and deed, in the

power of signs and wonders, in the power of the Spirit; so that from Jerusalem and round about as far as Illyricum I have fully preached the gospel of Christ. (15:17-19)

Although Paul was a priest only in a figurative sense, he was a preacher in the most literal sense. He was constrained by the love of God to minister God's Word (2 Cor. 5:14)."I am under compulsion," he declared in his first letter to Corinth;"for woe is me if I do not preach the gospel" (1 Cor. 9:16).

It was in regard to his preaching that he could declare with both boldness and humility: **Therefore in Christ Jesus I have found reason for boasting in things pertaining to God.**

In the next two verses Paul explains the nature of that boasting, and in doing so reveals five features of a faithful preacher.

First, Paul took no credit for himself. Lest he be misunderstood, he immediately explained, **I will not presume to speak of anything except what Christ has accomplished through me.** In other words, he was not boasting in what he had accomplished as an apostle but only in what Christ had accomplished through him.

In both of his letters to the church at Corinth, Paul admonished the immature and proud believers there:"Let him who boasts, boast in the Lord" (1 Cor. 1:31; 2 Cor. 10:17). We have no right to take credit for any spiritual effect we have had, but every right to boast in what God has done through us, though we are weak vessels.

From what we find in the New Testament, Paul would seem to have had more reason to boast than any of the other apostles, including Peter and John. He was used by God to reveal more of the New Testament than any other human writer, and the greater part of the book of Acts focuses on his ministry. But Paul discounted his own merits, both before and after his salvation. He referred to his eminent religious life before he was converted as "rubbish" (Phil. 3:8). He wrote Timothy, "I thank Christ Jesus our Lord, who has strengthened me, because He considered me faithful, putting me into service; even though I was formerly a blasphemer and a persecutor and a violent aggressor. And yet I was shown mercy, because I acted ignorantly in unbelief; and the grace of our Lord was more than abundant" (1 Tim. 1:12-14). He considered himself still to be the foremost of all sinners, and testified that it was for that very reason that he "found mercy, in order that in me as the foremost, Jesus Christ might demonstrate His perfect patience, as an example for those who would believe in Him for eternal life" (vv. 15-16).

On his "own behalf," however, Paul would "not boast, except in regard to [his] weaknesses. . . . Most gladly, therefore, I will rather boast about my weaknesses, that the power of Christ may dwell in me" (2 Cor. 12:5, 9). "God has chosen the foolish things of the world to shame the wise," he wrote in his previous letter to Corinth, "and God has chosen the weak things of the world to shame the things which are strong, and the base things of the world and the despised, God has chosen, the things that are not, that He might nullify the things that are, that no man should boast before God" (1 Cor. 1:27-29). Therefore, Paul declared, "May it never be that I should boast, except in the cross of our Lord Jesus Christ" (Gal. 6:14).

He commended the Thessalonian believers, saying that "we also constantly thank God that when you received from us the word of God's message, you accepted it not as the word of men, but for what it really is, the word of God, which also performs work in you who believe" (1 Thess. 2:13). They knew they had been saved not by Paul's word or power but by the word and power of the God he faithfully preached.

Paul's boast was never in himself. His boast was in the cross of Christ, in the grace and mercy of God to save unworthy sinners such as himself, and in the power of God to use him to bring other unworthy sinners to the Savior. Yet his was not a false humility that denied the great things God had clearly done through him. "We proclaim [Christ]," he said, "admonishing every man and teaching every man with all wisdom, that we may present every man complete in Christ. And for this purpose also I labor, striving according to His power, which mightily works within me" (Col. 1:28-29).

When Paul and Barnabas returned to Antioch, where they had been commissioned and sent out (Acts 13:2-3), "they began to report all things that God had done with them and how He had opened a door of faith to the Gentiles" (14:27). At the council in Jerusalem, "all the multitude kept silent, and they were listening to Barnabas and Paul as they were relating what signs and wonders God had done through them among the Gentiles" (Acts 15:12; cf. 21:19). In both instances those men made clear that they were not recounting what they themselves had accomplished but "what God had done through them."

Paul explained to the church at Corinth,

> We will not boast beyond measure, but within the measure of the sphere which God apportioned to us as a measure, to reach even as far as you. For we are not overextending ourselves, as if we did not reach to you, for we were the first to come even as far as you in the gospel of Christ; not boasting beyond our measure, that is, in other men's labors, but with the hope that as your faith grows, we shall be within our sphere, enlarged even more by you, so as to preach the gospel even to the regions beyond you, and not to boast in what has been accomplished in the sphere of another. (2 Cor. 10:13-16)

But even his boasting "within the measure of the sphere which God apportioned to us" was not self-boasting, as Paul goes on to make clear. "But he who boasts, let him boast in the Lord. For not he who commends himself is approved, but whom the Lord commends" (vv. 17-18).

The people God uses to accomplish His will are His instruments, and no Christian should take personal credit for what God does through him. No brush takes credit for a masterpiece it was used to paint. No violin takes credit for the beautiful music the musician makes with it. Neither should a Christian deny or belittle what God has done through him, because that would be to deny and belittle God's own work.

The second feature of a faithful preacher is emphasizing obedience to the Lord. Paul's preaching resulted **in the obedience of the Gentiles.** The gospel not only calls men to faith in Christ as Savior but to obedience to Him as Lord. At the beginning of this epistle Paul states clearly that "we have received grace and apostleship to bring the obedience of faith among all the Gentiles, for His name's sake" (Rom. 1:5). He never preached a gospel that did not include a call to obedience, because that call was integral to his apostolic mandate from God. Later in the letter he reminds believers in Rome "that though you were slaves of sin, you became obedient from the heart to that form of teaching to which you were committed" (6:17). In that context, obedience from the heart is a synonym for saving faith.

The third feature of a faithful preacher is personal integrity. Paul preached to the Gentiles **by word and deed.** His life was totally consistent with his message, without hypocrisy or self-righteousness. There is no greater deterrent to the work of God than a disparity in the life of a preacher between the message he proclaims and the life he lives.

The fourth mark of a faithful preacher is divine affirmation of his ministry. For Paul, that affirmation often was made evident **in the power of signs and wonders, in the power of the Spirit.** Divine affirmation does not require miracles. Much, perhaps most, of Paul's own ministry was not affirmed in such dramatic ways. But **the power of the Spirit** is always evidenced in some way when the gospel is rightly proclaimed, even by the simplest and most uneducated preacher who proclaims and glorifies Christ.

Before the full gospel message was recorded in what we now call the New Testament, God often used **signs and wonders** to authenticate true preaching and teaching. The ministry of the apostles, especially in the earliest days of the church, was accompanied by authenticating miracles.

Paul reminded the Corinthians that "the signs of a true apostle were performed among you with all perseverance, by signs and wonders and miracles" (2 Cor. 12:12). Although some dispute the genuineness of the last half of Mark 16, the truths it contains are consistent with the rest of the New Testament. It is therefore perfectly fitting to acknowledge that the apostles "went out and preached everywhere, while the Lord worked with them, and confirmed the word by the signs that followed" (Mark 16:20).

But even in the days of the apostles, the most miraculous authentication of the gospel was not through physical signs and wonders. The greatest miracle of miracles has always been the regeneration of a human soul from sinner to saint, from being an enemy of God to being a child of God, of being transformed from the kingdom of darkness to the kingdom of light. The greatest divine affirmation of ministry has always been the spiritual transformation of souls. The truth of the gospel today is authenticated by God's completed Word in the New Testament, but the power of the gospel is demonstrated by the lives that are transformed.

The fifth feature of the faithful preacher is that his work is thorough. He completes what God has called him to do. Paul could claim that **from Jerusalem and round about as far as Illyricum I have fully preached the gospel of Christ.**

From Jerusalem, in the far southeast, Paul travelled through Asia Minor, Macedonia, Greece, and even to **Illyricum,** the region roughly corresponding to the former eastern European country of Yugoslavia—a span of some 1,400 miles. The book of Acts does not record his going to **Illyricum,** but he probably visited that remote place during one of his stays in Macedonia.

The phrase **fully preached** can mean two things. It can refer to preaching the full gospel message (cf. Acts 20:27) or to preaching throughout the full geographical area in which he was called to minister. Paul obviously had the first meaning in mind when he told the Colossian believers, "Of this church I was made a minister according to the stewardship from God bestowed on me for your benefit, that I might fully carry out the preaching of the word of God" (Col. 1:25).

Both meanings appropriately describe Paul's ministry, but the context seems to indicate that the apostle here had the second meaning in mind. He was affirming that he faithfully and fully ministered in every place to which the Lord sent him. He permitted nothing to deter his selfless, bold, and fervent ministry. He informed the Corinthians that, beyond any other person who ministered among them, he had been involved in

far more labors, in far more imprisonments, beaten times without number, often in danger of death. Five times I received from the Jews thirty-nine lashes. Three times I was beaten with rods, once I was stoned, three times I was shipwrecked, a night and a day I have spent in the deep. I have been on frequent journeys, in dangers from rivers, dangers from robbers, dangers from my countrymen, dangers from the Gentiles, dangers in the city, dangers in the wilderness, dangers on the sea, dangers among false brethren; I have been in labor and hardship, through many sleepless nights, in hunger and thirst, often without food, in cold and exposure. (2 Cor. 11:23-27)

Paul was the ideal master preacher. He was humble, faithful, genuine, divinely blessed, thorough, and unswerving. Near the end of his life he could truthfully tell his beloved Timothy, "I have fought the good fight, I have finished the course, I have kept the faith" (2 Tim. 4:7).

Paul the Pioneer

And thus I aspired to preach the gospel, not where Christ was already named, that I might not build upon another man's foundation; but as it is written, "They who had no news of Him shall see, and they who have not heard shall understand." (15:20-21)

Even a superficial reading of the book of Acts reveals that Paul was a pioneer missionary, evangelist, and church planter. He preached **the gospel** where no one else had ministered, **where Christ was** not **already named.** Judging from the New Testament record, Paul ministered in more previously unevangelized areas than any other apostle or preacher. More than any other, he reached the unreached, because his calling and his desire were to **not build upon another man's foundation.** Such was surely the primary function of a New Testament evangelist.

It was not that it is wrong to build on another minister's foundation, because that process is part of God's plan for establishing and maintaining His church. Paul explained to the factious church at Corinth that he "planted, Apollos watered, but God was causing the growth" (1 Cor. 3:6). In that instance, Apollos had built on Paul's foundation, which was perfectly in accord with the calling of both men. It is still God's plan that some believers lay the foundation by bringing unbelievers to saving faith in Christ (evangelists) and that others build up those converts by ministering God's Word to them (pastors).

Quoting Isaiah 52:15 from the Septuagint, the Greek Old Testament, Paul declares that, **as it is written, "They who had no news of Him shall see, and they who have not heard shall understand."** The context of that passage in Isaiah indicates that its primary reference is to Christ's second coming. But in its broadest application it refers to the process of evangelism that began in Paul's day and will continue throughout church history until its ultimate fulfillment at Christ's return.

People who have **had no news of** Christ, **who have not heard** the gospel, are found everywhere. They can be found in every country, every city and town, and in every community and neighborhood. God does not call every believer to be an evangelist, but He calls every believer to be a witness. It therefore should be the desire and prayer of all believers that the unsaved will be given spiritual sight to see Christ as their only hope of salvation and that they will be given spiritual hearing in order to **understand** the gospel and turn to Him to be saved.

Ministering in the Will of God (Romans 15:22-33)

25

For this reason I have often been hindered from coming to you; but now, with no further place for me in these regions, and since I have had for many years a longing to come to you whenever I go to Spain—for I hope to see you in passing, and to be helped on my way there by you, when I have first enjoyed your company for a while—but now, I am going to Jerusalem serving the saints. For Macedonia and Achaia have been pleased to make contribution for the poor among the saints in Jerusalem. Yes, they were pleased to do so, and they are indebted to them. For if the Gentiles have shared in their spiritual things, they are indebted to minister to them also in material things. Therefore, when I have finished this, and have put my seal on this fruit of theirs, I will go on by way of you to Spain. And I know that when I come to you, I will come in the fulness of the blessing of Christ.

Now I urge you, brethren, by our Lord Jesus Christ and by the love of the Spirit, to strive together with me in your prayers to God for me, that I may be delivered from those who are disobedient in Judea, and that my service for Jerusalem may prove acceptable to the saints; so that I may come to you in joy by the

will of God and find refreshing rest in your company. Now the God of peace be with you all. Amen. (15:22-33)

Paul wrote the major part of his letter to the Roman church to establish himself with them doctrinally. In this epilogue, he establishes himself with them personally, indicating his heart's desire to minister to them and to fellowship with them.

Paul here makes additional comments about his ministry, especially his plans and hopes for future work in the Lord's service. These personal expressions do reveal some truths which are more implicit than explicit and are general rather than specific. As Paul bares his heart to a group of believers, most of whom he has never met and who lived in a place where he had never been, he provides some valuable principles for all who read.

Underlying the surface of this very personal passage is the basic principle that was the foundation of Paul's life, the principle that directed everything he thought, said, wrote, and did. He articulates that truth in verse 32: "by the will of God." The rest of the passage leads up to that statement and reveals in an intimate and unique way the attitudes, perceptions, and purposes of a believer who lives wholly in the knowledge of God's will.

Paul's life was centered in obeying his divine calling "to be a minister of Christ Jesus to the Gentiles" (Rom. 15:16; cf. Acts 9:15; 26:17-18). As seen in the last commentary chapter, he ministered as a priest, a preacher, and a pioneer. Although he typically began his ministry in a new area by preaching to Jews, his ultimate purpose was to use that Jewish base to reach unbelievers in Gentile lands, in order that his "offering of the Gentiles might become acceptable, sanctified by the Holy Spirit" (Rom. 15:16).

Paul's service was carefully focused exactly on God's will worked out with precision. He sought to follow the example of his Lord, who said, "I do not seek My own will, but the will of Him who sent Me" (John 5:30). As well as being careful regarding those to whom he preached, he also was carefully focused as to where he ministered. His three missionary journeys covered much of the same territories, although the second and third expanded on the first by his going to Macedonia and Achaia, the general area of what is modern Greece. During the second journey, after ministering again in Galatia, he and Silas had planned to travel north "into Bithynia, [but] the Spirit of Jesus did not permit them; and passing by Mysia, they came down to Troas," where Paul had a vision of a man calling them to Macedonia, after which they "sought to go into Macedonia, concluding that God had called [them] to preach the gospel to them" (Acts 16:6-10). Paul's personal plans were continually subject to God's direction and revision.

Paul knew from the beginning of his new life in Christ that following the divine call would lead him to endure suffering for his Lord (Acts 9:16). He told the elders from Ephesus that he was compelled to go to Jerusalem, not knowing exactly what would happen to him there, "except that the Holy Spirit solemnly testifies to me in every city, saying that bonds and afflictions await me" (Acts 20:22-23). "But I do not consider my life of any account as dear to myself," he continued, "in order that I may finish my course, and the ministry which I received from the Lord Jesus" (v. 24).

The personal cost of his ministry was of no consequence, however. "Now I rejoice in my sufferings for your sake," he wrote believers in Colossae, "and in my flesh I do my share on behalf of His body (which is the church) in filling that which is lacking in Christ's afflictions. Of this church I was made a minister according to the stewardship from God bestowed on me for your benefit, that I might fully carry out the preaching of the word of God. . . . And for this purpose also I labor, striving according to His power, which mightily works within me" (Col. 1:24-25, 29).

The faithful servant of God knows that true success in the Lord's work can be attained only as he wholly accepts his divine calling and unstintingly commits his heart, his mind, his time, his abilities, and his spiritual gift to fulfilling that calling. Genuine success sometimes can fail as much from trying to do more than we are called to do as from doing less. Paul did not try to do the work of several apostles but only the work to which the Lord had specifically called him. He demonstrated the same kind of economy of effort as Jesus, whose ministry was strictly focused on His Father's calling and will. He did not cure every illness in Palestine, nor did He attempt to preach to every Jew, much less every Gentile. Yet, after only three years of ministry, He could say to His Father in the Upper Room, "I glorified Thee on the earth, having accomplished the work which Thou hast given Me to do" (John 17:4), and could say on the cross before the world, "It is finished" (19:30).

Depth of ministry is always more important than breadth, thoroughness more significant than scope. God always demands depth of commitment, whether the field of service be large or small, constant or changing, public or private, and, in the world's eyes, noble or ignoble.

In Romans 15:22-32, Paul demonstrates in his own life six characteristics, or elements, of his own ministry that should be evidenced in the life and ministry of every believer who is committed to doing God's will. These may be categorized as providence (v. 22), planning (vv. 23-24), priority (vv. 25-28), prosperity (v. 29), purpose (v. 30*a*), and prayer (vv. 30*b*-32).

PROVIDENCE

For this reason I have often been hindered from coming to you; (15:22)

This reason refers to Paul's fulfilling his divine calling as "a minister of Christ Jesus to the Gentiles,... from Jerusalem and round about as far as Illyricum," in order that "they who had not news of Him shall see, and they who have not heard shall understand" (15:16, 19, 21). Faithfulness to his calling **hindered** him from doing many of the things he would like to have done, including, thus far, visiting the church at Rome.

Enkoptō **(hindered)** literally means to cut into or cut out. It was used of deep trenches that sometimes were dug across a road to impede an enemy army. It came to be used metaphorically of any hindrance or impediment. The imperfect tense of the Greek verb indicates continuation, and its being passive indicates that the cause was from the outside. Because of God's plan and control, Paul was providentially and continually prevented **from coming to** the church at Rome.

God has changed the natural course of events by direct, miraculous intervention, such as in opening the Red Sea for Israel to cross safely and then closing it on the pursuing Egyptian army. But God also—and most often, as far as our human understanding can perceive—controls men and events in non-miraculous and indirect ways that we cannot observe or be aware of. This is providence—God's sovereign control of everything exercised not through the miraculous, but through ordering all the complex natural events so that they accomplish His will. Even Paul, the most prominent of the apostles, who was used as a human instrument for recording much of God's Word in the New Testament, did not presume to fully understand the Lord's working in his life. But God's providence was a crucial element in achieving the intended purposes for Paul's service.

In the circumstance mentioned above, God did not explain to Paul His reason for not allowing him to minister in Bithynia. Somehow, Paul knew only that it was "the Spirit of Jesus [who] did not permit them" (Acts 16:7). And it was not until he and his companions had traveled on to Troas that their ultimate destination became clear.

The classic Old Testament illustration of God's indirect control to accomplish His will is found in the story of Joseph. During the time the events were unfolding, neither Joseph, his brothers, nor his father Jacob knew God's purpose in allowing the brothers to sell Joseph into slavery. It was many years later that Joseph's high position in Egypt was used by the Lord to save His chosen people from famine. As Joseph later realized and explained to his repentant brothers,"You meant evil against me, but God meant it for good in order to bring about this present result, to preserve many people alive" (Gen. 50:20). In a somewhat similar way, the Lord caused King Ahasuerus to choose Esther as his queen and thereby enabled her to intercede on behalf of her fellow Jews and save them from annihilation.

Jeremiah declared, "I know, O Lord, that a man's way is not in himself; nor is it in a man who walks to direct his steps" (Jer. 10:23). From Proverbs we learn that "the mind of man plans his way, but the Lord directs his steps" (Prov. 16:9), and that "many are the plans in a man's heart, but the counsel of the Lord, it will stand" (19:21). Paul reminded believers at Philippi that "it is God who is at work in you, both to will and to work for His good pleasure" (Phil. 2:13).

God effected His will in Paul's life by providentially controlling all the intricate circumstances around him.

Planning

but now, with no further place for me in these regions, and since I have had for many years a longing to come to you whenever I go to Spain—for I hope to see you in passing, and to be helped on my way there by you, when I have first enjoyed your company for a while— (15:23-24)

A second element for a believer who faithfully fulfills his divine calling is care in making plans for ministry. Contrary to how it may seem on first thought, sensible and careful planning by God's people does not necessarily indicate lack of trust in His providence. Waiting on the Lord's providence does not preclude personal planning.

Jesus asked rhetorically, "Which one of you, when he wants to build a tower, does not first sit down and calculate the cost, to see if he has enough to complete it? . . . Or what king, when he sets out to meet another king in battle, will not first sit down and take counsel whether he is strong enough with ten thousand men to encounter the one coming against him with twenty thousand?" (Luke 14:28, 31). In this instance, Jesus was speaking of the cost of discipleship (v. 33), but the principle of planning is also valid in regard to the way we fulfill our discipleship.

The prerequisite in every case, of course, is that our planning, no matter how carefully and sincerely made, be constantly and completely subject to the Lord's control and alteration—just as were Paul's plans to minister in Bithynia and to visit Rome.

He believed there was **no further place for** him **in these regions** where he had been ministering, and he **had for many years a longing to come to** Rome **whenever** he went **to Spain.** He did not claim that God was calling him to minister either in Rome or in **Spain,** but he strongly hoped for and planned for both ministries.

Spain included the city or region referred to in the Old Testament as Tarshish, the place to which Jonah sought to flee (Jonah 1:3) and from which ships brought King Solomon "gold and silver, ivory and apes and peacocks" every three years (1 Kings 10:22).

Spain was on the far western side of the continent and had become a major center of commerce and culture, made accessible by way of the renowned Roman roads. Ruins of impressive Roman architecture still exist there today. That province had produced such outstanding men as Martial, famous for his epigrams; the poet Lucan; the notable orator Quintilian; and the greatest Spaniard in the Roman Empire, Seneca, the notable statesman and Stoic philosopher who tutored Nero and was prime minister of the Empire. Yet, from the most reliable historical and archaeological evidence, **Spain** was not evangelized until the middle of the third century.

It therefore is understandable why Paul's plan was to minister in **Spain.** And he strongly desired **to see** the believers at Rome **in passing.** Because the church in Rome was well established and mature, Paul did not want, as he had already explained, "to preach the gospel ... where Christ was already named, that [he] might not build upon another man's foundation" (v. 20). But, although his intended layover in Rome was to be brief, it was of great personal importance to Paul. While visiting that church, he hoped **to be helped on** his **way there** (Spain), after he had **first enjoyed** the **company** of the Roman believers **for a while.**

To be helped is from the verb *propempō*, which, in the New Testament, is used in a rather specific and technical sense. It was always used of the custom in the early church of furnishing an escort, as well as supplies, for someone being sent out to minister in a distant field. After returning to the church in Antioch, which had originally commissioned and sent them out (Acts 13:2-3), Paul and Barnabas again were "being sent on their way *[propempō]* by the church" (15:3). The term is used of the Ephesian elders' "accompanying [Paul] to the ship" that would take him to Jerusalem. It is translated "escorted" in Acts 21:5; "send ... on [the] way" in 1 Corinthians 16:6, 11 and 3 John 6; and "help ... on [the] way" in Titus 3:13.

It was not that the churches in which he already had ministered were perfect, that they needed no more pastoral care, or that every professing believer was true or mature. As he had expressed in the opening comments of this epistle, his great hope was that, "perhaps now at last by the will of God I may succeed in coming to you. For I long to see you in order that I may impart some spiritual gift to you, that you may be established; that is, that I may be encouraged together with you while among you, each of us by the other's faith, both yours and mine. And I do not want you to be unaware, brethren," he continued, "that often I have planned to come to you (and have been prevented thus far) in order that I might obtain some fruit among you also, even as among the rest of the Gentiles" (Rom. 1:10-13).

Paul expressed other such personal plans, none of which compromised his still greater desire to fully obey God's will. He told the Thessalonian believers, "But we, brethren, having been bereft of you for a short while—in person, not in spirit—were all the more eager with great desire to see your face. For we wanted to come to you—I, Paul, more than once—and yet Satan thwarted us" (1 Thess. 2:17-18). Satan did not, of course, thwart God's plan, but God, for His own purposes, allowed Satan to thwart the plans of Paul.

Making sensible and careful plans for serving God does not conflict with reliance on His providence, and reliance on His providence does not excuse failure to plan.

But personal plans, no matter how unselfish and spiritually motivated, must be subject to God's plan. Paul's desire to visit Rome was strong, but his desire to obey God was stronger still. He had the self-discipline and steadfast dedication to fulfill what God had given him to do, setting his personal dreams aside until, and if, the Lord brought them to pass.

PRIORITY

but now, I am going to Jerusalem serving the saints. For Macedonia and Achaia have been pleased to make contribution for the poor among the saints in Jerusalem. Yes, they were pleased to do so, and they are indebted to them. For if the Gentiles have shared in their spiritual things, they are indebted to minister to them also in material things. Therefore, when I have finished this, and have put my seal on this fruit of theirs, I will go on by way of you to Spain. (15:25-28)

Paul illustrates a third element characteristic of a believer who faithfully fulfills his calling, namely that of setting clear priorities. Planning for future ministry must never cause a present ministry to suffer.

Before Paul would be free to go to Rome, much less Spain, it was necessary for him to go about a thousand miles in the opposite direction **to Jerusalem,** in order to serve **the saints** there.

His taking that journey seems to contradict his calling "to preach the gospel, not where Christ was already named" (15:20). The church was born in Jerusalem, and no city in the first century had more direct ministry by the apostles and other church leaders. But at the time Paul wrote this letter, probably in A.D. 58, the church in **Jerusalem** was suffering not only great persecution but great poverty. There was a famine throughout Palestine, and because of persecution by unbelieving Jews, many Christian men lost their jobs and many others were put in prison, making bad conditions still worse for their families. In addition to that, many foreign Jews who were visiting Jerusalem for the Feast of Pentecost were converted to Christ and decided to remain in the city, usually as guests of believers who lived there.

Because of that great need, Paul had made an appeal to the churches of **Macedonia and Achaia,** who were **pleased to make a contribution for the poor among the saints in Jerusalem.** During their previous trip to Jerusalem, Paul and Barnabas had been extended "the right hand of fellowship" by James, Peter, and John, "that we might go to the Gentiles," Paul had written to the Galatians some years earlier, "and they to the circumcised. They only asked us to remember the poor—the very thing I also was eager to do" (Gal. 2:9-10). This was part of assuring that the dividing wall between Jew and Gentile, broken down in Christ (Eph. 2:14), was not rebuilt.

In his first letter to Corinth, which was in the province of **Achaia,** Paul wrote, "Now concerning the collection for the saints, as I directed the churches of Galatia, so do you also" (1 Cor. 16:1). In his second letter to Corinth, he rejoiced in the generosity of the churches of **Macedonia.** "In a great ordeal of affliction their abundance of joy and their deep poverty overflowed in the wealth of their liberality. For I testify that according to their ability, and beyond their ability they gave of their own accord, begging us with much entreaty for the favor of participation in the support of the saints" (2 Cor. 8:2-4).

During this period there still was considerable animosity and distrust between Jewish and Gentile believers. The **contribution** from the primarily Gentile churches of **Macedonia and Achaia,** who, for the most part, were also poor, was a powerful gesture of love and reconciliation to the impoverished **saints in Jerusalem,** who were primarily Jewish. Paul was committed to taking that offering, along with representatives of the Gentile churches who gave it, in order to promote harmony in the Body of Christ.

Contribution translates *koinōnia* which has the basic idea of sharing and is most commonly rendered as "fellowship" or "communion." But here, as in 2 Corinthians 9:13, the context gives it the connotation of financial sharing, a gift. It seems that Paul's concern was to strengthen the *koinōnia* of spiritual fellowship between Jew and Gentile by means of the *koinōnia* of material support. Central to his ministry was proclaiming the truth that "now in Christ Jesus you [Gentiles] who formerly were far off have been brought near by the blood of Christ. For He Himself is our peace, who made both groups," Jews and Gentiles, "into one, and broke down the barrier of the dividing wall" (Eph. 2:13-14). God had given him special "insight into the mystery of Christ, which in other generations was not made known to the sons of men, as it has now been revealed to His holy apostles and prophets in the Spirit; to be specific, that the Gentiles are fellow heirs and fellow members of the body, and fellow partakers of the promise in Christ Jesus through the gospel" (3:4-6).

Believers in Macedonia and Achaia not only were willing to give generously, but **were pleased to do so.** They gave because the saints in Jerusalem were brothers and sisters in Christ and also because they realized that, as Jesus told the woman of Sychar, "salvation is from the Jews" (John 4:22). Isaiah prophesied that "the law will go forth from Zion, and the word of the Lord from Jerusalem" (Isa. 2:3).

On the human level, all Gentile Christians owe their spiritual lives to the Jewish apostles, prophets, teachers, and evangelists who first proclaimed the gospel of salvation in Jesus Christ. Therefore the Gentiles who contributed to the saints in Jerusalem acknowledged they were **indebted to** those Jews. **For if the Gentiles have shared in their spiritual things,** Paul continues to explain, **they are indebted to minister to them also in material things** (money).

Leitourgeō **(to minister)** is the Greek term from which we get "liturgy." It was often used of priestly service, to which Paul had referred in 15:16. Even their giving of **material things** was an act of spiritual service.

It was not that the Gentiles' being spiritually and materially **indebted** to the Jews made their generosity any less meaningful or loving. Duty does not exclude willing and joyful compliance. Even the most demanding duty or indebtedness can be fulfilled out of love. And the Macedonian and Achaian Christians fulfilled their duty and acknowledged their indebtedness in joyful willingness, not out of compulsion. As already noted, the letter of Romans was written in Corinth, a major city of Achaia, and believers there doubtless had heard many times the admonition Paul wrote to them in his second letter: "Let each one do just as he has purposed in his heart; not grudgingly or under compulsion; for God loves a cheerful giver" (2 Cor. 9:7). Many of them had become cheerful givers and thereby pleased God.

They were also pleasing to Paul. **Therefore, when I have finished this,** he said, **and have put my seal on this fruit of theirs, I will go on by way of you to Spain.** Paul was overjoyed with the generous gift that he and the delegation from those Gentile churches were bringing to Jerusalem. He wanted to **put** his **seal on this fruit of theirs,** confirming, both as a Jew and as an apostle, the genuine love and gratitude those Gentile representatives must have expressed as they presented their conciliatory contribution to the suffering Jewish saints in Jerusalem.

Paul mentioned again (see v. 24) his plan to visit the Roman church on his way **to Spain.** But his present priority was to demonstrate Gentile love toward Jewish believers by delivering the offering of the Gentile churches to the church in Jerusalem. It was this offering about which Paul wrote in his second letter to Corinth, assuring believers there that "the ministry of this service is not only fully supplying the needs of the saints, but is also overflowing through many thanksgivings to God. Because of the proof given by this ministry they [the Jewish saints in Jerusalem] will glorify God for your obedience to your confession of the gospel of Christ, and for the liberality of your contribution to them and to all" (2 Cor. 9:12-13). News of this forthcoming gesture of love apparently had already reached the Jerusalem church, because, Paul goes on to say, "they also, by prayer on your behalf, yearn for you because of the surpassing grace of God in you" (v. 14). That unselfish offering was further evidence to Jews that God's saving grace in the gospel of Jesus Christ did, indeed, extend to the Gentiles.

PROSPERITY

And I know that when I come to you, I will come in the fulness of the blessing of Christ. (15:29)

A fourth element characteristic of a person who faithfully fulfills his divine calling is spiritual prosperity. Paul's saying **I know** reflects his absolute assurance that when he came to Jerusalem it would be **in the fulness of the blessing of Christ.** Because he lived continually in obedience to the Lord, his life was always blessed. Obviously, that blessing did not exclude physical hardships and afflictions, as he mentions in verse 31 and in many of his other letters. But nothing physical could rob him of **the fulness of** that spiritual **blessing.**

What is often referred to as the "health and wealth gospel" was the furthest thing from Paul's mind. His obedience to Christ cost him dearly in both of those areas. Because of his service to Christ, he suffered imprisonments, beatings, stonings, dangers from Gentiles as well as Jews, and a host of other hardships (see 2 Cor. 11:23-27). But none of those outward problems could rob him of his inner blessing. To the contrary, he wrote, "my circumstances have turned out for the greater progress of the gospel, so that my imprisonment in the cause of Christ has become well known throughout the whole praetorian guard and to everyone else, and …most of the brethren, trusting in the Lord because of my imprisonment, have far more courage to speak the word of God without fear.…In every way,…Christ is proclaimed; and in this I rejoice, yes, and I will rejoice" (Phil. 1:12-14,18).

Paul's hardships gave him greater opportunity "to be a minister of Christ Jesus to the Gentiles" and to offer them as an offering to God, "acceptable, sanctified by the Holy Spirit" (Rom. 15:16) and thereby receive the **blessing** that only such selfless service to the Lord can bring. He knew "the peace of God, which surpasses all comprehension"; he knew "how to get along with humble means" and "how to live in prosperity"; and God supplied all his "needs according to His riches in glory in Christ Jesus" (Phil. 4:7,12,19).

Paul deeply believed the truth expressed in the sixteenth-century missionary Francis Xavier's beautiful hymn:

> My God, I love Thee; not because
> I hope for heaven thereby,
> Nor yet because who love Thee not
> Are lost eternally.
> Thou, O my Jesus, Thou didst me
> Upon the cross embrace;
> For me didst bear the nails and spear,
> And manifold disgrace.
> And griefs and torments numberless,
> And sweat of agony;
> And death itself; and all for me,
> Who was Thine enemy.
> Then why, O blessed Jesus Christ,
> Should I not love Thee well?
> Not for the sake of winning heaven
> Or of escaping hell.
> Not with the hope gaining aught,
> Not seeking a reward;
> But as Thyself has loved me,
> O ever-loving Lord?
> E'en so I love Thee, and will love,
> And in Thy praise will sing;
> Because Thou art my loving God,
> And my Eternal King.

PURPOSE

Now I urge you, brethren, by our Lord Jesus Christ and by the love of the Spirit, (15:30*a*)

A fifth implied characteristic of a person who faithfully fulfills his divine calling is that of having a clear purpose in his service for the Lord. The preposition **by** has the sense of "on behalf of," or "with regard to." **Now I urge you** introduces the exhortation to the readers to pray for his protection and ministry. Before giving that exhortation, Paul declared unequivocally that the overriding purpose for his request was to glorify **our Lord Jesus Christ.** He told the believers at Corinth, "I do all things for the sake of the gospel" (1 Cor. 9:23), which is to say for Christ's sake, the source and power of the gospel. "Whether, then, you eat or drink or whatever you do, do all to the glory of God" (10:31).

In a following letter to Corinth Paul declared, "We do not preach ourselves but Christ Jesus as Lord. . . . For we who live are constantly being delivered over to death for Jesus' sake, that the life of Jesus also may be manifested in our mortal flesh" (2 Cor. 4:5, 11). "Therefore I am well content with weaknesses," he confessed, "with insults, with distresses, with persecutions, with difficulties, for Christ's sake" (12:10). In his closing remarks to the Galatian churches Paul wrote, "From now on let no one cause trouble for me, for I bear on my body the brand-marks of Jesus" (Gal. 6:17). And to the Philippians he said, "I count all things to be loss in view of the surpassing value of knowing Christ Jesus my Lord, for whom I have suffered the loss of all things, and count them but rubbish in order that I may gain Christ" (Phil. 3:8).

The faithful Christian witnesses for the sake of those who need the Lord and he serves for the sake of those who need help, but his supreme motive always should be to serve his Lord and Savior, in whose name and by whose power he ministers to others.

Paul rejoiced in the fact that, if he succeeded in reaching Jerusalem with the contribution of the churches of Macedonia and Achaia, Christ would be glorified, within the church and before the onlooking world. The Lord would be glorified by the willing and loving generosity of the Gentile contributors as well as by the grateful reception of the gift by the Jews to whom it was sent. Christ is always honored and glorified when His church is unified in His name and in His service.

Not only did Paul minister on behalf of the glory of Christ but also for the sake of **the love of the Spirit.** This phrase and the idea it expresses are not found elsewhere in Scripture. Some have interpreted this phrase as meaning the Holy Spirit's love for Paul. As part of the Godhead, **the Spirit** certainly has the same love for the world as a whole and for believers in particular as do the Father and the Son. The context, however, seems to indicate that Paul was speaking of his love for **the Spirit,** rather than the Spirit's love for him. Paul's great love for God obviously included love for the Holy Spirit as well as for God the Father and God the Son. David expressed a similar sentiment when he wrote, "Teach me to do Thy will, for Thou art my God; let *Thy good Spirit* lead me on level ground" (Ps. 143:10, emphasis added). In both instances the Holy Spirit is praised and, by implication, is loved.

Devotion to the glory of the **Lord Jesus Christ** and love for His Holy **Spirit** should be the foremost and ultimate motive for all Christian living and service. In gratitude for the divine grace by which Christ saved us and for the divine power of the Holy Spirit who indwells us, everything we think, say, and do should express our love for them and bring them glory and honor.

PRAYER

to strive together with me in your prayers to God for me, that I may be delivered from those who are disobedient in Judea, and that my service for Jerusalem may prove acceptable to the saints; so that I may come to you in joy by the will of God and find refreshing rest in your company. (15:30*b*-32)

Perhaps the cardinal characteristic of a person who faithfully does the will of God is prayer. And Paul now urges his fellow believers in Rome **to strive together with me in your prayers to God for me.**

Sunagōnizomai **(to strive together)** is an intensified form of *agōnizomai,* which means to struggle or fight and is the term from which we get the English "agonize." The word was originally used of athletic events, especially gymnastics, in which contestants, such as wrestlers or boxers, struggled against each other. Jesus used the word when He told Pilate, "My kingdom is not of this world. If My kingdom were of this world, then My servants would be fighting [*agōnizomai*]" (John 18:36).

Prayer is often a battle. Sometimes the "opponent" is our old self, which continues to wage "war against the law of [our] mind, and [makes us] a prisoner of the law of sin which is in [our] members" (Rom. 7:23). Prayer is always, in one way or another, a struggle against sin and evil, whether in us or around us. Sometimes, as Isaiah attests, it is necessary to arouse ourselves, as it were, and "take hold of" God (Isa. 64:7). Although we do not wrestle with the Lord in the way that Jacob did (Gen. 32:24), the spiritual struggle of prayer may sometimes be equally intense. Paul's struggle on behalf of believers at Colossae and Laodicea doubtless included many hours of agonizing prayer on their behalf, that they would be rightly taught "a true knowledge of God's mercy, that is, Christ Himself," and would be protected from those who wanted to delude them (Col. 2:1-4). Near the end of that letter, Paul sent greetings from Epaphras, who was from their fellowship, and who was "always laboring earnestly for [them] in his prayers, that [they might] stand perfect and fully assured in all the will of God" (4:12).

Our finite minds cannot reconcile the power of prayer with God's absolute sovereignty. As with the Trinity, and many other clearly revealed but humanly unfathomable teachings of Scripture, we simply acknowledge their absolute truth. Any seeming inconsistencies are due to the limits of our human comprehension. We know from His own Word that God is sovereign and immutable. Yet we also know from that same Word that "the effective prayer of a righteous man can accomplish much" (James 5:16). We have our sovereign Lord's promise that "everyone who asks, receives; and he who seeks, finds; and to him who knocks, it shall be opened" (Luke 11:10). Any theology that belittles the power of prayer or intensity in prayer is heresy.

Although he asks for protection while in Judea, in this present passage Paul is not speaking primarily about struggling in prayer against the forces of evil. His emphasis here is rather on earnestly struggling along **with** his brethren in Rome in their prayers to God for him. He makes many similar requests in his letters. "With all prayer and petition pray at all times in the Spirit," he counsels the Ephesians, "and with this in view, be on the alert with all perseverance and petition for all the saints, and pray on my behalf" (Eph. 6:18-19). During his first imprisonment in Rome, he implored the Colossians, "Devote yourselves to prayer, keeping alert in it with an attitude of thanksgiving; praying at the same time for us as well" (Col. 4:2-3). In his second letter to Thessalonica, he said, "Finally, brethren, pray for us that the word of the Lord may spread rapidly and be glorified" (2 Thess. 3:1).

At the beginning of the letter to Rome, Paul assures believers there that "God, whom I serve in my spirit in the preaching of the gospel of His Son, is my witness as to how unceasingly I make mention of you, always in my prayers" (1:9-10). Now he asks those brothers and sisters in Christ to pray for him: for his safety in Judea when he visits Jerusalem (15:31a), for success in his ministry to the saints there (v. 31b), and for personal satisfaction, as he anticipates fellowship with his readers when he eventually reaches Rome (v. 32a, c).

SAFETY

that I may be delivered from those who are disobedient in Judea, (15:31a)

Disobedient is from *apeitheō*, which carries the basic idea of being obstinate and unpersuadable. In this context it refers to Jews who obstinately refused to believe the gospel and therefore were **disobedi-ent** to God, whose Son, the Messiah, they rejected. It is therefore rendered "do not believe" in the King James Version. The same verb is translated "disbelieved" in Acts 14:2 (*NASB*), referring to Jews who "stirred up the minds of the Gentiles, and embittered them against the brethren," specifically, Paul and Barnabas (see 13:50).

From the time that he first "began to proclaim Jesus in the synagogues, saying, 'He is the Son of God'" (Acts 9:20), Paul was marked for death by Jewish leaders in Damascus (v. 23) and shortly afterwards by Jews in Jerusalem when he began preaching the gospel there (v. 30). By the time he wrote the letter to Rome, he already had endured ridicule, imprisonments, lashings, beatings, and even stoning by Jews who fiercely opposed him and the gospel he preached (see, e.g., 2 Cor. 11:23-25; Acts 14:19; 18:12; 20:3,19).

Paul's request **to be delivered** was not for the purpose of his being spared further persecution or even death. He unselfishly wanted **to be delivered** only to the extent necessary for him to complete the ministry the Lord had given him. Long before he arrived **in Judea,** he knew that trouble awaited him. While his ship laid over at Miletus, he told the elders from Ephesus who came out to meet him, "Now, behold, bound in spirit, I am on my way to Jerusalem, not knowing what will happen to me there, except that the Holy Spirit solemnly testifies to me in every city, saying that bonds and afflictions await me. But I do not consider my life of any account as dear to myself," he continued, "in order that I may finish my course, and the ministry which I received from the Lord Jesus, to testify solemnly of the gospel of the grace of God" (Acts 20:22-24).

When Paul and his companions reached Caesarea, they stayed a few days at the house of Philip the evangelist. While there, "a certain prophet named Agabus came down from Judea. And coming to us," Luke reports, "he took Paul's belt and bound his own feet and hands, and said, 'This is what the Holy Spirit says: "In this way the Jews at Jerusalem will bind the man who owns this belt and deliver him into the hands of the Gentiles"'" (Acts 21:10-11).

Paul's prayer request **to be delivered from those who are disobedient in Judea** was therefore answered positively, to the extent that the unbelieving Jews in **Judea** were not allowed to take his life. He was beaten and imprisoned, but his life was divinely spared. While being held under guard by the Romans in Jerusalem, "the Lord stood at his [Paul's] side and said, 'Take courage; for as you have solemnly witnessed to My cause at Jerusalem, so you must witness at Rome also'" (Acts 23:11).

SUCCESS

and that my service for Jerusalem may prove acceptable to the saints; (15:31*b*)

Paul's second prayer request was that, regardless of what dangers might befall him, his **service for Jerusalem may prove acceptable to the saints.** In other words, he wanted his ministry to benefit the Lord's people there, at the birthplace of the church. He was not concerned for what might be called professional success. He once warned the Galatian believers that, "Even though we, or an angel from heaven, should preach to you a gospel contrary to that which we have preached to you, let him be accursed.... For am I now seeking the favor of men, or of God? Or am I striving to please men? If I were still trying to please men, I would not be a bond-servant of Christ" (Gal. 1:8,10).

Because he and his Gentile companions from Macedonia and Achaia were bringing a financial contribution to the church at Jerusalem, which was still largely Jewish, the service which Paul mentions doubtless referred, at least in part, to that offering. He wanted the saints in Rome to pray with him that the gift would not offend Jewish believers in Jerusalem but rather would **prove acceptable to the saints** there. He wanted it to be received with loving gratitude for what it was, a gesture of brotherly love and conciliation.

Paul's prayer for success in Jerusalem also was answered. "When we had come to Jerusalem," Luke says, "the brethren received us gladly. ...And after [Paul] had greeted them, he began to relate one by one the things which God had done among the Gentiles through his ministry. And when they heard it they began glorifying God" (Acts 21:17,19-20).

SATISFACTION

so that I may come to you in joy . . . and find refreshing rest in your company. (15:32*a,c*)

This is Paul's most personal prayer request of the three. Looking forward to the time when he finally would be able to **come to** the church in Rome, he hoped that he might do so **in joy.** He already had told them, "I hope to see you in passing, and to be helped on my way there by you, when I have first enjoyed your company for a while" (15:24).

In the closing comments of his first letter to Corinth, he said, "I rejoice over the coming of Stephanas and Fortunatus and Achaicus; because they have supplied what was lacking on your part. For they have refreshed my spirit and yours" (1 Cor. 16:17-18). He rejoiced in the blessings and joy of others. "Besides our comfort," he later wrote to the same church, "we rejoiced even much more for the joy of Titus, because his spirit has been refreshed by you all" (2 Cor. 7:13).

Paul's personal desire to minister in Spain was never realized, but he did reach Rome and found the joy and refreshing rest in their company for which he longed. When he and his companions arrived in Rome, "the brethren, when they heard about us, came from there as far as the Market of Appius and Three Inns to meet us; and when Paul saw them, he thanked God and took courage" (Acts 28:15).

Again we note that above all else, Paul was committed unalterably to **the will of God.** Soon after he and Barnabas were sent out by the Holy Spirit from the church in Antioch of Syria (Acts 13:2-3), Paul preached in the synagogue at Pisidian Antioch (v. 14), in Asia Minor. Twice he referred to David's obedience to God's will. Quoting 1 Samuel 13:14, he reminded his Jewish audience of the Lord's word concerning this greatest king of Israel: "I have found David the son of Jesse, a man after My heart, who will do all My will" (v. 22). Later in that sermon he noted again that "David ... had served the purpose of God in his own generation" (v. 36). From the moment of his conversion—whether as priest, prophet, or pioneer (see Rom. 15:14-21)—Paul sought to do nothing but **the will of God,** in order that, like David, he also might be a man after the Lord's heart.

Throughout his letter to the church at Rome, the apostle attests to that desire. As in the present text, he makes clear that his hope to visit Rome in person was qualified by its being in "the will of God" (Rom. 1:10). He previously has declared that one of the ministries of the Holy Spirit is to intercede "for the saints according to the will of God" (8:27), and urges believers, "by the mercies of God, to present your bodies a living and holy sacrifice, acceptable to God," and to "not be conformed to this world, but be transformed by the renewing of your mind, that you may prove what the will of God is" (12:1-2). He praised believers in Macedonia because they "gave themselves to the Lord and to us by the will of God" (2 Cor. 8:5). He cautioned believers in Ephesus not to "be foolish, but understand what the will of the Lord is" (Eph. 5:17), and admonished slaves to be "obedient to those who are your masters according to the flesh, with fear and trembling, in the sincerity of your heart, as to Christ; not by way of eyeservice, as men-pleasers, but as slaves of Christ, doing the will of God from the heart" (6:5-6).

In the opening verses of his two letters to the church at Corinth, his letters to the churches at Ephesus and Colossae, and his second letter to Timothy, Paul acknowledges that he was "an apostle of Jesus Christ by the will of God." The supreme focus of his personal life and of his public ministry was always **the will of God.**

When the believers at Caesarea begged Paul not to continue on

to Jerusalem because of the dangers he would face there, he responded, "What are you doing, weeping and breaking my heart? For I am
ready not only to be bound, but even to die at Jerusalem for the name
of the Lord Jesus" (Acts 21:13; cf. 20:24). What happened to him was
unimportant, as long as he was following the Lord's will in doing the
Lord's work.

When he testified about his conversion and calling before a
large crowd of Jews in Jerusalem, he recounted the words of Ananias,
who had said to him, "The God of our fathers has appointed you to know
His will, and to see the Righteous One, and to hear an utterance from
His mouth" (Acts 22:14).

As Paul has already testified in Romans 15, because of his ministering in the will of God, he knew spiritual triumph and could say
with perfect humility, "In Christ Jesus I have found reason for boasting
in things pertaining to God. For I will not presume to speak of anything
except what Christ has accomplished through me, resulting in the obedience of the Gentiles by word and deed" (vv. 17-18). By ministering
solely in the will of God he experienced the supernatural power "of
signs and wonders, in the power of the Spirit" and could claim "that from
Jerusalem and round about as far as Illyricum I have fully preached the
gospel of Christ" (v. 19).

BENEDICTION

Now the God of peace be with you all. Amen. (15:33)

Before extending personal greetings to various friends in Rome
and giving a final warning to be on guard against those who caused dissensions for their own selfish purposes, Paul gives this short but touching benediction.

In this chapter, he has spoken of "the God who gives perseverance and encouragement" (v. 5) and "the God of hope" (v. 13). Now he
asks that **the God of peace be with you all,** that is, all believers in
Rome.

God is the source of all true **peace,** the peace "which surpasses
all comprehension" (Phil. 4:7). In fact, "He Himself is our peace, who
made both groups," Jews and Gentiles, "into one" (Eph. 2:14; cf. vv. 11-13).

On the human level, Paul's life as an apostle was far from peaceful. As far as outward particulars were concerned, he lived in uncer-
tainty and often turmoil. He was under almost continual threat against
his physical safety and life. But he knew intimately **the God of peace,**
and he lived himself *in* the peace and settled tranquillity that God gives
to those who faithfully abide in His will. **Amen.**

Love for the Saints (Romans 16:1-24)

26

I commend to you our sister Phoebe, who is a servant of the church which is at Cenchrea; that you receive her in the Lord in a manner worthy of the saints, and that you help her in whatever matter she may have need of you; for she herself has also been a helper of many, and of myself as well.

Greet Prisca and Aquila, my fellow workers in Christ Jesus, who for my life risked their own necks, to whom not only do I give thanks, but also all the churches of the Gentiles; also greet the church that is in their house. Greet Epaenetus, my beloved, who is the first convert to Christ from Asia. Greet Mary, who has worked hard for you. Greet Andronicus and Juntas, my kinsmen, and my fellow prisoners, who are outstanding among the apostles, who also were in Christ before me. Greet Ampliatus, my beloved in the Lord. Greet Urbanus, our fellow worker in Christ, and Stachys my beloved. Greet Apelles, the approved in Christ. Greet those who are of the household of Aristobulus. Greet Herod ion, my kinsman. Greet those of the household of Narcissus, who are in the Lord. Greet Tryphaena and Tryphosa, workers in the Lord. Greet Persis the beloved, who has worked hard in the Lord. Greet Rufus, a choice man in the Lord, also his mother and mine. Greet Asyncritus, Phlegon, Hermes, Patrobas, Hermas and the brethren with them. Greet Philologus and Julia, Nereus and his sister, and Olympas, and all the saints who are with them. Greet one another with a holy kiss. All the churches of Christ greet you.

Now I urge you, brethren, keep your eye on those who cause dissensions and hindrances contrary to the teaching which you learned, and turn away from them. For such men are slaves, not of our Lord Christ but of their own appetites; and by their smooth and flattering speech they deceive the hearts of the unsuspecting. For the report of your obedience has reached to all; therefore I am rejoicing over you, but I want you to be wise in what is good, and innocent in what is evil. And the God of peace will soon crush Satan under your feet. The grace of our Lord Jesus be with you.

Timothy my fellow worker greets you, and so do Lucius and Jason and Sosipater, my kinsmen. I, Tertius, who write this letter, greet you in the Lord. Gaius, host to me and to the whole church, greets you. Erastus, the city treasurer greets you, and Quartus, the brother. [The grace of our Lord Jesus Christ be with you all. Amen.] (16:1-24)

Despite the great popularity of the book of Romans, chapter 16 is often neglected by preachers, teachers, and Bible students. It has almost no explicit teaching and includes several lists of people, many of whom we know nothing about except what little, if anything, is said of them here. But they doubtless were a representative cross section of believers in Rome and of Paul's companions at the time he wrote the letter.

This passage is by far the most extensive and intimate expression of love and appreciation to come from the tender heart and inspired mind of the apostle Paul. It is a rich and rewarding section that yields many insights into the life of Paul, into the lives of other early Christians, and into the nature and character of the first-century church. The apostle's comments about these mostly unknown individuals are all the more poignant because this great apostle takes time to speak so warmly and appreciatively of these "ordinary" Christians, who were as much his brothers and sisters in Christ as Peter, James, John, and other New Testament notables. He here reveals his deep affection for those whom he had served, for those who had served him, and for those who served with him.

Paul continues the personal epilogue that began in 15:14 and reveals still more of his inner thoughts and feelings, not so much as an apostle as a fellow servant of Jesus Christ. In 15:14-33 he focuses on his relationship to the Lord in his ministry. In chapter 16 he focuses on his relationship to other Christians with whom he has been associated in one way or another in his ministry. He specifically identifies, and sometimes briefly comments about, those to whom he felt the closest. He reveals his love for the community of the redeemed, his mutual accountability with them before God, and his dependence on them for his own ministry and for his own well-being. In many ways, this chapter reflects the personal and practical *agapē* love he has beautifully described in 13:8-10 and which, a few years earlier, he had portrayed in chapter 13 of his first letter to the church at Corinth.

In this beautiful account Paul reveals that love in four ways: through his commendation (vv. 1-2), through his cordiality (vv. 3-16), through his caution (vv. 17-20), and through remarks about and greetings from his companions (vv. 21-23), after which he adds a brief benediction (v. 24).

PAUL'S COMMENDATION

I commend to you our sister Phoebe, who is a servant of the church which is at Cenchrea; that you receive her in the Lord in a manner worthy of the saints, and that you help her in whatever matter she may have need of you; for she herself has also been a helper of many, and of myself as well. (16:1-2)

Paul devotes these two verses to the commendation of a single individual, **Phoebe, . . . a servant** and a member **of the church which is at Cenchrea.** Cenchrea was the neighboring port city of Corinth, from which Paul wrote this letter, and **the church . . . at Cenchrea** doubtless was a daughter church of the one at Corinth. It was from Cenchrea, at the end of his first ministry in Corinth, that Paul, Priscilla, and Aquila "put out to sea for Syria" (Acts 18:18).

Paul could **commend** this woman not only for what she had done as a faithful **sister** and **servant** of Christ but also for what she was soon to do in further service to their Lord. It is almost certain that **Phoebe** delivered this letter in person to the church at Rome, a responsibility of considerable magnitude.

The name **Phoebe** means "bright and radiant," and from Paul's brief comments about her, it seems that those words did indeed characterize her personality and her Christian life. Paul commends her to the church at Rome in three different ways: as a sister in Christ, as **a servant** and as **a helper of many,** including himself.

In Christ, we belong to God not only as "fellow citizens with the saints" in His divine kingdom but also are brothers and sisters in His divine "household" (Eph. 2:19). To refer to Phoebe as **our sister** meant that she was a devoted member of the family of God, and the context makes clear that she was especially dear to Paul.

Paul next commends **Phoebe** as **a servant** beloved by those she served in her home church **at Cenchrea,** and probably in the mother church at Corinth as well.

Servant translates *diakonos,* the term from which we get *deacon.* The Greek word here is *neuter* and was used in the church as a general term for *servant* before the offices of deacon and deaconess were developed. It is used of the household servants who drew the water that Jesus turned into wine (John 2:5,9), and Paul has used the term earlier in this letter (Rom. 13:4, twice) to refer to secular government as "a minister of God to you for good" and even of Christ as "a servant to the circumcision," that is, to Jews (15:8). When *diakonos* obviously refers to a church office, it is usually transliterated as "deacon" (see, e.g., Phil. 1:1; 1 Tim. 3:10,13).

In 1 Timothy 3:11, Paul declares that "women must likewise be dignified, not malicious gossips, but temperate, faithful in all things." Some argue that he is referring to wives of deacons, rather than to an office of women deacons. But it makes no sense that high standards would be specified for the wives of deacons but not for wives of overseers (or bishops, who are also called elders, see Titus 1:5), whose qualifications he has just given in verses 1-7. In this context (3:1-10, 12-13), the office of deaconess is clearly implied. The "likewise" in verse 11 ties the qualifications of these women to those already given for the offices of overseer and deacon. In verse 11, Paul did not refer to those women as deaconesses because *diakonos* has no feminine form.

During the first few centuries of the church, the role of a woman **servant** (*diakonos*) was to care for fellow believers who were sick, for the poor, for strangers passing through, and for the imprisoned. They also were responsible for helping baptize and disciple new women converts and to instruct children and other women.

Whether or not Phoebe held some official title or not, Paul commended her as a highly proven **servant** of Christ and implored the church at Rome to **receive her in the Lord.**

As mentioned above, Phoebe was entrusted with carrying this letter to the church at Rome. There were, of course, no copiers or carbon paper in those days, and even the simplest writing materials were very expensive. It is therefore highly unlikely that Paul, through the hand of Tertius (v. 22), made more than one copy of this letter. Since Paul realized that letter would become part of God's written Word, he knew that the truths he imparted in this letter had the mark of divine authenticity. He would therefore have made certain that this epistle to the Romans was entrusted only to the most reliable of persons.

Paul knew that the journey from Corinth to Rome would not be easy, and would involve considerable sea as well as land travel. When this special lady arrived in Rome and presented believers there with Paul's letter, they must have realized his great trust in her even before they read this personal commendation. It would be immediately evident that she deserved their greatest appreciation and respect.

Travel in those days was often hazardous, and the few inns that existed usually were connected with the worst sort of taverns, many of which were also brothels. The only safe places to stay were with a friend or a friend of a friend. Consequently, letters of commendation were routinely given to travelers by friends who had relatives or friends along the way who could provide food, lodging, and sometimes escort through dangerous areas. Such help was especially important for Christians and even more especially for those who were Jewish, who often were subjected to persecution not only by Gentiles but by unbelieving fellow Jews.

Such letters of commendation are mentioned several times in the New Testament. When Apollos "wanted to go across to Achaia, the brethren [at Ephesus] encouraged him and wrote to the disciples to welcome him" (Acts 18:27). Paul included a commendation of Titus and certain other faithful men in his second letter to Corinth, saying, "As for Titus, he is my partner and fellow worker among you; as for our brethren, they are messengers of the churches, a glory to Christ. Therefore openly before the churches show them the proof of your love and of our reason for boasting about you" (2 Cor. 8:23-24). John alludes to such a written commendation in verse 9 of his third epistle.

Phoebe was to be received into fellowship **in a manner worthy of the saints,** that is, as a true and faithful believer. Jesus promised that when believers minister to "one of these brothers of Mine, even the least of them," they do it for Him (Matt. 25:35-40). Christians are to **receive,** to love, to minister to each other in a way that is distinct from the world around us and that it cannot comprehend. We are to embrace, serve, and care for all those who genuinely name the name of Christ (cf. Matt. 18:5-10).

Paul requested that the Roman church **help** Phoebe **in whatever matter she may have need of** them for. **Matter** is from *pragma,* from which we get *pragmatic,* and refers to anything that was done or carried out. It was often used of business transactions, and probably carries that idea here, as indicated by the King James's rendering of "business." Paul not only was giving a commendation of Phoebe as a faithful Christian but also was giving a letter of reference, as it were, in regard to whatever business **matter** she may have had in Rome.

That idea is reinforced by Paul's speaking of her as a **helper,** which translates *prostatis,* which was commonly used to signify a patron, a wealthy person who encouraged and financially supported an organization or cause, as in a patron of the arts. In other words, Phoebe was no ordinary **helper,** but one of high esteem and integrity and likely was a businesswoman of considerable wealth. She used her influence and her financial means, as well as her personal time and effort, as **a helper of many** fellow believers **and of myself [Paul] as well.**

That statement says as much about Paul as it does about Phoebe. The esteemed apostle readily and graciously acknowledged his personal indebtedness to and love for a Christian sister, whom he memorialized in these two verses in the Word of God. And, although God inspired no woman to write a part of Scripture, he used Phoebe to transport the first copy of this marvelous letter, which is one of the bedrocks of New Testament theology. This woman was emblematic of those countless women of God whom He has used and honored with great distinction within the framework of His divine plan.

Paul's Cordiality

Greet Prisca and Aquila, my fellow workers in Christ Jesus, who for my life risked their own necks, to whom not only do I give thanks, but also all the churches of the Gentiles; also greet the church that is in their house. Greet Epaenetus, my beloved, who is the first convert to Christ from Asia. Greet Mary, who has worked hard for you. Greet Andronicus and Junias, my kinsmen, and my fellow prisoners, who are outstanding among the apostles, who also were in Christ before me. Greet Ampliatus, my beloved in the Lord. Greet Urbanus, our fellow worker in Christ, and Stachys my beloved. Greet Apelles, the approved in Christ. Greet those who are of the household of Aristobulus. Greet Herodion, my kinsman. Greet those of the household of Narcissus, who are in the Lord. Greet Tryphaena and Tryphosa, workers in the Lord. Greet Persis the beloved, who has worked hard in the Lord. Greet Rufus, a choice man in the Lord, also his mother and mine. Greet Asyncritus, Phlegon, Hermes, Patrobas, Hermas and the brethren with them. Greet Philologus and Julia, Nereus and his sister, and Olympas, and all the saints who are with them. Greet one another with a holy kiss. All the churches of Christ greet you. (16:3-16)

Paul continues his outpouring of love and affection for a host of beloved friends and fellow believers. Doubtless he could have included many more, but the ones he chose to acknowledge here were especially close and dear. As with his comments about Phoebe, he is not speaking as their authority so much as a friend in Christ.

Although he had not yet visited Rome, Paul names twenty-four individuals, seventeen men and seven women, along with many who are unnamed, such as those in the households of Aristobulus and Narcissus. In these verses the apostle gives a roster of choice Christians he knew and with whom he had worked. He had served them and been served by them.

The first to be greeted are **Prisca and Aquila,** a husband and wife who were **fellow workers in Christ Jesus** with Paul. They were not apostles or prophets but, nonetheless, were invaluable **workers** in the early church.

Paul first met this Jewish Christian couple on his first visit to Corinth, to which **Prisca,** whose diminutive name was Priscilla, **and Aquila** had fled from Rome when all Jews were expelled by the Emperor Claudias. It is possible that she was a Gentile, and perhaps a Roman citizen like Paul, and Aquila a Jew, but the expulsion would have applied to both of them, even if only one was Jewish.

During that period it was customary in synagogues not only that men and women sat on separate sides but that the men sat in groups according to profession or trade. It is therefore likely that Paul first met **Aquila** when he sat down as a visitor in the synagogue at Corinth. As it happened, he and **Prisca** were tentmakers like Paul, who stayed in their house while he began his ministry in Corinth (Acts 18:1-3). This remarkable couple is mentioned six times in the New Testament, three times by Luke in the book of Acts and three times by Paul, here and in 1 Corinthians 16:19 and 2 Timothy 4:19.

It is interesting that in four of those six references, Priscilla's name is given first. No reason for that unexpected order is given in the texts themselves. She may have been the more dominant and active of the two, or, as some have suggested, she may have had a higher social standing. No single explanation seems satisfactory, however, because both Luke and Paul use the names in both orders.

They were much more than fellow workers with Paul, for whom they **risked their own necks.** Probably more than once, they put their own lives in jeopardy to protect Paul's. From a human perspective, they prevented Paul's life and ministry from being cut short before he had fulfilled his role in God's plan. They obviously rendered selfless service to many other Christians as well, because Paul goes on to make the remarkable statement that to them **not only do I give thanks, but also all the churches of the Gentiles.** Wherever they traveled and lived, that Jewish couple ministered unstintingly and without prejudice.

Aquila and Priscilla later moved from Corinth to Ephesus. While there, they met a young Jewish preacher "named Apollos, an Alexandrian by birth, and eloquent man, . . . mighty in the Scriptures." He did not have a full understanding of the gospel, "being acquainted only with the baptism of John....But when Priscilla and Aquila heard him, they took him aside and explained to him the way of God more accurately" (Acts 18:24-26).

After Claudius died, Aquila and Priscilla returned to Rome, where they lived and ministered when Paul wrote this letter to the church there. By this time there were many believers in Rome, probably spread throughout the city. One of the congregations was meeting **in their house,** and Paul extended his greetings to them.

The noted commentator William Hendricksen makes the following observation:

> During his missionary career Paul had colleagues and fellow-workers. But he deemed it necessary to oppose Peter to his face (Gal. 2:11f.). With Barnabas he had such a sharp disagreement that the two parted company (Acts 15:39). There was a time when Paul refused to allow Mark to remain one of his companions (Acts 15:38). He was going to reprimand Euodia and Syntyche (Phil. 4:2). And Demas was going to desert him (2 Tim. 4:10). But even though Prisca and Aquila in a sense stood closer to him than any others—for they were his companions both in trade and in faith—as far as the record shows, between Paul, on the one hand, and Prisca and Aquila, on the other, there was always perfect harmony! (*Exposition of Paul's Epistle to the Romans* [Grand Rapids: Baker, 1981], 503)

Paul's next greeting is to **Epaenetus, my beloved, who is the first convert to Christ from Asia.** It is likely that **Epaenetus** was especially **beloved** of Paul for the very reason that he was **the first convert from Asia,** now sometimes referred to as Asia Minor, the general area of modern Turkey. Because Paul speaks of this man so affectionately, it could well be that he came to Christ through the preaching of Paul and was lovingly discipled by him.

First convert translates *aparchē* which literally means firstfruit. This believer was the **first convert from Asia** who became part of Paul's "offering of the Gentiles" to the Lord (Rom. 15:16). Through the intervening years, Paul had kept track of Epaenetus and was pleased that he now was part of the church at Rome.

Greet Mary, Paul continues, **who has worked hard for you.** We do not know where **Mary** came from, how or when she was converted, or anything else about her except that she had **worked hard** for the church at Rome. *Kopiaō* **(worked hard)** carries the idea of toiling at a task to the point of weariness and exhaustion. The phrasing of this verse suggests that **Mary** may not have been known to Paul personally and that he knew of her hard work from the reports of others, perhaps Aquila and Priscilla. The context also suggests that she had ministered in the church at Rome for some time, and possibly was a founding member who labored selflessly to establish and develop the fellowship of Christians in the capital of the empire.

Andronicus and Junias had a special and perhaps unique relationship to Paul. Because **Junias** may be a woman's name, these two might have been husband and wife. And because many of the individuals mentioned in this passage were Jews, **kinsmen** indicates not only that they were fellow Jews but probably means also that they, along with Herodion (v. 11) and Jason and Sosipater (v. 21) were Paul's relatives. If that is true, Paul must have felt a special warmth in seeing his **kinsmen** in the flesh become his **kinsmen** in spirit.

Besides being Paul's kinsmen, these two believers were at some time, perhaps even then, his **fellow prisoners.** Because Paul was often in prison (see 2 Cor. 11:23), their shared imprisonment could have been in any number of places. Because they were **outstanding among the apostles,** we can be sure that, like Paul, they were prisoners because of their faith. If they shared the same or adjoining cells, that imprisonment would have deepened and strengthened their personal and spiritual bond with each other.

The phrase **outstanding among the apostles** could have one of several meanings. It obviously does not refer to the office of apostle. The term itself means simply "sent ones," and in that sense refers to any believer whom the Lord sends forth in ministry. It seems likely that the meaning here is that Andronicus and Junias performed **outstanding** service in the Lord's work while working **among,** and possibly under, some of the ordained apostles, such as Paul and Peter. That interpretation is supported by Paul's remark that those two believers **were in Christ before me,** that is, were converted to Christ before he was. At the time of Paul's conversion, most converts were still living in or near Jerusalem, where several of the Twelve were leaders in the church. If, therefore, Paul's two kinsmen were converted before he was, it is likely that they lived in Jerusalem and performed their **outstanding** service **among the apostles** in that city.

Because those two believers were converted before Paul, it is quite possible that they had suffered persecution under Paul (then named Saul), whose great zeal against the church would not have been diminished by their being his relatives. It is also possible that the prayers of those relatives for Paul's salvation—and perhaps their witnessing to him—may have been instrumental in his eventual surrender to the Savior. If those things are true, the reconciliation of Andronicus and Junias with Paul when he came to Christ would have been all the more gratifying.

Ampliatus is greeted as Paul's **beloved in the Lord.** From history and archaeology we learn that **Ampliatus** was a common name among slaves. And because slaves were not allowed to bear the name of free men, this **beloved** friend of Paul must have been, and possibly still was, a slave. Many slaves in the imperial households of that day had that name, and because **Ampliatus** was then in Rome, it is conceivable that he was among the believers in "Caesar's household" mentioned by Paul in his letter to the church at Philippi (Phil. 4:22).

In one of the earliest Christian catacombs near Rome, the name **Ampliatus** can still be seen on a beautifully decorated tomb. Because free Romans always had three names, the fact that this grave marker contains only a single name could be further evidence that the Ampliatus mentioned here by Paul was, or had been, a slave. But the fact that his tomb was elaborately decorated indicates that he was held in special high esteem by his fellow Christians and was one of their **beloved** brethren as well as Paul's. Although James's strong admonition (James 2:1-9) indicates there were exceptions, for the most part, social or economic status carried little weight in the early church. Under persecution it carried even less weight, as believers endured common dangers and suffering in situations where wealth or status gave little, if any, protection. It seems evident that in the Roman church there was indeed "neither Jew nor Greek, there [was] neither slave nor free man, there [was] neither male nor female," because those believers genuinely considered themselves to be "one in Christ Jesus" (Gal. 3:28).

The next two saints to whom Paul sends greetings are **Urbanus** and **Stachys. Urbanus** was a common Roman name, suggesting that he may have been a Roman citizen. Paul speaks of him as **our fellow worker in Christ,** but gives no indication of how or where he ministered for **Christ. Our** could refer to Paul and any number of other coworkers, or it could refer to Paul and the church at Rome. If the latter, then **Urbanus** would have to have worked with Paul somewhere else before going to Rome and serving the church there.

Unlike **Urbanus,** the name **Stachys,** which means "ear of corn," was Greek and uncommon. Since he is called **beloved,** he would have been closely associated with Paul, but we do not know where or in what relationship. As mentioned above, many of those to whom Paul sends greetings were not outstanding leaders in the early church. That fact reveals the apostle's deep and sincere love for fellow believers and for fellow workers in particular, no matter how little known they were or how insignificant their service was from a purely human perspective.

We know nothing about Paul's relationship to **Apelles,** and cannot be certain how the two were personally acquainted. But whether from his own experience with this man or from reliable reports from others, Paul recognized **Apelles** as being **approved in Christ.** *Dokimos* **(approved)** carries the idea of being tried and tested, and was used of precious metals, such as gold and silver, that passed tests for purity. Whatever his field of service **in Christ** may have been, **Apelles** performed it well.

Paul's next greeting was to a group of believers whose names and number we do not know. They are simply identified as **those who are of the household of Aristobulus,** who himself is not identified. Because he is not greeted, it seems certain he was not a Christian. The Greek phrase says only "of Aristobulus," the word **household** being implied. How many of his **household** were Christians, and whether they were family members, servants, or both we are not told.

From his careful study of New Testament times, the noted biblical scholar J. B. Lightfoot suggests that **Aristobulus** may have been the brother of Herod Agrippa I and the grandson of Herod the Great. If so, he would have been a close ally of the Emperor Claudius. When **Aristobulus** died, his household—including his wife, children, slaves, and possessions—would have become the property of the emperor, although they would still have been referred to as **the household of Aristobulus.** It is therefore possible that this group of believers could have been part of the imperial household.

As with Andronicus and Junias (v. 7), Paul greets **Herodion** as **my kinsman,** who, for the same reason explained above, was Paul's physical kinsman and therefore a Jew, as well as his spiritual kinsman in Christ. As the name indicates, **Herodion** was related to the Herod family in some way and therefore may have been associated with the household of Aristobulus.

Like Aristobulus, **Narcissus** was probably not a believer, but some of **those of** his **household** were **in the Lord.**

Some scholars believe with J. B. Lightfoot that, like Aristobulus, the **Narcissus** mentioned here was closely connected to the Emperor Claudius as his secretary. Because all contact with the emperor had to be channeled through the secretary, he became extremely wealthy through the many bribes he received for granting access to, or simply for corresponding with, the emperor. It is therefore possible that at least two households within the palace had Christians in them. If so, those believers may have been among the saints "of Caesar's household" who joined Paul, then imprisoned in Rome, in sending greetings to the church at Philippi (Phil. 4:22).

In verse 12, Paul greets and commends three women. The first two, **Tryphaena and Tryphosa,** possibly were twin sisters, whose names mean "delicate" and "dainty," respectively. Those words may have characterized their lives before salvation, but spiritually they were active and faithful **workers in the Lord.**

Persis doubtless received her name from her native land of Persia. Not only was she **the beloved,** suggesting (by the definite article

the) she was loved by everyone who knew her, but she also was one who had **worked hard in the Lord.** Because the work of **Tryphaena and Tryphosa** is spoken of in the present tense and that of **Persis** in the past tense, it may have been that the first two were younger women and still active and that **Persis** was an older saint who had already lived her most productive years. But all three were noted for their work for and **in the Lord.**

Paul speaks of **Rufus** as **a choice man in the Lord.** *Eklektos* **(choice)** has the literal meaning of chosen, or elected. Paul could hardly be speaking about his being chosen for salvation, since, as made clear earlier in the epistle, every believer is "predestined to become conformed to the image of His Son" (Rom. 8:29). In that sense, every Christian is equally chosen "in [Christ] before the foundation of the world" (Eph. 1:4). The idea here, as the *New American Standard Bible* rendering indicates, is that **Rufus** was **choice** in the general sense in which that word is used today. He was an extraordinary Christian, known for his love and work for the Lord and for the Lord's people.

We learn from Mark's gospel, which was written in Rome after Paul wrote this letter to Rome, that Simon of Cyrene, a city on the Mediterranean coast of North Africa, who was pressed into service by the soldiers to carry Jesus' cross, was "the father of Alexander and Rufus" (Mark 15:21). Mark would have had no reason to include the names of Alexander and Rufus unless they were known to the church at large (through the wide distribution of Paul's letter to Rome) or at least known to the church in Rome. Scholars therefore agree that the **Rufus** mentioned here by Paul was one of those sons of Simon, who may have been brought to saving faith in Christ through that contact with Him on the way to Calvary. If so, he must have died before the Roman epistle was written, else he surely would have been greeted and commended by Paul. If Simon, the man privileged to have carried Jesus' cross and to have walked beside Him to Calvary, had become a believer, he would have been among the most honored of men in the early church. It is obvious that his wife, the **mother** of Rufus, believed, and it seems safe to assume from this text that Alexander likewise was converted, giving reason for Mark to mention him along with his brother. Alexander either was dead or did not live in Rome at the time, else Paul would have greeted him.

The greeting to **his mother and mine** does not mean Rufus was Paul's natural brother but that Rufus's **mother,** somewhere and in some way during Paul's travels and ministry, had cared for the apostle as if he were her own son. Like many other Jews converted at or soon after Pentecost, Simon and his family may have chosen to stay in Jerusalem and therefore have had the opportunity to know and befriend Paul during his visits there.

Paul makes no comment **about Asyncritus, Phlegon, Hermes, Patrobas,** and **Hermas.** The mention of **the brethren with them** indicates that the five men named here were leaders of one of the many assemblies of believers in Rome. In this context, **brethren** would include all believers there, including women.

Paul's greetings in verse 15 were to another such assembly of **saints,** in which **Philologus and Julia, Nereus and his sister, and Olympas** were outstanding members and leaders.

The careful research of William Barclay sheds light on one of the individuals Paul mentions in this beautiful passage. About **Nereus** Barclay writes:

> In A.D. 95 there happened an event which shocked Rome. Two of the most distinguished people in Rome were condemned for being Christians. They were husband and wife. The husband was Flavius Clemens. He had been consul of Rome. The wife was Domatilla and she was of royal blood. She was the granddaughter of Vespasian, a former Emperor, and the niece of Domitian, the reigning Emperor. In fact the two sons of Flavius Clemens and Domatilla had been designated Domitian's successors in the imperial power. Flavius was executed and Domatilla was banished to the island of Pontia where years afterwards Paula saw the cave where "she [Domatilla] drew out a long martyrdom for the Christian name." And now the point—the name of the chamberlain of Flavius and Domatilla was Nereus. Is it possible that Nereus the slave had something to do with the making into Christians of Flavius Clemens the ex-consul and Domatilla the princess of the royal blood? Again maybe it is an idle speculation, for Nereus is a common name, but again, maybe it is true. (*Letters to the Romans* [Philadelphia: Westminster, 1957], 237)

Paul ends this section with the admonition, **Greet one another with a holy kiss.** The practice of embracing and kissing friends on the forehead or cheek was common in Old Testament times. Men would sometimes be kissed on the beard. Such kisses were in no way romantic, much less erotic, and kissing on the mouth was rare, except for married couples. Kissing was common among relatives and close friends, especially when they first came together after a long separation and when they departed, as is common today. To kiss a person of high position was a sign of honor and respect.

The New Testament church, at first composed primarily of Jews, carried on the traditional practice of kissing among relatives and close friends. Because many new believers were made outcasts by their biological families, the spiritual kinship of Christians became all the dearer and was frequently manifested by what came to be called **a holy kiss.**

Paul admonished believers in Rome to maintain the practice when they would **greet one another.**

He gave the same admonition at the end of both of his letters to the church at Corinth (1 Cor. 16:20; 2 Cor. 13:12) and in his first letter to believers in Thessalonica (1 Thess. 5:26). Peter had in mind the same idea of demonstrating spiritual kinship when he said, "Greet one another with a kiss of love" (1 Pet. 5:14).

After Paul exhorted the elders from Ephesus who came out to meet him at Miletus as he was traveling to Jerusalem, "he knelt down and prayed with them all. And they began to weep aloud and embraced Paul, and repeatedly kissed him, grieving especially over the word which he had spoken, that they should see his face no more" (Acts 20:36-38).

While Jesus dined at the home of Simon the Pharisee, "a woman in the city who was a sinner," probably a prostitute, came into the house and proceeded to wash, anoint, and kiss Jesus' feet. Simon "said to himself, 'If this man were a prophet He would know who and what sort of person this woman is who is touching Him that she is a sinner.'" After telling a parable, Jesus "said to Simon, 'Do you see this woman? I entered your house; you gave Me no water for My feet, but she has wet My feet with her tears, and wiped them with her hair. You gave Me no kiss, but she, since the time I came in, has not ceased to kiss My feet'" (see Luke 7:36-45). Jesus not only approved of the woman's kissing His feet, but reminded Simon that he had neglected to greet Him with a kiss, implying that such a kiss not only was appropriate but was expected from a person who hosted an honored guest.

The practice of the holy kiss, or kiss of love, continued for many years in the early church. It probably came to an end by being corrupted by sensuous perversion. Some centuries later, it was somewhat revived in the form of a liturgical kiss, which was purely formal and ritualistic, not personal or spiritual.

In our own day, there is also danger of certain physical signs of affection being misunderstood and abused. Those dangers have always existed and will continue to exist until the Lord returns. But, if practiced with sensible discretion, a loving embrace and a truly holy kiss that reflect genuine, heartfelt love between Christians should not be jettisoned simply because of possible misunderstanding or misuse.

Paul extended greetings in behalf of **all the churches of Christ,** doubtless referring to congregations he had recently visited. We know from the New Testament that there were differences of opinions in the early church, even among the most spiritual leaders, including the apostles. Even serious factionalism, such as that in the church at Corinth, was not unknown, but there were no denominations as we know them today, no splinter groups within the body of orthodox believers.

They **all** simply were **the churches of Christ.** Those believers, Jews and Gentiles, wealthy and poor, free and slave, famous and unknown, enjoyed in Christ a depth of fellowship and partnership the world has no way of understanding.

But the world can observe it, and God's people should give the world more opportunity to do so. The Lord assured us, "By this all men will know that you are My disciples, if you have love for one another" (John 13:35). That love must be genuine and pure for it to strengthen the church or to have an impact on the world. For that reason, Paul has earlier commanded, "Let love be without hypocrisy. Abhor what is evil; cling to what is good. Be devoted to one another in brotherly love; give preference to one another in honor. . . . Rejoice with those who rejoice, and weep with those who weep. Be of the same mind toward one another; do not be haughty in mind, but associate with the lowly. Do not be wise in your own estimation" (Rom. 12:9-10,15-16).

That kind of love characterized the church at Ephesus, of whom Paul wrote that he had "heard of the faith in the Lord Jesus which exists among you, and your love for all the saints" (Eph. 1:15). Again linking faith in Christ with love for the brethren, he told the Colossian believers, "We heard of your faith in Christ Jesus and the love which you have for all the saints" (Col. 1:4; cf. v. 8). He could say of the church at Thessalonica, "You have no need for anyone to write to you, for you yourselves are taught by God to love one another" (1 Thess. 4:9).

Paul's Caution

Now I urge you, brethren, keep your eye on those who cause dissensions and hindrances contrary to the teaching which you learned, and turn away from them. For such men are slaves, not of our Lord Christ but of their own appetites; and by their smooth and flattering speech they deceive the hearts of the unsuspecting. For the report of your obedience has reached to all; therefore I am rejoicing over you, but I want you to be wise in what is good, and innocent in what is evil. And the God of peace will soon crush Satan under your feet. The grace of our Lord Jesus be with you. (16:17-20)

Godly love "does not rejoice in unrighteousness" (1 Cor. 13:6). It is the nature of love to warn against harm to those whom it loves. The greatest harm against believers is that which undermines God's truth in which they live. Love is ready to forgive all evil, but it does not condone or ignore evil, especially in the church. Paul therefore found it necessary to insert this caution into his greetings of love.

To truly love someone is to strive for what is good for them and to oppose whatever harms them. That is true of husbands' and wives' love for each other, of parents for their children, of pastors for their congregations, and of believers for all other believers.

Paul therefore demonstrates his love for the church at Rome as much by giving this caution as he does by expressing his commendations and his cordiality. **Now I urge you, brethren,** he implores, **keep your eye on those who cause dissensions and hindrances contrary to the teaching which you learned, and turn away from them.**

The mature Christian is to keep his **eye on those who cause dissensions and hindrances.** Paul is not talking about hair splitting over minor interpretations, or about immature believers who are divisive because of personal preferences, as disruptive and damaging as those things can be. We are to "shun foolish controversies and genealogies and strife and disputes about the Law, for they are unprofitable and worthless" (Titus 3:9). We are to "refuse foolish and ignorant speculations, knowing that they produce quarrels" (2 Tim. 2:23). Paul is here talking about something immeasurably more serious. He is warning about those who challenge and undermine **the teaching which you learned,** that is, the divinely-revealed apostolic **teaching** they had received.

Keep your eye on such men, Paul says. Mark them out as false teachers who are to be opposed and avoided. *Skopeō* **(keep your eye on)** carries the idea of looking at or observing with intensity. It is from the noun form of that word that we get the *scope* in telescope and microscope. It means more than simply to look at, but to examine and scrutinize carefully.

Paul is not talking about what today is often referred to as a "witch hunt," an effort that is determined to find fault whether it is there or not. Nor is he talking about legalistic and often mean-spirited and unloving "litmus tests" for an orthodoxy that is more rigid than Scripture.

Evangelicals who adhere strictly but unpretentiously to the inerrancy of Scripture and refuse to join ranks with those who claim to be Christian but who compromise or denigrate God's Word are often wrongly accused of being divisive. But God's true church is bonded by His Word and the power of His indwelling Spirit, who applies and builds the church on and through that Word. The ones who truly cause destructive division and disharmony, the ungodly **dissensions and hindrances** about which Paul speaks here, are those who promote and practice falsehood and unrighteousness. No institution or movement can rightly claim unity in Christ if they are not unified in and by His Word. Whatever spiritual unity they may have is based on the spirit of this age, which is satanic, not godly.

At the beginning of his letter to the churches of Galatia, Paul expresses with obvious emotion his great amazement that "you are so quickly deserting Him who called you by the grace of Christ, for a different gospel" (Gal. 1:6). To emphasize the gravity of the danger, he added, "But even though we, or an angel from heaven, should preach to you a gospel contrary to that which we have preached to you, let him be accursed" (v. 8).

Again, a caution about Paul's caution should be given. He was not teaching or implying that true believers have the right to do physical harm to heretics. During the Reformation, some Protestants as well as Catholics committed grave inhumanities in the name of Christ. When a group of Samaritans refused to render hospitality to Jesus and the disciples, James and John—whom Jesus had nicknamed "Sons of Thunder" (Luke 3:17)—asked, "Lord, do You want us to command fire to come down from heaven and consume them?" Jesus replied, "You do not know what kind of spirit you are of; for the Son of Man did not come to destroy men's lives, but to save them" (Luke 9:54-56). One of Jesus' several strong rebukes of Peter was given in response to that disciple's cutting off the ear of one of the high priest's slaves when the Jewish leaders brought Roman soldiers to arrest Jesus. "Put your sword back into its place," He said to Peter; "for all those who take up the sword shall perish by the sword" (Matt. 26:52; cf. John 18:10-11). Even protection of the Son of God did not justify the use of physical violence. That prerogative is God's alone, either directly by divine intervention or indirectly through divinely-instituted human government (Rom. 13:1-4).

The right response of believers to false teachers, especially those who teach their heresy under the guise of Christianity, is not debate or dialogue. We are to **turn away from them,** to reject what they teach and to protect fellow believers, especially new converts and the immature, from being deceived, confused, and misled. Paul often argued and debated with unbelievers, both Jew and Gentile. While in Athens, he "was reasoning in the synagogue with the Jews and the God-fearing Gentiles, and the market place every day with those who happened to be present," including Greek philosophers (Acts 17:16-17; cf. 9:29; 17:2; 18:4; 19:8-9). He did not, however, provide a platform for those who professed Christ but taught a false and perverted gospel. Such people are not to be debated but denounced.

Although it is helpful for Christians, especially preachers and teachers, to have some knowledge of what liberal Christianity and so-called Christian cults teach, it is spiritually unwise and dangerous to be overly exposed to their falsehoods, whether through reading their literature or becoming involved in their churches, colleges, seminaries, or other institutions. By doing such things, many ill-prepared but self-confident believers have had their faith as well as their doctrine seriously subverted, as they are "carried about by every wind of doctrine, by the trickery of men, by craftiness in deceitful scheming" (Eph. 4:14). Many seminarians, who typically are more familiar with Scripture than most other Christians of their age, have become so engulfed in dialogue with theological error that their effective ministry is all but forfeited. They do not, of course, lose their salvation, but they can easily have their usefulness to the Lord severely weakened and sometimes destroyed.

In the touching scene mentioned earlier, as Paul bade farewell to the elders from Ephesus, he reminded them that he "did not shrink from declaring to [them] the whole purpose of God." Because he loved them so dearly, he took special care to warn them with these sobering words:

> Be on guard for yourselves and for all the flock, among which the Holy Spirit has made you overseers, to shepherd the church of God which He purchased with His own blood. I know that after my departure savage wolves will come in among you, not sparing the flock; and from among your own selves men will arise, speaking perverse things, to draw away the disciples after them. Therefore be on the alert, remembering that night and day for a period of three years I did not cease to admonish each one with tears. And now I commend you to God and to the word of His grace, which is able to build you up and to give you the inheritance among all those who are sanctified. (Acts 20:27-32)

Jesus Himself repeatedly warned the disciples against false teachers and prophets. In the Sermon on the Mount, He said, "Beware of the false prophets, who come to you in sheep's clothing, but inwardly are ravenous wolves. You will know them by their fruits" (Matt. 7:15-16). On another occasion He warned that, in the end times, "false Christs and false prophets will arise and will show great signs and wonders, so as to mislead, if possible, even the elect" (Matt. 24:24).

Paul gives two negative reasons for turning away from false teachers. The first is that their motives are wrong. **Such men are slaves,** he explains, **not of our Lord Christ but of their own appetites.** No matter how seemingly sincere and caring false teachers or preachers may appear to be, they are never genuinely concerned for the cause of Christ or for His church. They are driven by self-interest and self-gratification—sometimes for fame, sometimes for power over their followers, always for financial gain, and frequently for all of those reasons. Many of them enjoy pretentious and luxurious lifestyles, and sexual immorality is the rule more than the exception. Such people "are enemies of the cross of Christ, whose end is destruction, whose god is their appetite, and whose glory is in their shame, who set their minds on earthly things" (Phil. 3:18-19)."These men are those who are hidden reefs in your love feasts when they feast with you without fear, caring for themselves," Jude testifies. They are "clouds without water, carried along by winds; autumn trees without fruit, doubly dead, uprooted; wild waves of the sea, casting up their own shame like foam; wandering stars, for whom the black darkness has been reserved forever" (Jude 12-13).

Many false teachers devote their lives to the study of Scripture, but because they have never trusted in Christ for salvation and because they view the Bible as man's ideas about God rather than God's revelation to man, they distort His Word and twist it to fit their own sinful predispositions. Because they have been in such close contact with God's truth,"it would be better for them not to have known the way of righteousness, than having known it, to turn away from the holy commandment delivered to them" (2 Pet. 2:21). Such scholars are "always learning and [are] never able to come to the knowledge of the truth. And just as Jannes and Jambres opposed Moses, so these men also oppose the truth, men of depraved mind, rejected as regards the faith" (2 Tim. 3:7-8). They reject the truth that Peter declares so clearly in his second letter:

> Know this first of all, that no prophecy of Scripture is a matter of one's own interpretation, for no prophecy was ever made by an act of human will, but men moved by the Holy Spirit spoke from God. But false prophets also arose among the people, just as there will also be false teachers among you, who will secretly introduce destructive heresies, even denying the Master who bought them, bringing swift destruction upon themselves. And many will follow their sensuality, and because of them the way of the truth will be maligned; and in their greed they will exploit you with false words; their judgment from long ago is not idle, and their destruction is not asleep. (2 Pet. 1:20-2:3; cf. 2:10-19)

Even the rare false teachers and leaders who live modestly and spend their lives sacrificially helping others are actually living for themselves. They try to please God by their good works rather than by faith in Him and obedience to His Word. They themselves do not know God or serve God and are a hindrance to others coming to know Him and serve Him.

Second, false teachers should be rejected because the results of their teaching are always destructive. **By their smooth and flattering speech, they deceive the hearts of the unsuspecting.**

The many popular and sentimentalized gospels of ecumenicity and ecclesiastical unity proclaimed today reflect such **smooth and**

flattering speech, which disguises itself as loving and beneficent, while denying the central truths of the gospel. In the name of strengthening and unifying Christ's church, they undermine its very foundation. In the name of bringing men closer to God, they drive them further from Him. Just as in Paul's day, **they deceive the hearts of the unsuspecting.**

In his second letter to the church at Corinth, Paul warned of "false apostles, deceitful workers, disguising themselves as apostles of Christ. And no wonder, for even Satan disguises himself as an angel of light. Therefore it is not surprising if his servants also disguise themselves as servants of righteousness; whose end shall be according to their deeds" (2 Cor. 11:13-15).

Any love that does not acknowledge God's truth has no part in God's love. No matter how cleverly disguised in religious congeniality and respectability, and no matter how great their claims to love God and His people, those who contradict or compromise His Word are enemies of God and of His people. The love that God commands and commends can never be separated from the truth He has revealed.

Because they pretend to speak for God and serve His people, the harshest of God's judgments in Scripture are reserved for false teachers and prophets, those who propose to speak for and serve the true God but who speak only for themselves and only serve themselves.

Paul also gives a positive reason for avoiding false teachers. **For the report of your obedience has reached to all.** The best protection against falsehood is adhering to God's truth, just as the best protection against sin is holding on to His righteousness.

Believers in Rome were protected against false teachers by their **obedience** to Christ and the truth of His gospel. Not only did their **obedience** protect themselves, but it also helped believers elsewhere who knew of and were encouraged by the Roman church's reputation for godliness. Early in this letter, Paul commended them for their faithfulness. "I thank my God through Jesus Christ for you all, because your faith is being proclaimed throughout the whole world" (Rom. 1:8). He therefore had good cause for **rejoicing** over them. The godliness of that church brought encouragement and joy to Paul, although he had never visited Rome and did not know most of the believers there.

Yet, knowing that even the most faithful believers can fall prey to Satan's traps, the apostle added, **but I want you to be wise in what is good, and innocent in what is evil.** He echoed Jesus' similar caution to His followers: "Behold, I send you out as sheep in the midst of wolves; therefore be shrewd as serpents, and innocent as doves" (Matt. 10:16). We will not be free from the allures of sin until Christ takes us to be with Himself. It is therefore necessary for Christians constantly to "abhor what is evil [and] cling to what is good" (Rom. 12:9). "Finally, brethren," Paul admonished believers at Philippi, "whatever is true, whatever is honorable, whatever is right, whatever is pure, whatever is lovely, whatever is of good repute, if there is any excellence and if anything worthy of praise, let your mind dwell on these things" (Phil. 4:8; cf. Col. 3:16).

Many Christians rationalize watching degrading movies and TV programs by claiming they need to be familiar with the ways of the world in order to better analyze secular culture and be better prepared to witness to those who are worldly. But it is not necessary to sift through garbage to recognize it for what it is, and the more we are around it the more we pick up its stench. The more willingly we associate with evil, the more it will drag us down to its level.

To be **innocent in what is evil** is not to be ignorant of it or to disregard it. We cannot abhor evil unless we have some idea of what it is. But, to use a popular analogy, the only reliable way to recognize a counterfeit bill is to be completely familiar with the genuine bill. The only reliable way to recognize evil is to be thoroughly familiar with the **good,** and the only reliable way to learn what is **good** is to learn God's Word.

For those who turn away from false teachers and who are wise in what is good and innocent in what is evil, **the God of peace will soon crush Satan under** their **feet.** Paul assures faithful believers that they can look forward to the day when their spiritual warfare will be over. Teachers of deceit and falsehood are instruments of the devil, and they will be destroyed when **the God of peace** crushes **Satan.** In Romans 15:33, Paul refers to "the God of peace" in relation to His divine provision for His children. Here **the God of peace** is spoken of in relation to His permanent victory over **Satan** and his minions on behalf of His children. Paul uses the figure of Genesis 3:15, where, after the Fall, God declares to the serpent **(Satan)** that "He [the Messiah] shall bruise you on the head," that is, inflict a mortal wound.

The phrase *en tochei*, here translated **soon,** has the meaning of speedily, or quickly, as it is rendered in Acts 12:7 and 22:18, and often carried the secondary connotation of unexpectedly. The closely related adverb *tachu* is used three times in Revelation 22 in relation to Christ's "coming quickly" (vv. 7, 12, 20). We know from the New Testament itself that Satan was not soon crushed from the perspective of believers living at that time. He is still not yet subdued.

It is encouraging that the Lord will **crush Satan under your feet,** the feet of God's people, as they join Christ in His triumph over Satan.

Paul now gives a second short benediction (see 15:33). **The grace of our Lord Jesus be with you.** "I know," the apostle says in effect, "that, even with your faithful obedience (v. 19), you need God's continuing grace to direct and strengthen you. You need His grace to give you wisdom to recognize false teachers. You need His grace to give you comfort and patience when you are attacked by Satan's emissaries while he is still in power over the world."

PAUL'S COMPANIONS

Timothy my fellow worker greets you, and so do Lucius and Jason and Sosipater, my kinsmen. I, Tertius, who write this letter, greet you in the Lord. Gaius, host to me and to the whole church, greets you. Erastus, the city treasurer greets you, and Quartus, the brother. [The grace of our Lord Jesus Christ be with you all. Amen.] (16:21-24)

Paul next sends greetings to the church at Rome in behalf of his companions, presumably men who were known by some of the believers in that city.

The first is **Timothy,** a choice **fellow worker** and protege. Paul reminded the church at Philippi, "You know of his [Timothy's] proven worth that he served with me in the furtherance of the gospel like a child serving his father" (Phil. 2:22). He commends, praises, and gives thanks for Timothy twice in 1 Corinthians (4:17; 16:10-11), once in 1 Thessalonians (3:2), and numerous times in his two letters to that beloved **fellow worker.**

Lucius may be the native of Cyrene who was one of the prophets and teachers in Antioch who, under the direction of the Holy Spirit, first commissioned Paul and Barnabas (Acts 13:1-3). Judging from the name alone, he could have been either Jewish or Gentile. Paul may have been using another form of *Luke*, who wrote the gospel that carries his name and was the only Gentile to write any part of Scripture. Paul refers to Luke as "the beloved physician" (Col. 4:14) and mentions him in two other letters (2 Tim. 4:11; Philem. 24). Luke and Paul were frequent companions, as indicated in the book of Acts when Luke uses "we" in regard to groups that included Paul (see, e.g., 16:11; 21:1-8).

Paul refers to **Jason and Sosipater** as **my kinsmen,** probably indicating simply that they were fellow Jews, not necessarily relatives. If the **Lucius** just mentioned was a Jew, he also would have been one of Paul's **kinsmen.** One of the first converts in Thessalonica was named Jason and apparently hosted Paul in his home for a short while before the believers there sent Paul and Silas to Berea for their safety (Acts 17:5-10). We learn from Acts 20:4-6 that a man from Berea named Sopater (a shortened form of **Sosipater)** was among the companions of Paul who met him at Troas after he left Ephesus. Sopater doubtless was among the Jews in Berea who "were more noble-minded than those in Thessalonica, for they received the word with great eagerness, examining the Scriptures daily, to see whether these things [that Paul preached] were so," and was among the "many of them [who] therefore believed" (Acts 17:10-12). The fact that the Jason and Sopater mentioned in Acts were from neighboring towns that Paul visited in succession gives strong support to the view that they are the **Jason and Sosipater** mentioned here, and that they not only were close friends of Paul but of each other.

Tertius was Paul's secretary, or amanuensis, who penned **this letter** that Paul dictated to him, and who here inserts his own greeting. The fact that Paul states that "the greeting is in my own hand—Paul," indicates that the main body of 1 Corinthians also was written for him (see 16:19-21). His saying, "See with what large letters I am writing to you with my own hand," may mean that he personally penned only the closing verses of Galatians (see 6:11). Just as Phoebe had the great privilege of delivering the book of Romans, **Tertius** had the great privilege of writing it for Paul.

Gaius was a **host to** Paul as well as **to the whole church,** probably referring to a congregation that met in his house. Because the book of Romans was written from Corinth, this **Gaius** almost certainly was among the many believers in Corinth who came to faith in Christ through the ministry of Paul and was one of the two men in that church whom Paul had baptized personally (1 Cor. 1:14). He is generally thought to be "Titius Justus, a worshiper of God, whose house was next to the synagogue" in Corinth (Acts 18:7) and whose full name would have been **Gaius** Titius Justus.

Erastus was **the city treasurer** of Corinth and therefore a man of prominence and high political office. Because his was such a common name, and because there is no clear New Testament evidence to suggest otherwise, this **Erastus** probably was not the man mentioned in Acts 19:22 or in 2 Timothy 4:20.

Quartus was the last of Paul's companions in whose behalf he sent greetings. He is identified only as **the brother,** which could mean he was the biological brother of Erastus, who has just been mentioned, or, more probably, simply that he was a **brother** in Christ.

As indicated by brackets in the *New American Standard Bible,* Paul's third short benediction (cf. 15:33; 16:20*b*) is not found in the earliest Greek manuscripts of the book of Romans. That is understandable, because these closing three verses form a longer, more explicit benediction, to which verse 24 adds nothing and seems a bit out of place. But the sentiment is fully consistent with the rest of Paul's gracious epilogue. **The grace of our Lord Jesus Christ be with you all. Amen.**

The Unveiling of God's Secret (Romans 16:25-27)

27

Now to Him who is able to establish you according to my gospel and the preaching of Jesus Christ, according to the revelation of the mystery which has been kept secret for long ages past, but now is manifested, and by the Scriptures of the prophets, according to the commandment of the eternal God, has been made known to all the nations, leading to obedience of faith; to the only wise God, through Jesus Christ, be the glory forever. Amen. (16:25-27)

The book of Romans ends with a beautiful doxology, praising God for what He has done through His Son, Jesus Christ.

Doxologies are found throughout Scripture. Sometimes a writer is so overwhelmed with gratitude that he breaks into inspired praise to God for His goodness and grace. That is especially evident in the Psalms, the hymnbook of ancient Israel. The 150 psalms are divided into five sections, generally referred to as books. Although praises to God are found throughout the Psalms, each of the five books ends with a special doxology. Book one ends with, "Blessed be the Lord, the God of Israel, from everlasting to everlasting. Amen, and Amen" (41:13). Except for the closing ascription to David (v. 20), book two ends with,

"Blessed be the Lord God, the God of Israel, who alone works wonders. And blessed be His glorious name forever; and may the whole earth be filled with His glory. Amen, and Amen" (72:18-19). Book three ends with, "Blessed be the Lord forever! Amen and Amen" (89:52). Book four ends with, "Blessed be the Lord, the God of Israel, from everlasting even to everlasting. And let all the people say, 'Amen.' Praise the Lord!" (106:48). Book five ends with Psalm 150, every verse of which is a grand doxology.

The New Testament is replete with doxologies. At the birth of Jesus, the angel and "a multitude of the heavenly host [were] praising God, saying, 'Glory to God in the highest'" (Luke 2:13-14). When Christ made His triumphal entry into Jerusalem, "the whole multitude of the disciples began to praise God joyfully with a loud voice for all the miracles which they had seen, saying, 'Blessed is the King who comes in the name of the Lord; peace in heaven and glory in the highest!'" (Luke 19:37-38). The prayer that Jesus taught His disciples, commonly known as the Lord's Prayer, ends with the doxology, "For Thine is the kingdom, and the power, and the glory, forever. Amen" (Matt. 6:13).

In the midst of this letter to the Roman church, Paul declares, "Oh, the depth of the riches both of the wisdom and knowledge of God! How unsearchable are His judgments and unfathomable His ways! For who has known the mind of the Lord, or who became His counselor? Or who has first given to Him that it might be paid back to him again? For from Him and through Him and to Him are all things. To Him be the glory forever. Amen" (Rom. 11:33-36). Likewise in the middle of his letter to Ephesian believers, Paul interjects a doxology that often is used at the close of worship services: "Now to Him who is able to do exceeding abundantly beyond all that we ask or think, according to the power that works within us, to Him be the glory in the church and in Christ Jesus to all generations forever and ever. Amen" (Eph. 3:20-21).

Near the end of the letter to the Hebrews, the author proclaims, "Now the God of peace, who brought up from the dead the great Shepherd of the sheep through the blood of the eternal covenant, even Jesus our Lord, equip you in every good thing to do His will, working in us that which is pleasing in His sight, through Jesus Christ, to whom be the glory forever and ever. Amen" (Heb. 13:20-21).

The book of Revelation is filled with hymns of praise. "The four living creatures and the twenty-four elders fell down before the Lamb . . . and they sang a new song, saying, 'Worthy art Thou to take the book, and to break its seals; for Thou wast slain, and didst purchase for God with Thy blood men from every tribe and tongue and people and nation'" (Rev. 5:8-9). They were joined by "the voice of many angels, . . . and the number of them was myriads of myriads, and thousands of thousands, saying, 'Worthy is the Lamb that was slain to receive power

and riches and wisdom and might and honor and glory and blessing'"
(vv. 11-12). Another great multitude in heaven sang,"Hallelujah! Salvation and glory and power belong to our God; because His judgments are true and righteous" (19:1-2).

There is a remarkable relationship between the last three verses of Romans and the first eleven. In 16:25 Paul speaks of **Him who is able to establish you,** and in 1:11 he talks of his readers being established. He speaks of **my gospel,** and in 1:1 of "the gospel of God." He speaks of **the mystery** of God **which has been kept secret for long ages past,** and in 1:2 of the gospel "which He promised beforehand." He mentions the **preaching of Jesus Christ,** and in 1:3 the gospel concerning God's Son. He speaks of **the Scriptures of the prophets,** just as he does in 1:2. He speaks of the gospel being **made known to all the nations, leading to obedience of faith,** and in 1:5 of bringing "about the obedience of faith among all the Gentiles."

Paul's closing doxology in Romans is unique, in that, in his praise of the Lord, he recapitulates major themes of the epistle. Perhaps taking the pen from Tertius (see v. 22), the apostle touches on the gospel that establishes men (v. 25*a*), the gospel that proclaims Jesus Christ (v. 25*b*), and the gospel that reveals God's mystery (vv. 25*c*-26).

THE GOSPEL THAT ESTABLISHES MEN

Now to Him who is able to establish you according to my gospel
(16:25*a*)

First of all, Paul praises God for the gospel that establishes men. God **is able,** that is, has sufficient power, **to establish** those who trust in Him **according to** the true **gospel** that Paul, and every true preacher and teacher, have clearly set forth.

Stērizō **(to establish)** means to make firm and stable, to make fast. In this context it refers to being mentally settled, firmly rooted in the truth of the **gospel.** The unbeliever has no certainty about God or His Word or the way of salvation. The majority of mankind does not even have an interest in finding the true God. They are perfectly satisfied with the religion they have inherited or been exposed to, or else have no concern about religion at all. Even those who attempt to find God by their own searching and discernment are "always learning and never able to come to the knowledge of the truth" (2 Tim. 3:7).

But, through the **gospel,** God **is able to establish** the minds and hearts of believers in the truth, to settle us, ground us, and make us firm in Him. No one but a Christian can be certain about God, certain about His truth, certain about His standards of righteousness, certain about His love and care, or certain about being with Him throughout eternity. Only the genuinely converted can truthfully say with Paul, "I know whom I have believed and I am convinced that He is able to guard what I have entrusted to Him until that day" (2 Tim. 1:12). The apostle assured the Corinthian Christians that "God is able to make all grace abound to you, that always having all sufficiency in everything, you may have an abundance for every good deed" (2 Cor. 9:8).

In praying for God **to establish** the believers at Ephesus, Paul petitioned the Lord "that He would grant you, according to the riches of His glory, to be strengthened with power through His Spirit in the inner man; so that Christ may dwell in your hearts through faith; and that you, being rooted and grounded in love, may be able to comprehend with all the saints what is the breadth and length and height and depth, and to know the love of Christ which surpasses knowledge, that you may be filled up to all the fulness of God" (Eph. 3:16-19).

In referring to **my gospel,** Paul was not speaking of his own personal view of the gospel. His gospel was the same as Peter's gospel, John's gospel, and the gospel preached by the other true apostles and teachers—the divinely-revealed gospel of Jesus Christ. As he explained to the Galatian believers, "I would have you know, brethren, that the gospel which was preached by me is not according to man. For I neither received it from man, nor was I taught it, but I received it through a revelation of Jesus Christ" (Gal. 1:11-12; cf. 2:2).

Through the **gospel** of Jesus Christ, whenever and by whomever it is rightly proclaimed, God will take a fallen, corrupted, vacillating, drifting, insecure, uncertain, chaotic mind and doomed soul and **establish** it forever in His truth by the power of His Spirit.

Many people try to squeeze out all the joy and meaning from life that they can, only to discover there is nothing there that satisfies. Life cannot have meaning apart from the Creator and Sustainer of life. Apart from Him, there is no purpose, no meaning, no satisfaction, no joy, no hope. There is only sin, disappointment, and judgment.

That is the theme of the first three chapters of Romans. Sinful man suppresses God's "truth in unrighteousness, because that which is known about God is evident within them; for God made it evident to them" (1:18-19). In rejecting what light they had from God, they turned to gods of their own making, "and exchanged the glory of the incorruptible God for an image in the form of corruptible man and of birds and four-footed animals and crawling creatures" (v. 23). The inevitable product of idolatry is immorality. "Therefore God gave them over in the lusts of their hearts to impurity," Paul continues, "that their bodies might be dishonored among them. . . . God gave them over to degrading passions; for their women exchanged the natural function for that which is unnatural, and in the same way also the men abandoned the natural function of the woman and burned in their desire toward one another, men with men committing indecent acts" (vv. 24, 26-27). Along with homosexuality came "unrighteousness, wickedness, greed, evil," and countless other forms of sin (vv. 28-30) that cause man to fall under the judgment of God.

In chapter 2 Paul says that God does not raise men up and establish them in righteousness because of His special favor for one group or person or another, "for there is no partiality with God" (v. 11). Nor does God forgive men because of ignorance, "for all who have sinned without the Law will also perish without the Law; and all who have sinned under the Law will be judged by the Law" (v. 12). God does not forgive and establish men on the basis of ritual, "for he is not a Jew [a true child of God] who is one outwardly; neither is circumcision that which is outward in the flesh. But he is a Jew who is one inwardly; and circumcision is that which is of the heart, by the Spirit, not by the letter; and his praise is not from men, but from God" (vv. 28-29).

In chapter 3 Paul asserts that "There is none righteous, not even one" (v. 10) and that "by the works of the Law no flesh will be justified in [God's] sight" (v. 20). As he earlier declared, only "the gospel ... is the power of God for salvation to everyone who believes, to the Jew first and also to the Greek" (1:16). In his beautiful and encouraging doxology, Jude reminds us that God "is able to keep you from stumbling, and to make you stand in the presence of His glory blameless with great joy" (Jude 24).

THE GOSPEL THAT PROCLAIMS JESUS CHRIST

and the preaching of Jesus Christ, (16:25*b*)

The only gospel of God that establishes men is the gospel that proclaims **Jesus Christ.** The major theme of Romans, like the major theme of all Scripture, is **Jesus Christ. The preaching of Jesus Christ** was Paul's supreme life commitment. "We preach Christ crucified," he said, "to Jews a stumbling block, and to Gentiles foolishness, but to those who are the called, both Jews and Greeks, Christ the power of God and the wisdom of God" (1 Cor. 1:23-24). In his second letter to the church at Corinth, he testified, "We do not preach ourselves but Christ Jesus as Lord. ... For God, who said, 'Light shall shine out of darkness,' is the One who has shone in our hearts to give the light of the knowledge of the glory of God in the face of Christ" (2 Cor. 4:5-6). "Faith comes from hearing," he explains in Romans, "and hearing by the word of Christ" (10:17).

In the second section of Romans (3:21-8:39), the apostle delineates virtually every blessing that the gospel brings to the lives of those who belong to Jesus Christ, those He has established. To give but a partial list: righteousness comes by faith in Christ (3:22); we are "justified as a gift by His grace through the redemption which is in Christ Jesus" (3:24); righteousness will be reckoned to "those who believe in Him [God] who raised Jesus our Lord from the dead" (4:24); "we have peace with God through our Lord Jesus Christ" (5:1); "if we have died with Christ, we believe that we shall also live with Him" (6:8); "the wages of sin is death, but the free gift of God is eternal life in Christ Jesus our Lord" (6:23); "we have been released from the Law, having died to that by which we were bound, so that we serve in newness of the Spirit and not in oldness of the letter" (7:6); we are indwelt by the Holy Spirit (8:9), have life in the Spirit (8:11), are led by the Spirit (8:14), have the Spirit's witness that we are God's children (8:16); have the first fruits of the Spirit (8:23), are interceded for by the Spirit (8:26), and cannot be separated "from the love of God, which is in Christ Jesus our Lord" (8:39).

The Gospel That Reveals God's Mystery

according to the revelation of the mystery which has been kept secret for long ages past, but now is manifested, and by the Scriptures of the prophets, according to the commandment of the eternal God, has been made known to all the nations, leading to obedience of faith; to the only wise God, through Jesus Christ, be the glory forever. Amen. (16:25c-27)

The gospel that establishes us and that proclaims Jesus Christ also reveals God's **divine mystery which has been kept secret for long ages past.**

This **mystery** (*mustērion*) does not carry the connotation that word has in modern English, as used, for example, of a mystery novel. In the New Testament it refers to something hidden in former times but now made known. Specifically, it refers to a part of God's truth that was not revealed, or was only partially revealed, in the Old Testament.

In 1 Corinthians Paul uses the term in a general way, speaking of the apostles and New Testament prophets, such as himself, Apollos, and Peter, as "stewards of the mysteries of God" (4:1; cf. 3:22). That is, they are bringing new revelation hidden from ages past (cf. Eph. 3:9; Col. 1:25-26).

There are many mysteries, such as "the mystery of lawlessness" (2 Thess. 2:7-8), "the mystery of godliness" (1 Tim. 3:16), the mystery of the rapture (1 Cor. 15:51),"the mystery of the kingdom of God" (Mark 4:11),"the mystery of His [Christ's] will" (Eph. 1:9),the mystery of Christ (Col. 2:2; 4:3), the mystery of Christ and the church (Eph. 5:32),"the mystery of the gospel" (Eph. 6:19), the mystery of Christ in believers (Col. 1:27),"the mystery of the faith" (1 Tim. 3:9),and several other mysteries mentioned in the book of Revelation (1:20; 10:7; 17:5, 7). But the most common mystery spoken of in the New Testament relates to God's providing salvation for Gentiles as well as Jews. Speaking of the divine truth revealed to him as an apostle, Paul wrote, "By revelation there was made known to me the mystery, as I wrote before in brief. And by referring to this, when you read you can understand my insight into the mystery of Christ, which in other generations was not made known to the sons of men, as it has now been revealed to His holy apostles and prophets in the Spirit" (Eph. 3:3-5). Specifically, the mystery is "that the Gentiles are fellow heirs and fellow members of the body, and fellow partakers of the body, and fellow partakers of the promise in Christ Jesus through the gospel" (v. 6; cf. v. 9). In other words, God's ultimate plan of redemption has always included the Gentiles in every way as much as the Jews, His specially chosen people under the Old Covenant. Through Jesus Christ, believing Gentiles are as fully saved, as fully the children of God, and as fully citizens of His divine kingdom as are believing Jews.

The **mystery** that **now is manifested** had been predicted in veiled words **by the Scriptures of the prophets, according to the commandment of the eternal God, [and] has been made known to all the nations, leading to obedience of faith.** Through Isaiah, God promised that "the Righteous One, My Servant, will justify the many, as He will bear their iniquities" (Isa. 53:11). Jeremiah foretold, "'Behold, days are coming,' declares the Lord, 'when I will make a new covenant with the house of Israel and with the house of Judah....I will put My law within them, and on their heart I will write it; and I will be their God, and they shall be My people'" (Jer. 31:31, 33). Through Ezekiel, the Lord said, "I shall give them one heart, and shall put a new spirit within them. And I shall take the heart of stone out of their flesh and give them a heart of flesh" (Ezek. 11:19).

Jews had always thought that such predictions, whatever they may fully have meant, applied only to them, the chosen race of God. "As to this salvation," Peter explains, "the prophets who prophesied of the grace that would come to you made careful search and inquiry, seeking to know what person or time the Spirit of Christ within them was indicating as He predicted the sufferings of Christ and the glories to follow" (1 Pet. 1:10-11). Even to God's inspired prophets under the Old Covenant, the full meaning of their prophecies was a mystery.

Yet, when God first made His covenant with Abraham, the father of His chosen people Israel, He alluded to His offering of grace to the whole world. "In you," He told Abraham, "all the families of the earth shall be blessed" (Gen. 12:3). When God made the covenant with His people through Moses at Mt. Sinai, He said, "You shall be to Me a kingdom of priests and a holy nation" (Ex. 19:6). In other words, it was God's design that Israel, *as a nation,* was to be a priest, a mediator of God, for the rest of the world.

Through Isaiah, the Lord told Israel that He not only had called her in righteousness and would hold her by the hand and watch over her, but also that He would appoint her "as a covenant to the people, as a light to the nations" (Isa. 42:6; cf. 49:22; 54:3; 60:5; 62:2; 66:19). Speaking of the Messiah, God predicted, "I will also make You a light of the nations so that My salvation may reach to the end of the earth" (Isa. 49:6), a passage that Paul and Barnabas quoted before a crowd of both Gentiles and Jews in Antioch of Pisidia (Acts 13:46-47).

That is the truth Paul emphasizes in the third major section of Romans (chaps. 9-16). God made "known the riches of His glory upon vessels of mercy,...not from among Jews only, but also from among Gentiles. As He says also in Hosea, 'I will call those who were not My people, "My people," and her who was not beloved, "beloved"' (9:23-25). "For the Scripture says, 'Whoever believes in Him will not be disappointed.' For there is no distinction between Jew and Greek; for the same Lord is Lord of all" (10:11-12). Paul spoke specifically of *"the mystery* ... that a partial hardening has happened to Israel until the fulness of the Gentiles has come in" (11:25, emphasis added), that is, until the Gentiles have had full opportunity to hear and receive the gospel.

In 12:3-8 Paul commands all believers, both Jews and Gentiles, to minister to each other with the gifts the Holy Spirit has given them. In chapter 13 he focuses on the responsibility of all believers to respect governmental authorities and to behave properly before the world. In chapter 14 he emphasizes the responsibility of believers not to offend one another's consciences, and in chapter 15 he reminds his readers again of God's extension of saving grace to both Jew and Gentile. In chapter 16, Paul's greeting Jews and Gentiles alike reflects his personal conviction of their oneness in Jesus Christ.

Paul crowns this marvelous letter with praise **to the only wise God,** the God of Jews and of Gentiles, the God of all creation. One may wonder why he does not say, "to the only powerful" or "only loving" or "only gracious" God. He has much to say about those divine attributes in his letters, including this one. Perhaps he calls attention here to God's wisdom in order to emphasize that only an infinitely wise mind could have designed and accomplished such a plan of redemption.

In his letter to the Ephesian church, Paul testified, "To me, the very least of all saints, this grace was given, to preach to the Gentiles the unfathomable riches of Christ, and to bring to light what is the administration of the mystery which for ages has been hidden in God, who created all things; *in order that the manifold wisdom of God might now be made known* through the church to the rulers and the authorities in the heavenly places. This was in accordance with *the eternal purpose* which He carried out in Christ Jesus our Lord" (Eph. 3:8-11, emphasis added).

It was **through Jesus Christ** that God supremely revealed not only His great grace but also His great wisdom. To Him, therefore, **be the glory forever. Amen.**

Indexes

Index of Greek Words

opheilō, 307

piptō, 117
porneia, 266
pragma, 361
proginōskō, 99
pronoia, 269
propempō, 344
pros, 274
proslambanō, 274, 318
prostatis, 361

sklērunō, 35
skopeō, 372
sōzō, 83
sperma, 48
stērizō, 383
sunagōnizomai, 351

tachu, 377

zēlos, 267

Index of Hebrew Words

yasha, 83

Index of Scripture

Index of Subjects

The MacArthur New Testament Commentary series includes:

www.MoodyPublishers.com | 1-800-678-6928